# The Liturgy of the Hours
## in East and West

# The Liturgy of the Hours in East and West

## The Origins of the Divine Office and Its Meaning for Today

*Second Revised Edition*
1993

## Robert Taft, S.J.

THE LITURGICAL PRESS
Collegeville, Minnesota

*Cover design by Cathleen Casey*

**Library of Congress Cataloging-in-Publication Data**

Taft, Robert F.
    The liturgy of the hours in East and West.

    Bibliography: p.
    Includes indexes.
    1. Divine office—Liturgy—History. I. Title.
BX2000.T34     1985          264'.1          85-24230
ISBN 0-8146-1405-1

In memory of
Bernard F. McSally
September 16, 1928–August 7, 1978

# Contents

## Part III: The Liturgy of the Hours in the Western Traditions

## Part IV: What It All Means

# Abbreviations

| | |
|---|---|
| AC | *Antike und Christentum* |
| ACC | Alcuin Club Collections |
| ALW | *Archiv für Liturgiewissenschaft* |
| AM | Aurelian of Arles, *Rule for Monks* |
| *ApTrad* | Hippolytus, *Apostolic Tradition* |
| AV | Aurelian of Arles, *Rule for Virgins* |
| BELS | Bibliotheca *Ephemerides liturgicae*, Subsidia |
| CCL | Corpus Christianorum Latinorum |
| CM | Caesarius of Arles, *Rule for Monks* |
| CS | Cistercian Studies Series |
| CSCO | Corpus scriptorum Christianorum orientalium |
| CSEL | Corpus scriptorum ecclesiasticorum Latinorum |
| CV | Caesarius of Arles, *Rule for Virgins* |
| DACL | *Dictionnaire d'archéologie chrétienne et de liturgie* |
| EL | *Ephemerides liturgicae* |
| HBS | Henry Bradshaw Society |
| HS | *Hispania sacra* |
| *id.* | *idem* (the same) |
| JTS | *The Journal of Theological Studies* |
| L | *Laudate* |
| LF | Liturgiegeschichtliche Forschungen |
| LMD | *La Maison-Dieu* |
| LQF | Liturgiewissenschaftliche Quellen und Forschungen |
| LXX | The Septuagint Greek OT |
| Mansi | J.D. Mansi, *Sacrorum conciliorum nova et amplissima collectio* |
| MGH | Monumenta Germaniae historica |
| NPNF | Nicene and Post-Nicene Fathers |
| NT | New Testament |
| OC | *Oriens Christianus* |
| OCA | Orientalia Christiana analecta |
| OCP | *Orientalia Christiana periodica* |
| OS | *L'Orient syrien* |
| OT | Old Testament |
| PG | Migne, *Patrologia Graeca* |
| PIO | Pontificio Istituto Orientale (Rome) |
| PL | Migne, *Patrologia Latina* |
| PO | Patrologia orientalis |
| POC | *Proche-orient chrétien* |
| RB | *The Rule of St. Benedict* |
| RevB | *Revue bénédictine* |
| RM | *The Rule of the Master* |
| SC | Sources chrétiennes |
| SRM | *Scriptores rerum Merovingicarum* (in MGH) |
| ST | Studi e testi |
| TU | Texte und Untersuchungen |

# Psalter Table

## The Numbering of the Psalms according to the Greek Septuagint (LXX), Latin Vulgate, Syriac Pšiṭta, and Hebrew Bible

The LXX and Vulgate numbering is the same. Modern translations generally follow the numbering of the Hebrew Bible. Syriac literature and liturgies follow the Pšiṭta numbering. The LXX-Vulgate system followed in all other eastern traditions, in the pre-Vatican II Roman Rite, and in all Christian sources before the advent of vernacular Bibles, is followed here. Where two numbers are given for one psalm, the second is the Hebrew number.

| LXX | Pšiṭta | Heb | LXX | Pšiṭta | Heb |
|---|---|---|---|---|---|
| 1 | 1 | 1 | 112 | 113 | 113 |
| 2 | 2 | 2 | { 113:1–8 | { 114A | 114 |
| 3 | 3 | 3 | { 113:9–26 | { 114B | 115 |
| 4 | 4 | 4 | 114 | { 115A | { 116A |
| 5 | 5 | 5 | 115 | { 115B | { 116B |
| 6 | 6 | 6 | 116 | 116 | 117 |
| 7 | 7 | 7 | 117 | 117 | 118 |
| 8 | 8 | 8 | 118 | 118 | 119 |
| { 9:1–21 | 9 | 9 | . . . | . . . | . . . |
| { 9:22–39 | 10 | 10 | 144 | 144 | 145 |
| 10 | 11 | 11 | 145 | 145 | 146 |
| 11 | 12 | 12 | 146 | 146 | { 147A |
| 12 | 13 | 13 | 147 | 147 | { 147B |
| 13 | 14 | 14 | 148 | 148 | 148 |
| . . . | . . . | . . . | 149 | 149 | 149 |
| . . . | . . . | . . . | 150 | 150 | 150 |

# Foreword

One familiar with the actual state of the Liturgy of the Hours through-out the length and breadth of most of Christendom experiences a giddy sense of unreality at the soaring periods in which Catholics apotheosize this form of prayer. Such ecclesiastical rhetoric provoked wry comment from J. D. Crichton in his discussion of numbers 83–101 of the Vatican II *Constitution on the Sacred Liturgy:*

> The Church holds a high doctrine of the divine office, yet its practice must be said to be low. In few churches, even cathedral churches, is the office sung or recited and in hardly any parish church is any part of the office ever heard. It is one sector of the liturgy of which the laity know hardly anything at all and which in recent times has given the clergy a great deal of anxiety.[1]

Carl Dehne, in a talk on the hours at the annual meeting of the Association of Jesuit Liturgists at Georgetown University, Washington, D.C., in January, 1980, said the same thing in different words. He recounted how exhilarated he would be reading, as a young high school student, liturgical-movement literature like Pius Parsch's *The Church's Year of Grace*, full of such resounding affirmations as: "During the nights of Advent . . . the Church prays her true Advent prayer, Matins . . . with a ring of joyful confidence . . . ." "At sunrise the Church calls out to us: 'Watch zealously; the Lord our God is near at hand.' " "At sundown the Church sings: 'You have appeared, O Christ, the Light from Light.' "[2] He soon discovered that practically nowhere in the world outside of monasteries was any voice raised to God at night, sunrise, sundown, or any other time, in these stirring words of the Church's prayer of hours.

Is someone pulling the wool over our eyes? Of course wishful thinking is a well-known ploy in churchly writings, a sort of ecclesiastical whis-

[1] J. D. Crichton, *The Church's Worship* (New York: Sheed and Ward, 1964) 187.
[2] Pius Parsch, *The Church's Year of Grace* (Collegeville: The Liturgical Press, 1957) I: 26, 114, 276.

tling in the dark in the hope that if we put the best face on theory, maybe reality will rise to the challenge. But in the case of the Divine Office this might well seem like giving a transfusion to a cadaver. The pages to follow are one man's Act of Hope that this be not true.

In any event, one cannot say that a new book on the Liturgy of the Hours is not needed. Whether or not this one fills the need, I leave for others to judge. But no major history of the Divine Office has appeared since the turn of the century, when the field was dominated by the "B's": Suitbert Bäumer's two-volume *Geschichte des Breviers* (Freiburg im B., 1895), Pierre Batiffol's *Histoire du Bréviaire romain* (Paris, 1898), and Jules Baudot's *Le Bréviaire romain* (Paris, 1907). The very titles betray their now outdated perspective: they are histories of the *breviary*, a book. We know now, and I trust the reader will too, that the Liturgy of the Hours is much more than a prayerbook—which is why the Vatican II-inspired reform of the Roman Office changed its name.

Since those early days, great advances have been made in the study of the Church's public prayer, and several important books have appeared: Joseph Pascher's *Das Stundengebet der römischen Kirche* (Munich, 1954), S. J. P. van Dijk and Joan Hazelden Walker's *The Origins of the Modern Roman Liturgy* (London, 1960), Pierre Salmon's *The Breviary through the Centuries* (Collegeville, 1962), and *L'office divin au moyen âge* (Paris, 1967). But these studies concerned themselves with the Latin offices exclusively. Previous to my recent study on Eastern offices, *The Liturgy of the Hours in the Christian East* (Cochin, 1984), I know of no general book on the Liturgy of the Hours that has included the Eastern material.

This is now necessary because of the revolution in liturgiology carried out in the past fifty years by historians of Eastern liturgy. The very distinction between cathedral and monastic liturgy, a concept that has changed radically our perpective on the early history of the Divine Office, was first developed by the German orientalist and founder of the school of comparative liturgy, Anton Baumstark (d. 1948). Further, Baumstark and those who came after him have shown that liturgiology, like philology, is a comparative discipline. One can no more be a liturgiologist knowing only one tradition than one can be a philologist knowing only one language. Gabriele Winkler's classic study of cathedral vespers showed the rich usefulness of this comparative approach to office studies.[3]

And so the advances in our knowledge of the origins, meaning, and later history of the Liturgy of the Hours have been produced of late in bits and pieces, often in highly technical and focused studies in learned

---

[3]Gabriele Winkler, "Über die Kathedralvesper in den verschiedenen Riten des Ostens und Westens," ALW 16 (1974) 53–102.

reviews, or in editions and commentaries of early monastic sources. Adalbert de Vogüé's work on the *Rule of the Master* and, with J. Neufville, on the *Rule of St. Benedict*, and Jordi Pinell's studies on the Iberian offices are but a few examples of the superb editions, commentaries, and specialized studies now available. A glance at the footnotes and bibliography will show the debt we owe to these and others.

But it is especially to my predecessors and colleagues in the Liturgical Section of the Faculty of Eastern Christian Studies at the Pontifical Oriental Institute in Rome that credit must be given. They have done more in the past half-century than any other single group of scholars to advance our knowledge of early and Eastern offices. Names such as J.-M. Hanssens, A. Raes, J. Mateos, and M. Arranz have become household words in the field of liturgiology. Mateos alone has revolutionized our study of the office in Late Antiquity.

The time has come, perhaps, to attempt a synthesis of these scattered recent findings and the new perspectives they have generated. For the early history of the office, this was done recently by Paul Bradshaw in his excellent book *Daily Prayer in the Early Church* (London, 1981). My own book, which covers a vaster sweep of history, grew, like liturgy, in bits and pieces. Baumstark said somewhere that "die Geschichte der Liturgie aus Sonderentwicklungen entsteht," and that is eminently true of this opus as well. Most of chapter 10 was originally a paper written in reaction to Bradshaw's book and presented at a meeting of the North American Academy of Liturgy (Douglaston, N.Y., January, 1983); it was later published in *Worship* (1984). Chapters 1–5, 12–15, 17, and 21–22 were written under pressure in four weeks during the Spring term of 1983. They began as a series of public lectures, the Placid Lectures, delivered in Rome, April 25–29, 1983. This annual series is in honor of Fr. Placid J. Podipara (1899–1985), a Carmelite priest of the Malabar Rite and former colleague on the faculty of the Pontifical Oriental Institute in Rome. My role in the 1983 lectures was due to the persistence of my friend Fr. Albert Nambiaparambil, c.m.i., then Director of the Centre for Indian and Interreligious Studies, Rome, which sponsors the Placid Lectures. Behind his persistence lay the lobbying of my numerous Indian graduate students at the Oriental Institute who wanted to see if I could talk about their traditions in English, too.

The enthusiastic reception of the lectures, coupled with more encouragement from Fr. Albert, resulted in the hasty production of a somewhat filled-out and documented redaction of what was said in the lectures. This was published in Cochin, Kerala, in January, 1984. Since things had gone that far, and the book was warmly received by those to whom I had sent it, I decided to do what I have often advised others *not* to do:

intrude on a field that extends beyond the limit of my specialty and round off the book for a larger public by adding chapters on the Western offices.

Since Western liturgy is so much more studied than Eastern, I presumed naively that this would be easy: not to worry, the work has been done—just read it and knit it all together. But somehow, Gaul seems to have been lost in the shuffle. I found nothing reliable on the Gallic offices, so I was forced back to the sources. Much of chapter 6 is the result of this fresh research. With this momentum, I was spurred also to take a look at the original sources for all the Western material—the Master, Benedict, the Iberian Fathers—though there, most of the work had been done, thanks to the scholars I cite, chiefly de Vogüé and Pinell.

Of course, in a work of this scope, one must be mindful of what Helmut Leeb says in the Introduction to his study of hagiopolite cathedral services:

> In our time what is required of research in the history of the liturgy is that it produce clear, sure results. In these results, established facts must be clearly distinguished from hypotheses. Because of the refined research methods of today's liturgical scholarship, with its attention to special, detailed questions, a wide-ranging one-author work covering a large area becomes daily more problematic and impossible. Too many uncertain assertions would have to be advanced, too many hypotheses risked, just because one person can no longer keep in view all the diverse sciences. Today the liturgical generalist like Anton Baumstark . . . is becoming more and more a rarity.[4]

So I cannot pretend to present here a complete history of the Liturgy of the Hours in all traditions, nor even in any one tradition. That would have required a volume for each single tradition.

My aim has been more modest. In Part I, I have attempted a thorough history of the origins and meaning of the Liturgy of the Hours during the formative peiord of Late Antiquity. I consider this absolutely essential to show what the Divine Office is really all about. As a historian of Christian liturgical traditions, it is my unshakeable conviction that a tradition can be understood only genetically, with reference to its origins and evolution. Those ignorant of history are prisoners of the latest cliché, for they have nothing against which to test it. That is what a knowledge of the past can give us. A knowledge of the future would serve equally well, but unfortunately that is not yet available to us.

This does not mean that our ignorance of the future leaves us enslaved by our past. For we do know the present; and in the present the

[4]Helmut Leeb, *Die Gesänge in Gemeindegottesdienst von Jerusalem (vom 5. bis 8. Jahrhundert)* (Weiner Beiträge sur Theologie 28, Vienna: Herder, 1970) 21.

past is always instructive, but not necessarily normative. What we do today is ruled not by the past but by the adaptation of tradition to the needs of the present. History can only help us decide what the essentials of that tradition are, and the parameters of its adaptation.

Part II attempts no more than a summary account of the main hours of the office in the chief extant traditions of the Christian East today. Part III offers the same for the Western hours, though the peculiar problems of the Western liturgical developments in this area have necessitated greater attention to the history of the office from the Middle Ages than was true for the East. Part IV is more reflective than scholarly, an attempt to get at the meaning of the Liturgy of the Hours in the life of the Church.

What I said in the public lectures that formed the original nucleus of this book was perforce directed at a broader audience than those with a professional interest in the study of liturgy. I hope the same is true of this book. It is the work of one who would like to think of himself as a liturgical scholar. It is also the work of one who loves to pray in common the Liturgy of the Hours. So, in spite of the technical portions of the book, it is my hope that it will be found readable by those whose piety is nourished by the common praise of God in the prayer of the Church.

With that in mind I have tried to reduce footnotes to the essentials. Where feasible I have treated well-known patristic and historical sources like the Bible: references to book, chapter, number, or verse are given in the body of the text without reference to an edition, wherever I judged that that would suffice. Anyone moderately acquainted with this literature should easily be able to find an edition of the original in one of the standard collections. References to secondary sources are also limited insofar as was compatible with the obligation to give credit for ideas that did not originate with me, or to indicate important studies in the field. For the same reasons, the bibliography is limited to the most important secondary works on the Divine Office. The reader who wishes to consult these works will find abundant reference to further bibliography.

The book is designed so that the reader interested in only one or a few of the traditions treated in Parts II–III can read those sections selectively with no loss of continuity. But Parts I and IV should be read in their entirety, and chapters 18–19 are essential to an understanding of the peculiar history of the hours in the West.

Many are those with whom I have had the privilege of offering God the sacrifice of praise that is the Liturgy of the Hours, especially the community of the Russian Catholic Church of St. Anthony the Abbot in Rome; students and colleagues in the Graduate Program in Liturgical Studies at the University of Notre Dame; and religious and monastic communities ranging from the Byzantine Basilian Sisters of Mount St. Macrina in Union-town Pennsylvania, St. Meinrad's Archabbey, St. John's Abbey, and Gethsemane Abbey in the U.S.A.; to Chevetogne in Belgium; Camaldo-li, the Abbazia di Praglia, the Badia Greca di Grottaferrata, and the Ukrainian Catholic Monastery of Studion at Castelgondolfo, all in Italy; and Dayr Abu Maqar in the Egyptian desert. They shared their prayer with me; I share my book with them. May it help them to understand better and love even more the praise of God in the Liturgy of the Hours.

# Acknowledgments

I am grateful to the editors of *Worship* and to The Liturgical Press, Collegeville, Minnesota, for permission to use in chapters 4 and 15 material from my article "Praise in the Desert: the Coptic Monastic Office Yesterday and Today" (*Worship* 56 [1982] 513–536); in chapters 5, 6, and 10, "*Quaestiones disputatae* in the History of the Liturgy of the Hours: the Origins of Nocturns, Matins, Prime" (*Worship* 58 [1984] 130–158); in chapter 21, "The Liturgical Year: Studies, Prospects, Reflections" (*Worship* 55 [1981] 2–23); to the editors of The Liturgical Press again for permission to use in chapter 17 some material from my "Sunday in the Eastern Tradition" (originally published in M. Searle [ed.] *Sunday Morning: a Time for Worship* [1982], 49–74). I also thank the editors of *Diakonia*, John XXIII Center, Fordham University, N.Y., for permission to use in chapter 21 part of my article "Thanksgiving for the Light: Toward a Theology of Vespers" (*Diakonia* 13 [1978] 27–50); and the editors of *Sobornost*, incorporating the now defunct *Eastern Churches Review* for permitting me to reuse in chapter 13 a few paragraphs of my article "On the Use of the Bema in the East-Syrian Liturgy" (*Eastern Churches Review* 3 [1970] 30–39).

I am also grateful to my colleagues Juan Mateos, s.j., of the Pontifical Oriental Institute, Rome, Hans Quecke, s.j., of the Pontifical Biblical Institute, Rome, Gabriele Winkler of St. John's University, Collegeville, and John Allyn Melloh, s.m., of the University of Notre Dame, for reading parts of the manuscript and making helpful suggestions; to Ms. Pat Palmer at the University of Notre Dame, and Suor Maria Grazia, s.d.c., and Sig. Maurizio Domenicucci at the Pontifical Oriental Institute for typing most of the manuscript; and to Michael Naughton, o.s.b., of The Liturgical Press, for his painstaking work in editing the book and seeing it through the press, as well as for his many valuable suggestions to improve the manuscript.

# PART I

# The Formation
of the Tradition

# 1

## PROLOGUE: CHRISTIAN PRAYER IN THE NEW TESTAMENT AND ITS JEWISH BACKGROUND

Apart from the question of temple worship, no two authors seem to agree about even the basics of Jewish services and prayer at the time of Christ. Were there public synagogue services daily or only on certain days? How many hours of private prayer were there daily? What were they? And why? I do not have the competence to answer these questions. What is more important, I do not think it is necessary to do so. The *details* of Jewish prayer systems were less important for the development of the Divine Office than is generally believed, and no direct link between the two can be demonstrated in spite of attempts to do so in the past. Jews pray at set times. So do Christians. The first Jewish-Christian converts may even have recited the same prayers at the same times as their Jewish contemporaries. Morning and evening prayer seem to have been the most constant and important hours of Jewish prayer. This will become true for Christians as well. And of course, Old Testament themes and types, and even texts, have formed part of the stuff of Christian prayer from the beginning. Beyond such generalities lie obscurity and speculation.

## New Testament Texts on Prayer

If we except those New Testament sayings concerning what today one calls "sacraments"—texts concerning the Lord's Supper, baptism, the imposition of hands, the anointing of the sick—we are left with four categories of texts concerning prayer in the New Testament:

1) references to Jesus and others at prayer
2) exhortations and commands to pray
3) instructions on how to pray
4) actual prayers and hymns.

From these texts we learn that Christians prayed "daily" (Acts 2:46), even "constantly" (1 Thess 1:2). They prayed when they were alone (Acts 10:9), when they were together (2:46), when they were separated (20:36–38; 21:5). They prayed at home (Acts 2:46; 10:9; 12:5, 12), in the temple (2:46; 3:1; Lk 24:53), or in the synagogue (13:14-15). In their prayer they used biblical psalms, canticles, and benedictions, or compositions of a like literary genre.[1] Their prayers included praise and blessing, thanksgiving, confession of faith;[2] and petitions to overcome temptation, to fulfill God's will, for the forgiveness of their persecutors, for the salvation of Israel, for aid in the preaching of the gospel, for the coming of the kingdom, for the forgiveness of sin, for rulers and the peace only they can assure us, for wisdom, holiness, sinlessness, strength and perseverance, faith, hope, love, health, revelation, enlightenment and the gift of the Spirit.[3] At times they were "filled with the Holy Spirit" (Acts 2:4), and prophesied or prayed in tongues (Acts 2:11; 10:46; 1 Cor 14).

As for explicit teaching and commands regarding prayer, the New Testament orders Christians to pray persistently (Matt 7:7-12; Luke 11:5-13; 18:1-8), even constantly (Luke 18:1; 21:36; Eph 6:18; Col 4:2; 1 Thess 5:16-18) with faith and confidence (Mark 11:24; Luke 18:1), yet humbly (Luke 18:9-14), and without hypocrisy or ostentation or many words (Matt 6:5-8). Finally, they are to be ever watchful (Luke 21:36; Col 4:2), watching and praying lest they enter into temptation (Matt 6:13;

[1]"Psalms and hymns and spiritual songs:" Col 3:16–17; Eph 5:18–20; specifically Christian hymns: Phil 2:6-11; Col 1:15–20; Eph 2:14–16; 5:14; 1 Tim 3:16; 1 Pet 3:18–22; Heb 1:3; Prologue of John; benedictions, etc.: Luke 1:46–55, 68–79; 2:29–32.

[2]Rom 1:8; 15:6, 9–11, 30–32; 1 Cor 1:4; 2 Cor 1:3ff.; 1 Thess 1:2; 2:13; 2 Thess 1:3; Eph 1:3, 9ff.; Col 1:3ff.; Phil 1:3ff.; 2 Tim 1:3; 1 Pet 1:3ff.; Phlm 4ff.

[3]See, for example, Matt 5:44; 6:9-15; 9:38 ;26:41; Mark 14:38; Rom 10:1; 1 Cor 1:4; 1 Thess 3:11–13; Eph 1:15ff.; 3:14–19; 1 Tim 2:1ff.

26:41; Luke 11:4). A model is provided in the Lord's Prayer (Matt 6:9–13; Luke 11:2–4): Christians are to pray to God as Father, and an exemplary, though by no means exhaustive, series of intentions is suggested. And they prayed in the name of Jesus (Matt 18:19–20; John 14:13–14; 15:16; 16:23–26; 1 Cor 1:2; Col 3:17). This New Testament teaching on prayer, more descriptive than exhaustive, contains one frequently repeated command that later tradition will apply to the Divine Office: the command to "pray without ceasing" (1 Thess 5:16–18; Col 4:2; Eph 6:18; Luke 18:1).

## Prayer in the New Testament and in First-Century Judaism

Were there any set forms and times of Christian prayer in this earliest period, forms and times that could be seen as the remote ancestor of our Liturgy of the Hours? It is difficult to generalize. In the first century, before the separation of Church and synagogue, and before the destruction of the Temple in A.D. 70, we know that Jewish Christians in Palestine participated in synagogue and temple worship. But some of that was a regression from an earlier, greater freedom vis-à-vis the Old Law.[4] And hellenistic Jewish Christians certainly looked on the temple cult as superceded (Acts 6:8ff.).[5] 1 Corinthians, a document of gentile Christianity, is the earliest and most explicit New Testament text regarding Christian worship. 1 Cor 11 has to do with the Lord's Supper, but chapter 14, the only New Testament text that is a real treatise on Christian worship,[6] describes a synaxis with speaking in tongues, revelations, prophecy, teaching, psalmody, blessings, thanksgiving, and formulas such as *"maranatha"* and "amen." Other epistles contain further formulas, the *pax*, etc.[7] But it does not seem possible to postulate any direct connection, except in the most general sense, between this data and what later became the Liturgy of the Hours.

More relevant, perhaps, than any direct relationship between Jewish or early Christian *forms* of public prayer and the later office, is the Jewish custom of praying *at set times.*[8] There is little agreement concerning

[4]F. Hahn, *The Worship of the Early Church* (Philadelphia: Fortress Press, 1973) 42.

[5]*Ibid.* 58ff.

[6]*Ibid.* 68.

[7]Rom 15:33; 16:16, 20, 27; 1 Cor 1:3; 12:13; 16:19–24; 2 Cor 1:2ff.; 13:12–14; Gal 1:3–5; 6:18; Eph 1:2; Col 1:2; 4:18; Phil 1:2; 4:9, 23; 1 Thess 1:1; 2:28; 2 Thess 1:2; 3:16, 18; 1 Tim 1:2; 6:21; 2 Tim 1:2; 2:18, 22; Titus 1:4; 3:15; Phlm 3; Heb 13:21; 1 Pet 1:2; 5:14; 2 John 3; 3 John 15; Jude 2:25; etc.

[8]In this section I am relying, in part, on R.T. Beckwith, "The Daily and Weekly Worship of the Primitive Church in Relation to its Jewish Antecedents," in R.T. Beckwith and others, *Influences juives sur le culte chrétien* (Textes et études liturgiques 4, Louvain: Abbaye du

the times of Jewish prayer in this period, and no wonder, for first-century Judaism was far from uniform. There were several schools of thought: Pharisees, Sadducees, Essenes. . . . Furthermore, most early Jewish-Christian converts were hellenistic Jews, and we are less well-informed about Jewish uses outside of Palestine. To compound the problem, Jewish liturgy of this period, though not totally amorphous, was largely uncodified.[9] So it is no longer possible simply to postulate a single Jewish pattern of two daily temple sacrifices (morning and evening), paralleled by two private prayer times at the same hours, which in turn lead supposedly to two chief Christian hours of morning praise and evensong. Instead, we see a mixed pattern: a *twofold* recitation of the Shema morning and evening, which in rabbinic circles is joined to a *threefold* daily private prayer—the additional prayer time being at the ninth hour, a pattern some think may have arisen from a shift of the evening hour of temple sacrifice from twilight to 3:00 P.M. Add to this the Essene uses as well as the Therapeutic practices described by Philo; the evidence of Dan 6:10, Ps 55/56:17, 2 Enoch 51:4; and finally the New Testament and early Christian testimony to a morning-noon-evening system in Judaism in the New Testament period—then the Jewish precedents for Christian prayer times appear much more muddled than they are sometimes made to seem. So I think all one can say about the influence of Jewish prayer times on Christian prayer in the apostolic period is the following.

Jewish prayer was centered in temple, synagogue, and home.

## I. TEMPLE

There were two daily sacrifices in the temple, morning and evening, and the New Testament tells us that the first Christians were "continually in the temple blessing God" (Luke 24:53), "and day by day attending the temple together. . ." (Acts 2:46). However, as Bradshaw has pointed out, Acts (3:11—4:31; 5:12-42) also makes it clear that these Christians gathered in Solomon's Portico as a separate group, to preach Jesus as the Christ, and that they were persecuted for it by the other Jews.[10] So these temple texts can hardly be taken to mean that the early Jerusalem Christians simply carried on their usual Jewish cult without further ado.

---

Mont César, 1981) 89–122; and P. Bradshaw, *Daily Prayer in the Early Church* (ACC 63, London: SPCK, 1981, and New York: Oxford University Press, 1982) chs. 1-2.

[9]On Jewish prayer forms and their codification, see especially J. Heinemann, *Prayer in the Talmud. Forms and Patterns* (Studia Judaica 9, Berlin/New York: Walter de Gruyter, 1977); L.A. Hoffman, *The Canonization of the Synagogue Service* (Notre Dame/London: University of Notre Dame Press, 1979).

[10]Bradshaw, *Daily Prayer* 24.

II. SYNAGOGUE

It is not clear just what corporate synagogue prayer comprised during the first Christian century, nor on how many days it was held. But it seems that there were public synagogue services at least on market days (Monday and Thursday), and of course on the Sabbath. Beckwith postulates a pattern of four services: morning prayer, additional prayer (at any hour), afternoon prayer, and evening prayer.[11] At least on the Sabbath, it seems, there were morning and afternoon services, and the morning assembly included a recitation of the Shema and *Tefillah* or benedictions,[12] plus readings from the Law and the Prophets. Luke 4:16–30 describes Jesus' participation in one such service. On the other hand, Epiphanius (*Adv. haer.* 29:9) speaks of only three hours of synagogue prayer among the Jews: ". . . in the morning and in the middle of the day and in the evening, three times a day when they say their prayers in the synagogues. . . ."

The New Testament tells us that Paul frequented the local synagogues on his missionary journeys before A.D. 61, but as the texts show, he went there to preach Christ, and was persecuted for his efforts (Acts 9:20–23; 13:5—14:7; 16:13–24; 17:1–17; 18:4–19; 19:8–10), so that can hardly be advanced as evidence for Christian worship in the synagogues. Indeed, it appears that the early Jewish Christians soon formed a synagogue unto themselves. The Letter of James, addressed to Jewish converts around A.D. 49–58, refers to "your synagogue" (2:2), and later around 70–80, Matthew's Gospel has Jesus advise his followers to pray at home rather than in the synagogue (6:5–6), and gives unmistakable evidence of tension between Church and synagogue at that time (10:17; 23:34).

III. HOME

With early Christian domestic prayer we are on surer ground. We know that the early Jewish Christians "with one accord devoted themselves to prayer" (Acts 1:14), and that this prayer was sometimes in common, in private homes (2:1, 46; 4:23–31; 12:5, 12). Was this formal prayer at set hours of every day? And if so, was it in direct continuity with Jewish prayer times? The problem in interpreting the times of Jewish statutory private prayer is that we have evidence for several distinct systems. First, there was the recitation of the Shema at the beginning and end of the day. The

---

[11]Beckwith, "Daily and Weekly Worship," 96ff. This is the *Tefillah* pattern in *Mishna*, Berakoth 4:1 (see note 13 below).

[12]On the Shema, see below. Two versions of the text of the benedictions are given in C.W. Dugmore, *The Influence of the Synagogue upon the Divine Office* (ACC 45, Westminster: The Faith Press, 1964) 114–125.

Shema, more a creed than a prayer, comprised four passages summarizing the Law: the Decalogue plus Deut 6:4-9; 11:13-21; and Num 15:37-41. These pericopes were preceded by two benedictions of thanksgiving, for creation and for revelation. The whole was concluded by a benediction in thanksgiving for redemption from Egypt and, in the evening, by a prayer for rest.

The Jewish prayer *par excellence* was the *Tefillah* or benedictions, recited privately three times a day (Dan 6:10). But when? The rabbinic custom was to pray the *Tefillah* morning, *afternoon*, and evening, but other texts—Ps 55:17 (54:18); 2 Enoch 51:4; Epiphanius, *Adv. haer.* 29:9—refer to prayer morning, *noon*, and evening. Though there is evidence for a connection between the evening temple sacrifice and private prayer (Ps 140/141:2; Ezra 9:5-15; Dan 9:20-21; Judith 9:1-14; Luke 1:10), it is not clear that the hours of *Tefillah* corresponded to the times of temple sacrifice or to the hours fixed for the recitation of the Shema, at least at the time of the New Testament. The *Mishna*, Berakoth 4:1,[13] allows the morning *Tefillah* at any time before noon, and the afternoon *Tefillah* at any time before sundown. The prayer during the day had no set time. Eventually, however, morning and evening benedictions were combined with the twofold recitation of the Shema.

In addition, there was also the prayer of such groups as the Essenes in Palestine, and the hellenistic Jewish Therapeutae in Egypt. The relevant Qumran texts are ambiguous at best, and open to several interpretations, but it seems that the Essenes, too, prayed three times a day—morning, noon, and evening.[14] In addition, they held vigils at night, dedicated to the study of the Law. Apart from some references in the psalms, this is the only evidence of night prayer in Palestinian Judaism. Philo (B.C. 13-ca. A.D. 45-50) in *The Contemplative Life* 27-28, 83-89, described the Therapeutae as praying privately at dawn and in the evening, and holding common vigil on the Sabbath. But another Egyptian source, *The Book of the Secrets of Enoch*, apparently written in Egypt by a hellenistic Jew at the beginning of the Christian era, and referred to by such Alexandrine Christian Fathers as Clement and Origen, testifies to the more traditional thrice-daily system of prayer: "It is good to go

[13]Berakoth 4:1: "The morning *Tefillah* [may be said any time] until midday. R. Judah says: Until the fourth hour. The afternoon *Tefillah* [may be said any time] until sunset. R. Judah says: Until midway through the afternoon. The evening *Tefillah* has no set time; and the Additional *Tefillah* [may be said] any time during the day. R. Judah says: Until the seventh hour." *The Mishnah*, trans. H. Danby (Oxford University Press, 1933) 5. The additional *Tefillah* was apparently done only in the synagogue: see *ibid.* Berakoth 4:7,

[14]See Bradshaw, *Daily Prayer* 4ff. for the texts and their conflicting interpretations.

morning, midday, and evening into the Lord's dwelling, for the glory of your creator" (2 Enoch 51:4).[15]

Finally, Flavius Josephus (B.C. 37–ca. A.D. 101), in his *Jewish Antiquities* 4, 212ff., seems to assign a privileged place to morning and evening prayer. Furthermore, he explains the spirit of this prayer in terms quite like those used later by the Fathers of the Church when speaking of Christian morning praise and evensong:

> Twice every day, at the dawn thereof and when the hour comes for turning to repose, let all acknowledge before God the bounties he has bestowed on them through their deliverance from the land of Egypt. Thanksgiving is a natural duty, and is rendered both in gratitude for past mercies, and to incline the giver to others yet to come.

So if we join and sift all the evidence of temple, synagogue, Shema and *Tefillah* prayer times, it seems hard to deny that morning and evening were the most general and privileged hours of prayer in the several traditions of Judaism in the period under discussion.

Did the early Christians observe these Jewish hours of prayer? It is impossible to give a definitive answer to this question. But the New Testament knew the Shema (Matt 22:37; Mark 12:29–30; Luke 10:26–27; 1 Cor 8:4–6), and also portrays Jesus as praying in the morning (Mark 1:35) and in the evening (Matt 14:23; Mark 6:46; John 6:15). Furthermore, like the Essenes and Therapeutae, Jesus also kept vigil at night (Luke 6:12). Later, in Acts, we see the disciples praying at the third (2:1, 15) sixth (10:9), and ninth hours (3:1; 10:3, 30). The latter, at least, is referred to explicitly as "the ninth hour of prayer," and it is possible that the other two hours were also set prayer times. In addition, the disciples imitated Jesus in praying at night (Acts 16:25; 2 Cor 6:5). And the vigil for the coming of the bridegroom in Matt 25:1–13 and related passages (Matt 9:14–15; Mark 2:18–20; 13:33–37; Luke 5:33–35; 13:35–40; cf. 1 Thess 5:2; Rev 3:3; 16:15; 19:9) may reflect an urchristian quartodeciman paschal watch at which, according to the Christian transformation of the later Jewish apocalyptic, the second coming of the Lord was awaited.[16]

---

[15]R.H. Charles, *The Apocrypha and Pseudoepigrapha of the Old Testament in English* (Oxford University Press, 1913) 2:461A. On the origins of this source, see *ibid.* 425.

[16]See, for example, *Targum Exodi* 12:42, trans. R. Le Déaut (SC 256) 96–99; Eusebius, *Church History* V, 24:2–5; *Gos. Heb.* (ca. 120–140), ed. A. Wilmart (ST 59) 58; Jerome (398), *Comm. in Matt* 4, 25:6; Lactantius (before 311), *Div. inst.* 7, 19:3. On this question see A. Strobel, *Ursprung und Geschichte des frühchristlichen Osterkalendars* (TU 121, Berlin: Akademie-Verlag, 1977) 29–46; R. Le Déaut, *La nuit pascale. Essai sur la signification de la Pâque juive à partir du Targum d'Exode XII 42* (Analecta Biblica 22, Rome: Pontifical Biblical Institute, 1963).

Later, we find liturgical material in the deutero-Pauline writings of the sub-apostolic period, such as Col 3:16–17 (cf. Eph 5:18–20):

> Let the word of Christ dwell in you richly, teach and admonish one another in all wisdom, and sing psalms and hymns and spiritual songs with thankfulness in your hearts to God. And whatever you do, in word or deed, do everything in the name of the Lord Jesus, giving thanks to God the Father through him.

This and other passages (e.g., 1 Cor 14:26; Eph 5:14; Jas 5:13) tell us really nothing more than that Christians had psalms, hymns, reading, and prayers in their meetings. So I must confess myself highly skeptical of all attempts to see a direct link between what begins to emerge in the third and fourth centuries as a gentile–Christian horarium of daily prayer at set times, and early Jewish-Christian participation in Jewish prayer during the New Testament period. As we shall see, the Old Testament command to offer sacrifice in the temple morning and evening certainly influenced the later Christian Liturgy of the Hours. But I would see this as part of the general spread of Old Testament themes in Christian thought from the third century, rather than as being in uninterrupted continuity with earlier Jewish Christianity. It is in this later period that the Sabbath is assimilated to Sunday as a day of Eucharist when fasting is forbidden, that themes of Old Testament priesthood are applied to the Christian ministry, and so on.

Of course I do not wish to deny all influence of Jewish cultic forms on early Christian prayer and worship. The *Didache* and book VII of the *Apostolic Constitutions* are proof positive of such influence, and we can also take as established the influence of the *berakah* and other Jewish prayer genres on Christian prayer, notably the anaphora. The writings of Audet, Bouyer, Ledogar, Ligier, Talley, Giraudo, and others, though not always in agreement, show clearly enough that the connection was there. As for the hours chosen for prayer, one can admit, as we shall see later, even a direct continuity in certain areas such as Palestine and Egypt, where the early Christian and Jewish communities were initially indistinguishable and long intermingled. Finally, it is perfectly obvious that the Bible, with its psalms and canticles and typology, provided the raw material and the symbols for what later would become the Liturgy of the Hours. A paradigmatic instance is the New Testament development of the theme of light and the later Christian use of sun imagery. This theme influenced the symbolism of Christian initiation, Easter, and Christmas (*Natalis solis invicti*); it influenced the question of orientation in prayer; and it influenced a key motif of cathedral morning praise and evensong. So the Liturgy of the Hours owes a clear debt to our Jewish heritage. But I cannot agree with Dugmore and others who try to see a greater continuity that the evidence just does not warrant.

## Conclusion

I think the most we can say about the Jewish and New Testament background of the Liturgy of the Hours is that Christians, like Jews, adopted the custom of praying at fixed times, and that the most important times for public liturgical prayer in commmon in both traditions were the beginning and end of the day. But these are natural prayer hours in any tradition. Some would like to see the three day hours—third, sixth, and ninth—as parallel to the Jewish times for private prayer. That may be a tenable view at least for Egypt, where hellenistic Jewish-Christian converts may well have followed Jewish customs more closely before the persecutions, especially under the emperor Hadrian (117–138), made identification with the Jews distinctly undesirable.[17] But even this is not certain. At any rate the office that has come down to us is the product of gentile Christianity, and a direct Jewish parentage cannot be demonstrated. Indeed, all the evidence points the other way: the absence of Ps 140 (141), the classic Christian evening psalm, in Jewish evening prayer is but one striking example.

Much more important than any such Jewish connection for the later history of the office is what is new and purely Christian in the New Testament: the belief that the Father has saved us in Christ Jesus, and that we live a new life in him. The New Testament is full of exultant hymns of joy and thanksgiving for this new creation,[18] and it is this that is at the basis of the hymn of praise that Christians have raised to the Father day in and day out, morning, evening, and night. And they shall continue to do so until the end of days.

[17]On early Egyptian Christianity and Judaism, see C.H. Roberts, *Manuscript, Society and Belief in Early Christian Egypt* (London: Oxford University Press, 1979).

[18]John 1:1–17; Phil 2:6–11; Col 1:15–20; Eph 1:3ff.; 2:14–16; 1 Tim 3:16; 1 Pet 3:18–20; Heb 1:3.

# 2

# DAILY PRAYER
# IN THE PRE-CONSTANTINIAN CHURCH

## The First Century

### I. THE DIDACHE

The first explicit, unambiguous reference to a system of daily prayer in the primitive Church is *Didache* 8, which gives the Matthean "Our Father" with the doxology "For yours is the power and the glory unto ages," followed by the rubric: "Pray thus three times a day." Some consider this a deliberate Jewish-Christian substitute for the twice daily recitation of the Shema. According to Audet, the *Didache* is an Antiochene composition dating from between A.D. 50–70,[1] not much later than the authentic Pauline corpus, and contemporaneous with the synoptic Gospels.

### II. CLEMENT OF ROME'S FIRST LETTER, TO THE CORINTHIANS

As for prayer at set times, the earliest Christian witness is *1 Clem.* 40:1–4, from the last decade of the first century. The hours are not specified, but the phrase "at set times" occurs in the chapter three times:

---

[1]J.-P. Audet, *La Didaché. Instructions des Apôtres* (Etudes bibliques, Paris: J. Gabalda, 1958) 219.

We should do in order (*taxei*) everything that the Master commanded us to do at set times (*kata kairous tetagmenous*). He has ordered oblations (*prosphoras*) and services (*leitourgias*) to be accomplished, and not by chance and in disorderly fashion but at the set times and hours (*ôrismenois kairois kai hôrais*) . . . .

What we have here is more an exhortation to Church order, based on Old Testament parallels, than a description of what was actually going on. More important for the Liturgy of the Hours is 1 *Clem.* 24:1–3, the earliest Christian text assigning a symbolic value to times of the day:

Let us consider, beloved, how the Lord continually manifests to us the resurrection to come, whose first fruits he made Christ by raising him from the dead. We see, beloved, that the resurrection was accomplished according to the time. Day and night make visible to us a resurrection. Night goes to sleep, the day rises; the day departs, the night follows.

# The Third Century

## I. CLEMENT OF ALEXANDRIA (D. CA. 215)

It is only at the beginning of the third century, in Egypt, that we see set times for prayer at the third, sixth, and ninth hours, as well as on rising, before retiring, and during the night. Clement of Alexandria insists that the true Christian must pray always, but from what he says it is clear that fixed hours for prayer were already an established custom in some circles: "Now if some assign fixed hours for prayer, such as the third, sixth, and ninth, the Gnostic, on the other hand, prays throughout his whole life. . ." (*Stromata* VII, 7, 40:3). Elsewhere Clement mentions prayer upon rising, before retiring, at night, and before, during, and after meals (*Pedagogue* II, 9–10; *Stromata* VII, 7, 49:3–4). But these times of prayer seem to be given more as examples of the Gnostic's unceasing prayer than as distinct, fixed hours of prayer.

In *Stromata* VII, 7, 43:6–7, Clement witnesses to the early Christian custom of orientation in prayer, based on the theme of Christ, light of the world and sun of justice, symbolized by the sun rising in the East:[2]

[2]On this theme see F.J. Dölger, *Die Sonne der Gerechtigkeit und der Schwarze* (LF 2 [14], Münster: Aschendorff, 1918); *id., Sol salutis. Gebet und Gesang im christlichen Altertum, mit besonderer Rücksicht auf die Ostung in Gebet und Liturgie* (LF 4/5 [16/17], Münster: Aschendorff, 1921); *id.,* "Sonne und Sonnenstrahl als Gleichnis in der Logostheologie des christlichen Altertums," AC 1 (1929) 271–290; *id.,* "Konstantin der Grosse und des Manichäis-

And since the dawn is an image of the day of birth, and the place from where the light, which shone forth first from the darkness, increases, there has also dawned on those wrapped in darkness a day of the knowledge of truth; prayers are made toward the sunrise in the East, in accord with the system of the sun.

This theme, as well as the practice of praying facing East, will become a commonplace in Christian tradition from the third century on.

Clement is also our first patristic witness to the eschatological character of Christian prayer at night. This, too, will become a fundamental trait of all Christian vigils. In the *Pedagogue* 2:9, Clement says:

> We must therefore sleep so as to be easily awakened. For it is said: "Let your loins be girt, and your lamps burning, and be like men who are waiting for their master to come home from the marriage feast, so that they may open to him at once when he comes and knocks. Blessed are those servants whom the master finds awake when he comes" (Luke 12:35–37). For a sleeping man is of no more use than a dead one. Therefore at night we ought to rise often and bless God. For blessed are they who watch for him, and so make themselves like the angels, whom we call "watchers." A man asleep is worth nothing, no more than if he were not alive. But he who has the light watches, and the darkness does not overcome him (John 1:5), nor does sleep, since darkness does not. Therefore he that is enlightened is awake towards God, and such a one lives. For what was made in him was life (John 1:3–4). "Happy is the man," says Wisdom, "who shall hear me, and the one who shall keep my ways, watching daily at my doors, waiting at the gates of my entrances" (Prov 8:34). "So then let us not sleep as others do, but let us keep awake," say the Scriptures, "and be sober. For those who sleep, sleep at night, and those who get drunk are drunk at night," that is, in the darkness of ignorance. "But since we belong to the day, let us be sober" (1 Thess 5:6–8). "For you are all sons of the light and sons of the day; we are not of the night or of darkness" (1 Thess 5:5).

"Vigilers" or "watchers" is the common term for angels in Syriac Christianity even today,[3] and the notion that the monks and nuns who keep

---

mus. Sonne und Christus im Manichäismus," AC 2 (1930) 301–314; *id.*, several brief notes in AC 3 (1932) 76–79, 282; *id.*, "Lumen Christi," AC 5 (1936) 1–43 (French trans. by M. Zemb, Paris: Cerf, 1958); *id.*, "Sonnengleichnis in einer Weinachtspredikt des Bischofs Zeno von Verona. Christus als Wahre und ewige Sonne," AC 6 (1940) 1–56; J. Pelikan, *The Light of the World. A Basic Image in Early Christian Thought* (New York: Harper and Brothers, 1962). See also chapter 3, note 15.

[3]See J. Gelineau, "Données liturgiques contenues dans les sept madrošé 'de la nuit' de saint Ephrem," OS 5 (1960) 107–121.

vigil at night while the world sleeps do so in imitation of the angels, who need no sleep and never interrupt their unending hymn of praise, will also become a commonplace in later tradition. The religious life will be an "angelic life" not only because of the ideal of absolute continence, but also because of the rule of uninterrupted prayer.

## ii. Origen (d. ca. 254)

Origen in his treatise *On Prayer* 32, also refers to the custom of praying facing East, "looking towards where the true light rises." In chapter 12:2 of the same work, he too knows only four hours of daily prayer: morning, noon, evening, and at night. The passage is also our earliest mention of Ps 140 in reference to evening prayer, a psalm which was later to become the nucleus of cathedral evensong throughout Christendom:

> He prays without ceasing who combines his prayer with necessary works, and suitable activities with his prayer, for his virtuous deeds or the commandments he has fulfilled are taken up as a part of his prayer. Only in this way can we take the saying "Pray without ceasing" (1 Thess 5:17) as being possible, if we can say that the whole life of the saint is one mighty integrated prayer. Of such prayer, part is what is usually called "prayer," and ought not to be performed less than three times each day. This is clear from the practice of Daniel, who, when great danger threatened him, prayed three times a day (Dan 6:10). And Peter, going up to the housetop to pray about the sixth hour, at which time also he saw the vessel let down from heaven, let down by the four corners (Acts 10:9, 11), gives an example of the middle of the three times of prayer spoken of by David before him: In the morning you shall hear my prayer; in the morning I will stand before you, and will look upon you (Ps 5:3). The last of the three is indicated in the words, "the lifting up of my hands like an evening sacrifice" (Ps 140:2). But not even the time of night shall we rightly pass without such prayer, for David says, "At midnight I rose to praise you for the judgments of your justice" (Ps 118:62), and Paul, as related in the Acts of the Apostles, at midnight together with Silas at Philippi prayed and sang praises unto God, so that the prisoners also heard them (Acts 16:25).[4]

With these three hours of prayer during the day in third-century Egypt it is possible that we have a reflection of Jewish usage. Origen cites Dan 6:10, and we have already seen that 2 Enoch 51:4 (an apocryphal text from

---

[4]Translation adapted from E. G. Jay, *Origen's Treatise on Prayer* (London: SPCK, 1954) 114–115.

hellenistic Jewry in Egypt at the beginning of the Christian era, one cited by both Clement and Origen in other writings) says: "It is good to go morning, midday, and evening into the Lord's dwelling, for the glory of your creator."[5] Early Alexandrine Christianity was closely linked to the large hellenistic Jewish community of Alexandria before the revolts and massacres of the Jews under Trajan (66–70), and again under Hadrian (117–138), forced Christians to distance themselves from their Jewish past.[6]

At any rate, Bradshaw is surely right in rejecting the usual interpretation of Alexandrine sources that try to fit Clement and Origen—or the *Didache*, for that matter—into a later "little hours" pattern of terce, sext and none.[7] Though Clement knew of prayer at the third, sixth, and ninth hours, the early Alexandrine pattern seems rather to have been prayer morning, noon, evening, and night. Bradshaw has proposed this as the "first pattern of daily prayer which is encountered at this period," to which he assigns an "apostolic origin."[8] But I am not sure that this primitive Egyptian pattern is really an horarium of daily prayer rather than just another way of saying "pray always," like our expression "morning, noon, and night."

### III. TERTULLIAN (D. AFTER 220)

Tertullian also knew the custom of orientation in prayer (*Apology* 16; *Ad nationes* 1:13), as well as other "rubrics" such as when to stand or kneel (*On Prayer* 23; *On Fasting* 14), all of which show a growing standardization of Christian prayer. Much more important for our purposes, we find in Tertullian's writings the first description of what was to become by the end of the fourth century the classic system of Christian daily prayer: obligatory prayer at the beginning and end of each day, with prayer highly recommended also at the third, sixth, and ninth hours, and at night.

Chapter 25 of his treatise *On Prayer*, written between 198 and 204, describes this daily prayer as follows:

> Concerning the time [of prayer], however, the external observance of certain hours will not be unprofitable. I mean those common hours that mark the intervals of the day: the third, sixth, and ninth, which are found to have been more solemn in the Scriptures. At the third hour the Holy Spirit was first poured out upon the gathered disciples

[5] See chapter 1, note 15.
[6] *Ibid.* note 17.
[7] *Daily Prayer* 47–50.
[8] *Ibid.* 57–59.

(Acts 2:15). Peter, on the day he experienced the vision of the whole community in that small vessel, had gone upstairs to pray at the sixth hour (Acts 10:9). The same one was going into the temple with John at the ninth hour when he restored the paralytic to health (Acts 3:1). Although these hours simply exist without any command for their observance, still it is good to establish a presumption that might reinforce the admonition to pray, and tear us away from our affairs for this duty as if by law, so that we at least pray not less than three times a day . . . which, as we read, Daniel also observed in accord, certainly, with Israel's discipline. Of course this is in addition to the statutory prayers, which are owed without any admonition at the beginning of light and of night.

Tertullian goes on to say that Christians should also pray before meals or before going to the bath, and when they are with guests (ch. 26), and even indicates psalmody as a part of such Christian common prayer (ch.27): "The more diligent in praying are accustomed to add in prayers the Alleluia and psalms of this type to the conclusions of which those who are together may respond. . . ." He seems to mean that psalms with Alleluia or some other responsory as part of the text itself—for example LXX Pss 110–118 and 145–150—were chosen so that the company could respond at the end of the verses.

Elsewhere Tertullian also mentions the custom of rising for prayer at night.[9] He even refers to assemblies at night (*"nocturnis conuocationibus"*) in *To his wife* II, 4:2. And in his *Apology* 39:18, written in A.D. 197, he provides our earliest evidence for the agape supper with its evening lamp ritual, remote ancestor of the lucernarium of cathedral vespers: "After the washing of hands and the lights, someone who is able is prompted to stand in the center and sing to God a hymn from Sacred Scripture or of his own composition . . . . And so the feast is likewise closed with prayer" [just as it began; see 39:17].

Tertullian does not explain just why he holds morning and evening prayer to be statutory and the other times only quasi-obligatory, but one can accept without hesitation the customary interpretation that he is referring to the precept of two daily temple sacrifices in Exod 29:38–41; 30:7–8; and Num 28:3–8. Both Chrysostom and Cassian (*Inst.* II, 3:1) later single out matins and vespers in the same way, and Chrysostom in his *Commentary on Ps 140*, 3, traces the obligation to the Old Testament precept.

What about the day hours? Tertullian implies that Christians have chosen them as prayer times because they were signalled publicly: ". . . these three hours, as more significant in human affairs, which divide the

---

[9]*To his Wife* (ca. 203) II, 5:2; *Apology* 39:18.

day, distinguish business affairs, which resound publicly . . . " (*On Fasting* 9:10). Chapter 25 of his treatise *On Prayer* cited above provides a similar motivation—"those common hours that mark the intervals of the day"—as well as citing scriptural texts that will become the classic justification for the "little hours" in later patristic writings.

Joan Hazelden Walker has pointed out that the custom of publicly announcing these divisions of the day was not general,[10] but Tertullian's suggestion does not rise or fall with whether or not there was an audible public signal to announce these hours. Twelve hours were normal divisions of the day, as we see in the parable of the laborers in the vineyard (Matt 20:3-5) and in the patristic texts already cited, just as the four watches were the normal divisions of the night (Mark 6:48; 13:35). It was customary to divide these twelve hours into groups of three. So the third, sixth, and ninth hours were normal points of reference in the ancient world, and I would agree with Dugmore[11] that they became Christian prayer times simply because they were such universal points of reference, used as reminders that we must pray always, "morning, noon, and night," as we would say today. Walker attempts to show that these hours of prayer could have had an apostolic origin in Rome, a usage she sees reflected in the Markan passion account. The Markan passion narrative does seem to have been framed to fit the conventional divisions of the Roman day, and the same is undoubtedly true of the several references to these hours in Acts. But that the Markan account reflects an actual Roman horarium of prayer at the third, sixth, and ninth hours is, I think, unlikely at such an early date.

## IV. Cyprian (d. ca. 258)

Cyprian in chapters 34–36 of his treatise *On the Lord's Prayer*, written around 250, confirms Tertullian's testimony concerning the prayer system of the third-century North African Church:

> [34]Now in celebrating prayer, we find that with Daniel the three boys strong in faith and victorious in captivity observed the third, sixth, and ninth hours, namely for a sacrament of the Trinity. . . . Having determined on these intervals of hours in a spiritual sense a long time ago, the worshipers of God were subject to them as the established and obligatory times for prayer. Later the fact was made manifest that these sacraments formerly existed, because the just used to

[10]"Terce, Sext and None. An Apostolic Custom?" *Studia Patristica* 5 (TU 80, Berlin: Akademie-Verlag, 1962) 206–212.

[11]Dugmore, *The Influence of the Synagogue* 66–67.

pray in this way. For the Holy Spirit came down upon the disciples at the third hour (Acts 2:15). . . . Likewise Peter, going up to the housetop at the sixth hour, was instructed by a sign and also by the voice of God (Acts 10:9). . . . The Lord also was crucified from the sixth to the ninth hours. . . .

[35]But for us, beloved brethren, besides the hours of praying observed of old, both the times and the sacraments have increased. For one must also pray in the morning, that the resurrection of the Lord may be celebrated by morning prayer. This the Holy Spirit meant formerly when he said in the psalms: "My king and my God, to you will I pray, O Lord, in the morning, and you shall hear my voice; in the morning I will stand before you and gaze upon you" (Ps 5:3-4). And again the Lord says through the prophet: "At dawn they shall watch for me, saying: Let us go and return to the Lord our God" (Hos 5:15—6:1).

Likewise at sunset and the passing of the day it is necessary to pray. For since Christ is the true sun and the true day, when we pray and ask, as the sun and the day of the world recede, that the light may come upon us again, we pray for the coming of Christ, which provides us with the grace of eternal light. For in the psalms the Holy Spirit declares that Christ is called the day. "The stone," he says, "which the builders rejected has become the cornerstone. This is the Lord's doing, and it is wonderful in our eyes. This is the day that the Lord has made; let us exult and rejoice in it" (Ps 117:22-24). Likewise the prophet Malachy testifies that he is called the sun, when he says: "But unto you that fear the name of the Lord the sun of justice shall arise, and in his wings there is healing" (Mal 3:20).

But if in the Holy Scriptures Christ is the true sun and the true day, no hour is excepted in which God should be adored frequently and always, so that we who are in Christ, that is, in the true sun and day, should be insistent throughout the whole day in our petitions, and should pray. And when by the laws of nature the return of night, recurring in its turn, follows, for those that pray there can be no harm from the nocturnal darkness, because for the sons of light, even in the night there is day. For when is one without light who has light in the heart? Or when does one not have the sun and the day, for whom Christ is sun and day?

[36]So let us who are always in Christ, that is, in the light, not cease praying even at night. This is how the widow Anna, always praying and keeping vigil, persevered in deserving well of God, as is written in the gospel: "She did not leave the temple, serving with fasting and prayers night and day" (Luke 2:37). . . . Let us, beloved brethren, who are always in the light of the Lord . . . count the night as day. Let us believe that we walk always in the light. Let us not be hindered by the darkness which we have escaped, let there be no loss

of prayers in the night hours. . . . Let us who by God's indulgence are recreated spiritually and reborn, imitate what we are destined to be. Let us who in the kingdom are to have only day with no intervening night, be as vigilant at night as in the light [of day]. Let us who are to pray always and render thanks to God, not cease here also to pray and give thanks.

Like Tertullian, Cyprian uses Daniel (with a Trinitarian twist), various other texts of the Old Testament, the image of the Trinity, and the traditional texts of Acts to support the custom of praying at the third, sixth, and ninth hours. For the last two hours he adds the passion of Jesus, a theme also mentioned by Tertullian, though less directly, in chapter 10 of his treatise *On Fasting*. More significant is the strong emergence of the light and resurrection themes in morning and evening prayer.

Note also that for Cyprian the "established and obligatory times for prayer—*statutis et legitimis temporibus*" (chapter 34 cited above) in Judaism are not the morning and evening temple sacrifices, but the three Jewish hours of private prayer in Dan 6:10, 13, which Cyprian applies (wrongly) to the Christian day hours. This weakens the popular theory, based on Tertullian's *"legitimae orationes,"* that the two pristine Christian prayer times were morning and evening, to which the "little hours" were later added. For Cyprian, the opposite was true: the older, obligatory Jewish times for prayer were the third, sixth, and ninth hours, to which Christians added prayer in the morning, in the evening, and at night.

In fact, we have no early text whatever that supports an initial pattern of only morning and evening prayer. Some early Egyptian sources have morning-noon-evening-night; the North-African sources have morning, third, sixth, ninth hours, agape, evening, and night. And as we shall see shortly, the *Apostolic Tradition* from Rome around 215 has the same horarium as the Africans, but with the addition of another night hour at cockcrow. What is true is that except for an occasional nocturnal vigil—see Tertullian, *To his Wife* II, 4:2—the only two times when Christians gathered regularly on weekdays was in the morning for instruction or in the evening for an agape supper.

## v. THE APOSTOLIC TRADITION (CA. 215)

We encounter these hours next in what is by far our most important third century liturgical source, a Greek text called the *Apostolic Tradition*, written presumably by Hippolytus of Rome around 215. However, this document is not without serious problems of text and interpretation.

If we put aside for the moment chapter 25 concerning the agape, the section that interests us begins with chapter 35, which treats of prayer at home on rising and, on occasion, an early morning catechetical instruction in common: *"per uerbum catecizatio."* I cite the text from the new translation of Geoffrey J. Cuming:[12]

> [35]The faithful, as soon as they have woken and got up, before they turn to this work, shall pray to God, and so hasten to their work. If there is any verbal instruction, one should give preference to this, and go and hear the word of God, to the comfort of his soul. Let him hasten to the church, where the Spirit flourishes.

This chapter is found in the earliest extant source of the document, a Latin version contained in several Latin palimpsest folia of codex *Verona LV (53)*.[13] These folia date from the end of the fifth century, and the Latin translation itself is thought to be from around 375. After the passage just cited, the Latin text continues with some canons on the Eucharist and on the sign of the Cross. Then there is a lacuna, and the text resumes on folio 81r with the motivation for prayer at the ninth hour. Modern editors have reconstructed the text by supplying the missing portion from our next oldest source, the Sahidic version of the Alexandrine *Sinodos* in codex *British Library Or. 1320*. The manuscript dates from A.D. 1006, but the Sahidic translation itself is thought to have been made from the Greek text before 700.

Of course such reconstructions are tenuous at best, but since the Latin version mentions prayer in the morning and, when the text resumes after the lacuna, at the ninth hour, it is not rash to suppose that the missing portion of the text would speak also of prayer at the third and sixth hours. At any rate, here is the reconstructed text, with the supplied Sahidic portion in brackets:

> [41][Let every faithful man and woman, when they have risen from sleep in the morning, before they touch any work at all, wash their hands and pray to God, and so go to their work. But if instruction in the word of God is given, each one should choose to go to that

[12]*Hippolytus. A Text for Students* (Grove Liturgical Study 8, Bramcote: Grove Books, 1976). For the critical edition of the reconstructed text, see B. Botte, *La Tradition apostolique de saint Hippolyte. Essai de reconstitution* (LQF 39, Münster: Aschendorff, 1963).

[13]E. Tidner (ed.), *Didascalia Apostolorum, canonum ecclesiasticum, Traditiones Apostolicae versiones latinae* (TU 75, Berlin: Akademie-Verlag, 1963) 142. For information on the sources of the reconstructed *ApTrad*, see the introductions to the works cited in note 12; also J.-M. Hanssens, *La liturgie d'Hippolyte. Ses documents, son titulaire, ses origines et son caractère* (OCA 155, Rome: PIO, 1969); *La liturgie d'Hippolyte. Documents et études* (Rome: Gregorian University, 1970).

place, reckoning in his heart that it is God whom he hears in the instructor.

For he who prays in the church will be able to pass by the wickedness of the day. He who is pious should think it a great evil if he does not go to the place where instruction is given, and especially if he can read, or if a teacher comes. Let none of you be late in the church, the place where teaching is given. Then it shall be given to the speaker to say what is useful to each one; you will hear things which you do not think of, and profit from things which the holy Spirit will give you through the instructor. In this way your faith will be strengthened about the things you will have heard. You will also be told in that place what you ought to do at home. Therefore let each one be diligent in coming to the church, the place where the holy Spirit flourishes. If there is a day when there is no instruction, let each one, when he is at home, take up a holy book and read in it sufficiently what seems to him to bring profit.

And if you are at home, pray at the third hour and bless God. But if you are somewhere else at that moment, pray to God in your heart. For at that hour Christ was nailed to the tree. For this reason also in the Old (Testament) the Law prescribed that the shewbread should be offered continually as a type of the body and blood of Christ; and the slaughter of the lamb without reason is this type of the perfect lamb. For Christ is the shepherd, and also the bread which came down from heaven.

Pray likewise at the time of the sixth hour. For when Christ was nailed to the wood of the cross, the day was divided, and darkness fell. And so at that hour let them pray a powerful prayer, imitating the voice of him who prayed and made all creation dark for the unbelieving Jews.

And at the ninth hour let them pray also a great prayer and a great blessing, to know the way in which the soul of the righteous blesses] God who does not lie, who remembered his saints and sent his word to give them light. For at that hour Christ was pierced in his side and poured out water and blood; giving light to the rest of the time of the day, he brought it to evening. Then, in beginning to sleep and making the beginning of another day, he fulfilled the type of the resurrection.

Pray before your body rests on the bed. Rise about midnight, wash your hands with water, and pray. If your wife is present also, pray both together; if she is not yet among the faithful, go apart into another room and pray, and go back to bed again. Do not be lazy about praying. He who is bound in the marriage-bond is not defiled.

Those who have washed have no need to wash again, for they are clean. By signing yourself with moist breath and catching your spittle in your hand, your body is sanctified down to your feet. For when (prayer) is offered with a believing heart as though from the font, the gift of the Spirit and the sprinkling of baptism sanctify him who believes. Therefore it is necessary to pray at this hour.

For the elders who gave us the tradition taught us that at that hour all creation is still for a moment, to praise the Lord; stars, trees, waters stop for an instant, and all the host of angels (which) ministers to him praises God with the souls of the righteous in this hour. That is why believers should take good care to pray at this hour.

Bearing witness to this, the Lord says thus, "Lo, about midnight a shout was made of men saying, Lo, the bridegroom comes; rise to meet him." And he goes on saying, "Watch therefore, for you know not at what hour he comes."

And likewise rise about cockcrow, and pray. For at that hour, as the cock crew, the children of Israel denied Christ, whom we know by faith, our eyes looking towards that day in the hope of eternal light at the resurrection of the dead.

And if you act so, all you faithful, and remember these things, and teach them in your turn, and encourage the catechumens, you will not be able to be tempted or to perish, since you have Christ always in memory.

There are four points worth noting in this text:

1) The daily horarium of prayer included seven hours—but not the seven we are used to in later sources. Rather, they are:

> on rising
> third, sixth, ninth hours
> evening agape (in ch 25)
> before retiring
> about midnight
> at cockcrow.

2) If the Sahidic version reproduces faithfully the third-century Greek text, it is our earliest source to interpret the day hours in terms of the Markan passion account. With respect to the supposed Roman origin of the *Apostolic Tradition*, recall Walker's attempt to trace the Markan passion horarium to an early Roman prayer cycle.[14]

3) In the earlier Latin version in the Verona fragments, the ninth hour is interpreted as the hour of Jesus' death, but that does not depend on the Markan chronology (*see* Matt 27:45–46; Luke 23:44), nor does it necessarily imply, as we shall see, the

[14]See note 10 above.

existence of the third and sixth hours with a passion interpretation.

4) In the latin text the evening and morning hours receive a paschal interpretation: sundown and sunrise are like the dying and rising of Jesus. The night hours are eschatological, looking to the second coming and to the resurrection of the dead.

5) Chapter 35 is repeated here in the Sahidic version, indicating, perhaps, a later expansion of the original horarium to include new material.

What, then, was the horarium of the Urtext of the *Apostolic Tradition*? It is possible that it comprised only:

> morning prayer
> ninth hour
> evening agape
> evening prayer
> midnight prayer
> prayer at cockcrow.

Bradshaw has proposed that the pristine Egyptian pattern of prayer, morning-noon-evening-night, was the earliest horarium.[15] To this first the ninth hour was added as an outgrowth of the service that concluded the station or fast on Wednesday and Friday, which Tertullian speaks of in chapter 10 of his treatise *On Fasting*. In this hypothesis, terce would have been added still later to round things off. Bradshaw supports this view by the fact that in fourth-century Jerusalem, according to Egeria's diary (24:2–3; 25:5; 27:3), there is no terce except in Lent. This argument is weakened, however, by the fact that Egeria's Jerusalem cycle has no "little hours" at all, not even sext, on Sunday (25:1–4). Furthermore, in his treatise *On Fasting*, ch. 10, a Montanist work written after 207, Tertullian attacks the Catholic practice of ending the stational fast at the ninth hour when the Lord died on the cross, rather than prolonging the fast until evening as the rigorist Montanists did. So I would prefer to see the reconstructed text of the *Apostolic Tradition*, including the third, sixth, and ninth hours, as a legitimate representation of early third-century Roman usage. This leaves us with the following prayer system:

| *Private Prayer:* | *Common Assemblies:* |
|---|---|
| on rising | |
| | morning instruction |

[15]Bradshaw, *Daily Prayer* 61ff.

| (Private Prayer:) | (Common Assemblies:) |
|---|---|
| third, sixth, ninth hours | |
| | evening agape |
| on retiring at midnight at cockcrow | |

Once again, the presence of two night hours of prayer should make one hesitate to homogenize our third-century evidence into one single pattern. In Egypt we saw a morning-noon-evening-night system of prayer; in Tertullian, a pattern of morning, third-sixth-ninth hours, evening, and night. And now with the *Apostolic Tradition* we find a system of *private* prayer like Tertullian's, but with *two* prayer times at night, and with the beginnings of a tradition of common synaxes morning and evening for catechesis and the agape.

The text of the *Apostolic Tradition* concerning the morning assembly is straightforward enough: it was an instruction, not a "matins" office. The agape, also mentioned by Tertullian in his *Apology* 39, did include a blessing of the evening lamp that is without doubt the ancestor of the lucernarium of cathedral evensong. This chapter 25 on the agape is not in the Verona Latin fragments. Indeed, it is found only in the Ethiopic version of our document, based on an earlier Arabic version, and dating from after 1295. But in spite of its late date, parallels in such earlier documents derived from the *Apostolic Tradition* as the *Canons of Hippolytus* from Egypt around 336–340, the *Apostolic Constitutions* from the environs of Antioch around 380, and the fifth-century Syriac *Testament of Our Lord Jesus Christ*, have induced modern editors to include the agape chapter in their reconstruction of the third-century Urtext, most of which has come to us in such disjointed fragments. Here is the text in question:

> [25]When the bishop is present, and evening has come, a deacon brings in a lamp; and standing in the midst of all the faithful who are present (the bishop) shall give thanks. First he shall say this greeting: "The Lord be with you."
> And the people shall say: "With your spirit."
> (Bishop:) " Let us give thanks to the Lord."
> And they shall say: "It is fitting and right: greatness and exaltation with glory are his due."
> And he does not say, "Up with your hearts," because that is said (only) at the offering.
> And he shall pray thus, saying: "We give you thanks, Lord, through your Son Jesus Christ our Lord, through whom you have shone upon

us and revealed to us the inextinguishable light. So when we have completed the length of the day and have come to the beginning of the night, and have satisfied ourselves with the light of day which you created for our satisfying; and since now through your grace we do not lack the light of evening, we praise and glorify you through your Son Jesus Christ our Lord, through whom be glory and power and honour to you with the holy Spirit, both now and always and to the ages of ages. Amen."

And all shall say: "Amen."

They shall rise, then, after supper and pray; and the boys and the virgins shall say psalms.

And then the deacon, when he receives the mixed cup of the offering, shall say a psalm from those in which "Alleluia" is written, and then, if the priest so directs, again from the same psalms. And after the bishop has offered the cup, he shall say the whole of a psalm which applies to the cup, with "Alleluia," all joining in. When they recite psalms, all shall say, "Alleluia, which means, "We praise him who is God; glory and praise to him who created every age through his word alone." And when the psalm is finished, he shall give thanks over the cup and distribute the fragments to all the faithful.

## Conclusion

The evidence from the first three Christian centuries, though not disparate, is diverse enough to exclude any facile attempt to harmonize it all and fit it into one system or horarium without doing violence to the facts.

### 1. THE CURSUS

Among the Egyptians we find a system of morning-noon-evening-night prayer that is close to Jewish and Essene usage. But the Egyptian sources also mention prayer before meals, and in general stress unceasing prayer, so that the times mentioned may have been just another way of saying that Christians must pray "morning, noon, and night"—in other words, always.

With the North Africans and the *Apostolic Tradition* we are closer to the full series of hours that will eventually coalesce into the fourth-century cursus:

> on rising
> [common catechesis in *ApTrad*]
> third, sixth, ninth hours

on retiring

during the night [*ApTrad*: midnight and cockcrow].

Not one source gives only morning and evening as *the* Christian hours of prayer, and so we should not make too much out of Tertullian's calling them *"legitimae."*

## II. CONTENT OF THE PRAYER SERVICES

What sort of prayer was this, what was its form, its structure, what did they actually do? We do not really know, but history does provide a few hints. Eusebius in his *Church History* VII, 30:10, recounts the problems created for the third-century Church by the popular hymns of the heretics, and we know that this had provoked a reaction against privately composed, non-scriptural hymns—*psalmoi idiotikoi*, as they were called—which in turn favored a broader use of biblical psalmody and canticles in Christian liturgy during the second and third centuries. Furthermore, Tertullian tells us that the early Christian daily prayers were said alone or in the company of others, that hymns and biblical psalms were used, and both he and the *Apostolic Tradition* indicate that sometimes the psalms were executed responsorially. Both these witnesses also describe the agape, which included a ritual of the evening lamp, psalmody, and prayer. The common morning service in the *Apostolic Tradition* was made up of Scripture and instruction. More than this we cannot say.

## III. MEANING

In this period we also see the beginnings of what will become the common interpretation of the Christian cursus of prayer— its "theology"—at least in cathedral usage. Evening and morning, at the setting and rising of the sun, the Church is reminded of Jesus' passover from death to life. The practice of orientation in prayer witnessed to by Clement, Origen, and Tertullian was also related to this symbolism of Christ as sun of justice and light of the world, as well as to the eschatological expectation of the second coming of the Lord, "for as the lightning comes from the East and shines as far as the West, so will be the coming of the Son of man" (Matt 24:27). The light of the evening lamp at vesperal prayer symbolizes Christ, the light of the world. The day hours recall the passion in the Markan account; the third hour is also a memorial of the descent of the Holy Spirit at Pentecost. Night prayer is eschatological, like the watch of the virgins for the coming of the bridegroom, and the unceasing praise of angels that will one day be ours too.

Was this "liturgical prayer" or "private prayer" or something in between? The very question is anachronistic in this early period. Christians prayed. Whether they did it alone or in company depended not on the nature of the prayer, but on who happened to be around when the hour for prayer arrived. The various "rubrics" about praying facing East, or with hands raised (Clement, *Stromata* VII, 7, 40:1); when to kneel and when not to; were equally observed alone or in company. The point was to pray. In times of persecution, or during the workday, that usually meant alone. When they could come together they did so, because the very nature of Church means to congregate. But alone or together, the prayer was the same except for those services like the agape or Eucharist which by their very nature were done only in common.[16]

---

[16]On the frequency and communal nature of the early Eucharist, see R. Taft, "The Frequency of the Eucharist throughout History," *Concilium* 152 (1982) 13–24.

# 3

# THE CATHEDRAL OFFICE
# IN THE FOURTH-CENTURY EAST

With the so-called Peace of Constantine in 312, the Church acquired the freedom to develop the public and external aspects of its life. The effects were immediately visible in church organization, in art and architecture, and in liturgy. Ecclesiastical dioceses and provinces were organized, synods held, monasteries founded, basilicas and baptistries built, mosaics created to adorn them. And Christian worship, formerly the furtive affair of a persecuted minority, became an integral part of the daily public life of the Roman Empire. The resulting flowering of liturgical uses was striking. The Constantinopolitan church historian Socrates, whose *Church History*, written between 439 and 450, and covering the first post-Nicene century (324–425), says:

> . . . It is impossible to find anywhere, among all the sects, two churches that agree exactly in their prayer ritual. . . . To give a complete catalogue of all the various customs and ceremonial observances in use throughout every city and country would be difficult—or rather, impossible (V, 22).

But in spite of the fact that Christian public worship bursts onto the scene with a veritable explosion of documentary evidence in the second half of the fourth century, what occurs is evolution, not revolution: it does not overturn what went before but builds on it. To us it seems revolutionary because it happens so suddenly, like spring in the far north, where temperatures rise dramatically, snow and ice melt, and seeds long buried under the snow burst suddenly into bloom. Something like that happens with the Divine Office or Liturgy of the Hours in this period. All of a sudden we see it everywhere as an established cycle of daily, common, public services.

J. Mateos divides the development of the office in this period into three types: 1) cathedral, 2) Egyptian-monastic, 3) urban-monastic.[1] These are not three successive chronological stages of the development of one office, but three distinct types of office that evolved in three separate areas of Church life. The first two evolve simultaneously from the mid-fourth century. The third, a synthesis of the first two, is already visible in the last quarter of the same century.

This distinction between "cathedral" and "monastic" offices goes back to the renowned German liturgiologist Anton Baumstark (d. 1948), founder of the school of comparative liturgy. It has become popular in recent years to challenge the historical basis on which this distinction depends, considering the monastic/cathedral distinction a mere mental construct, a conceptual framework describing not so much concrete offices that ever existed independently, but rather "ideal types" of liturgical forms found together in the same offices from the start. But the validity of Baumstark's distinction has been amply demonstrated in recent years by such scholars as Mateos, Arranz, Winkler, Bradshaw, and the present writer. And even a superficial glance at the present Coptic *Horologion* gives the lie to such skepticism, as we shall see in chapter 4.

The office of the secular churches is called "cathedral" rather than "parochial" because for centuries it was the bishop's church that was the center of all liturgical life. This office of the secular churches was a popular service characterized by symbol and ceremony (light, incense, processions, etc.), by chant (responsories, antiphons, hymns), by diversity of ministries (bishop, presbyter, deacon, reader, psalmist, etc.), and by psalmody that was limited and select rather than current and complete. That is, the psalms were not read continuously according to their numerical order in the Bible, but only certain psalms or sections of psalms were chosen for their suitability to the hour or service. Furthermore, the cathedral services were offices of praise and intercession, not a Liturgy of the Word. Contrary to another popular misconception, there were no Scripture lessons in the normal cathedral office except in Egypt and Cap-

---

[1]"The Origins of the Divine Office," *Worship* 41 (1967) 477–485.

padocia. The readings found today in some offices result from the later development of the festive calendar, and are not part of the basic structure of the ordinary cathedral offices.[2]

## Eusebius, First Witness to the Cathedral Office

Our first witness to such an office is the famous church historian Eusebius (ca. 263–339), bishop of his hometown, Caesarea in Palestine, from 313. In his *Commentary on Ps 64*, verse 9b (LXX): "You shall make the outgoings of the morning and evening rejoice," Eusebius explains that these morning and evening joys have been interpreted as hymns (*hymnologias*) and praises (*ainopoiêseis*), and then he tells why:

> For it is surely no small sign of God's power that throughout the whole world in the churches of God at the morning rising of the sun and at the evening hours, hymns, praises, and truly divine delights are offered to God. God's delights are indeed the hymns sent up everywhere on earth in his Church at the times of morning and evening. For this reason it is said somewhere, "Let my praise be sung sweetly to him" (cf. Ps 146:1), and "Let my prayer be like incense before you" (Ps 140:2).[3]

The reference to Ps 140 is significant, for although Eusebius does not say so, we shall see from other fourth-century sources that it was *the* psalm of cathedral evensong. The corresponding nucleus of morning praise was Ps 62, as Eusebius implies in his *Commentary on Ps 142*, verse 8.[4] And commenting on Ps 65:2, he speaks of the tradition of singing and psalmody throughout the whole Church of God, not only among the Greeks but

---

[2]On this question see R. Zerfass, *Die Schriftlesung im Kathedraloffizium Jerusalems* (LQF 48, Münster: Aschendorff, 1948). The East-Syrian (Assyro-Chaldean) office, one of the most primitive and purely "cathedral," has readings only on Easter Sunday. See A. J. Maclean, *East Syrian Daily Offices* (London: Revington, Percival and Co., 1894) 264, note 2; J. Mateos, *Lelya-Ṣapra. Les offices chaldéens de la nuit et du matin* (OCA 156, Rome: PIO, 1976²) 443. The gospel now read at vespers on certain days of Lent or before Sundays and feasts is not an original part of the office, but comes from the old Liturgy of the Presanctified or, in the case of Sundays and feasts, from the Mass of the following day. See S. Pudichery, *Ramsa. An Analysis and Interpretation of the Chaldean Vespers* (Dhamaram College Studies 9, Bangalore: Dhamaram College, 1972) 93ff., 184–198; C. Mousses, *Les livres liturgiques de l'Eglise chaldéene* (Beirut: Imprimerie orientale, 1955) 22.

[3]PG 23, 639.

[4]PG 24, 49.

also among the barbarians.[5] Finally, in his *Church History* II, 17:21–22, Eusebius refers to nocturnal vigils, especially (hence not exclusively?) during passiontide, at which the Scriptures were meditated on and a form of responsorial chant was in vogue.

Within a few years of Eusebius we find evidence for these offices in every province of the Christian East.

## Egypt

Our first Egyptian testimony to the fourth-century cathedral office comes from Athanasius of Alexandria (295–373). His *History of the Arians* 81 and *Defence of his Flight* 24 confirm the existence of cathedral vigils, attended by the monks as well as the laity, that comprised readings, responsorial psalmody, and prayers. A bit later John Cassian, who was in Egypt from about 380 to 399, in *Conferences* 21:26 has Abbot Theonas exhorting to morning prayer in Egypt say:

> And this kind of devotion even many of those that live in the world observe with the utmost care, since they rise before it is light, or very early, and do not engage at all in the ordinary and necessary affairs of this world before hastening to church and striving to consecrate in the sight of God the first fruits of all their actions and doings.

This text mentions only morning prayer, and it is not clear that it involved a common synaxis. But H. Quecke cites several later Coptic sources which make it clear that the Egyptian Church knew daily morning and evening prayer.[6]

The *Canons of Hippolytus*, a medieval Arabic document which according to its editor, R. Coquin, goes back to an original Greek text composed around 336–340 within the Patriarchate of Alexandria,[7] not only confirms the existence of a cathedral office in Egypt, but gives us precious information as to its contents:

> *Canon 21. Concerning the gathering of all the priests and people in the church every day.* Let the priests gather in church every day, and

---

[5]PG 23, 648.

[6]H. Quecke, *Untersuchungen zum koptischen Stundengebet* (Publications de l'Institut Orientaliste de Louvain 3, Louvain: Université Catholique de Louvain, 1970) 10–11.

[7]PO 31, 329ff. The canons cited below are translated from this edition. On the provenance of these canons see H. Brakmann, "Alexandreia und die Kanones des Hippolyt," *Jahrbuch für Antike und Christentum* 22 (1979) 139–149, who judges them to be from Egypt but not from Alexandria itself (cf. 149).

the deacons, subdeacons, readers, and all the people, at cockcrow. They shall do the prayer, the psalms, and the reading of the books and the prayers . . . .

In canon 26 entitled, "On the hearing of the Word and on prayer in church," we read that "everyone should take care to go to church every day that there are prayers" because of what one hears in church, which is the Word of God. And canon 27 says one should read the Scriptures at home at dawn when there is no prayer in church, and pray in the middle of the night and at cockcrow. These texts—especially canon 21, which is quite explicit—must refer to the office, since there was no daily Eucharist in Egypt in this period.[8] So we can conclude that the Word of God—probably not just psalmody but also Scripture lessons—was an integral part of the cathedral office in Lower Egypt.

Canon 27 of the same document, "concerning one who does not go to church, that he should read the books each day; and on the exhortation to pray in the middle of the night, or at cockcrow," resumes the eschatological and angelic praise themes of night prayer seen in the third-century sources:

> Let each one take care to pray with great vigilance in the middle of the night, for our fathers said that at that hour all creation is assiduous in the service of praising God, all the angelic hosts and the souls of the just bless God. For the Lord testifies to this, saying, "In the middle of the night there was a cry: Behold, the bridegroom has come, go out to meet him" (Matt 25:6). At cockcrow, again, is a time when there are prayers in the churches, for the Lord says, "Watch, for you do not know at what time the master will come, in the evening, or in the middle of the night, or at cockcrow, or in the morning" (Mark 13:35), which means we must praise God at every hour. And when a man sleeps in his bed, he must pray to God in his heart.

This same canon also makes it clear that the evangelical precept to pray without ceasing was not just for monks. Nor is this an Egyptian peculiarity. We see the same teaching in Chrysostom (*Sermon on Anna 4*, 5–6), Jerome (*Letter 46*, 12), and others.

Apparently there were readings also in the cathedral offices of Upper Egypt. In the second half of the fourth century Paphnutius, in his *History of the Monks of the Egyptian Desert*, quotes two friends from Souan (Aswan) who later became monks. "We used to go to church together daily, both evening and morning, and heard the Holy Scriptures that were read, and the lesson from the gospel that says, 'He who loves father or

---

[8] See Taft, "The Frequency of the Eucharist," 14.

mother more than me is not worthy of me . . . .' "[9] This text must also refer to the Liturgy of the Hours, for again, there was no tradition of daily Eucharist in fourth-century Egypt.[10] H. Quecke considers this an important witness to readings in the Egyptian office which, as he notes, was an Egyptian peculiarity.[11] He also refers to a later text, a ninth-century Arabic redaction of a homily attributed to Theophilus of Alexandria based on an earlier Greek original, which confirms the presence of Scripture lessons in the Egyptian cathedral offices: "A poor man who performs the prayers to which he is obliged, goes to church morning and evening and assists at the reading of the pericopes, receives the body of Christ and his blood, receives the pax, and preserves himself from all evil . . . ."[12]

## Cappadocia

Much of our evidence for the cathedral office in Cappadocia has to do with the large and prominent Christian family that produced three bishops, a monk, a nun, and a troop of saints: Basil the Great, bishop of Caesarea in Cappadocia and exarch of Pontus in 370, his sister St. Macrina, and his brothers Sts. Gregory of Nyssa and Peter of Sebaste, also bishops, as well as his mother and grandmother.

Gregory of Nyssa (d. 394) in his *Life of St. Macrina*, describes the death of his sister in 379.[13] The day before, Gregory wished to remain with the failing Macrina, "but the chant of the singers called to the thanksgiving for the light, and she sent me off to the church" (ch. 22).

The evening service began with the lighting of the lamps. This was a practical necessity, needed to provide light for the service. But even among non-Christians, the lighting of the evening lamp had a deeper meaning. In our age of abundant electricity "it is difficult for us to appreciate the wonder of flickering oil lamps piercing the settling darkness of the night. But pre-Edisonian cultures greeted artificial light with a sense of

[9]H. E. Wallis Budge, *Miscellaneous Coptic Texts in the Dialect of Upper Egypt* (London: British Museum, 1915) text, 437; see also 953, and O.H.E. Burmester, "The Canonical Hours of the Coptic Church," OCP 2 (1936) 82.

[10]See note 8.

[11]Private communication, and *Untersuchungen* 8–13.

[12]H. Fleisch, "Une homélie de Théophile d'Alexandrie en l'honneur de St. Pierre et de St. Paul. Texte arabe publié pour la première fois et traduit par H. Fleisch," *Revue de l'Orient chrétien* 30 (1935/1946) 398.

[13]The cited passages are translated from P. Maraval (ed.) Grégoire de Nysse, *Vie de sainte Macrine* (SC 178, Paris: Cerf, 1971) 212, 226.

grateful welcome."[14] Pagans were accustomed to greet the light with the exclamation *"Chaire phôs agathon* (Hail, good light)!" or *"Chaire phôs philon* (Hail, friendly light)!" And Clement of Alexandria in his *Protrepticus* 11, 114:1, recommends that we greet the true God with "Hail, light!" So even before the development of evensong into a formal liturgical office, Christian domestic piety had inherited the lucernarium, the practice of greeting the evening lamp with prayer and praise.

Whom they borrowed it from is a matter of dispute. Tertullian, in his *Ad nationes* 1:13, accuses the pagans of having borrowed "the Jewish lucernarium rite" and other Jewish practices "that are certainly foreign to your gods." But I am skeptical that this general pagan usage would have been borrowed from a despised minority such as the Jews. Furthermore, although there are parallels to the lucernarium in the Jewish ritual of the Sabbath eve and Hanukkah lights, I know of no Jewish parallel in the *daily* domestic or synagogue rituals of the Jews, and the pagan and Christian greeting of the evening lamp was a *daily* affair. So I am inclined to think the Christian lucernarium is a baptized pagan rite.[15]

In the *Apostolic Tradition* of Hippolytus (ca. 215) we saw that this early Christian lucernarium was in conjunction with the agape, and included a prayer of thanksgiving for the light. By the last quarter of the fourth century in Cappadocia, this ritual and its name have been incorporated into cathedral vespers. This is an exciting new development, which we see as early as 374 in Gregory Nazianzen's eulogy for his father, also Gregory, who was bishop of Nazianzus in Cappadocia, where the funeral oration was delivered in the presence of St. Basil the Great.[16] The relevant passage concerns the Easter vigil, but the lucernarium of the Easter vigil derives from that of vespers, not vice-versa.

But let us return to Gregory of Nyssa's life of his sister Macrina. His description in chapter 25 of the death scene the following evening shows that the domestic lamp ritual was still in vogue in spite of its adoption into the church service.

[14]A. Ciferni, "The Lucernarium," *Liturgical Prayer* 5 (Winter 1976/77) 32–33.

[15]The early Christian lucernarium and its pagan parallels are discussed in the works cited in ch. 2, note 2. See also J. Mateos, "Quelques anciens documents sur l'office du soir," OCP 35 (1969) 348–351; A. Tripolitis, "*Phôs hilaron*. Ancient Hymn and Modern Enigma," *Vigiliae Christianae* 24 (1970) 190ff.; A. Quacquarelli, *Retorica e liturgia antenicena* (Richerche patristiche 1, Rome: Desclée, 1960) ch. 7: "*Lux perpetua* e l'inno lucernare," 153–180. G. Winkler favors a domestic Jewish origin of the Christian lucernarium in her study "Über die Kathedralvesper in den verschiedenen Riten des Ostens und Westens," ALW 16 (1974) 60ff.

[16]*Oration 18*, 28–29, PG 35, 1017–1021, interpreted by F. van de Paverd, "A Text of Gregory of Nazianzus Misinterpreted by F. E. Brightman," OCP 42 (1976) 197–206.

And when evening had arrived and the lamp was brought in, she opened her eyes that had been closed until then and looked at the light, and made clear that she wished to say the thanksgiving for the light, but since her voice failed her, she fulfilled the offering with her heart and with the movement of her hands, while her lips moved in harmony with the inner impulse.

Basil, who also died in 379, the same year as his sister Macrina, provides us with the precious information that this "thanksgiving for the light" was the evening hymn *Phôs hilaron*, which is still the lucernarium hymn of Byzantine vespers according to the tradition of St. Sabas:

O joyous light of the holy glory of the immortal Father,
heavenly, holy, blessed Jesus Christ!
As we come to the setting of the sun and behold the evening light,
We praise you Father, Son and Holy Spirit, God!
It is fitting at all times that you be praised with auspicious voices,
O Son of God, giver of life.
That is why the whole world glorifies you!

This *epilychnios eucharistia*, one of the earliest extant Christian hymns, is a praise to Christ who is the true light shining in the darkness of the world and illuminating—i.e., saving—all men and women. In his treatise *On the Holy Spirit* 29 (73), Basil says the hymn was ancient even in his time, so old that he did not even know who wrote it:

It seemed fitting to our fathers not to receive the gift of the evening light in silence, but to give thanks immediately upon its appearance. We cannot say who was the father of the words of the thanksgiving for the light. But the people utter the ancient formula, and those that say "We praise you Father, Son and Holy Spirit of God" were never thought impious by anyone.

Basil's reading "Holy Spirit *of* God" is the original one, as can be seen in the ninth-century Sinai *horologion* edited by Mateos.[17]

Basil also seems to have known the "angel of peace" litany, traditional formula of dismissal, at the end of the evening office. In *Letter 11* he writes to an anonymous friend:[18]

After passing, by God's grace, the whole day in the company of our children, and having celebrated for the Lord a truly complete feast

[17]"Un horologion inédit de Saint-Sabas. Le Codex sinaïtique grec 863 (LXᵉ siècle)" *Mélanges E. Tisserant* III. 1 (ST 233, Vatican: Typis polyglottis Vaticanis, 1964) 56, 70ff.
[18]The letters of Basil cited here and below are translated from Y. Courtonne (ed.) S. Basile, *Lettres*, 2 vols. (Paris: Société d'édition "Les Belles Lettres," 1957/1961).

. . . we sent them on to your lordship in good health, after praying
God the lover of humankind to give them an angel of peace as an
aid and traveling companion . . . .

Basil also paraphrases this litany apropos of the monastic office in *Longer
Rules* 37:3, "asking of him guidance and instruction in what is profitable."
  So Cappadocian cathedral vespers in the second half of the fourth century had a light service with *Phôs hilaron*, probably Ps 140, and concluding intercessions. Ps 140 is not indicated in the Cappadocian documents,
but we can probably presume it on the basis of evidence from other areas,
as we shall see shortly. There may also have been Scripture lessons. Somewhat later Socrates of Constantinople in his *Church History* (ca. 439–450)
V, 22, a mixed salad of information on varying liturgical usages in Late
Antiquity, says: "Likewise in Caesarea in Cappadocia and in Cyprus on
Saturdays and Sundays, always in the evening at the lighting of the lamps
(*meta tês lychnapsias*) the presbyters and bishops explain the Scriptures."
So there was preaching, it seems, and perhaps even lessons, at cathedral
vespers on weekends in Cappadocia.
  Thus festive cathedral vespers in Cappadocia had something like the
following basic structure:

> Lucernarium with *Phôs hilaron*
> Ps 140
> Lessons and homily
> Intercessions with "angel of peace" petitions

We have less information for morning prayer, but Basil's Letter 207,
3, written to the clergy of Neocaesarea in reply to their criticism of Basil's
liturgical innovations in Caesarea (*plus ça change . . .* ), describes a vigil
that concludes with cathedral matins:

> [1]As for the accusation concerning the psalmody, with which espe-
> cially our calumniators frighten the more simple folk, I have this to
> say: [2]the customs now in use are in agreement and harmony with all
> the Churches of God. [3]Among us the people (*laos*) "keep watch after
> nightfall" (*ek nyktos orthrizei*: Is 26:9) in the house of prayer, [4]and
> in distress and affliction and continual tears make confession to God.
> [5]Finally, rising up from the prayers they begin the psalmody. [6]And
> now, divided into two sections, they chant alternately with one
> another, thus reinforcing the study of the scriptural passages, and at
> the same time producing for themselves attentiveness and an undis-
> tracted heart. [7]Then again, leaving it to one to intone the chant, the
> rest respond.
> [8]And thus after spending the night in a variety of psalmody inter-
> rupted by prayers, [9]when the day begins to dawn all in common, as

with one voice and one heart, raise the psalm of confession to the Lord, each one making his own the words of repentance.

[10]If you avoid us for these things, then you will shun the Egyptians, you will shun those of both [Upper and Lower] Libyas, Thebans, Palestinians, Arabs, Phoenicians, Syrians, and those who live by the Euphrates—in a word all those among whom vigils *(agrypniai)* and prayers and psalmody in common have been held in honor.

What was the nature of this vigil, which Basil as much as admits was a recent innovation? Mateos formerly believed it to be the nightly vigil of the Basilian ascetic communities.[19] But I have reexamined the question with him, and we agree with Bradshaw that this is by no means certain.[20] In the first place, as we shall see in the next chapter, this vigil does not accord with the uses of the ascetics in *Longer Rules* 37:5, which provides a period of rest between the nightly *mesonyktikon* or midnight office and the morning prayer of the ascetics. Furthermore, the text speaks of the "people" *(laos)*. Now it is true, as Mateos notes,[21] that Basil does not call his ascetics "monks," but the whole context of the passage of *Letter 207* on psalmody would lead one to think of cathedral practice. For instance, Basil justifies his liturgical usage by appealing to that of "all the Churches of God" (2) and numerous countries (10), whereas earlier in the same letter, when speaking of the ascetics, he appeals only to the three traditional cradles of monasticism: Egypt, Palestine, and Mesopotamia.[22] Furthermore, the absence of any explicit comparison with monastic usage elsewhere makes it more plausible that Basil is referring to an occasional cathedral vigil such as we see in Alexandria and Constantinople at this time.

Basil begins his description of the service (3) with a phrase from Is 26:9, which we shall also find in Chrysostom's Antiochene vigil, and which is still today the Lenten invitatory to nocturns in the Byzantine Sabaitic office. Further, the description of the psalmody, first antiphonal (6), then responsorial (7), and interrupted by prayers (8), is remarkably like the Friday-night vigil of the Bethlehem monks discussed in the next chapter (cf. Cassian's *Institutes* III, 8:4). Its basic structure was a liturgical unit of three antiphons, three responsorial psalms, and three lessons, repeated throughout the night. So it seems certain at least that Basil is describing an occasional, not a daily vigil.

[19]"L'office monastique à la fin du IVe siècle: Antioche, Palestine, Cappadoce," OC 47 (1963) 85–86.

[20]*Daily Prayer* 101–102.

[21]"L'office monastique," 86.

[22]*Letter 207*, 2, ed. Courtonne, vol. 2, 185.

This vigil may have opened (3) with Is 26:9ff. as invitatory, followed perhaps by Ps 118, then the liturgical unit as in Cassian, repeated several times. Cathedral matins opens (9) with Ps 50, and comprises "hymns and canticles" (*hymnoi kai odai*) according to Basil's *Letter 2*, 2, to Gregory Nazianzen.[23] This document is describing the prayer of an ascetic, but since the Cappadocian monastic office (cf. chapter 5) was a hybrid one containing elements of cathedral matins, we can take this as evidence for that office.

So I would hypothetically reconstruct the Cappadocian vigil as follows:

| | |
|---|---|
| *Vigil* | Is 26:9ff. |
| | Ps 118 |
| | Antiphonal psalmody; prayers |
| | Responsorial psalmody; prayers     } repeatedly |
| | [Lessons] |
| *Matins* | Ps 50 |
| | Hymns and canticles |
| | [Intercessions] |

# Cyprus

Epiphanius (ca. 315–403), a monk in Judea for thirty years before becoming bishop of Salamis (Constantia in Cyprus) in 367, also refers to the "morning hymns and prayers" and "the vesperal (*lychnikos*) psalms and prayers" in chapter 23 of his treatise *On the Faith* written ca. 374–377. Note that he speaks of morning hymns and prayers, and vesperal psalms and prayers—i.e., in the plural. I shall return to this point later apropos of the number of vesperal psalms in Egeria's diary, and the disputed question of the origins of lauds. Suffice it to say now that psalms and hymns followed by prayers of intercession were, and remain, the core of the morning and evening cathedral offices.

In chapter 24 of the same treatise Epiphanius says that frequent, assiduous, insistent prayer is commanded day and night at the established hours, without being any more explicit about just what those times were. But since this chapter concerns the laity, it is clear that attendance at the morning and evening synaxes did not exhaust their prayer obligations.

[23]*Ibid.*, vol. 1, 6.

## Antiochia

It is from Antiochia—Antioch and its environs—that we first find massive evidence for the cathedral offices hitherto seen only in a few passing allusions.

### 1. JOHN CHRYSOSTOM

Chrysostom in Antioch around 390 gives the motivation for the two daily cathedral synaxes in his *Baptismal Catechesis* VIII, 17–18.

> Be very diligent in coming here early in the morning (*orthron*) to bring prayers and praises to the God of all, and to give thanks for the benefits already received, and to entreat him to deign to be a close ally for protection in the future. . . . But let each one go to his affairs with fear and trembling, and so pass the time of day as one obliged to return here in the evening to give the master an account of the entire day and to ask pardon for failures. For it is impossible even if we are ten thousand times watchful to avoid being liable for all sorts of faults. Either we have said something inopportune, or listened to idle talk, or been disturbed by some indecent thought, or have not controlled our eyes, or have spent time in vain and idle things rather than doing what we should. And that is why every evening we must ask the master's pardon for all these faults. . . . Then we must pass the time of night in sobriety and thus be ready to present ourselves again at the morning praise. . . .[24]

In his *Commentary on Ps 140*, 1,[25] also from the Antiochene period of his ministry before 397, Chrysostom says Ps 140 is chanted "daily." Later, when he tells why it is chanted, it is clear he is referring to vespers. He also speaks of Ps 62 as the morning psalm:

> Many things in this psalm [140] are suitable for the time of evening. Not for this reason, however, did the fathers choose this psalm, but rather they ordered it to be said as a salutary medicine and forgiveness of sins, so that whatever has dirtied us throughout the whole length of the day, either in the marketplace or at home or wherever we spend our time, we get rid of it in the evening through this spiritual song. For it is indeed a medicine that destroys all those things.
>
> The morning psalm is of the same sort. . . . For it kindles the desire for God, and arouses the soul and greatly inflames it, and fills it with

[24]A. Wenger (ed.) Jean Chrysostome, *Huit catéchèses baptismales inédites* (SC 50, Paris: Cerf, 1957) 256–257.

[25]The relevant passages are in PG 55, 427, 430.

great goodness and love. . . . But let us see where it begins, and what it teaches us: "O God my God, I keep vigil before you, my soul thirsts for you"(Ps 62:1). Do you see how it shows the words of a soul afire? Where there is love of God, all evil departs; where there is remembrance of God there is oblivion of sin and destruction of evil. . . .

St. Basil in his *Longer Rules* 37:4 also affirms that vespers serves as a propitiation for the sins of the day, but since he is talking about the monastic office, we shall return to this text in chapter 5.

A bit later in the same *Commentary on Ps 140*, 3, when commenting on verse two: "Let my prayer rise like incense before you, the lifting up of my hands like the evening sacrifice," Chrysostom applies the Old Testament Levitical precept to cathedral matins and vespers, recalling Tertullian's *orationes legitimae* that we saw in the previous chapter:

> This was ordered and laid down by law for the priests, that . . . each morning and evening they sacrifice and burn a lamb. The former was called the morning sacrifice, the latter the evening sacrifice. God ordered this to be done, signifying through doing this that it is necessary to be zealous in worshiping him at both the beginning and the end of the day.

But Chrysostom seems not to have known a ceremonial use of incense in the Antiochene office, for he gives a purely spiritual interpretation to Ps 140:2, "Let my prayer rise like incense before you," in the context of vespers.[26] Perhaps the same can be said for a ritualization of the evening lamplighting. In his Lenten homily *In Gen. sermo 4*, 3, he complains that his Antiochene hearers pay less attention to the light of Sacred Scripture he is preaching to them than to the lights in church and to the one who at that very moment, apparently, was going through the church lighting the lamps.[27] These homilies were not necessarily preached at vespers—a ninth-hour communion service to break the fast would be equally plausible—but at any rate it appears from the text that the lamps were being lighted without fanfare during the sermon.

Finally, in his *Homily 6 on 1 Tim*, 1, Chrysostom speaks of the intercessions at the end of the daily offices. 1 Tim 2:1-4 is the classic Christian text concerning this intercessory prayer: "First of all, I urge that supplications, prayers, intercessions, and thanksgivings be made for all men, for kings and all who are in high positions. . . ." Chrysostom informs us that cathedral morning and evening prayer in fourth-century Antioch included such intercessions for various intentions: "What does this

[26]PG 55, 430-432.
[27]PG 54, 597.

'first of all' mean in the daily cult? The initiates [baptized] know how each day [supplications] are offered in the evening and in the morning: how we pray for the whole world, for the kings and for all those in authority.[28]

Chrysostom refers again to the daily intercessions in another Antiochene homily, *On the Obscurity of the Prophecies 2, 5.*[29] He notes that the catechumens were present—hence he is speaking of cathedral, not monastic services—and says we would not think we have the spiritual force to pray suitably for the bishop, for those present, and for everyone. But we dare to do so as a group because the community gives strength, and prayer offered by all the people together in church has great power. The catechumens cannot do this for they are not yet a part of this priestly, interceding people. In addition, Chrysostom mentions petitions for the whole world, for the entire Church all over the world, and for all bishops. This is obviously a description of the supplications that we know were at the end of Christian services, including the Liturgy of the Word. But such "daily" intercessions must refer to cathedral matins and vespers since Mass was not celebrated daily in Antioch at this time.[30]

In addition to these two common synaxes Chrysostom also exhorts the laity to pray assiduously during the day, wherever they happen to be, when possible even kneeling and raising their hands in prayer.[31]

## II. THE APOSTOLIC CONSTITUTIONS

The *Apostolic Constitutions*, a lengthy church order written in Greek around 380 by a Syrian from the environs of Antioch—though not from the city itself, it seems—provides the first full description of the structure and contents of the three cathedral offices of morning praise, evensong, and the Sunday resurrection vigil. In book II, 59, we read:[32]

> When you teach, bishop, command and exhort the people to frequent the church regularly, morning and evening every day, and not to forsake it at all, but to assemble continually and not diminish the Church by absenting themselves and making the Body of Christ lack a member. For it is not only said for the benefit of the priests, but let each of the laity hear what was said by the Lord as spoken to himself: "He who is not with me is against me, and he who does not gather with

[28]PG 62, 530.
[29]PG 56, 182.
[30]Taft, "The Frequency of the Eucharist," 15.
[31]*Sermon on Anna 4*, 5–6, PG 54, 666–668.
[32]The text is translated from F. X. Funk, *Didascalia et Constitutiones Apostolorum* (Paderborn: F. Schoeningh, 1905) vol. 1.

me scatters" (Matt 12:30). Do not scatter yourselves by not gathering together, you who are members of Christ, you who have Christ as your head, according to his own promise, present and communicating to you. Do not be neglectful of yourselves, nor rob the savior of his own members, nor divide his body, nor scatter his members, nor prefer the needs of this life to the Word of God, but assemble each day morning and evening, singing psalms and praying in the Lord's houses, in the morning saying Ps 62, and in the evening Ps 140.

But especially on the Sabbath, and on the Lord's day of the resurrection of the Lord, meet even more diligently, sending up praise to God who made all through Jesus and sent him to us and allowed him to suffer and raised him from the dead. Otherwise how will one defend oneself before God, one who does not assemble on that day to hear the saving word concerning the resurrection, the day on which we accomplish three prayers standing, in memory of him who rose in three days, on which day is accomplished the reading of the prophets and the proclamation of the gospel and the offering of the sacrifice and the gift of the holy food?

Here we see two daily services, morning and evening, with Ps 62 and Ps 140 as their nucleus, as well as a Sunday vigil service comprising the resurrection gospel and three "prayers" in honor of the resurrection on the third day (more about this vigil shortly), followed by the customary Liturgy of the Word, anaphora, and communion. Note that the corresponding chapter of the third-century *Didascalia*, of which the passage just cited is an expanded redaction, contains only a general exhortation to frequent church, especially on Sunday for the Eucharist, but with none of the references to the public daily offices, the Sabbath, or the Sunday vigil.[33] So these are clearly fourth-century innovations.

Book VII, 47, gives a redaction of the *Gloria in excelsis*, later to become a standard element in eastern matins, which one codex entitles "morning prayer." And chapter 48 gives an "evening hymn" comprising Ps 121:1 (*Te decet laus*) and the *Nunc dimittis* of Luke 2:29–32.

Of greater interest is book VIII, 34, which gives the full fourth-century cursus of the daily prayer of the secular churches, both private and public:

Accomplish prayers in the morning, and at the third and sixth and ninth hours, and in the evening, and at cockcrow; in the morning giving thanks because the Lord has enlightened you, taking away the night and bringing the day; at the third because at that hour the Lord received the sentence of condemnation from Pilate; at the sixth because at that hour he was crucified; at the ninth because everything trembled when the Lord was crucified; . . . in the evening giving

[33]*Ibid.* 170–173.

thanks because he has given you the night as a rest from the daily labors; at cockcrow because through that hour is heralded the good news of the coming of day for the doing of the works of the light.

But if it is not possible to go to the church because of the unbelievers, you shall assemble in a house. . . . But if it is not possible to assemble either in a house or in church, let each one sing psalms, read, pray by oneself, or two or three together, "For wherever," the Lord said, "there are two or three gathered in my name, there I am in the midst of them" (Matt 18:20). . . .

Chapters 35–39 of book VIII then describe the two daily public synaxes, giving even the texts of the lengthy concluding intercessions and prayers. Since the litanies for the various categories—catechumens, *energoumenoi, phôtizomenoi*, penitents, and faithful—are the same as those that conclude the Liturgy of the Word in book VIII, 6–10, the author refers back to those chapters without repeating the text, which fills six columns in the Migne edition or seven pages in the edition of Funk.[34] To each petition the faithful responded "*Kyrie eleison*":

. . . When evening has come, you shall assemble the church, bishop, and after the lamp-lighting psalm (*epilychnion psalmon*) has been said, the deacon shall proclaim [the petitions] for the catechumens and those disturbed [*energoumenoi*] and the *phôtizomenoi* and those in penance, as we said above [in chapters 6–9]. And after their dismissal the deacon shall say, "All we faithful let us pray to the Lord," and after he proclaims the [petitions] of the first prayer [above in chapter 10] he shall say:

Save us O God and raise us up by your Christ.
Arising, let us ask
for the mercies of the Lord and his compassion,
for the angel of peace,
for what is good and profitable,
for a Christian end,
for a peaceful and sinless evening and night.
And let us ask that the whole time of our life be
blameless.
Let us commend ourselves and one another to the living God
through his Christ.

At the end of the litany the bishop says the collect, praying in a similar vein for a peaceful and sinless evening and night, and for eternal life. Then the deacon cries, "Bow down for the imposition of hands," and the bishop says the "Prayer of Inclination" or final blessing over the bowed faithful,

[34]*Ibid.* 478–493, 544–555; PG 1, 1076–1088, 1137–1141.

asking God's favor and blessing, after which the deacon announces the dismissal: "Depart in peace."

The structure of morning prayer is the same except that the psalm is Ps 62, and the petitions and prayers are suited to the hour. The collect asks God to "receive our morning thanksgiving and have mercy on us," and in the blessing the bishop prays God to "preserve them in piety and righteousness, and grant them eternal life in Christ Jesus."

Thus the primitive nucleus of cathedral morning and evening prayer was:

> Psalmody (Ps 62 or 140)
>
> Litany, prayer of blessing and dismissal for each of the four categories (catechumens, *energoumenoi*, *phôtizomenoi*, penitents)
>
> Litany of the faithful
>
> Collect
>
> Prayer of Blessing
>
> Dismissal

### III. THEODORET OF CYR

Half a century later the cathedral services in Antiochia are still in full vigor, and have even developed ritually. Theodoret (ca. 393–466), a native of Antioch and Bishop of Cyr, a small town east of Antioch, from 423, recounts in his *Church History* II, 24 (cited below in chapter 9), how two laymen of Antioch, Flavian and Diodore, in 347–348, invented antiphonal psalmody for use at night vigils. And in his *Philothean History* 30:1, Theodoret describes how the Syrian virgin and ascetic St. Domnina attended the daily cathedral hours. "She goes at cockcrow to the sacred temple not far from there [where she lived] to offer with the others, both women and men, the hymnody to the God of all. This she does not only at the beginning but also at the end of day. . . ."[35]

In his *Questions on Exodus* 28, written sometime after 453, Theodoret, commenting on the Old Testament offering in Exodus, provides our first explicit testimony to the ceremonial embellishment of these services. The text in question is Ex 30:7–8: "And Aaron shall burn fragrant incense on it [the altar of incense]; every morning when he dresses the lamps he shall burn it, and when Aaron sets up the lamps in the evening, he shall burn

---

[35]P. Canivet, A. Leroy-Molinghen (eds.), Théodoret de Cyr, *Histoire des moines de Syrie*, tome 2: *"Histoire philothée"* (SC 257, Paris: Cerf, 1979) 241.

it, a perpetual incense before the Lord throughout your generations." Commenting on this in relation to Christian worship, Theodoret says, "We perform the liturgy reserved to the interior of the tabernacle [i.e., the offering of incense]. For it is the incense and the light of the lamps that we offer to God, as well as the service of the mysteries of the holy table."[36] So he clearly distinguishes between the Eucharist and the offering of incense and light, which undoubtedly refers to the two other Christian cathedral synaxes, morning and evening. This ceremonial development was new, for as I noted above, Chrysostom seems not to have known the use of incense in the Antiochene office. Ephrem (d. 373), however, in his *Carmina Nisibena* 17:4,[37] speaks of an "oblation of incense," which may refer to the use of incense in the office under the influence of Ex 30:7-8.

## Constantinople

We have very little evidence for the offices of New Rome in this early period. Sozomen in his *Ecclesiastical History* VIII, 7-8, written between 439-450, witnesses to the cathedral offices at Constantinople during Chrysostom's brief and ill-fated episcopate there in 397-404. The people "used the morning and night hymns" (*eôthinois kai nykterinois hymnois echrêto*), and Chrysostom himself introduced vigils and stational processions with antiphonal psalmody to compete with the services of the Arians.

## Jerusalem

We are richly informed on the pristine hagiopolite liturgy through the marvelously detailed account in the diary of the Spanish pilgrim nun Egeria, who trekked through the Holy Land stational services between 381-384, during the episcopate of St. Cyril (d. 386), one of the great liturgical leaders of this creative epoch. Together with the *Apostolic Constitutions*, this travel diary is the most important single document for the state of the Christian liturgy at the end of the fourth century.

Chapter 24 describes the services of an ordinary week. In reading it, one must remember that Jerusalem by this time had already become a great center of pilgrimage and was overrun by monks, nuns, ascetics, and pilgrims of every sort whose only aim in being there was to visit and pray at the shrines. So the hagiopolite liturgy not only had a sumptuous fullness and splendor found only in the great cities and pilgrimage centers of Late Antiquity, but had also absorbed certain monastic traits. Here is the text in the version of J. Wilkinson:[38]

[1] Loving sisters, I am sure it will interest you to know about the daily services they have in the holy places, and I must tell you about them. All the doors of the Anastasis are opened before cock-crow each day, and the "*monazontes* and *parthenae*," as they call them here, come in, and also some lay men and women, at least those who are willing to wake at such an early hour. From then until daybreak they join in singing the refrains to the hymns, psalms, and antiphons. There is a prayer between each of the hymns, since there are two or three presbyters and deacons each day by rota, who are there with the monazontes and say the prayers between all the hymns and antiphons.

[2] As soon as dawn comes, they start the Morning Hymns, and the bishop with his clergy comes and joins them. He goes straight into the cave, and inside the screen he first says the Prayer for All (mentioning any names he wishes) and blesses the catechumens, and then another prayer and blesses the faithful. Then he comes outside the screen, and everyone comes up to kiss his hand. He blesses them one by one, and goes out, and by the time the dismissal takes place it is already day.

[3] Again at midday everyone comes into the Anastasis and says psalms and antiphons until a message is sent to the bishop. Again he enters, and, without taking his seat, goes straight inside the screen in the Anastasis (which is to say into the cave where he went in the early morning), and again, after a prayer, he blesses the faithful and comes outside the screen, and again they come to kiss his hand.

[4] At three o'clock they do once more what they did at midday, but at four o'clock they have *Lychnicon*, as they call it, or in our language, Lucernare. All the people congregate once more in the Anastasis, and the lamps and candles are all lit, which makes it very bright. The fire is brought not from outside, but from the cave—inside the screen—where a lamp is always burning night and day. For some time they have the Lucernare psalms and antiphons; then they send for the bishop, who enters and sits in the chief seat. The presbyters also come and sit in their places, and the hymns and antiphons go on. [5]Then, when they have finished singing everything which is appointed, the bishop rises and goes in front of the screen (i.e., the cave). One of the deacons makes the normal commemoration of individuals, and each time he mentions a name a large group of boys responds *Kyrie eleison* (in our language, "Lord, have mercy"). Their voices are very loud. [6]As soon as the deacon has done his part, the bishop says a prayer and prays the Prayer for All. Up to this point the faithful

[38]*Egeria's Travels* (London: SPCK, 1971) for this and other citations from Egeria.

and the catechumens are praying together, but now the deacon calls every catechumen to stand where he is and bow his head, and the bishop says the blessing over the catechumens from his place. There is another prayer, after which the deacon calls for all the faithful to bow their heads, and the bishop says the blessing over the faithful from his place. Thus the dismissal takes place at the Anastasis, and they all come up one by one to kiss the bishop's hand.

7Then, singing hymns, they take the bishop from the Anastasis to the Cross, and everyone goes with him. On arrival he says one prayer and blesses the catechumens, then another and blesses the faithful. Then again the bishop and all the people go Behind the Cross, and do there what they did Before the Cross; and in both places they come to kiss the bishop's hand, as they did in the Anastasis. Great glass lanterns are burning everywhere, and there are many candles in front of the Anastasis, and also Before and Behind the Cross. By the end of all this it is dusk. So these are the services held every weekday at the Cross and at the Anastasis.

Juan Mateos has thoroughly analyzed the offices in this document and I shall follow his interpretation.[39] The day opens with a devotional vigil of the ascetics—monks and nuns—assisted by a few of the clergy who take turns at this ministry of assisting the devout in their prayer. The cathedral services properly so-called include matins, sext, none, and vespers or "lucernare," as Egeria calls it (24:4). The first three services follow the pattern we have seen in the Apostolic Constitutions: psalmody followed by intercessions. But there was apparently more than one psalm in the hagiopolite offices, though it is impossible to be more precise on this point, for Egeria uses nomenclature loosely, speaking of "hymns, psalms, antiphons" without specifying just what she means. (Note in this context, however, that "to say"—Greek legein, Latin dicere, Syriac emar—in ancient liturgical documents is a general term meaning to execute orally, and does not mean "say" or "recite" as opposed to "chant" or "sing" or "proclaim," as some liturgists have mistakenly presumed.)

So the Jerusalem form of service seems to differ from the usage at Antioch. Bradshaw[40] cites a passage from Chrysostom's Antiochene Homily 11 on Matthew, 7 as possible evidence for more than one psalm in the offices of Antioch, too, but van de Paverd interprets this text as referring to the Liturgy of the Word.[41] As Mateos has shown,[42] the Old Constan-

[39]"La vigile cathédrale chez Egérie," OCP 27 (1961) 281–312.

[40]Daily Prayer 74.

[41]See PG 57, 200, and F. van de Paverd, Zur Geschichte der Messliturgie in Antiocheia und Konstantinopel gegen Ende des vierten Jahrhunderts. Analyse der Quellen bei Joannes Chrysostomos (OCA 187, Rome: PIO, 1970) 124ff.

[42]"Quelques anciens documents," 360.

tinopolitan office, of Antiochene provenance, retained the Antiochene tradition of only one vesperal psalm, whereas the offices derived from that of Jerusalem (such as the Byzantine monastic office of St. Sabas, and Chaldean, Syrian, and Maronite vespers) all have three or more vesperal psalms—always including, of course, Ps 140. We saw above that Epiphanius of Salamis also speaks of "vesperal psalms" *(psalmoi lychnikoi),* but he was originally a monk in Palestine before becoming a bishop in Cyprus, and the office of his Church could reflect Palestinian usage. At any rate, extant Jerusalem-type cathedral vespers has more than one vesperal psalm, whereas in traditions of the Antiochene family there was only Ps 140, and this later structure seems to accord with what little evidence we can find for the pristine form of these services in fourth-century sources.

Vespers in Egeria includes not only psalms and antiphons, and the customary concluding intercessions and dismissals, but opens with a light service in which the vesperal light is brought out from the Holy Sepulcher, a rite clearly symbolizing the Risen Christ coming forth from the tomb to bring the light of his salvation to the sin-darkened world. Vespers is followed by brief stational services at the two shrines before and behind the cross.

In outline these hagiopolite vespers looked somewhat as follows:

> Lighting of the lamps
> Vesperal psalms, including Ps 140
> Antiphons
> Entrance of the bishop
> Hymns or antiphons
> Intercessions and blessing
> Dismissal
> Stations before and behind the cross, with prayers and
> blessings

Note that sext and none were also cathedral hours done in common in Jerusalem (terce was done only in Lent: 27:4–5), which is unusual at this early date, and probably attributable to the large number of monks, nuns, and ascetics who flocked to the Holy Land after the Peace of Constantine and participated, as Egeria tells us, in the basilical services at the Holy Places.

The services on Sunday began at cockcrow with a resurrection vigil. Those who arrived early for it prayed in the atrium until the basilica opened, but this prayer was not part of the cursus of offices. Egeria describes this in chapter 24:8–12:

> ⁸But on the seventh day, the Lord's Day, there gather in the courtyard before cock-crow all the people, as many as can get in, as if it was Easter. The courtyard is the "basilica" beside the Anastasis, that is to say, out of doors, and lamps have been hung there for them. Those who are afraid they may not arrive in time for cock-crow come early, and sit waiting there singing hymns and antiphons, and they have prayers between, since there are always presbyters and deacons there ready for the vigil, because so many people collect there, and it is not usual to open the holy places before cock-crow.
>
> ⁹Soon the first cock crows, and at that the bishop enters, and goes into the cave in the Anastasis. The doors are all opened, and all the people come into the Anastasis, which is already ablaze with lamps. When they are inside, a psalm is said by one of the presbyters, with everyone responding, and it is followed by a prayer; then a psalm is said by one of the deacons, and another prayer; then a third psalm is said by one of the clergy, a third prayer, and the Commemoration of All. ¹⁰After these three psalms and prayers they take censers into the cave of the Anastasis, so that the whole Anastasis basilica is filled with the smell. Then the bishop, standing inside the screen, takes the Gospel book and goes to the door, where he himself reads the account of the Lord's resurrection. At the beginning of the reading the whole assembly groans and laments at all that the Lord underwent for us, and the way they weep would move even the hardest heart to tears. ¹¹When the Gospel is finished, the bishop comes out, and is taken with singing to the Cross, and they all go with him. They have one psalm there and a prayer, then he blesses the people, and that is the dismissal. As the bishop goes out, everyone comes to kiss his hand.
>
> ¹²Then straight away the bishop retires to his house, and all the monazontes go back into the Anastasis to sing psalms and antiphons until daybreak. There are prayers between all these psalms and antiphons, and presbyters and deacons take their turn every day at the Anastasis to keep vigil with the people. Some lay men and women like to stay on there till daybreak, but others prefer to go home again to bed for some sleep.

Egeria's account of this vigil is a precious witness to the history of the cathedral hours, for remnants of this Sunday resurrection service can be found still in many extant offices in East and West. It was a popular service of great solemnity. Crowds flocked to it "as if it was Easter," Egeria tells us (24:8), and the bishop's presence during the entire service marked its signal importance in the weekly cycle. This was unusual for Jerusalem cathedral services. At other hours the bishop leaves the psalmody and chants to the lower clergy, delaying his solemn entrance until it is time for him to say the intercession collects and give the final blessings. But at the resurrection vigil he is there from the start, accompanied beyond doubt by his presbytery and deacons, awaiting the entrance of the people inside the chancel of the Holy Sepulcher.

The church is ablaze, brilliantly lighted by hundreds of flickering oil lamps. The service opens with three psalms, intoned in turn by a presbyter, a deacon, and another of the clergy, the people responding to the verses with a responsory or refrain. A collect follows each psalm. This threefold liturgical unit of psalmody and prayer corresponds to the "three prayers standing, in memory of him who rose in three days," in *Apostolic Constitutions* II, 59, cited above. Mateos has shown that the term "prayers" *(euchas)* here and in other services can be taken to include also psalms and canticles.[43] The usual intercessions follow the three antiphons. Then thuribles are brought into the Holy Sepulcher, probably in memory of the Myrrhophores, the women who brought spices to the tomb to anoint the body of the Lord and thus became the first witnesses to resurrection (Mark 16:1-8; Luke 23:55—24:1-11; cf. Matt 28:1-8). At least this is a standard theme in the remnants of this vigil in the Armenian and Byzantine traditions. After this symbolic preparation, the office reaches its climax with the proclamation of the gospel of the resurrection. From Egeria's description of the expressions of grief that this reading provoked, it is clear that the gospel lesson included the whole paschal mystery, not just the resurrection but also the passion and death on the cross. That the gospel was the highpoint of the service can be seen in Egeria's other references to the vigil (27:2; 43:1), where "Sunday gospel of the Lord's Resurrection" is shorthand for the whole service. In addition, the bishop himself— not the deacon or a reader, as one would expect— proclaims the gospel, announcing the resurrection like the angel before the tomb at the arrival of the Myrrh-bearing women. The office concludes with a brief station at the cross, as was customary in hagiopolite cathedral services.

So the Sunday resurrection vigil looked as follows:

Three responsories or antiphons with collects, in honor of
    the resurrection on the third day

General intercessions

Incensation

---

[43]"La vigile cathédrale chez Egérie," 299-301.

Paschal Gospel
Procession to the cross, with chanting
Station at the cross: Psalm and collect
Blessing and dismissal

Mateos is certainly right in supposing a hagiopolite origin for this vigil.[44] The link between its symbolism and its celebration in the Anastasis rotunda with the empty tomb or Holy Sepulcher is obvious. At the conclusion of the vigil the bishop and others depart, while the ascetics remain for their usual devotional vigil to await matins at daybreak, which in turn is followed immediately by Mass (25:1–2). The day hours are omitted on Sundays but vespers is held as usual (25:3).

Apropos of these cathedral offices Egeria remarks that "the psalms and antiphons they use are always appropriate, whether at night, in the early morning, at the day prayers at midday or three o'clock, or at Lucernare. Everything is suitable, appropriate, and relevant to what is being done"(25:5). This is precisely what distinguishes *cathedral* offices from the *monastic* psalmody that we shall encounter in the next chapter. Cathedral offices had *select* psalms, chosen because of their suitability for the particular service—e.g., Ps 62 at matins and Ps 140 at vespers. The psalmody of monastic offices was continuous, i.e., it simply followed the numerical order of the biblical psalter, with no attempt to coordinate the theme of the biblical text with the nature and spirit of the hour of prayer. There were differences also in the execution of the psalmody. The monks, as we shall see, simply recited the psalm verse by verse, or listened while a soloist did so. In cathedral usage popular participation in the psalmody was assured by the addition of responsories and antiphons or refrains. A soloist or soloists chanted the psalm verses, to which the congregation responded with a responsory—a fixed psalm verse or alleluia—or with an antiphon, i.e., a trope or refrain, a piece of ecclesiastical poetry. Other differences are the various ministerial roles (bishop, presbyter, deacon, etc.) and the use of ceremonial—light, incense, processions—both of which were completely foreign to monastic usage. We saw these characteristic

[44]*Ibid.*, 297. On the cathedral vigil and the remnants of it in other sources and extant rites, see also J. Mateos, "Les différentes expèces de vigiles dans le rite chaldéen," OCP 27 (1961) 47–63; *id.*, "Les matines chaldéenes, maronites et syriennes," OCP 26 (1960) 51–73; *id.*, Lelya-Ṣapra 55–66, 423–431; *id.*, "L'office dominical de la rèsurrection," *Revue du clergé africain* (May 1964) 263–288; *id.*, "Quelques problèmes de l'orthros byzantin," POC 11 (1961) 17–35, 201–220; esp. 203–205; J. Tabet, "Le tèmoignage de Bar Hebraeus (d. 1286) sur la vigile cathèdrale," *Melto* 5 (1969) 113–121; *id.*, "Le tèmoignage de Sévère d'Antioche (d. 538) sur la vigile cathédrale," *Melto* 4 (1968) 6–12; *id.*, L'office commun maronite. Etude du lilyō et du ṣafro (Bibliothèque de l'Universitè S.-Esprit, Kaslik [Lebanon], 1972) 210ff.

cathedral elements adumbrated in other sources. In Egeria the blueprint is complete.

## Conclusion

This is indeed a rich feast of services that we have found in the second half of the fourth century. With the exception of Egypt, where the picture is not clear, by the end of the century in Palestine, Syria, Asia Minor, and Constantinople we see an already well-established cursus of cathedral offices celebrated by the whole community—bishop, clergy, and people. Matins and vespers were the two privileged hours of daily prayer, and the offices comprised popular elements such as select psalms and canticles, chosen because of their suitability for the hour, and executed with popular participation through responsories and antiphons; the ceremonial use of light, incense, processions; and the usual petitionary intercessions for the needs dear to the people's hearts.

If we prescind from local peculiarities such as the Jerusalem stations, the skeleton of the principal hours of the cathedral cursus probably looked somewhat as follows:

DAILY                       SUNDAY

*Resurrection Vigil*

Three antiphons with prayers
Intercessions
Incense
Gospel
Blessing and dismissal

*Matins*

Morning psalms and canticles,
including Ps 62
Gloria in excelsis
Intercessions
Blessing and dismissal

*Eucharist*

*Vespers*

Light service and hymn
Vesperal psalmody, including
Ps 140

(Daily)                              (Sunday)

Incensation
"Hymns and antiphons"
Intercessions
Blessing and dismissal

Nor was there anything arcane about the rationale of these offices. The morning hour of prayer was a service of thanks and praise for the new day and for salvation in Christ Jesus. It was the Christian way of opening and dedicating the new day. And vespers was the Christian way of closing it, thanking God for the day's graces, asking his pardon for the day's faults, and beseeching his grace and protection for a safe and sinless night. The basic symbol of both services was light. The rising sun and the new day with its change from darkness to light recalled the resurrection from the dead of Christ, Sun of Justice. The evening lamp recalled the Johannine "light of the world" shining amidst the darkness of sin. And Christians did these prayers in common because, as Chrysostom and the *Apostolic Constitutions* affirm, their sole power was as the Body of Christ. To absent oneself from the synaxis is to weaken the body and deprive the head of his members.

# 4

## THE EGYPTIAN MONASTIC OFFICE
## IN THE FOURTH CENTURY[1]

While the formation of the cathedral Liturgy of the Hours was under-way in the secular churches during the second half of the fourth century, a parallel series of offices was evolving in monastic centers that had sprung up in Egypt and the Thebaid, Palestine, Mesopotamia, Syria, and Cap-padocia at the same time. Mateos divides these monastic offices into two families: 1) the "pure" monastic office of the Egyptian desert, and 2) the hybrid office of urban monasticism.[2] This distinction remains valid as long as we realize that it refers to "types" of offices, for we find more than one "pure" Egyptian monastic office, and several urban usages, too. Of special interest for our purposes are the two Egyptian monastic offices for which we have the most evidence: the tradition of Scetis and that of the Pachomian Tabennesiots.

---

[1]I am grateful to the editors of *Worship* and to The Liturgical Press, Collegeville, Minn., for permission to use in this chapter some material from my article "Praise in the Desert: the Coptic Monastic Office Yesterday and Today," *Worship* 56 (1982) 513–536.

[2]"The Origins of the Divine Office," 478.

## The Tradition of Scetis

In Lower Egypt in the fourth century there were three great monastic centers, Nitria, Kellia, and Scetis, located south of Alexandria in the Libyan or Great Western Desert west of the Nile Delta. The most important of these monastic "deserts" for our story is Scetis, the present Natron Valley or Wadi an-Natrun, sixty-five kilometers northwest of Cairo.

John Cassian, thought to have been born around 360 in Scythia Minor (present-day Rumania) near the Delta of the Danube, went to Egypt as a young monk, and he has left us a detailed description of the usage of Scetis. Cassian lived in Scetis from about 380 until 399 and undoubtedly visited the two nearby monastic centers of Nitria and Kellia about seventy kilometers to the north. He may have had contact with the Pachomians of the Monastery of the Metanoia at Canopus on the coast in the Delta (he knew the "Rule" of Pachomius since he refers to it in the *Preface*, 5, of his *Institutes*). But he never set foot on Tabennesiot ground in the Thebaid or Nile Valley of Upper Egypt.[3] In his *Institutes*, written around 417–425, some twenty years after leaving Egypt (he says himself he no longer trusts his memory [*Preface*, 4]), Cassian is attempting not a history of Egyptian monasticism, but a reform of Gallic monasticism along Egyptian lines. So he accommodates his experiences of the semi-anchoritic monasticism of Scetis to the framework of Gallic cenobitism. In making this adjustment, he presents a somewhat idealized Egyptian office that is apparently a synthesis of various elements, then claims universal authority for it as *the* tradition of "the whole of Egypt and the Thebaid" (*Inst.* II, 3–4). But in spite of similarities between the systems of Upper and Lower Egypt, it will become apparent that Cassian cannot be taken as a reliable witness to Pachomian uses. All this must be borne in mind when weighing Cassian's lengthy and detailed account of the Egyptian offices in Books II and III of his *Institutes*:[4]

> II,5 . . . One rose up in the midst to chant the Psalms to the Lord. And while they were all sitting (as is still the custom in Egypt), with

[3]J.-C. Guy, "Jean Cassien, historien du monachisme égyptien?" *Studia Patristica* 8 (TU 93, Berlin: Akademie-Verlag, 1966) 366–367; A Veilleux, *La liturgie dans le cénobitisme pachô-mien au quatrième siècle* (Studia Anselmiana 57, Rome: Herder, 1968) 150. On Canopus see D. Chitty, *The Desert a City. An Introduction to the Study of Egyptian and Palestinian Monasticism under the Christian Empire* (Crestwood, N.Y.: St. Vladimir's Seminary Press, n.d.) 54–55.

[4]For the translation of Cassian I use, with some changes, the English version of E.C.S. Gibson, *The Works of John Cassian* (NPNF, Grand Rapids: Eerdmans, 1964) series 2, vol. 11. For the Latin text, see J.-C. Guy (ed.), Jean Cassien, *Institutions cénobitiques* (SC 109, Paris: Cerf, 1965).

their minds intently fixed on the words of the chanter, when he had sung eleven Psalms, separated by prayers introduced between them, verse after verse being evenly enunciated, he finished the twelfth with a response of Alleluia, and then, by his sudden disappearance from the eyes of all, put an end at once to their discussion and their service.

⁶Whereupon the venerable assembly of the Fathers understood that by Divine Providence a general rule had been fixed for the congregations of the brethren through the angel's direction, and so decreed that this number should be preserved both in their evening and in their nocturnal services; and when they added to these two lessons, one from the Old and one from the New Testament, they added them simply as extras and of their own appointment, only for those who liked, and who were eager to gain by constant study a mind well stored with Holy Scripture. But on Saturday and Sunday they read them both from the New Testament; viz., one from the Epistles or the Acts of the Apostles, and one from the Gospel. And this also those do whose concern is the reading and the recollection of the Scriptures, from Easter to Whitsuntide.

⁷These aforesaid prayers, then, they begin and finish in such a way that when the Psalm is ended they do not hurry at once to kneel down, as some of us do in this country. . . . Among them, therefore it is not so, but before they bend their knees they pray for a few moments and while they are standing up spend the greater part of the time in prayer. And so after this, for the briefest space of time, they prostrate themselves to the ground, as if but adoring the Divine Mercy, and as soon as possible rise up, and again standing erect with outspread hands—just as they had been standing to pray before—remain with thoughts intent upon their prayers. . . . But when he who is to "collect" the prayer rises from the ground they all start up at once, so that no one would venture to bend the knee before he bows down, nor to delay when he has risen from the ground, lest it should be thought that he has offered his own prayer independently instead of following the leader to the close.

⁸That practice too which we have observed in this country—viz., that while one sings to the end of the Psalm, all standing up sing together with a loud voice, "Glory be to the Father and to the Son and to the Holy Ghost"—we have never heard anywhere throughout the East, but there, while all keep silence when the Psalm is finished, the prayer that follows is offered up by the singer. But with this hymn in honour of the Trinity only the whole Psalmody is usually ended. . . .

¹⁰When, then, they meet together to celebrate the aforementioned rites, which they term synaxes, they are all so perfectly silent that, though so large a number of the brethren is assembled together, you would not think a single person was present except the one who stands

up and chants the Psalm in the midst; and especially is this the case when the prayer is completed, for then there is no spitting, no clearing of the throat, or noise of coughing, no sleepy yawning with open mouths, and gasping, and no groans or sighs are uttered, likely to distract those standing near. No voice is heard save that of the priest concluding the prayer. . . . They think it best for the prayers to be short and offered up very frequently. . . .

[11]And, therefore, they do not even attempt to finish the Psalms, which they sing in the service, by an unbroken and continuous recitation. But they repeat them separately and bit by bit, divided into two or three sections, according to the number of verses, with prayers in between. For they do not care about the quantity of verses, but about the intelligence of the mind; aiming with all their might at this: "I will sing with the spirit: I will sing also with the understanding." And so they consider it better for ten verses to be sung with understanding and thought than for a whole Psalm to be poured forth with a bewildered mind. . . .

[III,2] . . . except Vespers and Nocturns, there are no public services among them during the day except on Saturday and Sunday, when they meet together at the third hour for holy communion.

From this description we learn that there were only two daily offices, one at night—that is, at cockcrow, in the wee hours of the morning (*Inst.* III, 6:1)—and one in the evening. The core of the offices comprised twelve psalms, doubtless "in course," with private prayer, prostration and a collect after each. The final psalm, apparently an "alleluia psalm," was followed by the *Gloria patri* and two lessons of Sacred Scripture. So both offices had exactly the same structure:

i. PSALMODY

Twelve psalms *currente psalterio*, as follows:

| | |
|---|---|
| *Seated*: | Psalm read *tractim* by a soloist, standing (*Inst.* II, 10). |
| *Standing*: | Silent prayer with arms extended. |
| *Prostration*: | Praying all the while. |
| *Standing*: | Silent prayer with arms extended; |
| | Collect by the presider (II, 7 and 10).[5] |

[5]Some think Cassian means there was but one collect, at the end of the whole office, but the context seems to require one here, since Cassian speaks of the collect when referring to the duration of the prostration which the collect, apparently, concluded (*Inst.* II, 7:2).

12th psalm is an alleluia psalm (II, 5, 11).
*Gloria patri* concludes the psalmody (II, 8).

ii. Lessons

Two readings from the Bible:

    *Weekdays:*    OT reading

                    NT reading

    *Saturday, Sunday, and Paschaltide:*

                    Epistle or Acts

                    Gospel

As we have seen, in the fourth century morning and evening were the two hours of obligatory public prayer in cathedral usage. And although there is less than complete precision in the still extant descriptions of the prayer-life of the ascetics of Lower Egypt,[6] three of the *Apophthegmata* referring explicitly to Scetis (Arsenius 24, Macarius 33, An Abba of Rome 1) support Cassian's assertion—which he repeats in *Conferences* 2, 26:2–3—that the embryonic cursus of Scetis, like that of the Tabennesiots, had only two daily prayer times: on rising, and after the one daily meal at the ninth hour (3:00 p.m.), just before retiring.

On Monday through Friday,the two daily offices were done by the monks in their cells, either alone or with whoever happened to reside with them or be visiting at the time. Only on Saturday and Sunday did all the monks of the laura gather in church for offices, Eucharist, and an agape or fraternal meal in common, after which each one drew supplies from the common storehouse to take back to his cell for the next five days of solitary prayer. "They come together in the churches only on Saturdays and Sundays, and meet one another. Many of them who die in their cells are not found for four days, because they do not see each other except at the Synaxis."[7]

---

[6]See the numerous references in such classical sources as the *Apophthegmata Patrum*, the *History of the Monks in Egypt* XX, 7–8, and XXIII, 1 (in the additions of Rufinus), trans. N. Russell, *The Lives of the Desert Fathers* (CS 34, Kalamazoo: Cistercian Publications, 1980) 106, 148–149, 153–154; Palladius, *Lausiac History* 7:5. Many of these citations have been collected (but not always rightly interpreted) in H. G. Evelyn-White, *The Monasteries of the Wâdi 'n Natrûn*, part II: *The History of the Monasteries of Nitria and Scetis* (New York: The Metropolitan Museum of Art Egyptian Expedition, 1932).

[7]*History of the Monks in Egypt* XX, 7. Here and elsewhere this source is cited from the trans. of Russell (see previous note). Note that in the sources of Lower Egypt the use of the term "synaxis" for the hours of prayer does not imply that the prayer was done in common, as we shall see later in this chapter. On the weekly cycle of work and prayer in Lower Egypt, see also A. Guillaumont, "Histoire des moines aux Kellia," *Orientalia lovaniensia periodica* 8 (1977) 193ff.

But when we get down to the details of the two offices, Cassian's description is not without its problems. Armand Veilleux considers it a composite of the "rule of the angel" with "Pachomian rubrics" for the prayers and prostrations of the type we see in the "Regulations of Horsiesios."[8] As for the two readings, no contemporary monastic source from Lower Egypt mentions them.[9] Cassian himself admits they are a later supplement added only for those that want them (*Inst.* II, 6), and hence not a fixed part of the general tradition like the twelve psalms believed to have been established by divine intervention. However, we know from sources cited in the previous chapter that there were Scripture lessons in the fourth-century Egyptian cathedral offices, and the same could well have been true of the monastic synaxes of Scetis.

## The Pachomian Office[10]

The other Egyptian monastic office about which we have some evidence is that of the cenobitic foundations initiated by Pachomius (d. 346) around 320 at Tabennesi in the Nile valley of the "Thebaid" north of Thebes. In the *Precepts of Our Father Pachomius* we find a passage (ch. 8) that describes the Tabennesiot office as psalmody, prayer, reading: "If it happens that during the psalmody or the prayer or in the midst of a reading anyone laughs or speaks, he shall unfasten his belt immediately and with neck bowed down he shall stand before the altar and be rebuked by the superior of the monastery."[11] This ordo is no different from what we saw in Cassian—and indeed, before Veilleux's recent study on the liturgy in the Pachomian cenobitic colonies of Upper Egypt,[12] most reconstructors of the Egyptian monastic office took Cassian at his word and extended the usage he describes to "the whole of Egypt and the Thebaid" (*Inst.* II, 3). However, this text of the *Precepts*, like the other components of the "Rule" of Pachomius, is part of a later anthology of material that cannot

---

[8]Veilleux, *La liturgie* 335ff.; see also 146ff., 279ff. For the "rule of the angel" in Palladius' *Lausiac History* and other sources, see *ibid.* 138–146, 324–334, and p. 72 below.

[9]Veilleux, *La liturgie* 337.

[10]For the Pachomian liturgical usage I rely on *ibid.*, especially ch. 6.

[11]I cite the Pachomian sources from the version of A. Veilleux, *Pachomian Koinonia*, 3 vols. (CS 45–47, Kalamazoo: Cistercian Publications, 1980, 1981, 1982).

[12]Veilleux, *La liturgie.* See also his "Prayer in the Pachomian Koinonia," W. Skudlarek (ed.), *The Continuing Quest for God. Monastic Spirituality in Tradition and Transition* (Collegeville: The Liturgical Press, 1982) 61–66.

be attributed to the most primitive Pachomian usage.[13] And Cassian was never in Upper Egypt, so whatever in his account is reliably Egyptian comes from *Lower* Egypt, and cannot automatically be extended to the Pachomians.

The Pachomian system was cenobitic, and the two customary daily offices at dawn and in the evening before retiring were held in common. In the morning all the monks of the monastery gathered for one common synaxis. In the slightly later *Institutes* of Pachomius (14), the evening office was said together by the monks of each house or dormitory before retiring.[14] In his *Preface* to *The Rules of Pachomius* (2), Jerome tells us a Pachomian monastery comprised thirty to forty houses, with about forty monks to a house.[15] Pachomian sources also refer to all-night watches that went right through the night from the evening synaxis until the dawn synaxis; but this was a private devotion done alone, not a service celebrated in common assembly, except at Easter or when a monk was being waked. There was also a difference in the horarium. It seems that the morning office in the Pachomian system did not begin at cockcrow, as in Lower Egypt, but at the normal hour of the morning service in the cathedral usage.

The "Regulations" attributed to Horsiesios, who took over the direction of the Tabennesiot monastic federation in 346 (Pachomius and his immediate successor Petronius died two months apart in the plague that year), gives some idea of what went on in these assemblies:

> [7]At the beginning of our prayers let us sign ourselves with the seal of baptism. Let us make the sign of the Cross on our foreheads, as on the day of our baptism, as it is written in Ezekiel (9:4). Let us not first lower our hand to our mouth or to our beard, but let us raise it to our forehead, saying in our heart, "We have signed ourselves with the seal." This is not like the seal of baptism; but the sign of the Cross was traced on the forehead of each of us on the day of our baptism.
>
> [8]When the signal is given for prayer, let us rise promptly; and when the signal is given to kneel, let us prostrate promptly to adore the Lord, having signed ourselves before kneeling. When once we are prostrate on our face, let us weep in our heart for our sins, as it is written, *Come, let us adore and weep before the Lord our maker* (Ps 94:6). Let absolutely no one of us raise his head while kneeling, for this shows a great lack of fear and knowledge.
>
> [9]When we rise again, let us sign ourselves; and after uttering the prayer of the Gospel, let us supplicate saying, "Lord, instill your fear

---

[13]Veilleux, *La liturgie* 116–132, and "Introduction" to *Pachomian Koinonia*, vol. 2, 7–11.

[14]*Precepts and Institutes* 14 (Veilleux, *Pachomian Koinonia*, vol. 2, 171). Veilleux (*La liturgie* 297) leans toward the view that this is a later development.

[15]Veilleux, *Pachomian Koinonia*, vol. 2, 142.

into our hearts that we may labor for eternal life and hold you in fear." Let each one of us say in his heart with an interior sigh, *Purify me, O Lord, from my secret sins; keep your servant from strangers. If these do not prevail over me, I shall be holy and free from a great sin* (Ps 18:13–14); and, *Create a pure heart in me, God, let a right spirit be renewed in my innermost self* (Ps 50:10).

[10]When the signal is given for us to be seated, let us again sign ourselves on the forehead in the form of the Cross. Then let us be seated and pay attention, heart and ears, to the holy words being recited, in accord with what we have been commanded in the holy Scriptures: *My son, fear my words, and having received them, do penance* (Prov 30:1) and again, *My son, take heed of my wisdom and incline your ear to my words* (Prov 5:1).[16]

From this and other Pachomian writings Veilleux has reconstructed the primitive office of the Tabennesiot cenobites.[17] At the synaxis the seated monks continued their traditional handiwork of weaving rushes into baskets and mats while the appointed individuals went in turn to the ambo to recite, probably from memory, a biblical passage (*not* necessarily a psalm). After each passage the reader gave a signal and all rose, made the sign of the cross on the forehead, and recited the Our Father with arms extended in the form of a cross. At a second signal they blessed themselves again and prostrated themselves on the ground, bemoaning their sins. Then they rose, blessed themselves again and prayed in silence. After a final signal they sat down once more to recommence the whole cycle. So the structure of the basic liturgical unit was as follows:

*Seated*:       scriptural passage recited by a monk standing at the ambo

*Standing*:    *signal*, sign of the cross on the forehead
Our Father with arms extended
*signal*, sign of the cross on the forehead

*Prostrated*:  penitential prayer in silence

*Standing*:    sign of the cross on the forehead
prayer in silence
*signal* to be seated.

It is not certain how often this liturgical unit was repeated at each synaxis. The evening prayer was called "The Office of the Six Prayers (or Six Sections of Prayers)," which may well mean that each soloist from

[16]*Ibid.*, vol. 2, 199–200.
[17]Veilleux, *La liturgie* 307ff.

the hebdomadary house or dormitory charged with the offices that week repeated six passages of Scripture with the accompanying prayers before ceding place to the next monk in order of seniority. At any rate there is no evidence whatever to interpret the "six" as six *psalms,* as almost everyone has done in the past.

The "Psalmody" or Sunday office, however, did comprise the chanting of psalms by the heads of the monasteries, and the brothers of the hebdomadary house responded to the soloist who was chanting the verses. On Sunday there was also a Eucharist and two catecheses or spiritual conferences by the superior.[18]

This is the most we can say about the original office of the Tabennesiots, in spite of van der Mensbrugghe's imaginative attempt to harmonize the disparate bits of evidence from different strata into a more complex structure and contrary to numerous attempts to apply the twelve-psalm-per-office rule to the Pachomian system.[19] The fact of the matter is that very few of the surprisingly numerous and illustrious early monastic travelers to Egypt ever got very far south into the Pachomian territory of the Thebaid, so they had first hand experience only of the uses of Nitria, Kellia, and Scetis in Lower Egypt.

## The "Pure" Monastic Office

As we have seen, the pure monastic office, like the contemporary cathedral system, had originally only the two common synaxes. So the monastic and cathedral cursus, if not the structure of the offices, were exactly the same: two services, one at the beginning and one at the end of the day. Since the monks of Lower Egypt went to bed at nightfall and rose again after a brief rest, their morning office actually began in the second half of the night and was over by dawn (*Inst.* III, 4–6). But these two prayer times correspond to morning and evening prayer in the cathedral usage. The basic tradition common to both cathedral and monastery was prayer at the beginning and end of the day. The monks just began the day earlier because they slept less. So it is mistaken to relate this monastic nocturnal prayer to the common nightly vigils for which we have evidence on weekends in other monastic traditions (see *Inst.* III, 8–11). The

[18]*Ibid.,* 313–315. Examples of the catecheses or spiritual conferences can be found in L. Lefort, *Oeuvres de S. Pachôme et de ses disciples* (CSCO 159–160, scr. copt. 23–24, Louvain: Secrétariat du CSCO, 1964), and Veilleux, *Pachomian Koinonia,* vol. 3.

[19]See A. van der Mensbrugghe, "Prayer-time in Egyptian Monasticism," *Studia patristica* 2 (TU 64, Berlin: Akademie-Verlag, 1957) 435–454, and the critque of Veilleux, *La liturgie* 280ff., 298ff. On the "rule of the angel" and the reliability of Palladius and Cassian as witnesses to Pachomian usage, see *ibid.* 138–158, 324–339.

sources often tell of the Egyptian monks praying privately at night.[20] But apart from the Easter vigil and the customary wakes or funeral vigils, in the Pachomian houses there were no common vigils as a regular part of the Egyptian monastic cursus,[21] though as we saw in chapter 3, according to Athanasius' *Defence of his Flight* 24, the monks in Lower Egypt sometimes attended the cathedral vigil. And by the time of the "Regulations of Horsiesios" we know that Pachomian monks who did not keep private vigil at night were expected to rise early and recite alone in their cells five to ten psalms before the common morning synaxis.[22]

## The Spirit of Early Monastic Prayer[23]

Far more important than the hours of the synaxes and their structure and content is the *spirit* of this pristine monastic prayer. From what we have seen it is obvious that the "pure" monastic office of the Egyptians was less a liturgical ceremony or service than a meditation in common on Sacred Scripture. F. Wulf states the difference between cathedral liturgy and early monastic prayer more bluntly:

> In the beginning the liturgy was not a part of the monastic life. Even the celebration of the Eucharist did not occupy any special place in it. All this was the affair of the clergy, not the monk. The monk's part was to pray in his heart without ceasing. That was his *Opus Dei*, his *Officium*, that is, fasting, watching, work, contrition of heart and silence.[24]

[20]The Bohairic *Vita* and First Greek *Vita* of Pachomius, Veilleux, *Pachomian Koinonia*, vol. 1, 78, 339; *History of the Monks in Egypt* VIII, 48, and the additions of Rufinus to ch. XXIII; Palladius, *Lausiac History* 22:6-8, 32:6-7; cf. Veilleux, *La liturgie* 289ff.

[21]See Cassian, *Inst.* III, 2; Veilleux, *La liturgie* 258-261, 287, 292ff., 302-305, 371ff.

[22]Veilleux, *La liturgie* 291.

[23]On early monastic prayer, in addition to the works of A. Veilleux already cited, see the classic commentary of A. de Vogüé, "Le sens de l'office divin," *La Règle de Saint Benoît* VII: *Commentaire doctrinal et spirituel* (SC hors série, Paris: Cerf, 1977) 184-248; *id.*, "Prayer in the Rule of St. Benedict," *Monastic Studies* 7 (1969) 113-140; A. Guillaumont, "Le problème de le prière continuelle dans le monachisme ancien," in H. Limet and J. Ries (eds.), *L'expérience de la prière dans les grands religions* (Homo religiosus 5, Louvain-la-Neuve: Centre d'histoire des religions, 1980) 285-293; I. Hausherr, "Comment priaient les pères?" *Revue d'ascétique et de mystique* 32 (1956) 33-58, 284-296; *id.*, "Opus dei," OCP 13 (1947) 195-218, English trans. in *Monastic Studies* 11 (1975) 181-204; *id.*, *The Name of Jesus* (CS 44, Kalamazoo: Cistercian Publications, 1978), ch. 3; E. Dekkers, "Were the Early Monks Liturgical?" *Collectanea Cisterciensia* 22 (1960) 120-137.

[24]"Priestertum und Rätestand," *Geist und Leben* 33 (1960) 250, trans. in A. Louf and others, *The Meaning of Monastic Spirituality* (N.Y.: Desclée and Co., 1964) 32.

So the dynamic of an Egyptian monastic synaxis was more like an Ignatian contemplation-with-colloquy done in common, than what we are used to in later monastic offices, in which psalmody becomes our praise of God rather than his saving Word to us. One can see this attention to interior prayer in Rufinus' additions to the *History of the Monks in Egypt* XXIII, with its amusing—and unfortunately, racist—account of the monks' distractions during a synaxis in mid-fourth century Scetis:

> One night a demon came and knocked on the door of his [Macarius']
> cell and said, "Get up, Macarius, and go to the meeting, where the
> brethren have met to celebrate vigils." But he . . . said, "You liar
> and enemy of the truth, what do you know about the meeting, when
> we are gathered together with the saints? Then the demon replied,
> "Don't you know, Macarius, that without us there is never any meeting
> or gathering of monks?" Macarius replied, "The Lord is in control
> of you, unclean demon." And turning to prayer, he asked the Lord
> to show him if the boast of the demon was true. Then he went to
> the meeting where the brothers had met to celebrate vigils, and again
> he prayed to the Lord to show him if this statement had been true.
> And behold he saw the whole church as it were filled with little black
> Ethiopian boys, running hither and thither and doing whatever they
> wanted to do. The brothers conducted themselves as usual, all being
> seated while one of them repeated a psalm and the rest either listened
> or made the responses. The Ethiopian boys ran among them, teasing
> each of those sitting down, and if they could put two fingers over
> their eyes they sent them to sleep at once. If they could put their fingers
> into their mouths, they made them yawn. After the psalm when the
> brothers prostrated themselves in prayer they ran to each of them,
> and as each threw himself forward to pray they assumed the appear-
> ance of women, while others made themselves into things to eat or
> drink, or did other things. And whenever the demons formed them-
> selves into something as if in mockery, distractions entered the minds
> of those praying; and yet there were some who when the demons be-
> gan to do something to them, repelled them as if by force and threw
> themselves forward so that they did not dare to stand in front of them
> or come alongside them, while they were able to play on the heads
> or the backs of the weaker brethren who were not intent on their
> prayers. When Saint Macarius saw this, he groaned heavily . . . After
> the prayers he called each of the brothers to him, to find out the truth,
> and before whichever face he had seen the demons playing in diverse
> ways and various images, he asked them if while they were praying
> or collecting their thoughts they had wandered away or followed any
> of the things which he had seen them imagining through the demons.
> And each confessed to him what had been in his mind as he urged
> them. And then he understood that all vain and superfluous thoughts

that anyone conceived during either the psalms or the prayers came from the illusions of the demons. Those who were able to keep control of their hearts were able to resist the black Ethiopians. He who joins his heart to God and remains intent at the time of prayer, can receive into himself nothing that is alien or superfluous.[25]

We are in the habit of distinguishing between "private" prayer and "liturgical" prayer, but for the early monks there was but one prayer, always personal, sometimes done in common with others, sometimes alone in the secret of one's heart. For the New Testament exhorts us not only to pray *adialeiptôs*, without ceasing (1 Thess 5:16–18; cf. Eph 6:18; Col 4:2; Luke 18:1; 21:36), but also to "be filled with the Spirit, addressing one another in psalms and hymns and spiritual songs, singing and making melody to the Lord with all your heart" (Eph 5:19; cf. Col 3:16). And writing to the Thessalonians, St. Paul also affirms:

> We were not idle . . . but with toil and labor we worked night and day, that we might not burden any of you . . . to give you in our conduct an example to imitate. For . . . we gave you this command: if any one will not work, let him not eat. For we hear that some of you are living in idleness . . . not doing any work. Now such persons we command and exhort in the Lord Jesus Christ to do their work in quietness and to earn their own living (2 Thess 3:7–12; cf. 1 Thess 2:9).

As A. Guillaumont has shown,[26] these two principles, *ora et labora*, continual prayer and incessant labor, were both the cornerstone and paradox of early monasticism. For how can one pray always if one must work? And how can one work at all if one must pray without ceasing? This is the problem Basil addresses in his *Longer Rules* 37:2, which I shall treat in the next chapter. Some extremists like the Messalians took literally the command of 1 Thess 5:17 to pray without ceasing, and refused to work. But the Fathers had a sure cure for that, as we see in the alphabetical collection of the *Apophthegmata*, Silvanus 5:[27]

> A brother came to the monastery of Abba Silvanus and when he saw all the brethren at work he said to the elder, "Do not labor for the bread that perishes. Mary has chosen the better part." At this the elder called a disciple and said, "Zachary, give this brother a book and show him to an empty cell." The ninth hour, which was the hour for dinner, came and passed. The guest was intently watching his door to

[25]Trans. Russell, CS 34, 153–154.

[26]See his article cited in note 23.

[27]Unless otherwise noted, translations of the *Apophthegmata* are from Hausherr, *The Name of Jesus* (note 23 above).

see if someone would come and get him for dinner, but no one called him. At length he rose and went to find the elder. "Abba," he said, "are the brethren fasting today?" "No, they have all eaten," replied the elder. "Why wasn't I invited?" "Because," answered the elder, "you are a spiritual person and have no need of bodily nourishment. But we, carnal as we are, are obliged to eat and this is why we work. You, however, have chosen the better part; you read all day long and have no desire for bodily nourishment." At these words the man made a prostration and said, "I beg your pardon, Abba." The elder pardoned him and concluded his lesson with the words, "That is how Mary herself stands in need of Martha. It was because of Martha that Mary could receive her praise."

So the ideal was not to avoid work, but to so live in unceasing labor and prayer that the whole of life was one, never ceasing to work while one prayed, never ceasing to pray while one worked, as we can see in the same alphabetical collection, Lucius 1:

Once some Euchites came to visit Abba Lucius in the Enaton, near Alexandria. When he asked them what type of work they did, they replied, "We never lift a finger to do manual labor; instead we pray without ceasing, in accordance with the Apostle's command." The elder said to them: "Don't you eat, then?" "We do," they assured him. "When you are eating, who prays in your place?" No answer. He asked them another question: "When you are sleeping, who keeps up your prayers?" They could give him no answer. Then he went on: "I beg your pardon, but you do not do what you say you do. Let me show you how I manage to pray always even when I busy myself at manual labor. I sit down with my supply of palm fronds soaking beside me and as I weave them together I say, with God's help, 'Have mercy on me, O God, according to your great goodness, and wipe out my transgressions according to your abundant mercy' (Ps 50:1). Tell me, is this not a prayer?" They assured him that it was. Then he said: "By working and praying like this all day long, I can complete around sixteen baskets. I give away two of these to any beggar who comes to my door. I make my living from the rest. And the man who has received the gift of two baskets prays for me while I am eating and sleeping. That is how, by God's grace, I manage to pray without ceasing."

As this passage shows, some monks even tried to fulfill the precept of unceasing prayer by arranging for continual prayer in shifts, an attitude that later gave rise to the monasteries of "sleepless" monks in both East and West, and at a later time to convents of "perpetual" adoration. But this fundamentalist construction of the evangelical precept was an exaggerated literal interpretation not shared by Fathers such as Origen, in his treatise *On Prayer* 12, which propounds a more balanced doctrine:

> He prays without ceasing who combines his prayer with necessary works, and suitable activities with his prayer, for his virtuous deeds or the precepts he has fulfilled are taken up as part of his prayer. Only in this way can we take the saying "Pray without ceasing" (1 Thess 5:17) as being possible, if we can say that the whole life of the saint is one mighty integrated prayer. Part of such prayer is what is customarily called "prayer." . . . [28]

According to Cassian the rule of unceasing prayer explains why the monks of Lower Egypt had ony two daily synaxes, with no "little hours." What other monks do at set times, the Egyptians are doing all the time:

> For manual labour is incessantly practiced by them in their cells in such a way that meditation on the Psalms and the rest of the Scriptures is never entirely omitted. And since they mingle suffrages and prayers with it at every moment, they spend the whole day in those offices which we celebrate at fixed times. Wherefore, except vespers and nocturns, there are no public services among them during the day . . . (*Inst.* III, 2).

But Cassian is wrong in implying that the institution of the day hours in monasteries outside Egypt was a relaxation of the ideal of ceaseless prayer, is obvious from the following anecdote from a Palestinian monastery in the alphabetical *Apophthegmata*, Epiphanius 3:

> The Abba of this cenobium wrote to Epiphanius, Bishop of Cyprus, saying: "Thanks to your prayers we have been faithful to our canonical hours. We never omit the office of terce, sext, none or vespers." But the bishop wrote back and reproached the monks in these terms: "Evidently you are neglecting the remaining hours of the day which you spend without prayer. The true monk should have prayer and psalmody in his heart at all times without interruption."

Furthermore, if the Egyptians saw a contradiction between set times of prayer and continuous prayer, why did they have any prayer times at all? In fact, as Veilleux has shown,[29] the earliest Egyptian anchoritic sources show no opposition between ceaseless prayer and a fixed daily *pensum*. In the Pachomian sources the first rule of prayer that the neophyte Pachomius received from his spiritual father Palamon was sixty prayers a day and fifty at night—but that was not a *substitute* for constant prayer: "Regarding the rule of the synaxis, [let it be] sixty prayers

---

[28]Trans. adapted from Jay (see ch. 2, note 4).
[29]*La liturgie* 288.

a day and fifty at night, not counting the ejaculations we do so as not to be liars, since we have been ordered to pray without ceasing."[30]

So it would be patently anachronistic to draw too sharp a distinction between "liturgical" and "private" prayer in early monasticism. In monastic literature during the foundational epoch the only difference between solitary prayer and common prayer was whether there was more than one person present. The following precept of Abba Isaiah of Scetis reflects this: "When you are at prayer in your dwelling, do not be negligent. . . . And when you do psalmody together, let each one say his own prayer. And if a traveler is with you, ask him with charity to pray. . . ."[31]

The very vocabulary of prayer in the earliest monastic documents betrays the same mentality.[32] In the *Apophthegmata*, "synaxis" is synonymous with "office," or a period or place of prayer, and "to do the synaxis" (*ballein tên synaxin*)[33] is used indifferently for common assemblies as well as for the prayer of solitaries. And although the Pachomian sources reserve "synaxis" for the common assemblies of the brethren, they use the same terms (*meletan, apostêthizein*) to refer to meditation on Sacred Scripture when at work alone throughout the day, when going to the church or refectory, or when hearing the pericopes recited by the soloist at the common synaxis.[34]

The point was not with whom one prayed, nor where, nor in what form, nor at what fixed times, nor in how many common synaxes, but that one's very life be totally prayer. When Abba Lot asked what he must do, Abba Joseph "rose and held his hands towards the sky so that his fingers became like flames of fire and he said: 'If you will, you shall become all flame.' "[35]

To unite prayer with all activities, even sleep, was the ancient ideal. The *Canons of Hippolytus* 27, an Egyptian source from around 336–340, says "When a man sleeps in his bed he must pray to God in his heart."[36] This ideal is resumed later and adapted to the active apostolate in the more modern axioms such as the Ignatian "contemplative in action," and "finding God in all things," as well as in such hallowed spiritual practices as purity of intention, the presence of God, recollection.

[30]Cited *ibid.* 288.

[31]V. Arras (ed.), *Collectio monastica* (CSCO 239, script. aethiopici 46, Louvain: Secrétariat du CSCO, 1963) 116.

[32]Veilleux, *La liturgie* 293ff.

[33]PG 65, 201; cf. 220.

[34]Veilleux, *La liturgie* 308.

[35]Cited in B. Ward, *The Wisdom of the Desert Fathers. "Apophthegmata Patrum" from the Anonymous Series* (Friaracres Publication 48, Oxford: SLG Press, 1981) xii.

[36]PO 31, 397.

It is probably to this rule of unceasing prayer that one must trace the Egyptian Urtradition concerning numbers and times of prayer according to the so-called "rule of the angel" of Palladius' *Lausiac History* 32, adapted by Cassian in *Inst.* II, 5–6, cited above. Veilleux has shown that the tradition found in unvaringly in all witnesses to this rule is twelve prayers *(euchas)* throughout the whole day *(dia pasês hêmeras)* and twelve during the night vigils *(en tais [nychterinais] pannychisi).*[37] Now it is not at all self-evident that originally "prayers" *(euchas)* here refers to psalms, nor that they were grouped into two synaxes of twelve each, morning and evening. The original sense seems to be that "prayers" were to be held twelve times a day and twelve times at night, that is, at every one of the twenty-four hours in the day—in other words, constantly. Veilleux[38] has gathered further evidence to support this interpretation. An ancient Egyptian text with a series of prayers for the twelve hours of the night which G. Maspero uncovered in the tomb of a Coptic monk may indicate a pre-Christian origin for the practice. And a Greek text called "the day and night canons of the psalms" attributed to Eusebius[39] distributes the psalter throughout the twenty-four hours of the day and night, twelve psalms per hour, in addition to the three psalms at matins and at vespers. And even today in Orthodox monasteries a distinction is drawn between the "office" and each monk's own private "canon" of prayer. Among Coptic Orthodox monks right up until our own day this "canon" of private prayer meant twelve times a day and twelve at night, as can be seen in the following Arabic rule from the Monastery of Dayr Anba Bakhum (St. Pachomius) in the Fayyum:

> V. **Prayer.** 1) PRIVATE PRAYER: The monk should practice public and private prayer. Concerning private prayer, he should pray twelve times a day and twelve times at night. 2) The private prayer should follow the psalter in accordance with the Church's *ordo*, and at the established hours. 3) PUBLIC PRAYER: The monks must assemble with one mind for the public prayer in the evening and in the morning.[40]

So the grouping of daily prayer into two daily synaxes of twelve psalms each is a later development in such sources as Cassian's *Institutes* II, 4–6, Palladius' *Lausiac History* 22, and the *Apophthegmata Patrum.*[41]

[37]Veilleux, *La liturgie* 324ff.

[38]*Ibid.* 329ff.

[39]PG 23, 1395.

[40]Johann Georg, Herzog zu Sachsen, *Streifzüge durch die Kirchen und Klöster Ägyptens* (Berlin/Leipzig: B.G. Teubner, 1914) 22.

[41]PG 65, 273–278, 385–389.

# Conclusion

Be that as it may, by the end of the fourth century we see that this continuous monastic prayer in Egypt has been grouped into two daily synaxes or offices at the beginning and end of the day, and that these services were more a quiet meditation on Scripture than a liturgical "ceremony" of the cathedral type. The point was to pray at all times. The when and the how, the where and the with whom, are all subject to change and evolution; but not the basic precept which is at the bottom of all Christian and especially monastic prayer then and now and forever.

# 5

# THE URBAN MONASTIC OFFICE
# IN THE EAST

Epiphanius of Salamis in his treatise *On the Faith* 23:2, written around 374–377, informs us that "some monks reside in the cities, others settle in monasteries and withdraw a great distance." And we saw Jerusalem overrun with ascetics by the time of Egeria. So at the end of the fourth century, in addition to the pure cathedral and monastic offices, mixed offices evolved, the product of monasticism in Palestine, Mesopotamia, Syria, and Cappadocia. Monks living near urban centers in these provinces were in contact with the life of the secular churches and adopted cathedral usages into their offices without, however, abandoning the continuous monastic psalmody inherited, seemingly, from Lower Egypt.

It is not difficult to explain why this came about. Although we now know there was more than one cradle of early monasticism, in the popular mind the Egyptian desert has always been *the* homeland of this movement, and the Egyptian monastic spirit and practices were the ideal that monks elsewhere strove to imitate. In Lower Egypt especially, the monastic movement spread with astounding rapidity. By the end of the fourth century there were over five thousand monks in Nitria and Kellia; in the sixth century there were 3500 in Scetis alone.[1] It was to these three deserts of

[1]Evelyn-White, *The Monasteries*, Part II, 333.

Lower Egypt that the constant stream of fourth-century monastic pilgrims made their arduous way. "It is a very perilous journey for travellers. For if one makes even a small error, one can get lost in the desert and find one's life in danger" (*History of the Monks in Egypt* XXIII, 1). But this did not daunt the intrepid voyagers who trekked across the burning sands in search of the way to God: Basil the Great, Melania the Elder, Rufinus of Aquileia, John Cassian, Jerome, Paula, Palladius, Evagrius of Pontus, Porphyrius of Gaza and the rest—the list reads like a *Who's Who* of the Early Church.

It is there that the dry stick immortalized in Ignatius of Loyola's *Letter on Obedience* was watered and took root (and the tree is still pointed out to the more comfortable if less credulous travelers of today). It is there that "the letter was begun but not ended," there that Benedict and later generations in East and West drew inspiration, via Cassian, or the *Philocalia*, or more recently from the Jesuit Alfonso Rodriguez's *Practice of Perfection and Christian Virtue*, with its endless anecdotes of "the foregoing confirmed by some examples" from the heroic lives of those halcyon days.

And it is from these three centers of Lower Egypt that most of the great literature of early monasticism derives: much of the *Apophthegmata Patrum*, a sixth-century collection of fourth-century stories; the *Lausiac History*, Palladius' eyewitness account written around 419–420; the anonymous *Historia monachorum in Aegypto*, whose author was in Egypt around 394–395 but never got to Scetis; to which one must add John Cassian's *Institutes* and *Conferences* written some twenty years after Cassian had left Scetis in 399. This literature, some of it already translated into Latin by the last quarter of the fourth century, was the staple of religious life in East and West right up until modern times. It is not surprising, therefore, to find the effects of this influence on monastic common prayer in other provinces of the Christian world in Late Antiquity, an influence openly acknowledged and often explicitly appealed to in order to lend the weight of tradition to the usages in question.

## Palestine

Once again, Cassian himself is our first witness to this hybrid urban monastic office. He had left home with his friend Germanus to become a monk in Bethlehem around 382–383 when only seventeen or eighteen years of age, and remained there a short time before moving on to Egypt sometime before 385–386. In his *Institutes*, written around 417–418 for the instruction of the monks in the monasteries he had founded in Marseilles, he also describes the office of the monks of Palestine and Mesopotamia. He begins by saying:

> The nocturnal system of prayers and psalms, as found throughout Egypt, has already, I think, been explained enough. . . . Now we must speak of the services of terce, sext, and none according to the rule of the monasteries of Palestine and Mesopotamia which mitigate by their institution the perfection and inimitable rigor of the discipline of the Egyptians (*Inst.* II, 1).

So these monasteries—and in *Institutes* III, 3, he expands the list to include those "of the whole Orient"—apparently had some pre-dawn synaxis of twelve psalms as in Egypt. To this they added prayer at the end of the third, sixth, and ninth hours, with three psalms and prayers apiece (III, 3:1; 4:2), and he goes on to justify these hours (III, 3:2-7) with the usual appeal to Dan 6:10, to the customary references to these times in Acts 2:15; 10:3, 9; 3:1; and to the crucifixion and harrowing of hell. The latter adds a slightly different nuance to the usual death on the cross theme of the ninth hour, and the reference to Cornelius' prayer at about the ninth hour in Acts 10:3 (III, 3) is peculiar to Cassian.

Then Cassian turns to vespers and matins, applying to them such traditional cathedral texts as Ps 140 and Ps 62, as well as new material. Since earlier (III, 1) he did not assert that *both* nocturns and vespers were the same as in Egypt, but only nocturns,[2] it is not unlikely that Palestinian monastic vespers contained some cathedral elements such as Ps 140. At any rate, here is what he says about the two main synaxes, morning and evening, in *Institutes* III, 3:8-11.

---

[2] In pure cathedral and monastic offices we saw just two daily synaxes, matins and vespers, at the opening and close of each day. In Lower Egypt, monastic offices began earlier than cathedral matins because the monks rose before the laity, but both hours were the opening service of the day. Later developments result in the following combinations. 1) Some hybrid urban-monastic offices, combining both systems, have two morning hours, one at cock-crow, one at dawn. To avoid confusion I follow Cassian and Gallic terminology in calling the earlier hour "nocturns," the later one "matins," except when discussing the *Rule of Benedict*. Benedict calls the morning office "matins" (RB 8:4; 12; 13:12), but for the night office he uses "nocturns" (10; 15:2) or "vigils" (8:3, 9:8; 11:10; 16:4) interchangeably, though "vigils" is more common, whereas in Gaul that term was used only for the longer occasional vigils, not for the daily night office. More recent western terminology, which calls nocturns "matins," and matins "lauds," is less satisfactory, and never had any currency outside the Latin tradition. I follow Benedict (RB 12:4; 13:11) and the Byzantines in restricting the term "lauds" to its narrow sense, using it only for what the Greeks call the *"Ainoi,"* i.e., Pss 148-150. 2) Other urban monastic offices kept matins at dawn and added to it the daily midnight office called *"mesonyktikon."* 3) Some authors use the term "vigil(s)" to refer indiscriminately to any night office, either the *daily* nocturns or *mesonyktikon,* or the longer *occasional*

But what is to be said concerning the evening sacrifices which are ordered to be offered continually even in the Old Testament by the law of Moses? For the fact that the morning holocausts and evening sacrifices were offered every day continually in the temple, although with figurative offerings, we can show from that which is sung by David: "Let my prayer be sent before your presence like incense, the lifting up of my hands like an evening sacrifice" (Ps 140:2), which we can understand in a still higher sense of either that true evening sacrifice which was given by the Lord our saviour in the evening to the apostles at supper, when he instituted the holy mysteries of the Church, and of that evening sacrifice which he himself, or on the following day, at the end of the ages, offered up to the Father by the lifting up of his hands for the salvation of the whole world; which spreading forth of his hands on the Cross is quite correctly called a "lifting up." For when we were all lying in hell he raised us to heaven, according to the word of his own promise, saying: "When I am lifted up from the earth, I will draw all men to myself" (John 12:32). But with regard to the morning service, that which it is customary every day to sing at it also teaches us: "O God, my God, since the dawn I keep watch before you" (Ps 62:2); and "I will meditate on you in the morning (Ps 62:7); and "I prevented the dawning of the day and cried;" and again, "My eyes have prevented the dawn, that I might meditate on your words" (Ps 118:147-8). At these hours too that householder in the Gospel (Matt 20:1-6) brought laborers into his vineyard. For thus he is also described as having hired them in the early morning, which time denotes our morning service; then at the third hour, then at the sixth, after this at the ninth, and last of all at the eleventh, by which the hour of the lamps is meant.

But this is not all Cassian has to say concerning the morning services, which were a special problem in Bethlehem. In the following chapter (III, 4) he recounts how a bit later a new service was instituted because the monks were going back to bed after nocturns, which went, as in Egypt, from cockcrow until dawn (*ante auroram*: III, 6:1). This going back to bed was unheard of in Egypt, where after the opening synaxis of the day the monks continued their prayer privately until daylight (II, 12:3; III, 5:2).

So according to Cassian the Palestinian monks developed their cursus in two stages. First they added the "little hours" to the original Egyptian two-synaxis cursus. Then came matins, a "new service" (*novella sollemnitas*), recently instituted for the first time in Cassian's own Bethlehem monastery. Its sole purpose was to make the monks get up at sunrise, for

---

night offices before certain special days of feasting or penance, such as the Easter vigil. The sense is usually clear from the context.

they had gotten into the habit of retiring again after nocturns and sleeping right through until terce (III, 4). This new celebration took place at sunrise (*primo mane*: III, 3:11; *ad ortum solis*: III, 4:2) and comprised three psalms (50, 62, 89) and three prayers (III, 4:2-6). So it had the same structure as the little hours, and some wish to see in it the origins of prime. This point will be discussed in chapters 6 and 10, along with the question of the origins of lauds, Pss 148-150, which Cassian says were attached to the end of Bethlehem nocturns without a break (III, 6).

So Cassian's Bethlehem daily cursus looked as follows:

> *From cockcrow until before day:* Nocturnal psalmody as in Egypt, followed by lauds (Pss 148-150).
>
> *At sunrise:* morning prayer, comprising Pss 50, 62, 89 with prayers
>
> *Third, sixth, ninth hours:* little hours, each with three psalms and three prayers.
>
> *Evening:* vesperal monastic psalmody, as in Egypt, probably with cathedral elements added.

Cassian also speaks of a psalm before and after supper (III, 12), and psalms before retiring (IV, 19:2), but he does not make it clear whether the psalm after supper and those before retiring are the same thing. Some wish to see compline in this bedtime psalmody, but I think that would be anachronistic, since Cassian omits all mention of such an office in his very detailed discussion of the Palestinian cursus. So I would prefer to consider these psalms as simply bedtime prayers before a formal office of compline had been introduced to serve this purpose.

What of Cassian's insistence that the new morning service originated in his Bethlehem monastery in his time? I shall return to both of these issues in chapter 10 when I analyze more closely some disputed questions in the history of the office.

What we see in the Palestinian monastic cursus is a mixed tradition. The day hours have been added to the two synaxes of the "pure" Egyptian monastic office. These two synaxes, in turn, have absorbed elements of the cathedral office such as lauds in the morning and possibly Ps 140 at vespers. And at a later stage there develops a new morning service made up of cathedral morning psalms, all three of which are reserved to lauds in the old Roman office and in the *Rule of St. Benedict*. On Sunday morning terce and sext are replaced by a single morning synaxis followed by Mass (III, 11). In addition, on Friday night there was an all-night vigil from evening almost until dawn (*usque ad aurorae uicinam*: III, 4:2), or during the long winter night until the fourth cockcrow (III, 8:1), comprising a threefold structure of three elements per section: 1) three antiphons standing, 2) after which they sat for three responsorial psalms intoned in turn by different monks, 3) and then three lessons (III, 8:4). This is what we saw in the vigil described in Basil's *Letter 207*, 3, to the clergy of Neocaesarea, cited above in chapter 3 apropos of the cathedral office in Cappadocia. Since these three elements alone would hardly make for an all-night vigil, I agree with Baumstark and Heiming that Cassian is describing a liturgical unit repeated several times in the course of the night.[3]

## Antioch[4]

When Cassian in *Institutes* III, 3:1 says a monastic office similar to that of Palestine is found also in monasteries of the whole Orient (*in monasteriis ac totius Orientis*), he was speaking undoubtedly of the civil *diocese* of Orient, not the *prefecture* of Orient which also included the diocese of Egypt (*Augustalis*). The diocese of Orient had Antioch as its metropolis, and John Chrysostom provides a description of the monastic office of that city before 397 that in fact does resemble in some points the usages of Bethlehem described by Cassian. The two Chrysostomian documents in question are probably reminiscences from Chrysostom's monastic days between 370 and 376, and so the practices he refers to antedate Cassian's account by a few years.

The first account is in his *Homily 14 on 1 Tim*, 4, which describes the monastic nocturnal office at Antioch:

> [1] . . . at the crowing of the cocks the superior comes immediately and gently touching the sleeper with his foot, rouses them all . . . . [2]Then as soon as they have risen they stand up and sing the prophetic hymns with much harmony and well-composed tunes . . . . [3]And the songs themselves are also suitable, and full of the love of God. "In the night," they say, "lift up your hands" (Ps 133:2) unto God, and again: "In the night my soul keeps vigil before you, O God, for your commandments are a light on the earth" (Is 26:9). [4]And the songs of David that cause fountains of tears to flow. For when he sings [Chrysostom cites

---

[3]A. Baumstark, *Nocturna laus. Typen frühchristlicher Vigilienfeier* (LQF 32, Münster: Aschendorff, 1957) 128; O. Heiming, "Zum monastischen Offizium von Kassianus bis Kolumbanus," ALW 7 (1961) 108.

[4]Some of the following material has appeared in a slightly different form in my article "*Quaestiones disputatae* in the History of the Liturgy of the Hours: the Origins of Nocturns, Matins, Prime," *Worship* 58 (1984) 130–158.

LXX Pss 6:7; 101:10; 8:5; 143:4; 48:17; 67:7; 118:164, 62; 48:16; 22:4; 90:5, 6; 43:23] he expresses their ardent love of God.[5]

Chrysostom is just citing appropriate verses at random, not giving a set order of psalms proper to this office. His quoting two verses of Ps 48 separately and in reverse order shows that clearly enough. So Mateos is right in interpreting this section as referring to the variable nocturnal psalmody customary in such offices.[6] But the next sentence, which cites Ps 148:1, seems to indicate that this is more than just another of the possible psalm verses that might occur in this office:

> [5]And again, when they sing with the angels—for angels, too, are singing then—"Praise the Lord from the heavens" (Ps 148:1). [6]And meanwhile we are snoring. . . . Think what it was for them to spend the whole night in this employment! [7]And when the day is coming on, they rest again. For when we begin our tasks they have a period of rest. [8]Each of us, when it is day, calls upon his neighbor. . . another visits the stage, another goes about his own business, but these again, after performing their morning prayers and hymns, dedicate themselves to the reading of the Scriptures. . . .

So the office began at cockcrow, apparently with a fixed invitatory comprising Ps 133 and Is 26:9ff (2–3), followed by variable psalmody (4). It concluded just before dawn (6–7) with the psalms of lauds, Pss 148–150 (5), giving the following structure:

> Invitatory:   Ps 133
> Is 26:9ff.
>
> Variable monastic psalmody *currente psalterio*
> Pss 148–150

Only Ps 148 is actually cited (5), but comparative liturgy makes it probable that the reference is to the *Ainoi* or lauds psalms as a unit. It is worth noting that Ps 133 is one of the fixed invitatories of nocturns in the Chaldean, Syrian, Tikritan, Maronite, Coptic, Ethiopian, and Old Constantinopolitan offices, whereas the Isaiah canticle serves the same purpose in the present Byzantine office of St. Sabas, a tradition of Palestinian origin.

Then, still in Chrysostom's description, after a brief rest (7), the monks rose for "morning prayers and hymns," a very short morning office since it was over, he tells us, by the time it was day (8)—probably sunrise, for the nocturnal vigil itself had concluded just before dawn (6–7). In another

---

[5]Text in PG 62, 576ff.; trans. here and below adapted from NPNF series 1, vol. 13 (Grand Rapids: Eerdmans, 1979) 456–457.
[6]Mateos, "L'office monastique," 56.

of his Antiochene homilies, *Homily 68 (69) on Matt,* 3, Chrysostom describes this brief morning service. The monks,

> [1] . . . as soon as the sun is up, or rather even long before sunrise . . . having risen then straightaway from their bed . . . and having made one choir . . . all with one voice, as from one mouth, [2]sing hymns to the God of all, honoring and thanking him for all his benefits, both particular and common. . . . [3]What is the difference between the angels and this company of them who on earth sing and say, "Glory to God in the highest. . . ?" [4]Then, after they have sung those songs, they bow their knees and entreat the God who was the object of their hymns for things, at the very thought of which some do not easily arrive. [5]For they ask nothing of things present, since they have no regard for these, but [they ask] that they may stand with boldness before the fearful judgment seat, when the Only-Begotten Son of God comes to judge the living and the dead, and that no one may hear the tearful voice that says, "I know you not," and that with a pure conscience and many good deeds they may pass through this toilsome life, and sail over the angry sea with a favorable wind. [6]And he who is their Father and their ruler leads them in their prayers. [7]After this, when they have arisen and finished those holy and continual prayers, [8]the sun being risen, they depart each one to his work, gathering from it a large supply for the needy.[7]

So Chrysostom's Antiochene monastic office, like cathedral matins in the *Apostolic Constitutions* seen above, comprised psalms or "hymns" (2), the *Gloria in excelsis* (3), concluding intercessions (kneeling: 4–6), and a concluding prayer after rising (7). The text of some of the intercessions (5) is similar to the *aitêseis* or "angel of peace" petitions found in the *Apostolic Constitutions* VIII 6–9; 37–39 and in Byzantine sources,[8] and also referred to by Basil in *Letter 11* cited above in chapter 3.

What were the opening "hymns" (4)? Chrysostom does not say. Could they have been the traditional opening psalm(s) of morning praise: Ps 62 as in the *Apostolic Constitutions* II, 59:2 (cf. VIII, 38:1) and the *De virginitate;* Ps 50 as in the Basilian documents; or both, plus Ps 89, as in Cassian, *Institutes* III, 6?[9] Since the *Apostolic Constitutions* is the nearest parallel document in time and place, Ps 62 is a likely choice. This would yield the following structure:

---

[7]Text in PG 58, 644–646; trans. adapted from NPNF series 1, vol. 10 (Grand Rapids: Eerdmans, 1978) 418.

[8]See R. Taft, *The Great Entrance* (OCA 200, Rome: PIO, 1978[2]) ch. 9.

[9]These documents are also studied in chapters 3, 6, and 10.

Ps 62
*Gloria in excelsis*
Intercessions
Concluding prayer(s)

Here too we see a hybrid office in which lauds have been appended
to the "pure" monastic psalmody of nocturns, and matins has been filled
out with even more elements of cathedral morning praise such as the *Gloria
in excelsis* and the intercessions. Just how all this came about will be developed in chapter 10.

In *Homily 14 on 1 Tim*, 4, Chrysostom also mentions "psalms and
hymns" at the third, sixth, and ninth hours and in the evening, as well
as after supper.

The similarities and differences between the Bethlehem and Antiochene
systems, observable in the first two synaxes of the day—the only ones
for which we have sufficient data to make a comparison—can be seen
in the following schema:

|  | BETHLEHEM | ANTIOCH |
|---|---|---|
| From cockcrow to just before dawn: | *vigil:* | *vigil:* |
|  |  | Ps 133 |
|  |  | Is 26:9ff. |
|  | variable psalmody | variable psalmody |
|  | Pss 148–150 | Pss 148–150 |
| At daybreak: | *novella sollemnitas:* | *morning office:* |
|  | Pss 62, 50, 89 with three prayers | Pss 50, 62 (?) |
|  |  | *Gloria in excelsis* |
|  |  | Intercessions |
|  |  | Concluding prayer(s) |

The rest of the horarium—terce, sext, none, vespers, mealtime and
bedtime prayers—is substantially the same in both traditions. From what
we know of later offices we can probably presume that the Antiochene
little hours also had three psalms, and that vespers included some continuous monastic psalmody. Did monastic vespers also have appended
to it cathedral elements such as a light ritual and Ps 140 with incense, as
we also see in later hybrid offices? We do not know, though Cassian in
*Institutes* III, 3:9, cited above, does comment on Ps 140 in the context

of "the hour of the lamps" in Bethlehem, and such elements are found in all later hybrid monastic-cathedral vespers in the Christian East.

What we find in the urban monastic office of Palestine and Antioch is, I think, basically a monastic cursus that has absorbed cathedral elements. This is betrayed by the fact that their more primitive office at the beginning of the day follows the horarium of Lower Egypt. The new morning service at daybreak or sunrise is a later addition. But when we turn now to Cappadocia we shall find, I think, the opposite: an urban monastic office that is rather a cathedral cursus onto which monastic hours have been grafted.

## Cappadocia[10]

### I. BASIL

We learn of the Cappadocian monastic office from the writings of St. Basil the Great (d. 379). Basil, a well-educated and cosmopolitan bishop, had visited the monastic centers of Syria, Palestine, Mesopotamia, and Egypt to learn their spirit and uses, and had lived the ascetic life with his friend Gregory Nazianzen (d. ca. 390) before becoming bishop of Caesarea in Cappadocia and exarch of Pontus in 370. His famous rules have had enormous influence on the whole history of cenobitic monasticism—St. Benedict relied heavily on Basil—right up to our own day.

To give seculars a living model of Christian life, Basil established his communities of ascetics in towns, and in *Longer Rules* 3:1 he explicitly rejects the idea that they are "monks." They were simply Christians taking the whole business seriously. For this reason the practices Basil describes are close to the usages of the secular churches—otherwise how could they be an example to the laity? But at the same time to ignore the ascetical heritage of Egypt, *the* cradle of religious life in the popular mind, was unthinkable. So these Basilian ascetics celebrated matins and vespers in imitation of the cathedral offices, adding to them terce, sext, none, and later compline, as well as something new, a *mesonyktikon* or nightly vigil not at cockcrow as in Palestine and Antioch, but at midnight. Clearly, this cursus is mainly a "liturgicizing" of the ancient horarium of Christian daily prayer.

In *Longer Rules* 37:2–5, after the customary affirmations concerning the rule of unceasing prayer, and how to reconcile the seeming contradic-

---

[10]Cf. Mateos, "L'office monastique," 69–87, though I depart somewhat from Mateos' interpretation.

tion between this evangelical precept and the rule of work, Basil describes the monastic cursus:[11]

[1]Now since some use prayers and psalmody as a pretext to avoid work, it is necessary to know that for certain other tasks there is a special time, as Ecclesiastes (3:1) says: "There is a time for everything." [2]But for prayer and psalmody . . . every time is suitable, so that while our hands move in work we may praise God with the tongue when this is possible, or rather when it is conducive to the edification of the faith. Or if not, then [we praise God] in the heart, with psalms and hymns and spiritual canticles (Eph 5:19; Col 3:16), as it is written, fulfilling the duty to pray in the midst of work. . . . [3]If this is not the way, how can there be mutual consistency in the sayings of the apostles, "pray without ceasing" (1 Thess 5:17), and "working night and day" (2 Thess 3:8)?

[4]Nor indeed, because thanksgiving at all times has been enjoined even by law . . . should the established times of prayer in the brotherhood be neglected, [5]times which we have chosen necessarily because each has its own special reminder of blessings received from God.

[6]In the morning [we pray] so that the first movements of the soul and mind may be consecrated to God, and nothing else be taken into consideration before we have been delighted by the thought of God, as it is written, "I remembered God and was delighted" (Ps 76:3), and so that the body may not engage in work before the saying is fulfilled: "To you will I pray, O Lord; in the morning you shall hear my voice, in the morning I will stand before you and keep watch" (Ps 5:4–5).

[7]Again at the third hour we must stand up to pray and gather the brotherhood . . . and recalling the gift of the Spirit given to the apostles at the third hour (Acts 2:15), all should worship together with one accord so that they also may become worthy to receive sanctification, asking of him guidance and teaching in what is profitable, according to the words: "Create a clean heart in me, O God . . . " (Ps 50:10–12), and elsewhere: "Your good spirit shall guide me to level ground" (Ps 142:10). And so we apply ourselves to our tasks again.

[8]And if some, perhaps, are absent owing to the nature or place of their work, they are of necessity obliged to observe there all that is prescribed for common observance, without any hesitation, "for where two or three are gathered together in my name, there am I in the midst of them" (Matt 18:20).

[9]And we judge prayer to be necessary at the sixth hour, in imitation of the saints who say: "Evening and morning and at noon I will speak and declare, and he shall hear my voice" (Ps 54:17). And so that we may be delivered from mishap and from the noonday devil (Ps 90:6), at the same time Ps 90 is also said.

[11]Text in PG 31, 1012ff.

[10]The ninth [hour], however, was handed down to us as necessary for prayer by the apostles themselves in Acts, where it is related that "Peter and John went up to the temple at the ninth hour of prayer" (Acts 3:1).

[11]And when the day is finished, thanksgiving should be offered for what has been given us during the day or for what we have done rightly, and confession made of what we have failed to do—an offence committed, be it voluntary or involuntary, or perhaps unnoticed, either in word or deed or in the very heart—propitiating God in our prayers for all our failings. For the examination of past actions is a great help against falling into similar faults again. Wherefore it says: "The things you say in your hearts, be sorry for on your beds" (Ps 4:5).

[12]And again, at the beginning of the night we ask that our rest may be without offence and free from phantasies, and at this hour also Ps 90 must be recited.

[13]And Paul and Silas have handed on to us midnight as necessary for prayer, as the story of Acts proves, saying: "And at midnight Paul and Silas praised God" (Acts 16:25), and the psalmist also, saying: "I rose at midnight to praise you for the judgments of your righteousness" (Ps 118:62).

[14]And again we must rise to anticipate the dawn with prayer, so that we are not caught by the day asleep in bed according to him who said: "My eyes have prevented the morning, that I might meditate on your words" (Ps 118:148).

[15]None of these times should be neglected by those who have chosen a life dedicated to the glory of God and his Christ. [16]But I think diversity and variety in the prayers and psalmody at the fixed hours is desirable for this reason: through routine the soul often grows weary somehow, and is distracted, whereas by alternation and variety in the psalmody and Scripture at each hour, its desire is refreshed and its sobriety renewed.

We see here a full cycle of seven hours: matins (6, 14), terce (7), sext (9), none (10), vespers (11), compline (12), and the midnight vigil (13). At the end of the cursus Basil returns again to matins (14), but in both places (6, 14) he refers to it as the office of dawn (*orthros*) and is obviously speaking of one, not two morning services.

Some of this cursus is referred to in other writings of Basil. His *Letter 2* to Gregory Nazianzen written around 358 speaks of matins from daybreak until after sunrise, of prayer while at work, *lectio divina*, the practice of the presence of God, prayer before and after meals, and prayer at midnight.[12] His *Ascetical Discourse*, which resumes many of the points in the *Longer Rules*, knows only six hours, so that sext is divided

[12]Ed. Courtonne, vol. 1, 5–13.

in two to make up the classic number of seven referred to in Ps 118:164.[13] But this document's authenticity is not absolutely certain. In *Longer Rules* 37:2-5, Basil also gives information on the contents of these hours. He affirms explictly that Ps 90 is recited at sext (9) and again at compline (12), and it is possible that some of the other psalms he mentions to justify certain other hours were part of the offices—especially Ps 54 at sext (9) and Ps 118 at *mesonyktikon* (13), which are also applied to these hours in the *Ascetical Discourse*. The following table compares the psalms of the present Byzantine Sabaitic horologion with the ones Basil gives (the asterisk means that the *Ascetical Discourse* also locates the psalm in the office in question; the midnight office in the horologion column refers to the original Sabaitic *mesonyktikon*, now the nocturns of matins):

|  | HOROLOGION | BASIL |
|---|---|---|
| *terce:* | 16 | |
| | 24 | |
| | *50* | *50* and *142* |
| *sext:* | 53 | |
| | *54* | *\*54:18* |
| | *90* | *90* |
| *none:* | 83 | |
| | 84 | |
| | 85 | |
| *compline:* | *90 (Great Compline)* | *90* |
| *midnight:* | | *\*118* |

Matins consisted of Ps 50 followed by hymns and canticles, and probably concluded with intercessions, as we saw in chapter 3.

Basil also gives the rationale of the hours. Apropos of the day hours he cites the usual texts of Acts for terce and none, but not for sext. Psalm verses are also adduced in support, but not the classic text of Dan 6 nor the passion horarium of the gospels, though the *Ascetical Discourse* does mention the passion with respect to the ninth hour. More important, Basil's reasons for morning and evening prayer parallel exactly what Chrysostom says regarding these hours in cathedral usage (see ch. 3).

## II. De Virginitate

An even more fully developed pattern of monastic night and morning prayer emerges clearly in the treatise *De virginitate* 20. This document is at-

[13]PG 31, 877.

tributed to Athanasius of Alexandria, but M. Aubineau has challenged its authenticity, and in the process has shown that the treatise's vocabulary is akin to that of Cappadocian writers around 370.[14] Furthermore, its liturgical material, which seems to me of Cappadocian rather than Alexandrine vintage, only confirms this skepticism regarding its Athanasian provenance. The liturgical pattern of this treatise *On Virginity* is repeated in extant eastern offices such as the Chaldean and, formerly, the Byzantine,[15] and we know from Basil that the Cappadocian ascetics were in close contact with the life of the secular churches. Here is the text:[16]

> [1]At midnight arise and hymn the Lord your God, for at that hour our Lord rose from the dead and hymned the Father. For this reason it befits us to hymn God at that hour. [2]On rising, say first this verse: "I rose at midnight to praise you for the judgments of your righteousness" (Ps 118:62), and pray, and begin to say the whole of Ps 50 up to the end, [3]and these things are set down for you to do each day. [4]Say as many psalms as you have the strength to say standing, [5]and after each psalm, say a prayer and make a prostration, [6]with tears confessing your sins to the Lord, asking him to forgive you. [7]After three psalms, say the alleluia. [8]And if there are [other] virgins with you, let them sing the psalms and perform the prayers one by one.
>
> [9]At dawn say this psalm: "O God my God, I keep vigil before you, my soul thirsts for you"(Ps 62:1). [10]And at daybreak: "All the works of the Lord bless the Lord, sing hymns . . ." (Dan 3:35), [11]" Glory to God in the highest," [12]and the rest.

The author of the document obviously considers "the rest" (12) to be a part of morning prayer so well-known to the reader that he does not need to spell it out. The most reasonable supposition is that he is referring to Pss 148–150. So here there are two separate offices, one at midnight (1)—i.e., in the period between midnight and cockcrow—of variable length depending on how many psalms the virgins can manage (4), the second at dawn (9). The nocturnal office has the classic structure of such vigils: a fixed invitatory (2), followed by variable psalmody (4), undoubtedly "in course," with each psalm followed by prayer and a prostration

---

[14]M. Aubineau, "Les écrits de s. Athanase sur la virginité," *Revue d'ascétique et de mystique* 31 (1955) 144–151.

[15]See the following works of J. Mateos: *Lelya-Ṣapra, passim;* "Les matins chaldéenes, maronites et syriennes," OCP 26 (1960) 54–55, 58ff., 61ff., 68, 72; "L'invitatoire du nocturne chez les syriens et les maronites," OS 11 (1966) 353–366; "Un office du minuit chez les chaldéens?" OCP 25 (1959) 101–113; "Les differentes espèces de vigiles dans le rite chaldéen," OCP 27 (1961) 48ff.; "Quelques problèmes de l'orthros byzantin," POC 11 (1961) 22–31.

[16]E.F. von der Goltz (ed.), *De virginitate. Eine echte Schrift des Athanasius* (TU 29, Heft 2a, Leipzig: J.C. Hinrichs, 1905), 55–56.

(5–6). The psalter is divided into groups of three psalms—the basic grouping in most traditions, as Mateos has shown[17]—with the alleluia after each group of three (7). Matins also has a fixed invitatory psalm (9), followed perhaps by other psalms, for it is not until daybreak that the fixed conclusion is added (10), comprising the *Benedicite* of Dan 3:35–68 (10), the *Gloria in excelsis* (11), and probably Pss 148–150, as follows:

NOCTURNS:

> Ps 118:62
>
> Prayer
>
> Ps 50
>
> Variable psalmody with prayers and prostrations; alleluia after
> each set of three psalms

MATINS:

> Ps 62
>
> Variable psalmody (?)
>
> *Benedicite*
>
> *Gloria in excelsis*
>
> Pss 148–150 (?)

These three final elements, the *Benedicite, Gloria in excelsis,* and lauds, have become a standard part of later cathedral and hybrid morning offices. Rufinus (ca. 345–410) in his *Apologia in S. Hieronymum* 2, 35, says that the *Benedicite* is sung in churches all over the world.[18] A century later we see it as the canticle of Sunday lauds in the rules of the Master (39) and Benedict (12); in eastern arrangements the *Benedicite* with the *Gloria in excelsis* is still a part of the morning office or cathedral vigil at least on Sunday in all extant traditions except the West Syrian, which does not have the *Benedicite,* and the Maronite, which does not have the *Gloria.*[19]

---

[17] J. Mateos, "Office de minuit et office du matin chez s. Athanase," OCP 28 (1962) 175–176.

[18] PL 21, 613–614.

[19] In addition to the relevant chapters below in Part II, for the Syrian traditions, see the schemata in Mateos, "Les matines chaldéenes, maronites, et syriennes;" for the Byzantine tradition see his "Quelques problèmes de l'orthros," 31–34. In the Armenian rite the *Benedicite* occurs in that part of the Sunday morning office that was the old cathedral vigil: see *ibid.,* 31, 217, and G. Winkler, "The Armenian Night Office," II: *Revue des études arméniennes* 17 (1983) 471–551, esp. 500–505. In the Coptic rite there is none of this cathedral office in the monastic *Horologion* except for the *Gloria in excelsis,* but the *Benedicite* is one of the elements of the old cathedral vigil still found in the Coptic cathedral morning office known as the Psalmodia of the Night: see Taft, "Praise in the Desert," 529, 531 ff. and ch. 15 below. For further information on the history of the *Gloria in excel-*

## Conclusion

By the end of the fourth century monks in or near urban centers outside Egypt had carried the evolution of the Liturgy of the Hours three steps
further: 1) they had filled out the daily horarium by creating common
synaxes or formal liturgical hours—the "little" or "day" hours of terce,
sext, none—at the traditional fixed times of Christian private prayer; 2)
they effected a synthesis of monastic and cathedral usages by adopting
elements of cathedral morning prayer and evensong, while retaining the
continuous monastic psalmody at the beginning and end of the monastic
order of the day; 3) they introduced a new office, compline, as bedtime
prayer, thus duplicating vespers in both the cathedral and pure monastic
cursus. For as we saw in the previous chapter, the Egyptian monks ate
at the ninth hour, after which the vesperal psalmody ended the day. And
in the cathedral system it was—and still is—at vespers that we review and
conclude the day, thanking God for graces received, begging pardon for
faults committed, and requesting protection from sin and danger throughout the coming night.

But the hybrid urban monastic horarium and offices were not the same
everywhere. The sources seem to agree that three psalms formed the core
of the "little hours," and that compline included Ps 90. Our information
on vespers is less explicit, but that office continued to share with the new-
er compline its original purpose as a service of thanksgiving, examination of conscience, and forgiveness. As for the structure of the evening
service, Cassian implies that urban monastic vespers in Bethlehem was
not just a replica of the Egyptian monastic psalmody, so it probably had
incorporated at least such classic cathedral elements as the lucernarium
with hymn, Ps 140 with incense, and intercessions, giving the following
tentative and ideal structure that we see repeated in later hybrid eastern
vesperal rites:

> Continuous monastic psalmody
> Light ritual with hymn of light
> Ps 140 with incense
> Intercessions

To this skeleton in a later period, and maybe already at this time, other
elements such as antiphons, responsories, lessons, canticles, were added.

---

sis and *Benedicite* in the liturgy see J. Mearns, *The Canticles of the Christian Church, Eastern
and Western in Early and Medieval Times* (Cambridge: The University Press, 1914) *passim.*

The significant differences occur in the offices that open the monastic day: nocturns and matins or cathedral lauds. In Palestine and Antioch, lauds were appended to the nocturnal office, which went from cockcrow—around 3:00 A.M. it seems—to before dawn. Later, another matins service was added at daybreak, comprising matins psalms and, in Antioch, other elements borrowed from cathedral morning praise such as the *Gloria in excelsis* and concluding intercessions. But in Cappadocia, the office of cathedral matins, celebrated at dawn, apparently retained its integrity, including the psalms of lauds, and a separate monastic vigil of continuous psalmody was introduced at midnight. So it seems that the Palestinian monks started with an essentially Egyptian monastic system, opening the day with the traditional monastic psalmody at cockcrow, and added cathedral elements. The Cappadocian ascetics took as their point of departure cathedral matins-lauds at dawn, and added a vigil service of continuous monastic psalmody at midnight.

I have already outlined these nocturnal and morning services above in the preceding pages of this chapter, and in chapters 6 and 10 I shall give a more detailed analysis of some of the outstanding hermeneutical problems involved in interpreting the texts concerning vigils, matins-lauds, and prime.

# 6

# THE MONASTIC OFFICE IN THE WEST: NORTH AFRICA, GAUL, IRELAND, AND THE IBERIAN PENINSULA

The beginning of the fifth century was also the beginning of the end for the Roman Empire in the West. At the end of 406, the Germanic tribes crossed the Rhine, sacking Mainz, burning Trier, and devastating the countryside. In 409 they crossed the Pyrenees and took most of Spain. Meanwhile the Goths were in the ascendant. Rome fell to the Visigoths under Alaric in 410. They entered Gaul in 412, Spain the following year. The Goths made war on the other tribes, were eventually allowed by the Romans to settle in Gaul as "*foederati*," and gradually spread their power throughout the whole West. By 476 they held all of Southern France and a third of Italy. The end came that same year when Odoacer deposed the usurper Romulus Augustulus to become the first barbarian King of Italy (476–493). It is in the context of this momentous historic change that the development of the Divine Office in the West must be considered.

Contrary to what we saw in the East, where the evidence for a cathedral office is much more abundant and detailed than for monastic usage before the end of Late Antiquity, in the fifth–sixth century West the opposite is true: we have several accounts of the monastic cursus complete in almost every detail, but little is known directly about cathedral usage save the fact of its existence. Hence I shall reverse the order of treatment and deal first with the monastic office in the West.

## The *Ordo Monasterii*

Perhaps the oldest western monastic cursus for which we have evidence is the *Ordo monasterii*, a primitive monastic rule in elegant Latin attributed to Alypius of Thegaste in North Africa around 395.[1] Not only was the *Ordo* later incorporated by St. Augustine into his rule;[2] Caesarius of Arles also used it in composing his *Rule for Monks*.[3]

Chapter 2 of the *Ordo* gives the cursus of hours as follows:[4]

> We shall describe how we ought to pray or execute the psalmody. At matins let three psalms be said: the 62nd, the 5th, and the 89th; at terce: first a responsorial psalm (*psalmus ad respondendum*), then two antiphons (*antiphonae*), a reading, and the conclusion (*completorium*); sext and none likewise; but at lucernarium: one responsorial psalm (*psalmus responsorius*), four antiphons, again one responsorial psalm,[5] a reading, and the conclusion.
>
> And at a suitable time after the lucernarium let readings be read to all seated; but after this let there be said the usual psalms before sleep. As for the nocturnal prayers, in the months of November, December, January, and February: twelve antiphons, six psalms, three lessons; in March, April, September, and October: ten antiphons, five psalms, three lessons; in May, June, July, and August: eight antiphons, four psalms, two lessons.

The terminology of this text presents certain difficulties, but Lambot is undoubtedly correct in taking *antiphonae* to mean antiphonal psalms as in the *Rules* of the Master and Benedict, rather than antiphons in the narrow sense, i.e., the refrains that accompanied the psalm. Otherwise the little hours would have one psalm only, vespers but two, nocturns

[1]L. Verheijen, *La Règle de s. Augustin*, II: *Recherches historiques* (Etudes augustiniennes, Paris, 1967) 125 ff. See also G.P. Lawless, "*Ordo Monasterii*. Structure, Style and Rhetoric," *Augustinianum* 22 (1982) 469–491; *id., Ordo monasterii*. A Double or Single Hand?" *Studia Patristica* 17/2 (Oxford: Pergamon, 1982) 511–518. In the latter article Lawless reviews all opinions and argues against Verheijen's attributing the *Ordo* to Alypius, but all seem to agree it comes from the time and milieu of St. Augustine.

[2]Verheijen, *La Règle* 205ff.

[3]C. Lambot, "La Règle de S. Augustin et S. Césaire," RevB 41 (1929) 337–341, where the *Ordo* is called the *Regula secunda* of Augustine.

[4]Text edited in D. de Bruyne, "La première règle de s. Benoît," RevB 42 (1930) 318–319.

[5]Concerning "de Bruyne's comma," crucial for interpreting this passage, see Heiming, "Zum monastischen Offizium," 111.

six, five, or four.[6] Furthermore, *completorium* must refer to the conclusion of the hour, like *conplere* in the *Rule of the Master* (52:1–4, 55:8, 56:8, etc.),[7] or like Benedict's description of the conclusion of lauds: ". . . *canticum de evangelia, litania, et completum,*"[8] which Benedict more often calls *missae.*[9] Less certain is Lambot's interpretation of the unqualified *psalmus* as a psalm chanted *in directum* by all the monks together, *psalmus responsorius* or *ad respondendum* as a psalm *in directum* by a soloist, and *antiphona* as alternate psalmody by all the monks divided into two choirs. A study of the kinds of psalmody in the West in this early period would carry us too far afield. But I consider it far more likely that *antiphona* means a psalm with antiphon, for this is what *antiphona* means in the *Rule of the Master;*[10] and *psalmus responsorius* or *ad respondendum* is a psalm with responsory, as in almost all other documents. "*Psalmus*" unqualified in matins and nocturns is ambiguous. But the ternary structure of the psalmody in all other hours, in threes or multiples of threes, or in a two-to-one proportion of two antiphonal psalms to one responsorial,[11] leads me to agree with Heiming and Baumstark that the "*psalmus*" of nocturns is synonymous with the responsorial psalm(s) of the other hours.[12]

Several arguments recommend this hypothesis:

1)     It gives the hours a uniform structure except for matins, which remains an exception perhaps because that hour, the *novella sollemnitas* we saw in Cassian, was an innovation in monastic usage.

2)     It would make the *Ordo* agree with the *Rule of the Master*, where there are also only these two types of psalmody, antiphonal and responsorial, in the normal office.[13] *Directaneus* execution is found at table prayer in the refectory (RM 38, 43), or in the hours recited by those prevented by work from being present at the office in the oratory (RM 55:18).

---

[6]C. Lambot, "Un 'ordo officii' du Ve siècle," RevB 42 (1930) 79–80.

[7]See Heiming, "Zum monastischen Offizium," 109–110, and the index to RM in J.-M. Clément, J. Neufville, D. Demeslay, *La Règle du Maître* III: *Concordance verbale . . .* (SC 107, Paris: Cerf, 1965) 84.

[8]RB 12–13; cf. Heiming, "Zum monastischen Offizium," 79.

[9]RB 17; cf. Heiming, "Zum monastischen Offizium," 109–110.

[10]A. de Vogüé, *La Règle du Maître* vols. I–II: *Introduction, texte, traduction et notes* (SC 105–106, Paris: Cerf, 1964) I, 60.

[11]*Ibid.* I, 53; Heiming, "Zum monastischen Offizium," 111, cf. 93.

[12]Heiming, "Zum monastischen Offizium," 112; Baumstark, *Nocturna laus* 113.

[13]Cf. Heiming, *loc. cit.*

3)  It brings nocturns into conformity with the threefold
structure of the occasional vigil we saw in Cassian and
Basil: antiphonal psalms, followed by responsorial
psalms, followed by lessons. Here, however, it is a single-
unit, fixed daily office, as is clear from the set number
of psalms and readings in each season, whereas in Cassian and Basil it was a unit to be repeated throughout
the night.[14]

In summary, then, the office of the *Ordo* comprised:

| | |
|---|---|
| *Matins:* | Pss 62, 5, 89 |
| *Terce-sext-none:* | 1 responsorial psalm |
| | 2 antiphonal psalms |
| | reading |
| | conclusion |
| *Lucernarium:* | 1 responsorial psalm |
| | 4 antiphonal psalms |
| | 1 responsorial psalm |
| | reading |
| | conclusion |
| *Nocturns:* | 12/10/8 antiphonal psalms |
| | 6/5/4 responsorial psalms |
| | 3/3/2 readings |
| | [conclusion] |

Though the text does not say so, Heiming supposes that nocturns, like
the other hours except matins, concluded with the *completorium*.[15] He
also leans toward presuming a period of silent prayer following the psalms,
as we shall see in Caesarius and Aurelian of Arles, and in Columban, but
I think this may have been true only of nocturns.[16]

## Cassian in Southern Gaul

But North African monasticism had its own independent history, and
it is to the traditions of the European continent that we must look for the
background of our present Western offices. By the last quarter of the fourth
century we have evidence for the existence of monasticism in Northern

---

[14]See above, pp. 39–41, 79–80.
[15]Heiming, "Zum monastischen Offizium," 111.
[16]Cf. *ibid.* 113.

Italy, Rome, and Campania to the south; in Gaul; and in the Iberian peninsula.[17] But most of the sources, apart from general references to psalmody and vigils, tell us nothing about the structure of monastic prayer until Cassian gave the movement coherence.

In Gaul the oldest monastic cursus is that which Cassian legislated for his Monastery of St. Victor in Marseilles and for the Monastery of Lerins founded by his disciple Honoratus. These monasteries were the cradle of numerous bishops, the most celebrated of whom was St. Caesarius of Arles. It was these bishops who spread this office throughout France.

Above in chapter 5 we reviewed Cassian's testimony concerning the urban monastic office of Bethlehem in his *Institutes*, written around 417–425. There we learn of the Gallic office only as reflected in the mirror of Cassian's description of the uses of Egypt and Palestine. What he says, basically, is that the office in Gaul was like that of Bethlehem apart from the exceptions noted:

1) In Gallic usage each psalm, not just a unit of psalms as in Egypt and Palestine, was concluded with the *Gloria Patri (Inst.* II, 8). This difference still distinguishes eastern and western monastic psalmody.

2) Nocturns, an office of continuous psalmody followed by two readings as in Egypt, went from cockcrow until before day as in Bethlehem (*Inst.* II, 1). In Bethlehem, however, lauds were attached to the end of nocturns; this was not true in Gaul (III, 6).

3) For in Gaul the morning office at sunrise comprised not Pss 50, 62, 89 as in Bethlehem (III, 4:2-6), but Pss 62, 118:147-148, and lauds: Pss 148-150 (III, 3-6).

4) Terce-sext-none comprised three psalms each in both usages (III, 2-3).

5) The eleventh hour or vespers, as in Bethlehem, had an Egyptian-type continuous psalmody with readings, preceded, perhaps, by cathedral elements such as Ps 140 and a lucernarium (III, 3:8-11).[18]

6) A vigil was held Friday night, as in Bethlehem (III, 8:1-2).

The only real problems of interpretation here concern the structure of the morning office. We saw in chapter 5 that the Palestinian monks

---

[17]On early Western monasticism see J. Lienhard, *Paulinus of Nola and Early Western Monasticism* (Theophaneia 28, Cologne: P. Hanstein, 1977).

[18]This point was discussed in the previous chapter.

had introduced a "new service" to make the monks get up before terce. This office, celebrated at sunrise, comprised Pss 50, 62, 89 (*Inst.* III, 3:11; 4:2–6). It did not contain lauds (Pss 148–150), which in Bethlehem, Cassian tells us, were appended to the end of the previous hour of nocturns. In Gaul, however, lauds were part of the morning office, not an appendix to nocturns. That, at least, is how I would interpret *Institutes* III. But since the problems of this difficult text are more than hermeneutical, let us look at the original:[19]

> III,3 . . . De matutina uero sollemnitate etiam illud nos instruit, quod in ipsa cotidie decantari solet: *Deus, Deus meus, ad te de luce uigilo,* et: *In matutinis meditabor in te,* et: *Praeueni in maturitate, et clamaui,* et rursum: *Praeuenerunt oculi mei ad diluculum: ut meditarer eloquia tua.* . . .
>
> 4Sciendum tamen hanc matutinam, quae nunc obseruatur in occiduis uel maxime regionibus, canonicam functionem nostro tempore in nostroque monasterio primitus institutam. . . . Usque ad illud enim tempus matutina hac sollemnitate, quae expletis nocturnis psalmis et orationibus post modicum temporis interuallum solet in Galliae monasteriis celebrari, cum cotidianis uigiliis pariter consummata reliquas horas refectioni corporum deputatas a maioribus nostris inuenimus.

Here is what Cassian appears to be saying:

> III,3 . . . Concerning the morning office, that which it is customary to sing at it daily also teaches us: "O God my God, to you do I keep watch at break of day" (Ps 62:2), and "I will meditate on you in the morning" (Ps 62:7); and "I anticipated the dawning of the day and cried out" (Ps 118:147), and "My eyes have anticipated the break of day, that I might meditate on your words" (Ps 118:148). . . .
>
> 4One should know, however, that this matins, which is now observed especially in western regions, was first instituted as a canonical office in our time and in our monastery. . . . For up until that time we find that when this morning office (which in the monasteries of Gaul is customarily celebrated after a short interval after the psalms and prayers of nocturns have been finished) was ended [in Bethlehem] together with the daily vigils, the remaining hours were assigned by our elders to bodily rest.

Cassian goes on to observe (III, 5) that this second period of rest was abused by the monks, who slept from after nocturns right through until terce. So the new morning office at sunrise was instituted to make them

---

[19]Texts are cited from the ed. of Guy, 102, 108. The interpretation I give here was also published in my "*Quaestiones disputatae,*" 139–142.

get up earlier. This new office, like terce and sext, had three psalms with prayers. As to which three, Cassian returns to this question in III, 6, a passage that has become the *crux interpretum*:

III,6Illud quoque nosse debemus nihil a nostris senioribus, qui hanc eandem matutinam sollemnitatem addi debere censuerunt, de antiqua psalmorum consuetudine inmutatum, sed eodem ordine missam quo prius in nocturnis conuentibus perpetuo celebratam. Etenim hymnos, quos in hac regione ad matutinam excepere sollemnitatem, in fine nocturnarum uigiliarum, quas post gallorum cantum ante auroram finire solent, similiter hodieque decantant, id est centesimum quadragensimum octauum psalmum, cuius initium est *Laudate Dominum de caelis* et reliquos qui sequuntur. Quinquagensimum uero psalmum et sexagensimum secundum et octogensimum nonum huic nouellae sollemnitati fuisse deputatos. Denique per Italiam hodieque consummatis matutinis hymnis quinquagensimus psalmus in uniuersis ecclesiis canitur, quod non aliunde quam exinde tractum esse non dubito.

III,6This too we ought to know, that no change was made in the ancient usage of the psalms by our elders [in Bethlehem] who decided that this morning office should be added: the dismissal was always celebrated in their nocturnal assemblies in the same order as before. For they still sing in the same way today, at the end of the nocturnal vigils (which they [in Bethlehem] are accustomed to finish after cockcrow, before dawn), the hymns which in this region [Provence] they reserve for the morning office, that is, Ps 148, beginning "Praise the Lord from the heavens," and the rest that follow. But the 50th psalm and the 62nd and the 89th have been assigned to this new service. Finally, throughout Italy today when the morning hymns have ended, Ps 50 is sung in all the churches, which I have no doubt is derived only from this source.

The *crux interpretum* here is the following passage from *Inst.* III, 6, just cited: "Etenim hymnos, quos in hac regione ad matutinam excepere sollemnitatem, in fine nocturnarum vigiliarum, quos post gallorum cantum ante auroram finire solent, similiter hodie decantant, id est centesimum quadragensimum octauum psalmum . . . et reliquos qui sequuntur. . . ." As Froger has indicated,[20] this could also be translated: "For they still sing in the same way today the hymns which in this region [Provence] they reserve for the morning office at the end of the nocturnal vigils. . . ." But this version would make the practice of Gaul no different from that of Bethlehem, and render unintelligible the con-

[20]J. Froger, "Note pour réctifier l'interpretation de Cassien, *Inst.* III, 4–6 proposé dans *Les Origines du Prime,*" ALW 2 (1952) 97–99.

*trast* Cassian is drawing between these two *divergent* uses of the morning office. So what Cassian seems to be saying is:

1) In Bethlehem, nocturns ends with Pss 148–150. Then after a short rest the monks rise again at sunrise for a brief morning office, recently instituted, comprising Pss 50, 62, 89.

2) In Gaul, however, Pss 148–150 were not the conclusion of nocturns, but part of a separate morning office that followed nocturns after a brief interval.

3) The same system as the latter was in force also in Italy where, in addition, the psalms of lauds were *followed* (not preceded) by Ps 50/51. I shall save this point for the following chapter.

So the first two hours of the Provençal cursus looked as follows:

| | |
|---|---|
| at cockcrow: | *vigil* |
| | variable psalmody |
| at daybreak: | *morning office* |
| | Ps 62 |
| | Ps 118:147–148 |
| | lauds: Pss 148–150 |

In Egypt the monastic psalmody was followed by readings, but Cassian makes a point of telling us (*Inst.* II, 6) that the Egyptians added lessons "simply as extras and of their own appointment, only for those who liked, . . ." and never mentions them in the context of the Bethlehem or Provençal offices.

## The Office of Lerins/Arles[21]

Our next important Gallic evidence shows the later transformation of Cassian's system in the rules of Saints Caesarius and Aurelian of Arles.

[21]Caesarius, *Rule for Virgins* (=CV), ed. G. Morin, *Sancti Caesarii Arelatensis opera omnia* (Maredsous, 1942) II, 101–124; *id., Rule for Monks* (=CM), *ibid.* 149–155; trans. of CV in M. C. McCarthy, *The Rule for Nuns of St. Caesarius of Arles: A Translation with a Critical Introduction* (The Catholic University of America Studies in Medieval History, New series, 16, Washington D.C.: The Catholic University of America Press, 1960); Aurelian, *Rule for Monks* (=AM), PL 68, 387–396; *id., Rule for Virgins* (=AV) PL 68, 399–406; French versions of both authors in *Règles monastics d'occident, IV<sup>e</sup>-VI<sup>e</sup> siècle, d'augustin à Ferrèol*, introductions et notes par V. Desprez, préface par A. de Vogüé (Vie monastique 9,

For Aurelian's rule is based on Caesarius', who states, in turn, that his cursus "follows for the most part the Rule of the Monastery of Lerins" (CV 66:2) founded by Cassian's disciple Honoratus (d. 429-430). These two offices maintain Cassian's basic structure of psalms and lessons in that order, but the number of psalms and types of psalmody are increased, new elements—hymns and *capitella*—are added, and the cursus is expanded to include other hours and more frequent and more fully developed vigils.

St. Caesarius of Arles was the most prominent Gallic bishop of his times. [22] Born in Châlon-sur-Saône around 470, he entered the Monastery of Lerins around 490. Later he served as a priest in Arles, was named superior of the monastery there, and then metropolitan of the city from 503-542. As bishop he founded the Monastery of St. John for nuns, and it was for them that his *Rule for Nuns* was composed. Adapted and completed over the years, its final redaction, including the *Recapitulationes* (chapters 48-65) containing most of the liturgical information that interests us here, dates from 534. His *Rule for Monks*, composed betweeen 534-542, probably for the monks he addresses in *Sermons 233-238*, is dependent on the *Rule for Nuns*, as de Vogüé has shown. [23]

St. Aurelian, second successor to Caesarius as bishop of Arles (546-551), also wrote two rules for the monasteries he founded there, one for the monks of Holy Apostles and Martyrs Monastery founded in 547, the other for the later foundation of nuns at St. Mary Monastery. [24] Aurelian's *Rule for Monks* depends on the rules and other writings of Caesarius, as well as drawing on sources such as Cassian, Augustine, Basil, the so-called *Second Rule of the Fathers* (or *of Macarius*), the Gallic synods, and even one papal letter. [25]

Aurelian's description of the office is more detailed than that of Caesarius, but the significant differences between the two can be reduced to the fact that Aurelian has daily prime, and twelve psalms at the little hours for the monks. His *Rule for Virgins* is an abridgement of the *Rule*

---

Bégrolles-en-Mauges: Abbaye de Bellefontaine, 1980) 157-255. For background, in addition to the excellent short introductions in *ibid.* 158-168, 224-227, see F. Prinz, *Frühes Mönchtum im Frankenreich* (Munich-Vienna: R. Oldenbourg, 1965), Teil I: *Das altgallenische Mönchtum (bis 590).*

[22]*Règles monastiques d'occident* 158-161.

[23]A. de Vogüé, "La Règle de S. Césaire d'Arles pour les moines: un résumé de sa Règle pour les moniales," *Revue d'ascetique et de mystique* 47 (1971) 369-406.

[24]*Règles monastiques d'occident* 224-227.

[25]*Ibid.* 225; A. Schmidt, "Zur Komposition der Mönchsregel des Hl. Aurelian von Arles," *Studia monastica* 17 (1975) 237-256; 18 (1976) 17-54.

*for Monks*, with the same office except that the psalmody is halved and the nuns recited the main hours in the Basilica of St. Mary, open to the public so the laity could attend, whereas the office of Aurelian's monks was inaccessible to the public.[26]

The substance of Caesarius' legislation is found in his *Recapitulationes*, and CV 68–70, though scattered references are found also in CV 10, 15, 18–19, 21–22, and in CM 20–21, 25. Aurelian details the office in the lengthy chapters AM 56–57; there is information also in AM 28–29, 31, 59.

## I. STRUCTURAL ELEMENTS OF THE OFFICE IN GAUL

Before attacking the problem of the structure of the individual hours, let us try to untangle the three types of psalmody and other constitutive elements as presented in these Gallic rules.[27]

### 1. The monastic psalmody:

When Caesarius and Aurelian refer to "psalms" *tout court* they always mean current monastic psalmody, found in the office in varying multiples of three psalms (6, 12, 18) depending on the hour, liturgical season, or rule in question. In each unit of three psalms the third was an alleluia psalm, unlike Egypt where only the final psalm of twelve was. This monastic psalmody is never found in the cathedral hours of matins and lucernarium as described in these rules. Aurelian tells us these monastic psalms were read, in turn, by soloists, each monk doing three psalms (AM 56:2, 10). As Heiming notes,[28] it is surprising that neither rule mentions the customary silent prayer after each psalm or unit of psalmody. For in *Sermon 76*, 1, Caesarius clearly refers to prayer after psalms,[29] and canon 30 of the Council of Agde held under Caesarius in 506 recommends prayer and a collect after the antiphons of the cathedral offices.[30] However, *Sermon 76*, apparently, and the canon for sure, refer to the cathedral office.

### 2. The directaneus (breuis/parvulus):

Every matins and lucernarium opens with an invitatory psalm designated *directaneus breuis* or *parvulus* (CV 66:7, 69:12–16; AM 56:7), or simply *directaneus* (CM 21:7; AM 56:12, 51), which I take to mean the

---

[26]*Règles monastiques d'occident* 277.
[27]Heiming, "Zum monastischen Offizium" 115ff.
[28]*Ibid.* 124.
[29]The sermons are edited in CCL 103–104.
[30]Mansi 8, 329–330.

same thing. This was a psalm done straight through, without refrain, responsory, or alternation, as in RM 55:7 and RB 12:1, 17:6.

### 3. Antiphons:

It is obvious from the text that *antiphonae* refers to the whole unit of psalm plus refrain or, sometimes, alleluia. The antiphons of nocturns are called "minor" (CV 66:12; AM 56:21), which probably means that only a part of the psalm was sung. In general one finds in the hours a ratio of one antiphonal psalm per six *"psalmi"*—i.e., psalms of the current monastic psalmody. Just how the antiphonal psalms were executed we are not told.

### 4. Responsorial psalms:

Responsorial psalmody is also mentioned, though again, with no information as to its mode of execution.

### 5. Lessons:

There are no readings in the two cathedral hours of matins and lucernarium, but the ordinary monastic hours have from one to three lessons, all biblical. In addition, vigils have units of readings and psalmody, referred to as *missae*. A *missa* comprised three *orationes*—three lessons, each followed by an oration—then three psalms, as will be seen below when we come to vigils.

### 6. Hymns:

New to monastic tradition in the West are the hymns that we find for the first time in the rules of Arles. The little hours had one fixed hymn for the entire year. The other major hours had two proper hymns for use on alternating days, except for festive and Sunday matins, and during Easter week:[31]

Matins:

| | |
|---|---|
| daily (Mon.–Fri.): | 1) *Splendor paternae gloriae* |
| | 2) *Aeternae lucis conditor* (AM 56:38) |
| festive: | *Te deum* and |
| | *Gloria in excelsis* (CV 69:11–12; CM 21:10–11; AM 56:17, 57:7) |
| Easter week: | *Hic est dies verus dei* (CV 66:7; AM 56:8) |

[31]For a complete index of Latin hymns see U. Chevalier, *Repertorium hymnologicum. Catalogue des chants, hymnes, proses, séquences, tropes an usage dans l'Eglise latine des origines jusqu'à nos jours*, 2 vols. (Louvain: Lefever, 1892).

Prime:   *Fulgentis auctor aetheris* (CV 69:13; AM 56:40)
Terce:   *Iam surgit hora tertia* (CV 66:4; AM 56:3, 47)
Sext:    *Iam sexta sensim volvitur* (CV 66:5; AM 56:5, 49)
None:    *Ter hora trina volvitur* (CV 66:6; AM 56:6, 49)
Lucernarium:

| | |
|---|---|
| daily: | 1) *Deus qui certis legibus* |
| | 2) *Deus creator omnium* (CV 69:16; AM 56:51–53) |
| Easter week: | *Hic est dies verus dei* (CV 66:7; AM 56:8) |
| Duodecima: | 1) *Christe, precamur, annue* |
| | 2) *Christe qui lux es et dies* (CV 66:8–9) |

Nocturns:

| | |
|---|---|
| 1st nocturn: | 1) *Rex aeternae domine* (AM 56:29; CV 69:2–3) |
| | 2) *Mediae noctis tempus est* (only in CV 69:2–3) |
| 2nd nocturn: | *Magna et mirabilia* (CV 69:3; AM 56:29) |

### 7. Kyrie eleison:

Aurelian puts a triple *Kyrie eleison* at every office (*in omni opere dei*) at the beginning, after the monastic psalmody, and after the concluding *capitellum* (AM 56:4). Though not mentioned by Caesarius in his rules, canon 3 of the Second Council of Vaison held under his leadership in 529 orders the *Kyrie eleison* introduced into cathedral matins and vespers, and at Mass.[32] Since the two cathedral hours in the rule of Arles, matins and vespers, already conclude with the *Kyrie* twelve times, and have no monastic psalms, Aurelian added three sets of triple *Kyrie* to the monastic hours only.

### 8. Capitellum:[33]

Each office concludes with the *capitellum*—or at least I have so presumed, for though Caesarius occasionally neglects to mention it, it appears to be a set concluding piece in his system. Aurelian gives the plural form, *capitella consuetudinaria*, once, at the end of compline (AM 56:55). What was this liturgical piece, found where we would normally expect some sort of concluding intercessions or litany or prayer? Canon 30 of

---

[32]Mansi 8, 727.
[33]See Heiming, "Zum monastischen Offizium," 121.

the Council of Agde presided over by Caesarius in 506 exhorts that "at the conclusion of matins or vesper services (*missae*), after the hymns, verses (*capitella*) from the psalms be said."[34] And, indeed, Aurelian indicates "*Fiat domine*," the final verse (22) of Ps 32, as the *capitellum* of terce: "May your mercy, O Lord, be upon us, for we have placed our hope in you" (AM 56:47). So the *capitellum* or *capitella* comprised one or more intercessory petitions drawn from the psalms, a sort of psalmic litany to conclude the hour.

## II. The Cursus

The daily cursus of Arles as described by Caesarius comprised:

    Nocturns
    [Vigils]
    Matins
    [*Sat., Sun., feasts:* Prime]
    Terce
    Sext
    None
    Lucernarium
    Duodecima
    [Vigils]

Vigils of readings filled in the interstices before and after nocturns, depending on the feast or season. To this cursus Aurelian adds daily prime and a brief compline (AM 56:55), already adumbrated in the bedtime psalmody of the *Ordo monasterii* and in Cassian (*Inst.* IV, 19:2), and seen earlier in Cappadocia in the writings of Basil.[35] As should be immediately apparent from a glance at this cursus, matins and lucernarium are cathedral additions to an already complete monastic horarium, with nocturns and *duodecima* the exact parallel to the two synaxes that opened and closed the monastic day in Cassian.

## III. The Structure of the Hours

If we prescind for the moment from Aurelian's compline, the basic liturgical unit is the same in all these hours:

    Monastic psalmody
    Antiphonal psalmody (except at prime and 2nd
      nocturns)

---

[34]Mansi 8, 329–330.
[35]See above, 79, 86–87.

> (Hymn at prime, sext, none)
> Lesson(s)
> Hymn (except at prime, sext, none)
> Capitellum

With the exception of prime and second nocturns, which have no antiphons, and the little hours except festive terce, which inexplicably put the hymn before the readings, all that varies is the quantity of each element, depending on the hour or author in question.

In addition, at the more important hours of nocturns and *duodecima*, the psalmody opens with a fixed invitatory psalm, executed *in directum*. And of course Aurelian adds the triple *Kyrie eleison* at the beginning and end of each office, and after the monastic psalmody (AM 56:4). This gives us the following structures.

**1. Little hours (except festive terce)** (CV 66:5–6, 68:3, 69:13–15;
AM 56:47–50; AV 41–42):

> Kyrie eleison 3x
> 6 psalms (Aurelian: 6 for nuns, 12 for monks)
> Kyrie eleison 3x
> 1 antiphonal psalm
> Hymn
> Reading(s)
> Capitellum
> Kyrie eleison 3x

Prime has two readings, one from the Old Testament and one from the New, and no antiphonal psalm is mentioned (CV 69:13–15; AM 28, 56:40). Historically this is the earliest clear reference to prime, and Aurelian (AM 28) gives the same motivation for its introduction as Cassian did for his *novella sollemnitas*: to keep the monks from retiring again after matins. The fact that in Caesarius prime is celebrated only on Saturdays, Sundays, and feasts, and that neither author mentions it in Easter Week (CV 66:3; AM 56:2)—reflecting Baumstark's law of the greater conservatism of high liturgical seasons—all point to its very recent origin.

**2. Festive terce:**

Why terce should be singled out for special treatment on Saturdays (CV 68:4; AM 57:8) and during Easter week (CV 66:3–4; AM 56:2–4) is not stated, but I presume it must be because of the monks' communion. As we shall see below, festive terce had the same function as the *typika* (Slavonic *izobrazitel'nye*, *obednitsy*) in the Byzantine monastic tradition: it was originally a presanctified monastic communion rite on days when no Mass was celebrated.[36] In Caesarius (CV 68:4), Saturday-Sunday terce has prefixed to it six psalms and three readings: from the prophets, apostle, and gospel. Aurelian (AM 57:8) mentions only the readings. At Easter, terce has its usual structure, but with twelve psalms, six antiphons, three readings: Acts, apostle, gospel (CV 66:3-4; AM 56:2-4). And since monasteries generally had no priest, and the monks and nuns did not leave the enclosure for Mass even on Sundays and holydays—one more proof that we must never absolutize our present view of how things "must" have been—Aurelian tells us that on Sundays and feasts terce is followed by the Our Father, and then all communicate *"psallendo,"* for Mass is celebrated only when the abbot sees fit (AM 57:11-12).[37]

### 3. Duodecima (CV 66:8-11; 68:5 AM 56:9-10, 54):

The twelfth hour preserves the same structure as these day hours and, in Caesarius, probably the same number of psalms, for he explicitly increases the number only for feasts (CV 66:16; 68:5), which have at *duodecima* twelve psalms and three antiphonal psalms, whereas in Aurelian (AM 56:54) daily *duodecima* has eighteen psalms and one antiphon. In both authors, Easter *duodecima* has eighteen psalms, three antiphonal psalms, and two lessons: from the apostle, and a resurrection gospel. Further, the office opens with an invitatory, the *directaneus breuis* Ps 103:19b[-24a]—both authors give the incipit; the end is my guess. Caesarius tells us in *Sermon 136,* 1, that Ps 103 "is said at the twelfth hour in both churches and monasteries throughout the world."

### 4. Compline:

Compline, found only in Aurelian (AM 56:55), comprises Ps 90 *in directum,* and the *capitella consuetudinaria*[38]—i.e., in the plural, possibly signifying more than one petitionary verse.

### 5. Nocturns (CV 66:12-14; 69:1, 3; AM 56:9-11, 20-21, 26-29):

Daily nocturns has the exact same structure as Easter *duodecima:*

> Kyrie eleison 3x
> Invitatory (Ps 50)

---

[36]See Mateos, "Un horologion inédit," 64-68.

[37]On the Eucharist in monastic usage see Taft, "The Frequency of the Eucharist," 17-18; *id., Beyond East and West* (Washington D.C.: Pastoral Press, 1984) 68-70.

[38]At least this is how I understand "Quando repausaturi estis, in schola in qua manetis completa dicatur: imprimis directaneus, psalmus nonagesimus dicatur, deinde capitella consuetudinaria" (PL 68, 395). But since "imprimis directaneus (parvulus)" is Aurelian's set phrase for an invitatory, after which he mentions the psalm(s) (*ibid.* 393-395), the text could be repunctuated to mean an invitatory *in directum,* plus Ps 90 and the *capitella.*

> 18 psalms
> Kyrie eleison 3x
> 3 antiphonal psalms with alleluia
> 2 readings
> Hymn
> Capitellum
> Kyrie eleison 3x

The antiphons were "little antiphons" with alleluia (CV 66:12; AM 56:21); the two lessons in Easter week were from the apostle and gospel (AM 56:10); otherwise from the apostle or prophets (AM 56:12).

In winter, from October 1 until Easter when the nights were longer, a second nocturn was added (CV 69:1, 3; AM 56:26–29), comprising:

> Invitatory (Ps 56)
> 18 psalms
> 2 readings (prophets or Wisdom)
> Hymn

The *capitellum* is not mentioned, so I presume the second nocturn was simply inserted between the hymn and *capitellum* of the first nocturn, leaving one *capitellum* to conclude the entire service.

6. **Vigils** (CV 10; 19; 66:16; 68:1–2; 69:5–9, 11, 17–27; CM 20–21; AM 29; 31; 56:24–25, 30–34, 56:1–6):

Monastic vigils in Arles were not so much an office as the occasional insertion between the usual night offices of units of readings referred to as *missae*. A *missa* comprised three *orationes* followed by antiphonal and responsorial psalmody, one *oratio* being a lesson followed by an oration, executed as follows:

> *seated*      oratio 1: reading, prayer
>              oratio 2: reading, prayer
>              oratio 3: reading, prayer
> *standing*   psalm 1: antiphonal
>              psalm 2: responsorial
>              psalm 3: antiphonal

The psalms followed the order of the psalter. Except on Sundays and at least some feasts, the readings were a *lectio continua* from both Old and New Testaments, each lesson a short selection of two to three pages maximum (CV 69:23–24; CM 20:2; AM 56:30–31). On Sundays, at the first *missa* of the vigil, the resurrection accounts were read in a four-Sunday cycle, according to the order of the four Gospels (CV 69:17–19; CM 21:4–6). During this resurrection gospel all remained standing, whereas normally the three *orationes* lessons were heard seated. On the vigils of martyrs' feasts the lessons of the first *missa* were from the passion of the martyrs (CV 69:20; AM 56:30–31). At Christmas and Epiphany the lessons were from the Gospels and Isaiah (Christmas) or Daniel (Epiphany) (CV 68:1–2; AM 57:1–3).

From Easter to October, vigils were held only before Saturdays, Sundays, and feasts (CV 66:14, 68:1–2, 69:11, 17–21; AM 56:23–25; 57:6), but during the winter there were *missae* every night (CV 69:1–7, 22; CM 20; AM 56:30–34).

On days when there were vigils the night office looked as follows:

> *In summer* (CV 66:16; AM 56:24; 57:6):
> Duodecima
> 6 missae
> 18 psalms
> 3 antiphonal psalms (only in CV 66:16)
> Nocturns
> 3 missae (2 on Sat. in AM 56:24) until dawn, then
>    immediately,
> Matins
>
> *In winter* (CV 69:5–9, 2; CM 20; AM 56:24–25,
>    57:6):
> Duodecima
> 1st nocturn
> 2nd nocturn
> 3, 4, or 5 missae (6 on Sunday)
> Matins

Furthermore, when a monk or nun died the body was waked with *missae* throughout the night. The religious shared this vigil in two shifts, before and aftermidnight (CV 70; AM 58:1–2; AV 38:5). As we saw in chapter 4, such wakes were also a custom in Pachomian monasticism.

The main difference between Caesarius and Aurelian is in the arrangement of the vigils of Christmas and Epiphany, from the third hour of the night until dawn.[39] Caesarius places six *missae* both before and after nocturns (CV 68:1–2); Aurelian puts the first six between first and second nocturns (AM 57:1–3).

---

[39]In Antiquity day and night were divided equally into twelve periods variable from season to season depending on the relative length of daylight and darkness. Thus monastic vespers or *hora duodecima*—the twelfth hour—was the last daylight hour. The third hour of the night would be 9:00 P.M. When day and night were equal and *duodecima* was 6:00 P.M.

All this adds up to a staggering night *pensum*. One can understand why our authors advised the monks to stand up if they felt drowsy at vigils (CV 15; AM 29)! Otherwise they remained seated, as in Egypt, doing their handiwork while meditating on the sacred text being read (CV 15; AM 29)—work which, unlike in Egypt, was forbidden at other times of the psalmody (CV 10; AM 31). Nor did matins end the ordeal, for, Aurelian notes, the monks did not retire after matins but said prime immediately, then continued their *lectio divina* until terce (AM 28).

Lessons, not continuous psalmody, form the core of these Gallic monastic vigils. We shall return to this point later. Suffice it to note here the overriding importance of Scripture lessons in the office of Arles. But the spirit of this prayer was no different from that of monastic prayer elsewhere: *pray always*. When praying the psalms and hymns with their lips, they meditated in their hearts what their voices were saying, and at work, when there was no reading, they ruminated on the passages of Sacred Scripture they knew by heart (CV 18, 22). In *Sermon 76*, (cited below in chapter 8), Caesarius makes clear that the psalmody in no way exhausts the obligation to pray but is rather a stimulus to prayer, the point of the lance but not the whole spear.

## iv. Cathedral Hours In The Monastic Office Of Arles

As I have said, the horarium described above already represents a full monastic cursus, with nocturns and *duodecima* the traditional monastic offices at the beginning and end of the day. To this purely monastic cursus Caesarius adds—but as separate hours, not as appendices or integral parts of the monastic hours as in some offices—cathedral matins and vespers. Still later, Aurelian adds an embryonic compline, as we saw. The cathedral character of these matins and vespers is apparent not only from the content and structure of the offices, but also from the fact that on feasts they are celebrated in the public oratory for the people (CV 69:12, 16).

### 1. Lucernarium:

Cathedral vespers or lucernarium has the same structure in Caesarius (CV 66:7; 69:16) and Aurelian (AM 56:7–8, 51–53), if we presume the *capitellum* in Caesarius for the reasons already expressed:

> Short invitatory psalm *in directum*
> 3 antiphonal psalms
> Capitellum

Aurelian adds further precisions. During Easter week there were two short invitatories for alternating days: Ps 67:33[–36] and Ps 112:1[–3] (AM 56:7–8). Aurelian gives only the incipits of the invitatories; the verses in brackets represent what I presume the *directaneus parvulus* included (CV 66:7; 69:16; AM 56:7). This is obvious in the case of Ps 67, where verse 36 ends the psalm; and with the choice of verses for Ps 112 made by parallelism with Ps 67, and because Ps 112:1–3 is a self-contained sense unit with a reference to sunrise in verse 3:

> ¹Laudate, pueri, dominum,
>     laudate nomen domini.
> ²Sit nomen domini benedictum
>     ex hoc nunc et usque in saeculum.
> ³A solis ortu usque ad occasum
>     laudabile nomen domini.

The third antiphon was, as usual, an alleluia psalm (AM 56:52), but we have no other information on what psalms were used for these antiphons. Since they remain unspecified, they were undoubtedly variable and followed the order of the psalter, as in parallel instances in the offices of Arles.

Both authors mention the same three hymns, one for Easter week (*Hic est dies verus dei:* CV 66:7; AM 56:8), two others to use on alternating days the rest of the year (*Deus qui certis legibus; Deus creator omnium:* CV 69:16; AM 56:53). Caesarius tells us that festive vespers is celebrated in the public oratory on Sundays and feasts so the people can attend (CV 69:16).

Note that what we find in this Provençal horarium is exactly the opposite of what we saw in the East where in hybrid offices the monastic psalmody *precedes* the cathedral lucernarium. In Arles the monastic evening psalmody, *duodecima,* follows the cathedral remnant.

### 2. Festive matins (Saturdays, Sundays, and feasts):

Matins, also purely cathedral, is characterized by fixed psalms executed antiphonally: with antiphons daily; with alleluia on Saturdays, Sundays, and feasts. Both authors provide fuller details for festive matins (CV 66:7; 69:8–12; CM 21:7–11; AM 56:12–19; 57:4–7), so I shall begin there. Elements witnessed to only by Aurelian are in parentheses; those in brackets are my hypothetical reconstruction:

> Invitatory *directaneus breuis:* Ps 144[:1–2]
> Ps 117 with antiphon (alleluia: AM 56:14)
> (Pss 42, 62, with alleluia)

Ex 15 with alleluia
Pss 145(–147) with alleluia
Dan 3:57–88 with alleluia
Pss 148(–150) with alleluia
(Sundays, major feasts, Easter week: *Magnificat*
with antiphons or alleluia)
*Te deum*
Sundays, major feasts, Easter week: *Gloria in
excelsis*
Easter week: hymn *Hic est dies verus dei*
Capitellum

Although only Aurelian (AM 56:15) explicitly mentions all the matins psalms (145–147, 148–150), I interpret Caesarius' reference to Pss 145 and 148 as simply the head of the two series, since he speaks of "all the matins [psalms] with alleluia" (CV 69:10). Furthermore, it seems that the proper hymn for Easter week did not replace the *Gloria in excelsis* on Easter Sunday, but was added to it (CV 66:7; 69:12; CM 21:10–11; AM 56:8, esp. 17–19), though here too there is room for doubt.

**3: Daily matins** (Monday–Friday):

For daily matins Caesarius stipulates "the canonical morning psalms with antiphons" (CV 69:8). Aurelian, as usual, is more specific, if none too clear (AM 56:34–38; 57:7). Here is the text of AM 56:34–38; the brackets contain my additions:

[1]    . . . dicite matutinos [psalmos] canonicos:
[2]    id est primo canticum in antiphona,
[3]    deinde directaneum
        *Judica me deus* [Ps 42];
        *Deus, deus meus, ad te luce vigilo* [Ps 62];
        *Lauda anima mea dominum* [Ps 145];
        *Laudate dominum quoniam bonus est psalmus*
            [Ps 146];
        *Lauda Hierusalem dominum* [Ps 147];
[4]    deinde: *Laudate dominum de coelis* [Ps 148],
                *Cantate domino canticum
                    novum* [Ps 149],
                *Laudate dominum in sanctis
                    ejus* [Ps 150],
    cum antiphona.

[5]    Dicite hymnum . . .
[6]    et capitellum,
[7]    et *Kyrie eleison* duodecim vicibus.
[8]    Omnibus diebus quotidianis sic impleatur.

The "antiphonal canticle" [2] said *primo*, must have been Ps 117, again by comparison with the festive structure. Caesarius does not include it among the "matins psalms" (CV 69:10), and it always follows the invitatory immediately. The interpretation of the rest of this text will depend on how one punctuates it. One could argue that only Ps 42 was executed *in directum.* But we know from CM 21:2 that Ps 144, not Ps 42, was the invitatory for weekdays as well as feasts, so there is no reason to restrict the *directaneus* mode to Ps 42. Furthermore, *deinde* [4] seems a clear divider between the group of psalms *in directum* and lauds, done antiphonally, just as the earlier *deinde* [3] separates the antiphonal canticle [2] from the following series of *directaneus* psalms. So I would interpret the rubric *"in directum"* as applying to Pss 42, 62, 145–147. This, however, disagrees with the practice in Caesarius, who states clearly that the psalms in daily matins are done antiphonally: "Then let them say the canonical morning psalms, on ordinary days with antiphons, on feasts with alleluia" (CV 69:8; cf. CM 21:2).

Hence I would reconstruct ordinary weekday matins as follows:

Invitatory *directaneus breuis:* Ps 144:1–2
Ps 117 with antiphon
Caesarius: Pss 145–147 with antiphons
(Aurelian: Pss 42, 62, 145–147 *in directum*)
Pss 148–150 with antiphons
Hymn
Capitellum
Kyrie eleison 12x

In conclusion, note the influence of the developing calendar on the office. The cathedral hours, still firmly rooted in the daily cycle, take on festive coloration only in Easter week, with a proper hymn. The monastic night watch makes some concessions to a weekly cycle in the resurrection gospel of Sunday, and in the incipient sanctoral with readings from the passion of the martyrs on their feast days.

## The Irish Monastic Cursus in St. Columban

In chapter 7 of his *Regula monachorum* St. Columban (ca. 543–615) gives a brief description *"De cursu,"* i.e., of an Irish monastic cursus of his time.[40] Its main characteristic, common also to later Irish offices, is a backbreaking *pensum* of night psalmody, especially in the longer winter nights, though the saint sniffs that "some Catholics *(quidam catholici)"* have a *pensum* of only twelve psalms in their night offices.

Columban divides the office into six hours, three of the day and three at night. The three day hours have the traditional psalms each, seen almost everywhere in the little hours. But the night hours of the beginning *(initium noctis)* and middle *(medium noctis)* of the night had twelve psalms each, and matins *(matutinum)* bore the staggering load of thirty-six psalms on weekdays (twenty-four in summer), increasing to seventy-five on Saturdays and Sundays in winter (thirty-six in summer). This adds up to ninety-nine psalms during those weekend nights in winter, and to 108 in the complete Saturday-Sunday winter cursus if we add the nine psalms of the day hours.

The psalms of the night hours were grouped into units of three called *chora*, the first two psalms of each unit being without antiphon, the third with, though how the non-antiphonal psalms were executed is not stated, nor is anything said about the day-hour psalmody.[41]

Columban's other rule, the *Regula coenobialis* chapter 9, adds the precision that after each psalm the monks knelt and prayed, or, at Eastertide, bowed and said privately three times, "O God, come to my assistance, O Lord make haste to help me" (Ps 69:2).[42]

The *Rule of Benedict 18*, says:

> . . . monks who in a week's time sing less than the full psalter with the customary canticles betray extreme indolence and lack of devotion in their service. We read, after all, that our holy Fathers, energetic as they were, did all this in a single day. Let us hope that we, lukewarm as we are, can achieve it in a whole week.[43]

Columban's winter cycle comes closer to this presumed ancient ideal than any early source I know of. Later Irish *horaria* such as the ninth-century monastic rules of the Céli Dé and of the monastery of Tallaght have the whole psalter in three units of fifty psalms every day, and most Irish

[40]G. S. M. Walker, *Sancti Columbani opera* (Scriptores latini Hiberniae vol. 11, Dublin: The Dublin Institute for Advanced Studies, 1957) 128–132; text also in Heiming, "Zum monastischen Offizium," 125–126.

[41]Heiming, "Zum monastischen Offizium," 128–130.

[42]Walker, *S. Columbani opera* 158.

[43]T. Fry (ed.), *RB 1980. The Rule of St. Benedict in Latin and English with Notes* (Collegeville: The Liturgical Press, 1981) 215.

psalters arrange the psalms in this way.[44] But I know of no early evidence to support Benedict's assertion that, apart from the occasional *agrypnia* or all-night vigil, it was usual to do the entire psalter *every single day*. At any rate this staggering *pensum* should make one appreciate all the more the moderation of later western monastic legislators like Benedict. As Gelineau once noted, throughout Church history most reformers have reduced, not increased, ritual and liturgical prayer.

## The Monastic Hours In Spain

### I. ISIDORE OF SEVILLE[45]

St. Isidore of Seville (ca. 560–633), a monk between 590 and 600, wrote his *Rule for Monks* while abbot of a monastery in Betica (Andalusia) in that period.[46] It is the most important document of early Spanish monasticism. Later, as bishop of Seville from 600 to 636, he wrote for his brother, Fulgentius, bishop of Ecija, a work *De origine officiorum* which we know as Book I of the *De ecclesiasticis officiis*.[47]

#### 1. The cursus:

Chapter 6 of the *Rule* is our oldest description of the monastic office in Spain. After exhorting the monks to hasten to the office at the signal

[44]Information from P. Jeffery, "Eastern and Western Elements in the Irish Monastic Prayer of the Hours," unpublished paper delivered at the International Conference of Medieval Studies, Kalamazoo, Mich., May, 1985. I am indebted to Prof. Jeffery for providing me a copy of his paper. For Tallaght, Jeffrey refers to E.J. Gwynn, "The Rule of Tallaght," *Hermathena* 44, 2nd supplemental volume (1927) 51-55. For the psalters see H.M. Bannister, "Irish Psalters," JTS 12 (1911) 280-284. On Céli Dé see P. O'Dwyer, *Céli Dé Spiritual Reform in Ireland, 750–900* (Dublin: Editions Tailliura, 1981) which was not available to me. See also M. Curran, *The Antiphonary of Bangor and the Early Irish Monastic Liturgy* (Dublin: Irish Academic Press, 1984) esp. Part III.

[45]For a full bibliography of sources on the history of the office in Spain, see J. Pinell, "El oficio hispáno-visigótico," HS 10 (1957) 385-399; *id., De liturgiis occidentalibus, cum speciali tractatione de liturgia hispanica* (Rome: Sant' Anselmo, 1967-pro manuscripto) 52-54. A basic study is W.S. Porter, "Early Spanish Monasticism," *Laudate* 10 (1932) 1-15, 66-79, 156-167; 11 (1933) 199-207; 12 (1934) 31-52. The section on the office has been published in Spanish: "Monasticismo español primitivo. El oficio monastico," HS 6 (1953) 1-34.

[46]Porter, "Early Spanish Monasticism," L 10 (1932) 66. The text of the *Rule* is in PL 83, 867-894.

[47]Porter, "Early Spanish Monasticism," L 11 (1933) 199. *De officiis eccl.* I is in PL 83, 737-778.

and not to leave until it is over, Isidore describes the déroulement as follows:

> [6:1]. . . while the monks are reciting [the psalms], after the completion of each psalm all together make adoration prostrate on the ground, then quickly rising up let them begin the psalms that follow, and in this way let them do every office.
>
> [2]When the spiritual sacraments of the psalms are celebrated, let the monk shun laughter or conversation; but let him meditate in his heart what he psalms with his mouth. At terce, sext, or none, let three psalms be said, one responsory (responsorium), two lessons from the Old or New Testament, then lauds, a hymn, and a prayer (oratio). But at vespers, first the lucernarium, then two psalms, one responsory, and lauds, the hymn, and prayer are to be said.

After vespers the brethren gather for a sort of recreation to reflect on and discuss some pious topic. Then comes compline, not described, and the monks retire in silence until vigils (6:3). The night and morning office are described as follows:

> [6:4]But in the daily office of vigils, first the three canonical psalms (psalmi canonici) are to be recited, then three missae of psalms, a fourth of canticles, the fifth of the office of matins. On Sundays, however, or martyrs' feasts, let another missa be added because of the feast. In vigils it is usual to recite (recitandi), whereas in matins it is the custom to chant and sing (psallendi canendique), so that in each way the minds of God's servants may be exercised in pleasing variety and more abundantly moved to praise God without boredom.
>
> [5]After vigils there is rest until matins. After matins there is work or reading . . .

### 2. The psalmody:

Jordi Pinell, internationally known expert on Iberian liturgy, has shown that the missa was a liturgical unit of three psalms or canticles, not a unit of readings as in the rules of Arles. After each missa there was a responsory, at least in later sources, and each psalm or canticle had its own collect.[48]

From Isidore's De ecclesiasticis officiis I, 13:1 as well as from later Iberian sources, we know that the laudes of which he speaks were not Pss 148–150 but an alleluia responsory comprising a few psalm verses—two to five in the later sources—with alleluia one or more times as response.[49]

---

[48]Pinell, "El oficio hispáno-visigótico," 404. On the manifold meanings of missa in Latin liturgical nomenclature, see C. Mohrmann, "Missa," Vigiliae christiana 12 (1958) 67–92; K. Gamber, Missa romensis (Studia patristica et liturgica 3, Regensburg, 1970) 170–186.

[49]Porter, "Early Spanish Monasticism," L 11 (1933) 201; 12 (1934) 32ff.

*De ecclesiasticis officiis* I, 7 and 9, describe the execution of the antiphons and responsories. The antiphons are chanted by two choirs alternately. For the responsories, formerly one but now two or three soloists do the verses of the psalm while the rest chant the response in choir. Though this document is describing the cathedral offices, it is undoubtedly applicable to the antiphons and responsories, both cathedral elements, in monastic usage too.

### 3. The little hours:

The day hours—note the absence of prime—are clear enough, and traditional:

> 3 psalms *currente psalterio,* with prostration for
>     prayer after each
> Responsorial psalm
> 2 Scripture lessons
> Lauds
> Hymn
> Prayer

### 4. Vespers:

Vespers is basically the same, with one less psalm, and the whole preceded by a lucernarium. Was Ps 140 part of the lucernarium? It does figure as part of *duodecima* in later Spanish Offices.[50] But we know next to nothing about early monastic vespers in Spain apart from what Isidore tells us. The later *Ordo officii* of a monastery of nuns at Bobadilla in Galicia, preserved in an eleventh century manuscript though the office itself is much older, is clearly dependent on Isidore: ". . . At lucernarium, however, three psalms, then the responsory and lauds and completurium."[51] Here "lucernarium" seems the *name* of the entire vesper service, whereas in Isidore's *Rule* 4:2 cited at the beginning of this chapter, it is just the opening part of vespers: "But at vespers, first the lucernarium, then two psalms, one responsory, and lauds, the hymn, and prayer are to be said." There is abundant evidence for a light service in later Iberian cathedral vespers , as we shall see, but whether the lucernarium referred to here in Isidore is a light ritual or just a double evening office, as with the lucernarium and *duodecima* of Arles, I cannot say.

---

[50]*Ibid.* 12 (1934) 47.

[51]*Ibid.* 11 (1933) 201; Pinell, "El oficio hispáno-visigótico," 401. Porter translates the text from the edition of D. de Bruyne, RevB 42 (1930) 341–342.

### 5. Vigils:

Vigils opened with three "canonical" psalms, i.e., fixed psalms, as in the terminology of Southern Gaul. Later documents of the Spanish Office show these psalms to have been Pss 3, 50, 56 with antiphons, on Sundays; Ps 3 only, on ferias.[52] Then came "missae" of psalms and canticles. Isidore does not identify the canticles of vigils, but they are innumerable in the later Mozarabic sources.[53]

### 6. Matins:

As for the psalms of the missa of matins, Porter presumes they are Pss 148-150,[54] which is not unreasonable in the light of what we know of the later Iberian system as reconstructed by Pinell:[55]

> Invitatory: Ps 3 with antiphon and collect
> One or more missae of 3 "antiphons" each. An
>     antiphon comprised:
>     2 variable psalms with antiphons and collects
>     "alleluiaticum" or "laudes" = 1 alleluia
>     psalm with collect
>     responsory with collect
> Ps 50 with antiphon and collect
> Canticle with antiphon and collect
> Benedictiones: canticle of Dan 3, usually
>     abbreviated (or on ferias a psalm), with
>     antiphon and collect
> Pss 148-150 with antiphons
> Sono (Hymn)
> Verse
> Supplicatio (petitions)
> Completuria (final prayer)
> Our Father
> Petitio (embolism of Our Father)
> Blessing

One sees a certain ambiguity between the nomenclature here—laudes, alleluiaticum, missa—and what we saw in Gaul, but Iberian experts agree

---

[52]Pinell, "El oficio hispáno-visigótico," 403–404; id., "Las 'missas', grupos de cantos y oraciones en el oficio de la antigua liturgia hispana," Archivos Leonenses (León) 8 (1954) 145-185.

[53]A.W.S. Porter, "Cantica mozarabici officii," EL 49 (1935) 126-145. See also J. Szövérffy, Iberian Hymnody. Survey and Problems (Classical Folia Editions, 1971).

[54]"Early Spanish Monasticism," L 11 (1933) 200.

[55]El oficio hispáno-visigótico," 402-404; id., "El 'matutinarium' en la liturgia hispana," HS 9 (1956) 3-4. See also Jungmann, Pastoral Liturgy (New York: Herder, 1962) 122-151.

on this outline, with more or fewer elements depending on the stage of evolution of this ultimately highly complex office. Apart from this variety in nomenclature the similarity of these Iberian offices with those of Gaul is evident at a glance. Their later extensive development can be followed in the literature already cited.

## II. FRUCTUOSUS OF BRAGA

St. Fructuosus of Braga (d. ca. 665), son of a rich landowner general in the army of the Visigoths and founder of several monasteries in Galicia, is the most important figure in Iberian monasticism in the Visigothic era.[56]

The monastic office in the two rules of Fructuosus, which were followed in the monasteries of Galicia and Northern Portugal until the second half of the eleventh century, is not easy to reconstruct.[57] In the *Common Monastic Rule* 10 (ca. 660) he lists, with the indicated scriptural warrant, the hours of prime (Matt 20:1), terce (Acts 2:15), sext and none (Matt 27:45-50), vespers (Ps 140:2), midnight (Matt 25:6), and cockcrow when Jesus rose from the dead. These are the "canonical hours" observed everywhere in East and West, and they are obligatory. But if need be, other "special hours"—*horae peculiares*—can be added: the second, fourth, fifth, seventh, eighth, tenth, and eleventh hours, somewhat akin to the later Byzantine monastic *mesoria*.

The earlier *Rule for Monks* was written for the Monastery of Compludo west of Astorga around 630-635. Chapters 2 and 6 mention prime, second, terce, sext, none, *duodecima*, and vespers. The "first hour of the night" has six prayers, ten psalms, praise *(laus)*, and benedictions. Then comes compline, also mentioned in chapters 3 and 17, at which the monks take leave of one another with a mutual confession and absolution. This service has three psalms "according to custom," *laus*, a blessing, and the creed. In chapter 3 the description continues. Rising before midnight the monks do twelve psalms *"per choros,"* as is customary. Then after a pause

[56]On the life of Fructuosus and his rules, see Valerius, *Vita S. Fructuosi*, PL 87, 459-470; Porter, "Early Spanish Monasticism," L 10 (1932) 156-167; *Iberian Fathers*, vol. 2: *Braulio of Saragossa, Fructuosus of Braga*, trans. C. W. Barlow (The Fathers of the Church, Washington DC: The Catholic University of America Press, 1969)—though this translation of Fructuosus is not always liturgically reliable.

[57]The two documents are: *Rule for monks*, PL 87 1099-1110; *Common Monastic Rule*, PL 87, 1111-1150. On the offices of Fructuosus, in addition to the works cited above in note 45, see J. Pinell, "San Fructuoso de Braga, y su influjo en la formación del oficio monacal hispánico," *Bracara Augusta* 22, fasc. 51-54 (63-66) (Braga, 1968); Porter, "Early Spanish Monasticism," L 11 (1963) 202-204. For the later history of the office of Braga, see P. R. Rocha, *L'office divin dans l'Église de Braga: originalité et dépendances d'une liturgie par-*

they do the midnight office, with four responsories for each unit of three psalms—hence twelve psalms in all, the equivalent of Isidore's three *missae*. In winter they have a lesson and a homily on it by the abbot or prior, though in summer when the nights are shorter this is done between vespers and compline. After the twelve psalms they go back to bed. At cockcrow they celebrate the "morning sacrifice" *(matutinum sacrificium)* corresponding to Isidore's fourth *missa*: three psalms, *laus*, and *benedictio*. Then they go to the place of meditation, do three more psalms (the fifth *missa*), and thus concluding the prayer, they meditate until sunrise.

Isidore in his *De officiis ecclesiasticis* I, 22, concerning vigils, seems to imply this same threefold night office in his reading of Luke 12:38 on the faithful servants who keep watch for the arrival of their master: "And if he comes at the second watch, and if at the third watch, and finds them waiting, blessed are those servants." Isidore paraphrases these times: "If he comes at the vesperal hour or at midnight or at cockcrow and finds them keeping vigil, blessed are those servants." Such a threefold vigil structure we have already seen in Ireland, as well as in Palestine and Cappadocia.[58]

In all the offices, each psalm ends with the *Gloria Patri*, at which the monks prostrate themselves for prayer, then rise again to pray with outstretched hands. On Saturdays and Sundays the number of *missae* is increased, and especially at the night offices on the eve of great feasts, a sixth *missa* is added, as in Isidore.

By comparison with what we know of other Iberian offices we can conclude that in compline and matins the "praise" *(laus)* is an alleluia responsory,[59] and the "benediction" is obviously the final blessing we see in most of the Hispanic sources.[60] The customary psalmody "by choirs" may refer to antiphonal psalmody, with two choirs alternating the refrains (antiphons), a custom referred to earlier by Isidore in his *De ecclesiasticis officiis* I, 7. For the responsories, a soloist (formerly), or in Isidore's time two or three soloists together, chanted the verses of the psalms, while the rest responded in choir.[61]

---

*ticulière au moyen âge* (Cultura medieval e moderna 15, Paris: Fundação Calouste Gulbenkian/Centro Cultural Português, 1980).

[58]See above, pp. 39–41, 79–80, 114.

[59]Isidore, *De eccl. officiis* I, 13:1: "Laudes, hoc est, *alleluia* canere, canticum est Hebraeorum, cujus expositio duorum verborum interpretatione consistit, hoc est, *laus Dei* . . ." (PL 83, 750).

[60]See *ibid.* I, 17, PL 83, 754.

[61]*Ibid.* I, PL 83, 744.

# 7

# THE MONASTIC HOURS IN ITALY

It is obviously impossible to study in detail every one of the innumerable monastic "rules" in circulation in the West before the Carolingian period, by which time the *Rule of Benedict* had imposed itself on almost the whole of Western monasticism. Cassian, in his day, had already found "that many in different countries, according to the fancy of their mind . . have made for themselves in this matter various norms and rules" (*Inst.* II, 2), and by the eighth century, Western monastic rules abounded. Benedict of Aniane (750–812) lists them in the *Codex regularum*[1] of his *Concordia regularum*,[2] perhaps the first attempt at putting some order into the multiplicity of Western monastic usages. Many of these rules are just a short collection of precepts, like those of Pachomius, or a series of counsels, like the two rules of Basil. But others are rules in the modern sense, a veritable rule of life encompassing the entire spiritual and material life of a monastic community.[3]

[1]PL 103, 423-700.

[2]PL 103, 717-1376.

[3]On Western monastic rules up to the 8th century, see A. de Vogüé, "The Cenobitic Rules of the West," *Cistercian Studies* 12 (1977) 175-183. Versions of the texts are found in the works cited in chapter 6, note 21, and in *Early Monastic Rules. The Rules of the Fathers and the Regula Orientalis* (Collegeville: The Liturgical Press, 1982); A. de Vogüé, *Les Règles des saints péres*, 1-2 (SC 297-298, Paris: Cerf, 1982). For RB and RM see the editions cited below in notes 4 and 31.

## The Rule of the Master[4]

The longest and surely the most important of pre-Benedictine Latin rules is the *Rule of the Master,* probably from Campania, southeast of Rome, in the first quarter of the sixth century. Three times as long as the *Rule of Benedict,* it is important not only because of its detail, but especially because it was a major source used by Benedict in the composition of his own *Rule* around 530–560.

As its editor, the great contemporary Benedictine expert on the Western monastic rules, Adalbert de Vogüé, has pointed out, the prescriptions on the Divine Office in RM 33–49 are all that those in previous sources are not: "This limpid *ordo* and the confused mass of incomplete rubrics in the *ordines* of the two bishops of Arles have nothing in common."[5] Chapters 33–38 deal with the number of psalms in the hours; the cursus and its underlying principles are set out in chapters 38–49.[6] The times of the hours are strictly adhered to (RM 34), without any of Benedict's delays or anticipations, except for the possibility of moving up vespers in summer (RM 34:12–13).

### I. THE STRUCTURE OF THE HOURS

The structure of the hours is the one we are already familiar with from our other Western offices: psalmody with prostrations and prayer, followed by lessons and concluded by intercessions. Except for nocturns, the hours differ structurally only in the amount of psalmody and in the location of the verse, (before or after the lessons). Nocturns simply doubles the basic larger unit of antiphons plus responsory, and prefixes the whole with an invitatory. Prime (RM 40) has been completely assimilated to the other little hours: nothing distinguishes it or betrays its recent origin, as in Arles. The entire day is opened before nocturns and closed at the end of compline with verses that form the framework of the whole daily cycle.

The structure of the individual hours is as follows:

**1. Nocturns** (RM 33; 44–45):

Opening verse 3x
Invitatory responsory: Ps 94

---

[4]Critical edition and excellent commentary in de Vogüé, *La Règle du Maître,* from which all citations are made; English version in L. Eberle, *The Rule of the Master* (CS 6, Kalamazoo: Cistercian Publications, 1977). I depend on de Vogüé for all questions of dating and history.

[5]de Vogüé, *La Règle du Maître* I, 60.

[6]*Ibid.* I, 47.

9 [6] antiphons without alleluia
Responsory without alleluia

4 [3] antiphons with alleluia
Responsory with alleluia

Apostle
Gospel

Verse
Rogus dei

## 2. Matins (RM 35:1; 38) and vespers (36; 41):

4 antiphons without alleluia
2 antiphons with alleluia
Responsory
Verse
Apostle
Gospel and its responsory
Rogus dei

## 3. The little hours (35; 40):

2 antiphons without alleluia
1 antiphon with alleluia
Responsory
Apostle
Gospel
Verse
Rogus dei

## 4. Compline (37; 42):

2 antiphons without alleluia
1 antiphon with alleluia
Responsory
Apostle
Gospel
Rogus dei
Closing verse

## II. Liturgical Units

### 1. Psalmody:

The basic liturgical unit of psalmody, regardless of its mode of execution (antiphonal, responsorial) was the *inpositio*, which comprised (RM 33:32, 43–45):

Psalm
Gloria Patri
Prostration
Prayer

It is not altogther clear if this prostration for prayer after the *Gloria Patri* was silent prayer followed by prayer aloud, but that is how I would prefer to interpret RM 33:32, 43–45, especially in the light of 55:15–18; 56:1–8. Further, RM 55:16 and 73:15 seem to imply that the prayer aloud was spontaneous rather than a fixed collect. The Master (33:42–45) insists that psalms never be run together, but that each be executed separately, with its own concluding *Gloria Patri*, lest the prayers *(orationes)* be lost and "the glories" diminished. Heiming thinks the *Gloria Patri* followed the prayer after the psalm, and de Vogüé leans toward the same opinion, but this is unlikely.[7] The Master states clearly that the *Gloria Patri* is the signal for prayer and the end of each psalm (RM 33:42–45).

On Sundays and feasts, and during Eastertide and the Nativity-Epiphany season, there were no prostrations, and all the antiphons had alleluia as refrain (RM 39:6–7; 41:4; 45). Sundays (RM 45:12–15) and saints' days have a few other particularities (RM 45:16–18).

The distribution of the psalms is regulated by two basic principles, which de Vogüé calls "the rule of the twenty-four impositions," and "the rule of two-thirds."[8] According to the first rule, the twenty-four psalms, divided between the two hours of the Egyptian tradition according to Cassian, were so distributed throughout the Master's cursus that the day and night hours each had twenty-four impositions (RM 33–38) except in summer, when the brevity of the shorter nights forced an abbreviation of nocturns (33:35–41). Compline for some reason—perhaps because it was a later addition—remained outside the system.[9] The execution of the psalms antiphonally or responsorially had no affect on this count:

*Day hours:*

Prime, terce, sext, none: 3 antiphons and 1
    responsory each = 16 impositions
Vespers: 6 antiphons, 1 responsory, 1 gospel
    responsory = 8 impositions

---

[7]*Ibid.* I, 49–50 note 1; Heiming, "Zum monastischen Offizium," 94.
[8]de Vogüé, *La Règle du Maître* I, 49ff.
[9]*Ibid.* I, 50–55.

*Night hours:*

Nocturns: 13 antiphons (summer: 9), 3 responsories
  = 16 (12) impositions
Matins: 6 antiphons, 1 responsory, 1 gospel
  responsory = 8 impositions

Note the harmony of this system. Vespers and matins correspond, whereas the sum of the little hours equals the psalmody of nocturns.

The "rule of two-thirds" refers to the arrangement of the entire corpus of antiphonal psalmody in units of threes or multiples of threes, with each unit subdivided into psalms without or with alleluia, in a ratio of two to three. We have already seen similar triplets in other Western offices. Thus the little hours and compline have two antiphons without alleluia to one with, matins and vespers four to two, and summer nocturns six to three. The rule breaks down only with the thirteen antiphons of winter nocturns, unevenly divided into nine without and four with alleluia according to de Vogüé's reconstruction.[10]

The Master tells us that except at compline and matins, the antiphonal psalms were *currente semper psalterio* (RM 33:29, 36; 35:2, 36:1; 40:2; 41:2; 44:2, 7; 46:1). But since there is no fixed *pensum* term—e.g., the whole psalter in one week, as in Benedict—any psalm would eventually appear in any hour in the course of the normal numerical execution of the psalter. Hence unlike Cassian (*Inst.* II, 11:3), it is clear that the Master uses alleluia with other than the biblical alleluia psalms. Indeed, he also uses the biblical alleluia psalms without the alleluia refrain, at least in the case of Ps 148 of lauds, as we shall see shortly. But the responsories for each hour seem to have been fixed psalms, the antiphons of matins had fixed cathedral psalms or canticles (Pss 50, 148–150, Dan 3:52–90),[11] as we shall see, and it is highly probable that compline, as in all Latin monastic rules, comprised fixed psalms such as Ps 90 (91).

Note the overwhelming predominance of the antiphonal mode of execution and the complete absence of the *directaneus* psalmody characteristic of other monastic offices, except when the hours are recited out of choir for some reason (RM 55:8).[12]

### 2. The verse and rogus dei:

The verse was apparently a psalm verse. The *rogus dei* has been variously interpreted as a litany, or a silent prayer, or even (improbably) as

[10]*Ibid.* I, 52.
[11]*Ibid.* I, 59.
[12]*Ibid.* I, 62.

the Our Father.[13] I would agree with Heiming and de Bhaldraithe that it is a litany, since silent prayer immediately after the silent prayer of the gospel *inpositio* is unlikely.[14]

### 3. The euangelia:

It is not altogether clear if the *euangelia* at matins and vespers is a lesson, or a gospel canticle such as the *Benedictus* or *Magnificat*, which de Vogüé thinks likely, to which Heiming would add the *Nunc dimittis*.[15] In support of this latter view is the fact that the *euangelia* is counted, along with the antiphons and responsory, as the eighth and final *inpositio* (RM 36:1-2). This would hardly suit a lesson, and indeed the *euangelia* is clearly distinguished from the *lectiones* in RM 36:

> [36:1]Psalmi lucernariae in hieme dici debent
> sex, currente semper psalterio,
> responsum unum,
> uersum,
> lectionem apostoli et euangelia, quae semper abbas dicat,
> post hoc et rogus Dei,
> [2]ut tam istae cum responsorio et euangelia [octo] inpositiones psallentium sine uersum et lectiones . . . [7]Similiter et tempore aestatis octo debent fieri in lucernaria cum responsoria et euangelia inpositiones extra uersum et lectiones . . . .

Furthermore, RM 41 (cf. 38:2), when speaking of the antiphons with alleluia, also lumps the *euangelia* with the psalms:

> [41:1]Psalmi lucernariae cum antifanis psalli debent, [2]in quibus duo ultimi cum alleluia, currente semper psalterio, [3]singula responsoria, uersum, lectionem apostoli et *euangelia*, quae semper abbas dicat sine alleluia, in dominica uero cum alleluia. [4]Nam omnes antifanae ipso die a benedictionibus dictis cum alleluia psallantur. . . .

In both texts for matins and vespers note that the Latin does not say "the reading of the apostle, reading of the Gospels," as it does for the little hours (RM 40:3, "lectionem apostoli, lectionem euangeliorum"), but "reading of the apostle, and the Gospels" (*euangelia* = nominative). What, then, of the plural *lectiones* in RM 36:2, 4, 7, cited above (see also RM 33:30; 33:36)? If there is but one apostle lesson, one would expect the singular

---

[13]For various interpretations see *ibid.* II, 183 note 30; Heiming, "Zum monastischen Offizium," 102.

[14]Heiming, *loc. cit.*; E. de Bhaldraithe, "The Morning Office in the Rule of the Master," *Regulae Benedicti Studia, Annuarium Internationale* 5 (1976) 220.

[15]de Vogüé, *La Règle du Maître* II, 192; Heiming, "Zum monastischen Offizium," 100.

*lectio.*[16] De Bhaldraithe attempts to reconcile these contradictions.[17] He argues at length from comparative liturgy, and convincingly, that the *euangelia* included indeed a gospel reading, but this lesson was followed at matins and vespers by a responsory, and the alleluia with this responsory on Sundays and some other days is simply the alleluia responsory of the gospel lesson, for which de Bhaldraithe sees parallels in the Roman Office in *Ordines romani XIV*, and especially *XXVII*, as well as in other later sources.

### 4. The lessons:

The first lesson or "apostle" was from St. Paul. The gospel was always read by the abbot himself (RM 41:3; 46:3-4). Is this gospel a relic of the old cathedral vigil resurrection gospel or just a matins gospel? De Bhaldraithe argues in favor of the latter option, again convincingly, showing that in several traditions, Eastern and Western, one must distinguish two morning gospels: that of the Sunday resurrection vigil, and the ordinary Sunday gospel of matins.[18]

### III. MATINS

Matins poses special problems. RM 39:4 states that matins contains Ps 50, lauds (Pss 148-150), two canticles, and on Sundays the *Benedictiones* of Dan 3. Now we saw that matins has six antiphons and one responsory, seven antiphons or *inpositiones* in all:

> 4 antiphons without alleluia (except Sundays, feasts)
> 2 antiphons with alleluia
> Responsory
> Verse
> Apostle
> Gospel and its responsory
> Rogus dei

The problem is how to fit the specified fixed units—Pss 50, 148-150, two canticles, and Dan 3—into this framework. P. Jasmer has suggested that Ps 50, the canticles, and lauds may be in addition to the six antiphons of matins,[19] but I consider this impossible since it would destroy

---

[16] de Vogüé, *La Règle du Maître* II, 192-193 note 2; de Bhaldraithe, "The Morning Office," 204.

[17] "The Morning Office," 202-205.

[18] *Ibid.* 211-215.

[19] P. Jasmer, "A Comparison of the Monastic and Cathedral Vespers up to the Time of St. Benedict," *The American Benedictine Review* 34 (1983) 347 note 48.

the count of impositions in RM 35:1; 36:1-6, a symmetry which is part of the essential structure of the cursus of the Master.

Though RM does not indicate any order for the six antiphons, Roman and Benedictine matins had Ps 50 at the beginning and lauds at the end,[20] and I think it is as good as certain that the same was true of the related Italian office in RM. Against this, of course, is the explicit testimony of Cassian, *Institutes* III, 6: "Finally, throughout Italy today when the morning hymns have ended *(consummatis matutinis hymnis)*, Ps 50 is sung in all the churches." Since he goes on to say that this custom must have come from Bethlehem, where we know Ps 50, first psalm of the new morning solemnity, came *after* Pss 148-150, which concluded nocturns there,[21] it is perfectly obvious that Cassian is affirming the presence of Ps 50 *after*, not *before* lauds in the morning office throughout Italy. Bradshaw rightly sees this as an argument in support of his theory that the end of nocturns, and not matins, is the original *Sitz im Gottesdienst* of Pss 148-150.[22] But in the face of the almost complete unanimity of all other witnesses, East and West, and especially of all our Italian sources, which put Ps 50 at the beginning of matins and not after the psalms of lauds,[23] I am at a loss how to interpret Cassian except to presume on the basis of comparative liturgy that he must be wrong—though of course a historian can never be really comfortable in dismissing evidence in this way.

Since Pss 148-150 are all biblical alleluia psalms, it is likely that Pss 149-150 furnished the two weekday alleluia antiphons, leaving Ps 148 as the fourth antiphon without alleluia. The first three non-alleluia antiphons were Ps 50 and the two canticles. What were these canticles? It is probable that they were fixed. De Bhaldraithe proposes the *Magnificat* and *Benedictus* as in RB, thus giving matins in RM a structure remarkably like that of early Palestinian Sabaitic orthros.[24]

That leaves the *Benedictiones*.[25] My initial temptation was to presume it was simply the proper Sunday canticle, as in Byzantine Sabaitic orthros, followed as there by the combined *Magnificat-Benedictus* as the second

---

[20]See the discussion of the various possibilities in A. de Vogüé, *La Règle de S. Benoît* V: *Commentaire historique et critique* (SC 185, Paris: Cerf 1971) 483ff.

[21]See above, 99-100.

[22]*Daily Prayer*, 108-110.

[23]See de Vogüé, *La Règle de S. Benoît* V, 483-487; the Cappadocian sources cited above pp. 47, 108; and the place of Ps 50 in the Armenian, Byzantine, Maronite, and Ethiopian matins, in the respective chapters below.

[24]"The Morning Office," 215-217, 220.

[25]de Vogüé, *La Règle du Maître* I, 59 note 3, says the *Benedictiones* were Dan 3:52-56, 57-90, as at Arles.

canticle.[26] But a close reading of RM 39:5, 7; 45:12, 14, 16–17 confirms, I think, de Bhaldraithe's hypothesis that at festive matins Dan 3 replaces Ps 50 as the first antiphon.[27] For the Master repeats five times that the prohibition against kneeling on Sundays and festivities begins with the *Benedictiones*, which can only mean with the beginning of matins. Furthermore, the Master's prohibition against combining psalms is equally applicable to all impositions, including the two canticles, and to simply add Dan 3 to the other two canticles would destroy the Master's strictly fixed and balanced number of impositions.

But I do not understand why de Vogüé and de Bhaldraithe have the *Benedictiones* without alleluia.[28] RM 39: 6–7, 41:4; 45:12–13 all say that the antiphons and responsories *"a benedictionibus dictis cum alleluia psallantur et genua non flectantur."* If one takes this to mean that the alleluia is added only *after* the *Benedictiones*, then one must logically interpret the prostration prohibition in the same way, i.e., that Dan 3 was without alleluia and was followed by a prostration even at festive matins. But this would make no sense whatever. So what RM obviously means is that both the alleluia refrain and the prohibition to kneel begin with matins—and matins begins with the *Benedictiones*.

We can now reconstruct matins in RM as follows:[29]

| *Ferial:* | *Festive:* |
|---|---|
| Ps 50 with antiphon, prostration, prayer | Dan 3 with alleluia, prayer |
| *Magnificat* with antiphon, prostration, prayer | *Magnificat* with alleluia, prayer |
| *Benedictus* with antiphon prostration, prayer | *Benedictus* with alleluia, prayer |
| Ps 148 with antiphon, prostration, prayer | Ps 148 with alleluia, prayer |
| Ps 149 with alleluia, prostration, prayer | Ps 149 with alleluia, prayer |
| Ps 150 with alleluia, prostration, prayer | Ps 150 with alleluia prayer |

[26]See *ibid.* 215–216 and below, ch. 17.

[27]de Bhaldraithe, "The Morning Office," 215–221. For de Vogüé's view, which has vacillated, see *La Règle du Maître* II, 197, note to RM 39:4–5; *La Règle de S. Benoît* V, 500 note 6.

[28]de Vogüé, *La Règle de S. Benoît* V, 500 note 4; de Bhaldraithe, "The Morning Office," 220–221.

[29]Except for a few differences my reconstruction agrees basically with de Bhaldraithe, *loc. cit.*

| | |
|---|---|
| Responsory, prostration, prayer | Responsory with alleluia, prayer |
| Verse | Verse: Sunday, Ps 149:5 (RM 46:14;cf.57:26) |
| Apostle lesson | Apostle lesson |
| Gospel lesson | Gospel lesson |
| Gospel responsory, prostration, prayer | Gospel responsory with alleluia, prayer |
| Litany *(Rogus dei)* | Litany |

IV. CONCLUSION

In RM as in the rules of Arles we note a characteristic of Western monastic offices: whereas matins is almost totally cathedral in provenance, vespers shows almost no cathedral characteristics. But I have already observed that the responsory of the hours, which RM seems to exclude from the *psalmodia currens*, may have been a fixed psalm, and could well have been Ps 140:2 at vespers, as Jasmer has suggested.[30]

In its basic characteristics this office, like the old Roman hours, is more an ancestor of Benedict's cursus than linked to the non-Italian Latin offices we have seen in Gaul, the Iberian peninsula, and Ireland.

## The Old Roman Hours and the Rule of St. Benedict[31]

The two greatest influences on the office in the *Rule of Benedict* were the *Rule of the Master* and the Roman Office of Benedict's time. We have already studied the Master's cursus; we have much less information for that of "The City," as its residents still call Rome today.

[30]"A Comparison," 347 note 48, 351ff. *passim.*

[31]Critical edition and excellent commentary in J. Neufville-A. de Vogüé, *La Règle de S. Benoît,* 7 vols. (SC 181–186; vol. 7 hors série, Paris: Cerf 1972–1977) = vols. 1-2: critical edition by Neufville, introd., trans. and notes by de Vogüé, vol. 3: Neufville, *Instruments pour l'étude de la tradition manuscrite;* vols. 4–6: de Vogüé, *Commentaire historique et critique;* vol. 7 (hors série): de Vogüé, *Commentaire doctrinal et spirituel*—the latter also in English: *The Rule of St. Benedict. A Doctrinal and Spiritual Commentary* (CS 54, Kalamazoo: Cistercian Publications, 1983). Edition with English trans. and commentary in Fry, *RB 1980,* where Appendix 3: "The Liturgical Code in the Rule of Benedict" by N. Mitchell is especially good for our purposes.

1. THE MONASTIC OFFICE IN THE CITY OF ROME

From the fourth and fifth centuries we have but a few scraps of information concerning the monastic office in Rome. First of all, some of the references (Cassian, Arnobius) adduced in chapters 6 and 8 could apply here too. The same can be said for what follows below concerning the cathedral office in Rome, for we do not know to what extent the cathedral-monastic distinction existed there.

But some sources refer clearly to monastic groups in The City. Jerome speaks in several letters of prayer or psalmody at dawn, at the third, sixth, and ninth hours, at the coming of evening, and during the night.[32] In *Letter 22, 37*, written in 384, he says, "one should rise two or three times at night to go over parts of Scripture that we know by heart," whereas in the letters written in 404 he speaks just of rising at night for prayers and psalms (*Letter 107, 9*), or "at midnight" (*Letter 130, 15*). Now some of these letters (*22, 107, 130*) were written to aristocratic Roman ladies—widows and virgins—living at home, and it is not always possible to know if Jerome was writing about prayer in an embryonic monastic community, about participation in "cathedral" services, or about the domestic devotions of his devotees. At least one text, *Letter 107* to Leta (treated in the next chapter), can be interpreted as referring to "cathedral" prayer—though again, it is not at all clear that in Rome there was much difference between cathedral and monastic offices. The reason for this is to be found in the peculiar history of urban monasticism in Rome.

Though the earliest monastic foundation in Rome was Sixtus III's (432–440) Monastery of St. Sebastian *in catacumbas*, monastic life of a more or less organized sort existed in Rome before this.[33] Shortly after 383 St. Augustine testified to monastic life for men in Rome and Milan in his *De moribus ecclesiae catholicae*,[34] and Jerome in *Letter 127, 8*, speaks of "many monasteries of virgins, and an innumerable multitude of monks *(crebra virginum monasteria, monachorum innumerabilis multitudo)*." Numerous other references can be adduced to prove the existence of monastic life in fourth-century Rome,[35] but "it is not possible to ascertain

---

[32]*Ep. 108*, 19; *23*, 35, 37; *15*, 11. Jerome's *Letters* are edited in CSEL 54–56. On Jerome and Roman monasticism see L. Gutierrez, "El monaquismo romano y San Jerónimo," *Communio* 4 (1971) 49–78.

[33] G. Ferrari, *Early Roman Monasteries. Notes for the History of the Monasteries and Convents at Rome from the V through the X Century* (Studi di antichità cristiana 23, Vaticano: Pontificio Istituto di Archeologia Cristiana 1957) xiii, xvi, 163–165.

[34]PL 32, 339–1340.

[35]See Ferrari, *Early Roman Monasteries* xiv–xvi, and G. D. Gordini, "Origine e sviluppo del monachesimo a Roma," *Gregorianum* 37 (1956) 220–260.

to what extent these ascetics lived in community, nor is it clear how these communities were organized, or where they were located."[36] Indeed, it is known that many Roman virgins and ascetics in the early period continued to live at home.[37]

But beginning with the Lateran and St. Peter's in the fifth century, the basilicas of Rome began to be served by small monastic communities, and their office became that of the churches that served the people—a situation unheard of in other urban centers this early in Late Antiquity.[38] When Benedict states that he follows the Roman way of psalmody (RB 13:3,10) it is this Roman urban monastic office he is talking about. So whatever there was of a pure cathedral Roman Office before this period must be sifted from this monastic setting.

As for the urban monastic office of these Roman basilical communities, predecessors of the later Western "canons regular,"[39] it would take us too far afield to attempt more than a brief synthesis of what is known about this usage. The problem is to get behind the Benedictine office in the *Rule* to the earlier Roman stratum, for although Benedict states his dependence on earlier Roman usage (RB 13:3,10), the earliest explicit documents of it such as the eighth-century *Ordines romani XVIII* and *XIX*— the latter once thought to be the work of John, the famous archicantor of St. Peter's in Rome—refer in turn to the *Rule of Benedict* as the core, but not the only source, of their monastic legislation.[40] Furthermore, scholars doubt the reliability of these *Ordines* as direct witnesses to Roman usage since they were probably composed in France on the basis of what could be known of Roman uses of the time.[41] "Research into the pre-Benedictine Roman Liturgy of the Hours is confronted with pitch-darkness that can be pierced only with great difficulty," is how Joseph Pascher opens his study on the topic.[42]

---

[36]Ferrari, *Early Roman Monasteries* xv.

[37]*Ibid.*

[38]*Ibid.* xix, 365–375.

[39]*Ibid.* 382ff. and L. Hertling, "Kanoniker, Augustinerregel und Augustinerorden," *Zeitschrift für katholische Theologie* 54 (1930) 335–359.

[40]See M. Andrieu, *Les "Ordines romani" du haut moyen âge* (Spicilegium sacrum lovaniense, Etudes et documents, fasc. 24, Louvain: Université catholique, 1961) III: *Les textes* (suite) (*Ordines XIV–XXXIV*) 20–21, 65–66; Ferrari, *Early Roman Monasteries* 392ff. The references to RB are in *Ordo XVIII*, 4, Andrieu II, 205; *Ordo XIX*, 29, *ibid.* 222.

[41]Ferrari, *Early Roman Monasteries* 396–397.

[42]"Der Psalter für Laudes und Vesper im alten römischen Stundengebet," *Münchener theologische Zeitschrift* 8 (1957) 255–267.

## 1. Matins:

Primitive Roman matins as reconstructed by Pascher were remarkably like what we saw in the Master:[43]

> Ps 50 (92?)
> Ps 62
> Ps 66
> Pss 148–150

Later developments can be seen in the following table:[44]

| Primitive Roman: | RM: | Classical Roman: | RB: |
|---|---|---|---|
| Ps 50 | 50 | 50 | 66, 50 |
| 62 | Canticle | Variable psalm | 2 variable psalms |
| 66 | Canticle | 62, 66 | Canticle |
| Lauds | Lauds | Lauds | Lauds |

The office concluded as follows:[45]

| RM: | Roman: | RB: |
|---|---|---|
|  |  | Epistle lesson (Apoc. on Sundays) |
| Responsory |  | Responsory |
|  |  | Hymn |
| Verse | Verse | Verse |
| Epistle |  |  |
| Gospel | Gospel canticle | Gospel canticle |
| Gospel responsory |  |  |
| *Rogus dei* | *Preces* | Litany |
|  | Our Father | Our Father |
|  | or collect |  |

In the psalmody it is clear that Benedict depends more on Rome than on RM, whereas in the concluding part of the offices he has introduced non-Roman elements from RM.

## 2. Vespers:

All we know about primitive Roman vespers is that it once had six psalms as in RM, later reduced to five in the second half of the fifth cen-

---

[43]*Ibid.* 256; cf. de Vogüé, *La Règle de S. Benoît* V, 485.
[44]de Vogüé, *La Règle de S. Benoît* V, 487.
[45]*Ibid.* V, 492.

tury,[46] and finally to four in the Benedictine reform of the following century.

### 3. The little hours:

These sources knew daily prime as a fully accepted part of the *horarium* rather than as an innovation to be justified and insisted on (RM 34:2, 4; 35:2; 40:1; RB 15:3; 16:2, 5; 17:2; 18:2, 4–5; 48:3). So de Vogüé supposes that the origins of prime in Central Italy may antedate our first explicit proof of its existence in Arles.[47]

The other little hours have the traditional three-psalm structure in all the sources. The main difference is that while the Roman variable psalter was divided between vigils and vespers, with fixed psalms daily at matins, the little hours, and compline, Benedict, 1) by spreading the variable weekly *pensum* of 150 psalms over the other hours except compline, which retains its three fixed Pss 4, 90, 133, and 2) by removing from the variable vigils-vespers psalter all the fixed psalms taken daily in matins, the little hours, and compline, reduced the burden of psalmody to more manageable proportions, as can be seen in the table on pages 136–137.[48]

## II. THE FINAL SYNTHESIS IN THE RULE OF BENEDICT

### 1. Structure of the hours:

The following outlines show the Roman monastic office in its final, Benedictine form.[49] Once again we remark here what characterizes all Western monastic offices: the heavily cathedral content of matins, and the apparently complete absence of cathedral elements in vespers. P. Jasmer has proposed that the response and versicle, together in RM but split in RB by the addition of the hymn, may be a remnant of cathedral vespers: Ps 140 with its responsory versicle Ps 140:2.[50] We shall return to this point in the next chapter, when discussing the question of cathedral vespers in the West.

A. VIGILS (RB 9–11):

Opening verse 3x
Ps 3

[46]*Ibid.* V, 495–498; Pascher, "Der Psalter," 256–262.
[47]de Vogüé, *La Règle de S. Benoît* V, 516.
[48]From M. Righetti, *Storia liturgica* vol. 2 (Milan: Ancora, 1955) 501.
[49]More detailed outlines with all variable parts indicated in Fry, *RB 1980,* 390–397.
[50]"A Comparison," 357–360.

    Ps 94
    Hymn

*1st nocturn:*

    6 psalms + refrain
    Versicle
    Blessing by the abbot
    3 lessons + responsories in winter, 1 in summer,
      4 on Sundays

*2nd nocturn:*

    6 psalms + alleluia
    Epistle
    Versicle
    Litany

*[Sundays: 3rd nocturn:*

    3 canticles + alleluia
    Versicle
    Blessing by the abbot
    4 NT lessons + 4 responsories
    *Te deum laudamus*
    Gospel
    *Te decet laus*
    Blessing]

B. MATINS (LAUDS) (RB 12–13):

    Ps 66
    Ps 50 + refrain (Sundays: alleluia)
    2 variable psalms
    Canticle (Sundays: Dan 3:52–56, 57–90)
    Lauds: Pss 148–150
    Epistle (Sundays: Apoc)
    Responsory
    Hymn
    Versicle
    Gospel canticle
    Litany
    Our Father

C. LITTLE HOURS (RB 17–18):

    Opening verse
    Hymn
    3 variable psalms, with or without refrain

# Roman Psalter (5–6th c.)

| | Sun | | Mon. | Tues. | Wed. | Th. | Fri. | Sat. |
|---|---|---|---|---|---|---|---|---|
| **Vigils** | | | | | | | | |
| | . . . . . . . . . . . . . . . . . . . . . . . . . . . . . . . . . . . . . . . . . . . . . . | | | | | | | |
| 1 Noct. | 1 | 2 Noct. 15 | 27 | 39 | 53 | 68 | 80 | 96 |
| | 2 | 16 | 28 | 40 | 54 | 69 | 81 | 97 |
| | 3 | 17 | 29 | 41 | 55 | 70 | 82 | 98 |
| | 6 | 18 | 30 | 43 | 56 | 71 | 83 | 100 |
| | 7 | 19 | 31 | 44 | 57 | 72 | 84 | 101 |
| | 8 | 20 | 32 | 45 | 58 | 73 | 85 | 102 |
| | 9 | 3 Noct. 21 | 33 | 46 | 59 | 74 | 86 | 103 |
| | 10 | 22 | 34 | 47 | 60 | 75 | 87 | 104 |
| | 11 | 23 | 35 | 48 | 61 | 76 | 88 | 105 |
| | 12 | 24 | 36 | 49 | 63 | 77 | 93 | 106 |
| | 13 | 25 | 37 | 51 | 65 | 78 | 94 | 107 |
| | 14 | 26 | 38 | 52 | 67 | 79 | 95 | 108 |
| **Lauds** | | | | | | | | |
| | . . . . . . . . . . . . . . . . . . . . . . . . . . . . . . . . . . . . . . . . . . . . . . | | | | | | | |
| | 92 | | 50 | id . | id . | id . | id . | id. |
| | 99 | | 5 | 42 | 64 | 89 | 142 | 91 |
| | 62+66 | | id. | id. | id. | id. | id. | id. |
| | Canticle | | Cant. | Cant. | Cant. | Cant. | Cant. | Cant. |
| | 148–150 | | id. | id. | id. | id. | id. | id. |
| **Prime** | | | | | | | | |
| | 117 | | 53 | id. | id. | id. | id. | id. |
| | 118, 1–4 | | id. | id. | id. | id. | id. | id. |
| **Terce** | | | | | | | | |
| | 118, 5–10 | | id. | id. | id. | id. | id. | id. |
| **Sext** | | | | | | | | |
| | 118, 1–16 | | id. | id. | id. | id. | id. | id. |
| **None** | | | | | | | | |
| | 118, 17–22 | | id. | id. | id. | id. | id. | id. |
| **Vespers** | | | | | | | | |
| | 109 | | 114 | 121 | 126 | 131 | 137 | 143 |
| | 110 | | 115 | 122 | 127 | 132 | 138 | 144 |
| | 111 | | 116 | 123 | 128 | 134 | 139 | 145 |
| | 112 | | 119 | 124 | 129 | 135 | 140 | 146 |
| | 113 | | 120 | 125 | 130 | 136 | 141 | 147 |
| **Compline** | | | | | | | | |
| | 4 | | id. | id. | id. | id. | id. | id. |
| | 90 | | id. | id. | id. | id. | id. | id. |
| | 133 | | id. | id. | id. | id. | id. | id. |

## Psalter in RB 9–18

| | Sun. | Mon. | Tues. | Wed. | Th. | Fri. | Sat. |
|---|---|---|---|---|---|---|---|
| **Vigils** | | | | | | | |
| | 3 | id. | id. | id. | id. | id. | id. |
| | 94 | id. | id. | id. | id. | id. | id. |
| **1 Noct.** | 20 | 32 | 45 | 59 | 73 | 85 | 101 |
| | 21 | 33 | 46 | 60 | 74 | 86 | 102 |
| | 22 | 34 | 47 | 61 | 76 | 88,1 | 103,1 |
| | 23 | 36,1 | 48 | 65 | 77,1 | 2 | 2 |
| | 24 | 2 | 49 | 67,1 | 2 | 92 | 104,1 |
| | 25 | 37 | 51 | 2 | 78 | 93 | 2 |
| **2 Noct.** | 26 | 38 | 52 | 68,1 | 79 | 95 | 105,1 |
| | 27 | 39 | 53 | 2 | 80 | 96 | 2 |
| | 28 | 40 | 54 | 69 | 81 | 97 | 106,1 |
| | 29 | 41 | 55 | 70 | 82 | 98 | 2 |
| | 30 | 43 | 57 | 71 | 83 | 99 | 107 |
| | 31 | 44 | 58 | 72 | 84 | 100 | 108 |
| **Lauds** | | | | | | | |
| | 66 | id. | id. | id. | id. | id. | id. |
| | 50 | id. | id. | id. | id. | id. | id. |
| | 117 | 5 | 42 | 63 | 87 | 75 | 142 |
| | 62 | 35 | 56 | 64 | 89 | 91 | Cant.,1 |
| | Canticle | Cant. | Cant. | Cant. | Cant. | Cant. | 2 |
| | 148–150 | id. | id. | id. | id. | id. | id. |
| **Prime** | | | | | | | |
| | 118, 1–4 | 1 | 7 | 9,2 | 12 | 15 | 17,2 |
| | | 2 | 8 | 10 | 13 | 16 | 18 |
| | | 6 | 9,1 | 11 | 14 | 17,1 | 19 |
| **Terce** | | | | | | | |
| | 118, 5–7 | 118, 14–16 | 119 | id. | id. | id. | id. |
| | | | 120 | id. | id. | id. | id. |
| | | | 121 | id. | id. | id. | id. |
| **Sext** | | | | | | | |
| | 118, 8–10 | 118, 17–19 | 122 | id. | id. | id. | id. |
| | | | 123 | id. | id. | id. | id. |
| | | | 124 | id. | id. | id. | id. |
| **None** | | | | | | | |
| | 118, 11–13 | 118, 20–22 | 125 | id. | id. | id. | id. |
| | | | 126 | id. | id. | id. | id. |
| | | | 127 | id. | id. | id. | id. |
| **Vespers** | | | | | | | |
| | 109 | 113 | 129 | 134 | 138,1 | 141 | 144,2 |
| | 110 | 114 | 130 | 135 | 2 | 143,1 | 145 |
| | 111 | 115+116 | 131 | 136 | 139 | 2 | 146 |
| | 112 | 128 | 132 | 137 | 140 | 144,1 | 147 |
| **Compline** | | | | | | | |
| | 4 | id. | id. | id. | id. | id. | id. |
| | 90 | id. | id. | id. | id. | id. | id. |
| | 133 | id. | id. | id. | id. | id. | id. |

Lesson
Versicle
Litany
Dismissal

D. VESPERS (RB 13:12; 17:7-8; 18:12-18):

Opening verse (?)[51]
4 variable psalms
Lesson
Responsory
Hymn
Versicle
Gospel canticle
Litany
Our Father
Dismissal

E. COMPLINE (RB 17:9-10; 18:19):

Opening verse (?)[52]
Pss 4, 90, 133, without refrain
Hymn
Lesson
Versicle
Litany
Blessing
Dismissal

### 2. How the office was celebrated:

Just how Benedict intended the psalms, hymns, and canticles to be executed has been disputed by later interpreters of the *Rule.* Here, as in other sources, one can make no argument from the variety of verbs Benedict uses to describe the performance: "to sing" *(cantare, canere, modulare:* RB 9:5-6, 9; 11:2-3; 17; 18:12), "to psalm" *(psallere:* 17:6), or simply "to say" *(dicere:* 11:6; 18:15). This is clear from RB 11:3, where Benedict says that "the *Gloria* is said by the one singing *(dicatur a cantante gloria)."*[53] The same is true in liturgical Greek or Syriac, where such verbs as *legein* or *emar,* the equivalents of *dicere,* "to say," just indicate vocalization indifferently, with no implication of "saying" as distinct from "chanting"

---

[51]RB does not mention the verse for vespers or compline but I have presumed it.
[52]See the preceding note.
[53]Mitchell, "The Liturgical Code," 403.

or "singing." Furthermore, traditional early monastic opposition to music does not mean the monks did not chant. It was worldly music, musical instruments, and—initially at least—non-scriptural refrains and chants they set their faces against. So we can take it as certain that Benedict and those before him did not intend the hours to be "spoken," though we know nothing of the nature of their chant in this early period.

Nor is it altogether clear just what Benedict means by antiphonal psalmody.[54] In early monastic usage, psalms were executed either *directly* (*in directum, directaneus:* RB 17:6, 9), that is, in their entirety, by a soloist or by the whole community together; or *alternately*, with the congregation divided into two choirs alternating the verses. If the biblical text of the psalm included an "alleluia" response, the psalm might be chanted *responsorially*, with the entire congregation responding "alleluia" to each verse proclaimed by a soloist. Later monastic usage followed the cathedral churches in extending the responsorial method beyond the repertoire of biblical alleluia psalms to the entire psalter by simply selecting a verse of any psalm to serve as its response. *Antiphonal* forms of psalmody appear from the fourth century as further elaborations of the responsorial mode. The *Gloria Patri,* never found in responsorial psalmody, is added to conclude the unit; non-biblical refrains sometimes replace the scriptural antiphons, especially in the East; and the congregation, divided into two choirs, responds to the verses alternately, sometimes with the same refrain, sometimes each choir with its own refrain, to the verses chanted by the soloist or, at times, by two soloists alternating the verses, one at the head of each choir.

Note that the refrain or antiphon was repeated after each verse and not just at the beginning and end of the psalm, and that two soloists, not two choirs of monks, alternated the verses, contrary to what one sees in more recent Latin usage. The evidence is not always clear, but I would take modern Western antiphonal usage, with the soloist's role and the repetition of the antiphon after each verse suppressed, to represent but the debris of the pristine structure of this liturgical unit as intended by Benedict in the *Rule.*

Since this antiphonal system worked only when there were enough monks to divide into soloists and two choirs, RB 17:6 eliminates the antiphons if the community is too small: "Si maior congregatio fuerit, cum antiphonis, si vero minor, in directum psallantur."

---

[54] Cf. *ibid.* 401ff., and J. Mateos, "La psalmodie dans le rite byzantin," POC 51 (1965) 107–126, reprinted in *id., La célébration de la parole dans la liturgie byzantine* (OCA 191, Rome: PIO, 1971) 7–26.

The *Rule* does not specify the pericopes for the Scripture lessons, so I would presume that they were a *lectio continua* from books chosen according to the season of the liturgical year.

### III. CONCLUSION

The advantages of Benedict's revisions are immediately apparent.[55] His redistribution of the variable, current monastic psalmody of the weekly psalter to cover lauds and the day hours, too, not only eliminates repetitions, but also introduces variety into those hours while lightening vigils *pensum* to twelve psalms daily and that of vespers from five to four. But Benedict did more than render the Roman psalmody less burdensome and less repetitious. He also introduced hymnody, not a Roman custom in the hours, though we find hymns in the offices of Milan, Gaul, and the Iberian peninsula. Further, he relieved the monotony of the nocturnal psalmody by placing the lessons after the first six psalms of vigils, instead of at the end of the traditional twelve. In so doing he abandoned the tradition, passed on from Egypt via Cassian, the Master, and Roman usage, of placing the lessons after all twelve psalms.

This moderation and pastoral good sense, so characteristic of Benedict and his *Rule*, also led to the suppression of all-night vigils in the Benedictine cursus (see ch. 9).

Although the office of Benedict was no more than a revision of the Roman cursus, especially the psalter, with the addition of elements from the office of RM, it did not succeed in supplanting older Roman usages in The City itself. And it is those usages, and not Benedict's office, from which the later Roman breviary derived. But in monasteries throughout the Latin West, the adoption of Benedict's wise *Rule* brought with it his revision of the Roman cursus, and by the second millenium the office of RB had become *the* monastic office of the Western Church.

---

[55]For a more detailed analysis see de Vogüé, *La Règle de S. Benoît* V, esp. ch. 9, and Mitchell, "The Liturgical Code," 397ff.

# 8

# THE CATHEDRAL HOURS IN THE WEST

Our earliest evidence for cathedral hours in the West is both later and vaguer than that for the East. Apart from Winkler's classic study on cathedral vespers,[1] this material has never been subjected to an exhaustive analysis, and such is obviously beyond the scope of this book. So I shall limit myself to what can be gleaned from the fourth to sixth century sources.

## Milan[2]

Ambrose (339–397) witnesses to the existence of cathedral services in Milan, where he was bishop from 374 until his death in 397. The meager available references indicate that Ambrose's Church knew the usual psalmody at the beginning and end of the day, as well as at night: "The psalm is the blessing of the people, the praise of God . . . the voice of the Church . . . a weapon at night, a teacher by day. . . . The break of day echoes with a psalm, its close resounds with one," he tells us in *Explan. ps. 1, 9*.[3]

[1] Winkler, "Über die Kathedralvesper."
[2] I am following V. Monachino, *S. Ambrogio e la cura pastorale a Milano nel secolo IV* (Milan: Centro Ambrosiano di documentazione e studi religiosi, 1973) 139–151.
[3] CSEL 64, 7.

## 1. Matins:

In *Expositio ps. 118*, 19:22, 30, 32,[4] Ambrose gives the usual symbolism for prayer at sunup, and affirms this to be a daily common synaxis that Christians were expected to attend:

> [30] . . .let us anticipate the sunrise, let us hasten to its beginning before-hand, let us say: behold, here I am. The Sun of Justice wishes and waits to be anticipated. . . . Be sure to anticipate this sun which you see, "rise sleeper and arise from the dead and Christ shall give you light" [Eph 5:14]. If you anticipate this sun before it rises, you receive Christ the giver of light. It is he who shines in the secrecy of your heart, he who says to you, "In the night my spirit kept watch before you" [Is 26:9]; the morning light shall shed light in times of darkness, if you meditate on the words of God. For when you meditate [on them], there is light, and seeing not a temporal light but the light of grace, you say: "For your commandments are a light" [Is 26:9]. When therefore the day finds you meditating on the divine word, and so worthy a work of prayer and psalmody has delighted your mind, you say again to the Lord Jesus: "You make the outgoings of the morning and evening rejoice" [Ps 64:9].
>
> [32] . . . In the morning hasten to church, bring the first fruits of your pious devotion; and afterwards, if worldly affairs summon you, you will not be prevented from saying, "My eyes anticipated the morn-ing, to meditate on your words" [Ps 118:148]. . . . How pleasant it is to begin the day with hymns and canticles, with the Beatitudes which you read in the gospel. . . .

In these passages Ambrose cites some of the traditional components of classical cathedral morning prayer—Ps 118:148, Is 26:9, canticles—as well as the Beatitudes. Elsewhere he repeats the Sun of Justice symbolism, and refers to psalms and hymns.[5] And it is well known that Ambrose him-self composed hymns for use at the hours.

## 2. Vespers:

In *Hexaemeron (Exameron)* V, 12:36, Ambrose speaks of closing the day with a celebration of the psalms,[6] and in *Expos. ps. 118*, 8:48, describ-ing the Christian's day, he refers to the Eucharist at noon on some days, and to the "evening sacrifice" (Ps 140:2), which suggests the use of that classic vesper psalm in Milanese cathedral evensong.[7] In *De virginibus* III, 4:18 Ambrose cites Ps 118:164, "Seven times a day I praised you," and

---

[4]CSEL 62, 433, 437–439.
[5]*De Helia et ieiunio* 15:5, CSEL 32/2, 445.
[6]CSEL 32/1, 170.
[7]CSEL 62, 180.

Matt 26:41, "Watch and pray, lest you enter into temptation;" and speaks of private prayer on rising, when we go out, before and after meals, and "at the hour of incense, when at last we are going to rest."[8] The reference may just be to the hour of the evening offering of incense in the temple in Ex 30:8. It might also be the earliest western evidence for the use of incense at vespers, along with the testimony of the Spanish poet Prudentius' (348–after 405) *Hymnus ad incensum lucernae.*[9] Finally, Augustine in his *Confessions* IX, 12 (31) reminds us that Ambrose composed the vesperal hymn *Deus creator omnium,* probably sung at every evening prayer in Milan.

### 3. Vigils:

Ambrose also makes reference to prayer at night, apparently private prayer at home.[10] And there were public all-night vigils on certain occasions, as we shall see in the following chapter.

## Rome

References to a cathedral office in Rome and environs are even less precise. Indeed, as I said in the previous chapter, we cannot even be sure that the cathedral-monastic distinction is applicable there. In that chapter I examined Cassian's reference to lauds followed by Ps 50 at the morning office "throughout Italy . . . in all the churches" (*Inst.* III, 6). And Arnobius the Younger, an African who lived as a monk in Rome in the middle of the fifth century, says in his *Commentary on Ps 148* that Ps 148 is sung daily, at dawn: ". . . We who daily, throughout the whole world, as soon as the dawn of day begins to show its very first signs, by the sound of this psalm call upon everything in heaven and on earth to praise and bless God."[11]

Jerome was in Rome from 382 to 385. His *Letter 107, 9,* to Leta, though largely concerned with the spiritual formation of Leta's daughter, contains elements that could refer to cathedral prayer. "Hymns" are specified in the morning, and "the evening sacrifice" at the hour of lamplighting. The virgin should

> . . . rise at night for prayers and psalms; sing hymns in the morning;
> at the third, sixth, and ninth hours stand in the [battle] lines like a

[8]PL 16, 225.
[9]CSEL 61, 25–32.
[10]*Expos. ps. 118,* 7:31, 8:45–52, CSEL 62, 145, 178–183; *Explan. ps. 36,* 65, CSEL 64, 124.
[11]PL 53, 566.

warrior of Christ; and with lamp lit, offer the evening sacrifice. So
let the day pass, and so let the night find her at work. Let reading
follow prayer, and prayer reading.[12]

Just south of Rome, Uranius' letter on the death of Paulinus (d. 431),
bishop of Nola in Campagna, refers to matins, to preparing "a light *(lu-
cernam)* for my Christ" at "the time of the evening *(lucernariae)* devotion," as well as to keeping vigil with the dying saint.[13]

Elsewhere in Italy Rufinus of Aquileia (d. 410), well-traveled in Italy
and the East, affirms in his *Apologia in S. Hieronymum* II, 35 that "every
Church all over the world *(omnis ecclesia per orbem terrarum)"* sings the
canticle of Dan 3[14]—undoubtedly in matins, since that is where we see
it almost everywhere as a standard OT canticle on Sundays and feasts.


## North Africa

Augustine in his *Confessions* V, 9 speaks of his saintly and beloved
mother Monica (d. 387) "twice a day, morning and evening, coming to
your church without fail . . . in order that she might hear you in your
words, and you her in her prayers." And in his *Enarr. in ps. 49,* 23 he
implies the existence of cathedral matins and vespers when describing the
attitude of those who look on religious practice as a sort of commerce
with God, saying to themselves: "I'll get up every day, go to church, join
in the singing of one morning hymn, a second at vespers, a third or fourth
at home; daily I offer the sacrifice of praise, and make an offering to my
God."[15] He also speaks of one who like an "ant of God gets up every day,
runs to church, prays, listens to the reading, sings the hymn, thinks over
what he has heard . . ."[16] Furthermore, Augustine was a great lover of
church singing, psalmody, and hymns, and we can perhaps presume that
his praises of music signals its importance to the cathedral office of his
Church.[17]

The *Vita Fulgentii* 29 (59) attributed to Fulgentius' student, the Car-
thaginian deacon Ferrandus, recounts how the great theologian Fulgen-

[12]CSEL 55, 300.
[13]4, PL 53, 861–862.
[14]PL 21, 613–614.
[15]PL 36, 580; cf. *Enarr. 2 in ps. 33,* 14, PL 36, 316.
[16]*Enarr. in ps. 66,* 3, PL 36, 805.
[17]Cf. F. van der Meer, *Augustine the Bishop* (London: Sheed and Ward, 1978) 325–337.

tius (467–533), bishop of Ruspe, a small town in the North African Province of Byzacena, instructed the clergy to chant and pronounce well the psalmody, and "ruled that each week all the clergy and widows, and whoever of the laity was able, were to fast Wednesday and Friday, ordering everyone to be present at the daily vigils, fasts, and morning and evening prayers."[18]

## Gaul in the Fourth and Fifth Centuries

Much fuller evidence is available for the cathedral office in Gaul. Already in the fourth century the widely-traveled Bishop Hilary of Poitiers (d. 367), commenting, like Eusebius before him, on Ps 64:9, says that "The progress of the Church in the delights of morning and evening hymns are a great sign of God's mercy in the Church. The day is begun with God's prayers, the day is ended with God's hymns."[19]

A century later canon 14 of the Council of Vannes, Brittany, in 465, obliges priests to be present at the "morning hymns *(matutini hymni)*," and canon 15 exhorts that there be a uniform usage and rule for the office and psalmody.[20] In the same period we have our first lectionaries for use, apparently, in the Divine Office, such as the one prepared by Musaeus (d. ca. 460), a presbyter of Marseilles, for his bishop St. Venerius.[21]

In the Rhone Valley, we see matins and vespers plus the little hours in Lent, at least in Orange under Bishop Eutropius (ca. 463—after 475).[22] The *Life of St. Severius*, a priest at Vienne (d. after 450), also refers to a full cursus, distributed among the churches of the city: matins and nocturns in the cathedral, terce and sext at St. Stephen's Basilica, none at St. Lawrence's, vespers and duodecima at St. Alban's outside the walls.[23]

---

[18]PL 65, 147.

[19]*Tract. in ps. 64*, 21, CSEL 22, 244.

[20]Mansi 7, 955.

[21]Gennadius, *Liber de viris inlustribus* 80, ed. E. C. Richardson (TU 14/1, Leipzig: J. C. Hinrich, 1896) 88–89; cf. G. Dix, *The Shape of the Liturgy* (Westminster: Dacre Press, 1945) 558–559.

[22]*Vita S. Eutropii, Bulletin du Comité des monuments écrits de l'histoire de France, Histoire* I (1849) 57, cited in H. G. Beck, *The Pastoral Care of Souls in South-East France during the Sixth Century* (Analecta Gregoriana 51, Rome: Pontifical Gregorian University, 1950) 117 note 94. I owe several references in this section to Beck.

[23]*Vita S. Severii Viennensis* 8, *Analecta Bollandiana* 5 (1886) 421–422; Beck, *The Pastoral Care of Souls*, 117. However, the *Vita* itself seems not to antedate the 7th c. *(ibid.* xlv–xlvi).

## Gallic Offices in the Sixth Century:
## The Church under the Franks

By the sixth century our evidence for the cathedral office in Gaul becomes more frequent, more complete, more cohesive, especially in the Rhone Valley. But first let us look at the evidence for the Frankish Kingdoms of Clovis (d. 511) and his heirs.

Tours, on the left bank of the Loire, came under the Franks as Clovis extended his conquests south, crossing the Loire into Visigothic Gaul in 507. One of our main sources of information on the history and usages of the Church under the Franks is St. Gregory, bishop of Tours (538–594), at that time the religious center of Gaul. In his *History of the Franks* X, 31 he informs us that Injurius, bishop of Tours (529–546) introduced terce and sext into the cathedral cursus of his Church, and in *De virtutibus S. Iuliani*, 20, he speaks of evensong as *"gratia vespertina,"* a name that recalls the *epilychnios eucharistia* of the Cappadocians.[24]

More interesting is Gregory's *Vitae patrum* VI, 7 on the death, in 551, of his uncle St. Gaul, bishop of Clermont. The passage describes a Sunday morning office held in church at dawn *(albascente jam coelo)*. To the dying bishop's question about what was being sung in church *(quid in ecclesia psalleret)*, those with him replied:

> . . . "They are chanting the blessing *(benedictio)*." And when Ps 50 and the blessing had been chanted, and the *alleluiaticum* with the *capitellum* finished, he completed matins. With the office done, he said: "We say goodbye to you, brethren." And saying this he opened his arms and sent his spirit, eager for heaven, to the Lord.[25]

The recurrence of the cathedral offices of morning praise and evensong at deathbed scenes of the saints in both East and West (St. Macrina, St. Gregory Nazianzen, St. Gaul) is but one more sign of the great importance assigned this liturgical prayer in Antiquity.

There is general agreement that the *benedictio* of this text is the *Benedicite* or *Benedictiones* of Dan 3, a standard Sunday matins canticle in East and West. The *alleluiaticum* is most likely the lauds Pss 148–150. We are already familiar with the *capitellum* or psalmic intercessory verse(s). The resulting outline of matins is close to what we see in other Gallic sources of the period:

> Ps 50
> OT canticle: Dan 3

[24]MGH, SRM III, 519 and SRM I, 573.
[25]MGH, *Serm.* I, 685 = PL 71, 1034.

Lauds: Pss 148-150
Capitellum

## Southern Gaul under the Visigoths

It is in the sixth century in the region of the Rhone Valley under the influence of the great bishop St. Caesarius of Arles (503-542) that our evidence first becomes rich and coherent enough to provide a basis for at least a general, synthetic view of the cathedral hours in Southern Gaul.

### I. THE GALLIC SYNODS

One of the great shifts in world history occurred toward the end of the fifth century, as the Roman Empire in the West came to an end in 476 under the pressure of the newly forming federation of barbarian kingdoms. During this period, much of our information for the office in the Visigothic Kingdom under Alaric (d. 507) in Southern Gaul and the Iberian peninsula comes from the canons of numerous local synods held in Gaul as the Church tried to adjust to the new situation.[26]

#### 1. Agde (506):

One of the most important of these local councils, convoked at Agde in September 506 under the leadership of Caesarius, gathered bishops from every province of the Kingdom of Alaric—at that time Gaul except for the North and Burgundy controlled by the Franks and the Burgundians, and most of Spain.

Canon 30 of this synod decrees:

> And since it is fitting that church order be kept equally by all, strive to see that after the antiphon, collects *(collectiones)* be said in order by the bishops or presbyters, as is done everywhere, and let the morning *(hymni matutini)* and evening hymns be sung every day, and at the end of the morning and evening services *(missae)*,[27]after the hymns, let *capitella* from the psalms be said; and at vespers after a collect *(collecta)* by the bishop let the people be dismissed with a blessing.[28]

---

[26]For the circumstances of these councils see J. Hefele and H. Leclerq, *Histoire des conciles* II.2-III.2 (Paris: Letouzey et Ané, 1908-1910).

[27]On the various meanings of *missae*, see K. Gamber, *Missa Romensis* (Studia patristica et liturgica 33, Regensburg: Pustet, 1970) 170-186. Here *missae* means chants and prayers (*ibid.* 185), though Gamber's explanation of *missa* in the *Rule* of Caesarius is unsatisfactory.

[28]Mansi 8, 329-330.

So the bishop and his presbyters held matins and vespers daily for the people. The services comprised antiphons (undoubtedly psalmody), each followed by a collect. This is the first reference to "psalm collects," collections of which have survived from Africa (the earliest), Italy, and Spain, from the fifth, sixth, and seventh centuries.[29] Each hour was concluded with a hymn and intercessions: we already saw in chapter 6 that the *capitella* were intercessory verses from the psalms.

Were the lauds psalms a part of these *"matutini hymni"*? Most probably. In chapter 3 we saw in Eusebius and Egeria a similar expression to describe the Eastern cathedral office of morning praise, it was usual for biblical psalms to be called "hymns" or "antiphons," and Cassian (*Inst.* III, 6) calls Pss 148–150 "the morning hymns" in use in Gaul and Italy.[30]

### 2. Epaon (517):

Canon 27 of the Synod of Epaon (Eponum, Epao) in the Rhone Valley south of Vienne, convoked in 517 by the recently converted King Sigismund of the Burgundians, rules that the offices be celebrated in provincial churches according to the order used by the metropolitans of the province.[31]

### 3. Vaison II (529):

In 529, canon 3 of the Second Synod of Vaison (in Vico Vaseni, Vasio), also in Burgundy but part of the ecclesiastical Province of Arles and hence presided over by Caesarius, orders the *Kyrie eleison* added to matins, vespers, and Mass, as was customary "in the Apostolic See and throughout all the provinces of the East and of Italy."[32] Just how the *Kyrie* was used—as a litanic response, or simply repeated three times as in the monastic offices of Aurelian—is not indicated. Furthermore, canon 1 provided for a sort of rudimentary seminary. It orders that the presbyters of every parish receive into their household young lectors to be trained in psalmody and reading, in order to secure the succession of the clergy.[33]

---

[29]See L. Brou, "Où en est la question des 'Psalter Collects'?" SP 2 (TU 64, Berlin: Akademie-Verlag, 1957) 17–20; *id.* and A. Wilmart, *The Psalter Collects from V–VIth Century Sources* (HBS 83, London: Harrison and Sons, 1949); H. de Sainte Marie, "The Psalter Collects," EL 65 (1951) 105–110; C. Mohrmann, "Apropos des collects du psautier," *Vigiliae Christianae* 6 (1952) 1–19; J. Pinell, *Liber orationum psalmographicus* (Monumenta Hispaniae sacra, serie liturgica 9, Barcelona, 1972); P. Salmon, *The Breviary through the Centuries* (Collegeville: The Liturgical Press, 1962) 55–59; F. Vandenbroucke, "Sur la lecture chrétienne du psautier au Vᵉ siècle," *Sacris erudiri* 5 (1953) 5–26.

[30]On Cassian see chapters 6, 10.

[31]Mansi 8, 562.

[32]*Ibid.* 727.

[33]*Ibid.* 726.

## 4. Tours II (567):

With the consent of the Frankish King Charibert, the Second Council of Tours on November 18, 567, decrees in canon 18 the same order of psalmody in the Basilica of St. Martin and all other churches, and determines the number of psalms:

> On summer days[34] let six antiphons of two psalms [each] be done. In August let there be vigils (*manicationes*[35]), because in this month there are the feasts and *missae* of the saints; in September, seven antiphons of two psalms; in October, eight of three psalms; in November, nine of three psalms; in December, ten of three psalms; in January and February likewise, up until Easter. It is also possible for one to do more, another less, according to ability. Still, twelve psalms are set for matins, since the statutes of the Fathers have ordered it, and at sext let six psalms be said with alleluia, and twelve at *duodecima*, likewise with alleluia, which also they taught, as shown by the angel. If twelve psalms are done at *duodecima*, why not twelve likewise at matins? Whoever says fewer than twelve at matins, let him fast until vespers. . . .

What we see here is an already highly monasticized cathedral office, not unlike the cathedralized monastic usage in the rules of Arles. Indeed, one can say that in the West the distinction between the two types of services has already begun to blur.

Canon 23 of the same synod declares that besides the Ambrosian hymns "in the canon *(in canone)*," other suitable hymns may also be sung provided their authors' names are indicated in the margin,[36] undoubtedly to forestall the unwitting introduction of suspect authors into the prayer of the Church. So when some Iberian synods exclude all non-biblical chants in the office, this was apparently a later move against Priscillianism, and must not be interpreted as proof that no sixth-century offices in Gaul and Spain had non-scriptural hymns.[37] As noted in chapter 6, there were hymns in the office of Arles as described in the rules of Caesarius and Aurelian, and the Spanish poet Prudentius' (348–after 405) *Hymn at the Evening Incense* seems to indicate the same for the cathedral office in Spain long before these prohibitions appear.[38] Furthermore the *Te deum* testified to

---

[34]The text in Mansi 9, 796, reads "in diebus festis," but others give what seems a more coherent reading: "in diebus aestivis." See S. Bäumer, *Histoire du Bréviaire* (Paris: Letouzey et Ané, 1905) I, 225 note 3.

[35]The verb *manicare* from *mane* (morning), means to come in the morning. So *manicatio* means early rising and, by extension, the chanting of the early morning service.

[36]Mansi 9, 803.

[37]Cf. Bäumer, *Histoire du Bréviaire* I, 224.

[38]See note 9 above.

in the rules of Arles for matins, a service with unmistakable cathedral traits, is witnessed to also in a letter of Cyprian, Bishop of Toulon, to Maximus, bishop of Geneva, written between 524 and 533: "But in the hymn which the whole Church throughout the entire universe has received and sings, we pray daily: *Tu rex gloriae, Christus; tu Patri sempiternus es filius.* . . ."[39] As Bradshaw rightly cautions, we must take the reference to "the entire universe" with a grain of salt.[40] But the text at least proves that the chant was known in Provence and Burgundy, areas into which the sons of Clovis extended Frankish control after his death in 511. The Kingdom of the Burgundians was annexed in 534, Provence was ceded by the Ostrogoths in 537. And even when under the control of different barbarian kingdoms, the various church provinces of this Frankish-Gothic region were in close ecclesiastical contact.

### 5. Narbonne (589):

Finally, on November 1, 589, canon 2 of a provincial synod at Narbonne, not far from Agde, in that part of Southern Gaul occupied by the Goths, ordered the *Gloria Patri* added at the end of each psalm or section of the longer psalms.[41]

## II. NON-CANONICAL SOURCES: ST. CAESARIUS OF ARLES

Our other sources from the Rhone Valley in the same period only confirm this impression of a church life of great intensity and importance in the life of the people, with an increasingly full and sophisticated cycle of cathedral offices.

At Vienne, for instance, we have a reference to psalmody in two choirs from St. Avitus (d. 518), bishop there, in his *De virginitate:* "Nam quoties sanctum compleveris ordine cursum, alternos recinens dulci modulamine psalmos."[42] At nearby Lyons, too, the office was done in two choirs, as the epitaph of St. Nicetius, Bishop of Lyons (d. 573) recalls.[43] Nicetius is depicted by Gregory of Tours, *Liber vitae patrum* VIII, 4, at matins in his cathedral: two antiphons followed by a responsorial psalm intoned by a deacon are mentioned, as well as "the Sunday canticles."[44] But far

---

[39]MGH, *Epistolae* III = *Epist. merowingici et karolini aeui* I, 436.

[40]*Daily Prayer* 119.

[41]Mansi 9, 1015.

[42]U. Chevalier, *Oeuvres complètes de S. Avit* (Lyons: Librairie générale catholique et classique E. Vitte, 1890) 92.

[43]MGH, SRM III, 519.

[44]*Ibid.* I, 694.

and away the most important source after the synodal canons are the homilies of St. Caesarius of Arles. Caesarius served as Metropolitan of Arles for almost forty years (503–542) and had enormous influence on the Church throughout Gaul in his lifetime, when the world that was to become medieval Latin Christianity was aborning. He was also the greatest Latin preacher since Augustine, and a veritable Western Chrysostom for the innumerable tidbits of liturgical information he provides in his sermons.[45]

That the Church of Arles knew a cathedral office under Caesarius is beyond challenge. In *Sermon 80*, 3, he tells his flock that "one who is faithful to the prayer and psalmody in church is like one who seeks to offer God an odor of sweetness from the holy thurible of the heart." As for those unlettered peasants, both men and women, who complained that they couldn't remember the prayers and chants of the services, Caesarius tells them roundly in *Sermon 6*, 3, that they find it easy enough to remember and sing diabolical and lascivious love songs. "They'd do much better to learn the creed, the Lord's Prayer, and other antiphons, and to learn and remember Pss 50 and 90, and say them more often. . . ." His own devotion to the hours is testified to in his *Vita* I, 11, where we learn that while still a deacon under Bishop Eonius he was the first in church for matins and the last to leave.[46] Later, *Vita* I, 19 informs us how as bishop he made provision for the active participation of the people in the offices:

> He added also and provided that the lay inhabitants memorize psalms and hymns, and chant, some in Greek, others in Latin, sequences *(prosas)* and antiphons with a high and melodious voice, like the clergy, so as not to have any time to waste on gossip while in church.

### 1. Vigils:

There is a certain amount of confusion in Caesarius' writings concerning the first synaxis of the day, because it seems to have been a composite office of vigils followed immediately by morning praise or matins in the strict sense of the term. He tells us that matins, which he usually calls vigils (*Sermon 76*, 3; *86*, 5; *188*, 6; *195*, 4; *196*, 2; *211*, 5; *212*, 6), began in the early morning (*196*, 2; *212*, 6) before dawn (*72*, 1). The office lasted about half an hour (*76*, 3), and included Ps 50 (*76*, 3), the chanting of psalms (*72*, 1), prayers (*72*, 1-3; *76*, 1), scriptural lessons (*72*, 1; *76*, 3; *118*, 1; *196*, 2, 4), and sometimes a homily (*76*, 3; *195*, 4; *211*, 5; *212*, 6).

---

[45]They are in CCL 103-104. I shall simply refer to them by number in the text.
[46]Caesarius' *Vita* is in MGH, SRM III, 457-501. See also *Serm. 86*, 5 and *196*, 2.

But if we sort out this jumble of elements with the help of the information Caesarius provides, it appears that matins in the strict sense was
the short office about a half-hour long referred to in *Sermon 76, 3*. So
I would interpret Caesarius to mean that the cathedral cursus in Arles
opened with a nocturnal vigil, followed immediately by matins, for the
following reasons:

1) There is no way in which all the elements enumerated
by Caesarius as comprising vigils-matins could have
been accomplished in a half-hour.

2) When there was to be preaching, Caesarius tells us that
Ps 50 was said "earlier *(maturius)*," so that the office
might not drag on beyond the usual time of dismissal, lest the people be late for work (*75, 3; 118, 1*).
This can only mean that Ps 50 was the end of vigils
or, more likely, the beginning of matins, and that
Caesarius was in the habit of delaying his sermon until then, by which time even the laggards would have
arrived for the obligatory morning prayer. Otherwise
what he says in *Sermons 76, 3*, and *118, 1* about beginning Ps 50 earlier on days when there was preaching would make no sense. For if the homily preceded
the opening of matins with Ps 50, the psalm could be
left at its usual time without causing any delay in the
dismissal, which was the point of it all.

3) Presumably in Arles and elsewhere the laity were expected to be present at cathedral morning prayer. But
since Caesarius constantly exhorts his faithful to come
to the morning synaxis "earlier *(maturius)*," something
must have preceded the half-hour matins service (*76,
3; 86, 5; 188, 6; 195, 4; 196, 2; 211, 5; 212, 6*). Hence
the lessons he refers to in the context of vigils-matins
must have been before Ps 50. One would normally
have expected the preaching to have accompanied
these readings, but Caesarius delayed it until matins
in order to reach a larger audience.

4) This is confirmed by what we saw above in chapter
6 in the cathedral hours of Arles described in the rules
of Caesarius and Aurelian. There were no scriptural
lessons in matins. Rather, they were part of the *missae* of lessons, psalmody, and prayer that *preceded* the
morning office.

So I would agree with Bradshaw that the readings at the early morning synaxis were a part of vigils that preceded matins,[47] and not part of the morning office or matins in the strict sense. Ps 50 was moved up because of the homily, which lengthened matins, so that the dismissal would not be delayed beyond the usual time.

Apparently, then, it was customary for the faithful to drift in to vigils when they arose, somewhat like the sporadic assistance at "forty-hours exposition" in Latin churches of later generations, though it was undoubtedly bad form not to be there at least by the opening of matins with Ps 50. So Caesarius constantly exhorts the people to show greater fervor by coming as early as possible to the vigil.

Most of the liturgical information in Caesarius' homilies concerns these vigils, to which he assigned great importance, undoubtedly because of the primacy of proclaiming and preaching the Word of God in Caesarius' pastoral-liturgical program (*72*, 1; *76*, 3; *118*, 1; *192*, 2, 4). Nor was this emphasis on the Word, so characteristic of Caesarius, limited to the public services. In *Sermon 6*, 2–3, he tells his hearers they could well occupy their evenings reading or, if illiterate, listening to the reading of the Scriptures, instead of wasting time on endless banquets and drinking half the night.

The vigil lessons were interspersed with psalmody (72, 1), and the prayers following the psalms were said kneeling, as the faithful had to be reminded in *Sermon 76*, 1 (cf. *76*, 3):

> I beg you dearly beloved and admonish you with fatherly care that as often as a prayer is said, anyone who perhaps cannot kneel because of some infirmity should at least not neglect to bend the back or bow the head. What good does it do you to sing the psalms faithfully if, when you stop singing, you do not want to entreat God? Let each one who has ceased chanting pray and entreat the Lord with all humility, so that what he utters with the lips he may deserve with God's help to fulfill in deed. Just as singing the psalms, brethren, is like sowing a field, praying is like the sower who cultivates it by burying and covering the ground. . . . So whenever a person stops chanting, let him not stop praying if he wants a harvest of divine mercy to grow in the field of his heart.

Since we already know from the Synod of Agde that there were collects, what we have here is undoubtedly the traditional prayer-structure of later Latin services: the command to kneel, silent prayer kneeling, the command to rise, and the collect.

---

[47]*Daily Prayer* 121–122.

*Flectamus genua!*
    all kneel and pray in silence
*Levate!*
    all rise

*Collect* by the presiding bishop or presbyter

This text also expresses Caesarius' theology of the Liturgy of the Hours. In ancient usage, as de Vogüé has noted, the psalmody, like the lessons, was God's Word to us, not ours to him.[48] Personal prayer is what followed each psalm, stimulated by the meditative recitation of the Sacred Word.

### 2. Matins:

As we just saw, matins apparently opened with Ps 50, lasted about half an hour, and occasionally included a homily, which, with remarkable candor since he was the homilist, Caesarius tells us the people found annoying (76, 3). If there was preaching, the opening Ps 50 was begun earlier than usual, so that the dismissal might take place at the usual time (76, 3; 118, 1) and the people could be about their work on time.

The canticle of Dan 3 was also sung in the services, undoubtedly at matins. In *Sermon 69*, 1, Caesarius implies it was proper to the festive office: "You have heard in the *Benedictiones*, and you have heard on every feast when they are read, how everything in heaven and on earth praises God. . . ." This agrees with what we saw in chapter 6 concerning matins in the *Rules* of Caesarius and Aurelian.

Finally, we learn from *Sermon 76*, 2 that a prayer of blessing was preceded by the command to bow down (*"inclinate capita vestra"*), as is still customary today—though even this seemed to tax the strength of Caesarius' indifferent congregation: "I both advise and urge, brethren, that as often as you are told to bow down for a blessing, don't make it such a burden for you to incline your heads, for you are not bowing down before man but before God."

Can we pull together these elements of cathedral matins, almost all of which seemed to cause boredom if not outright annoyance to poor Caesarius' motley flock? The basic outline seems to have been somewhat as follows:

Ps 50
(Festive matins: canticle of Dan 3)
Antiphons: psalms with antiphons or alleluia, each
    followed by silent prayer kneeling and a collect

[48]de Vogüé, *Le Règle de S. Benoît* VII, 206–221.

(Homily on some occasions)
(Festive: *Te deum*)
Hymn
Psalmic intercessions *(capitella)*
Prayer of Inclination

Though the cathedral sources do not specify the nature of the antiphons, it is not unreasonable to suppose they were like what we saw in the obviously cathedralized matins in the monastic rules of Caesarius and Aurelian, i.e., that the antiphons included such classic cathedral elements as biblical canticles (festive) and the traditional Pss 148–150 of lauds. Probable also would be the *Gloria in excelsis* on Sundays and major feasts. It is a standard element in festive matins just about everywhere in East and West, including the Gallic monastic rules, and there is no reason to suppose its absence here. But the two traditions clearly differed in some respects, for cathedral—but not monastic—matins follows the Italian usage of Ps 50 as invitatory of matins.

### 3. The little hours:

In *Vita* I, 15, we read that Caesarius introduced monastic hours into the cathedral cursus on becoming bishop in 503: ". . . he immediately arranged for the clergy to sing the offices of terce, sext, and none daily in St. Stephen's Basilica, so that if some secular or penitent wanted to perform a good work, he could attend the office daily without any excuse."[49]

### 4. Vespers:

We have much less information on cathedral vespers—a situation characteristic of Western sources, as Winkler has shown in her definitive study on the topic.[50]

From Caesarius' *Vita* we learn that vespers is called lucernarium (I, 43, 59), could include a homily (I, 59), and concluded with the bishop's blessing (I, 43; II, 16). Not a word, however, about Ps 140.[51]

In the following citation from *Sermon 136*, 1–4, Caesarius is speaking of *duodecima*, the monastic evening psalmody which in Southern Gaul followed the cathedral service of vespers or lucernarium. He not only applies the familiar light theme to evening prayer. He also affirms that Ps 103 (104) "throughout the world is said in both churches and monasteries at the twelfth hour *(duodecima)*." We saw it to be the invitatory psalm of monastic *duodecima* in the rules of Arles, and it still serves the same

[49]See note 46 above.
[50]"Über die Kathedralvesper."
[51]See note 46 above.

purpose in the monastic synaxis of Byzantine Sabaitic vespers (see below, chapter 17). Note that Caesarius considers this monastic office part of the cathedral cursus:

> [136, 1]Dearly beloved brethren, that psalm which is recited in both churches and monasteries throughout the whole world at the twelfth hour is so well known to almost everyone that the majority of humankind have it by heart. . . . [2]As you know, that psalm contains: "The sun knows its setting; you bring darkness and it is night" (Ps 103: 19–20). . . . [3]Now what the psalmist said, "The sun knows its setting," is not to be taken concerning that sun, but with regard to that one of whom the prophet says: "For those who fear your name there will arise the sun of justice with healing in its wings" (Mal 4:2). Of him we read in Solomon that the wicked will say: "The sun did not rise for us" (Wis 5:6). Therefore the true sun of justice is Christ. He knew his setting when he lay down in his passion for our salvation; for when he was crucified, night and darkness took hold of the souls of his disciples. . . . [4]At the crucifixion of Christ when the darkness of unbelief took possession of the souls of the apostles, those spiritual beasts began to go about seeking to devour souls. However, while they went about: "The sun rises and they congregate" (Ps 103:22). What is the sense of this "The sun rises, and they congregate," unless that Christ rose and all the spiritual beasts were gathered together? "And they lay down in their dens" (Ps 103:22). For when at the sun's rising the splendor of faith again began to shine in the apostles, those spiritual beasts lay down in their dens. . . .

## Spain

Our earliest, albeit oblique reference to cathedral hours in the Iberian peninsula comes from the intrepid pilgrim nun Egeria. Although it is now agreed that our famous pilgrim was indeed named Egeria and was roaming the Holy Land in 381–384, her homeland is still disputed. There are two theses: Gaul (Aquitaine or Narbonnaise), and Galicia in Northwest Spain, with the evidence running in favor of the latter.[52]

Speaking of Jerusalem vespers in chapter 24:4 of her diary, she says ". . . at four o'clock they have *lychnikon*, as they call it here, though we

---

[52]For Egeria see chapter 3 on the cathedral office in the East. The latest edition is P. Maraval (ed.), Egérie, *Journal de voyage (Itinéraire)* (SC 296, Paris: Cerf, 1982). On the question of her homeland, see *ibid.* 21, 38, and P. Devos, "Une nouvelle Egérie," *Analecta Bollandiana* 101 (1983) 57–58. It would also seem that she was indeed a religious, in spite of doubts to the contrary (Devos 54–57, against Maraval 23–27).

say *lucernare* (quod appellant licnicon, nam nos dicimus lucernare)." She seems to have found nothing notably different about the service at home and in Jerusalem except the name.

I have already cited the fourth-century Spanish poet Prudentius' (348–after 405) *Hymnus ad incensum lucernae* as possibly indicating a use of incense in Iberian vespers at that time.[53]

### I. ISIDORE OF SEVILLE

Not until two centuries later does another ecclesiastical author provide us some information on Iberian cathedral services. As we saw in chapter 6, St. Isidore of Seville, last of the Latin Fathers, wrote his *De ecclesiasticis officiis* while bishop of that city from 600 to 636. In Book I, 7 and 9, he refers to such elements of the cathedral offices as antiphonal and responsorial psalmody, as well as *laudes*—not Pss 148–150 but a short alleluia responsory of a few verses (I, 13).

In I, 17 he compares the blessing of the priest, which, as noted elsewhere, terminated the offices, to the blessing in Num 6:24. For the rest, among the scriptural texts he cites to justify the offices are some of the classic psalms and canticles: Is 26:9, Ps 118:62, for vigils (I, 22); Pss 118:148 and 62:7–8 for morning prayer (I, 23); Ps 140:2 for vespers (I, 20); and Ps 131:3–5 for compline (I, 21). But he gives no details about the content or structure of the hours.[54]

### II. THE IBERIAN COUNCILS

The Iberian peninsula also furnishes a large corpus of canonical legislation concerning the cathedral celebration of the hours of prayer.[55]

#### 1. Toledo I (400):

Canon 9 of the First Council of Toledo, held during September of the year 400 in still Roman Spain, forbids the celebration of lucernarium except in church unless a bishop, presbyter, or deacon is present.[56]

#### 2. Terragona (516):

A century later the Spanish provinces occupied by the Visigoths knew a period of prosperity in 511–526 during the regency of Theodoric, King

[53]Note 9 above.
[54]PL 83, 743–760.
[55]The sources are listed in Pinell, "El oficio hispáno-visigótico," 386–389.
[56]Mansi 3, 1000.

of the Ostrogoths, and three synods were held, two of which interest us here. On November 6, 516, canon 7 of the Synod of Terragona orders the daily celebration of matins and vespers by a hebdomadary presbyter and deacon assigned to this ministry. But all are to be present at Saturday vespers, and the canon condemns any lack of clergy that would impede the celebration of *luminaria* (i.e., lucernarium) in the basilicas.[57]

### 3. Gerona (517):

A year later at Gerona, on June 8, canon 1 orders that throughout the Province of Terragona the *ordo psallendi* of the metropolitan church be followed, and canon 10 asks that the priest say the Our Father at the end of daily matins and vespers.[58]

### 4. Barcelona (ca. 540):

In the same metropolitan province Serius, archbishop of Terragona, held a provincial council at Barcelona around 540 which deals with details of the office:[59]

> 1) Ps 50 is to be said "before the canticle"—undoubtedly of matins (canon 1).
> 2) At the end of matins and vespers a blessing is to be imparted to the people (canon 2).
> 3) When a bishop is present, the presbyters say the orations (canon 5)—probably the collects of the psalms, Pinell suggests—the final collect and blessing being reserved to the bishop.[60]

### 5. Braga (563):

The Council of Braga in Galicia (now in Portugal), held in 563 when the area was under the Suevi with their recently converted King Ariamir, again insists on liturgical unity.[61] Canon 1 decrees that there be one order of psalmody in matins and vespers, adding, "and let no different, private or monastic customs be mixed with the ecclesiastical rule" (canon 1). Alas, as we know from the later history of the Liturgy of the Hours in the West, this pastorally wise resistance to the monasticization of the cathedral hours did not win the day. The very notion that there was ever any such thing as a cathedral office was eventually lost in the mists of history, as we shall

---

[57]Mansi 8, 542.
[58]*Ibid.* 549–550.
[59]Mansi 9, 109–110.
[60]Pinell, "El oficio hispáno-visigótico," 386 note 5.
[61]Mansi 9, 777–778.

see when we come to the liturgical reform of Vatican II, where some of those engaged in the reform of the Roman Breviary did not have a clue that the office had ever been or could be anything but a prayerbook for priests and a choir obligation for religious.

Canon 2 orders uniformity for the vigils or *missae* before feasts: all should do the same readings at them. Canon 3 seeks to enforce unity even in short formulae—greetings like *Dominus vobiscum* and the introductions to the lessons—and canon 12 forbids the chanting of non-scriptural compositions in church. This ancient principle, reintroduced here because of the struggle with Priscillianism, may be the reason for the enormous number of scriptural canticles in the Iberian offices.[62]

### 6. Toledo IV (633):

The Fourth Council of Toledo, convoked by King Sisenand on December 6, 633, gathered sixty-two bishops of Spain and the neighboring Province of Narbonne in Southern Gaul under the presidency of St. Isidore of Seville.[63] It, too, seeks to impose liturgical uniformity, this time on a considerably vaster scale: canon 2 decrees one order of psalmody and one use for vespers and matins in all the provinces of Spain and Southern Gaul. Other canons give further particulars:

1) The doxology in its Iberian form, *Gloria et honor Patri,* is to be sung at the end of each psalm (canons 15–16).

2) The *Gloria in excelsis* and other non-biblical hymns such as those of Ambrose or Hilarius may be admitted in the offices (canon 13).

3) Canon 14 says that the *Benedictiones* of Dan 3, sung by the Catholic Church throughout the whole world (undoubtedly at matins, though that is not stated), is neglected by some priests on Sundays and martyrs' feasts. This abuse is proscribed.

4) Other permissible components of the office listed are *missae,* prayers *(preces),* orations *(orationes),* commendations *(commendationes),* and the imposition of hands (canon 13). We have already seen what *missae* were in Spain.[64] The orations were undoubtedly the collects that followed the psalms and canticles, and concluded the offices. The imposition of hands refers to the final blessing. *Commendationes* in the

---

[62]See note 37 above, and Porter, "Cantica mozarabici officii."
[63]Canons in Mansi 10, 616–624.
[64]See chapter 6 at note 48.

Latin of the time means prayers for the departed, though I am unable to identify them further in the context of the Iberian hours. *Preces* probably refers to the petitionary verses seen in later Iberian sources under the names *miserationes* and *clamores.*[65]

### 7. Mérida (666):

Later cathedral vespers in Visigothic Spain (450–711) can be seen in canon 2 of the provincial synod of the Province of Lusitania held at Mérida on November 6, 666: "It is fitting therefore to observe also in our churches that which is done in other churches at vespers time: after the oblation of the light, let the vesperal psalm *(vespertinum)* be said, just before the hymn *(sonus)* on feast days."[66]

### 8. Toledo XI (675):

Finally, the Eleventh Council of Toledo on November 7, 675, reiterates in canon 3 the demand for uniformity in the order of psalmody, vespers, and matins in each province, following the usage of the metropolitan see. This also applied to monasteries, which had their own monastic horarium, but "it is not allowed to celebrate the other public offices, i.e. vespers, matins, or Mass, except as in the principal church," that is, the cathedral church of the province.[67]

### III. CONCLUSION

On the basis of the available evidence, scant as it sometimes is, and with notable lacunae, it is possible to draw some conclusions concerning the structure of cathedral vespers and matins in the Hispanic sources.

### 1. Iberian Vespers:

It is clear that Spain knew a light ritual, the *oblatio luminis,* at the beginning of vespers. This was followed by an evening psalm, the *vespertinum,* originally probably a fixed psalm, undoubtedly Ps 140, though later most Western offices opted for variety here as at lauds. There was also a hymn, the *sonus,* and the customary concluding intercessions and prayers. On the basis of the evidence we have seen, and by filling in a

---

[65]Porter, "Early Spanish Monasticism," L 12 (1934) 32–52 *passim;* texts in W. Meyer, *Die Preces der mozarabischen Liturgie* (Abhandlungen der königlichen Gesellschaft der Wissenschaften zu Göttingen. Philologisch-historische Klasse, n. F. Bd. 15. Nr. 3. Berlin: Weidmannsche Buchhandlung, 1914).

[66]Mansi 11, 77.

[67]*Ibid.* 138.

few gaps in it with the help of some later sources adduced by J. Pinell,[68] we can reconstruct Iberian cathedral vespers tentatively as follows:

> Oblation of the light
> Vesperal psalm with antiphon, doxology, and
> 　collect
> Hymn
> Supplication[69]
> Completuria (final prayer)
> Our Father
> Petition (embolism of Our Father)
> Blessing
> [Psallendum]

The light ritual or "oblation of the light" consisted, according to later Iberian sources, in the elevation of a lighted candle before the altar, with the proclamation, "In the name of Our Lord Jesus Christ, light and peace!" to which the people responded *"Deo gratias!"* This is what we see, for example, in our oldest extant Iberian liturgical formulary, the *Orationale* of Verona composed ca. 725, and in the letter of Eutherius, bishop of Osma, and Beatus of Liébana, against Elipandus, bishop of Toledo, written around 783–800.[70]

The *vespertinum* was later reduced to only the antiphon with a few verses, but Pinell presumes it was once the vesperal psalm.[71] Among the vesperal psalms in the later sources of the rite, in addition to Ps 140, we find the following, all reflecting the light theme of cathedral lucernarium:[72]

> Ps 35 (:10), "In you, O Lord, is the source of
> 　life; in your light we shall see light."
> Ps 26 (:1), "The Lord is my light and my salvation,
> 　whom shall I fear?"
> Ps 111 (:4), "In the darkness there has risen a light
> 　unto the just."

---

[68]"El oficio hispáno-visigótico," 401. For a more detailed analysis of the stages of growth of vespers in Spain see Winkler, "Über die Kathedralvesper," 83–91; also J. Bernal, "Primeros vestigios del lucernario en España," *Liturgica* 3 (Montserrat, 1966) 21–49.

[69]On these intercessions see J. Pinell, "Una exhortación diaconal en el rito hispánico: La supplicatio," *Analecta sacra Terraconensia* 36 (1963) 3–23.

[70]Winkler, "Über die Kathedralvesper," 85; *Heterii et S. Beati ad Elipandum epist.* I, 66, PL 96, 935; cf. Pinell, *loc. cit.*; also *id.*, "Vestigis del lucernari a occident," *Liturgica* 1 (Montserrat, 1956) 110–117.

[71]Pinell, "El oficio hispáno-visigótico," 401.

[72]Pinell, "Vestigis del lucernari," 110–115.

> Ps 117 (:105), "Your word is a lamp to my feet,
> O Lord, and a light to my path."
> Ps 96 (:11), "A light has dawned for the just one,
> a joy for the upright of heart."
> Ps 131 (:17b), "I have prepared a lamp for my
> Christ."
> Ps 17 (:29), "Since you are my lamp, O Lord,
> my God, enlighten my darkness."
> Ps 4 (:7), "The light of your face has set its mark
> upon us, O Lord."

Pss 140 and 4 are used with special frequency.[73]

The *psallendum* at the end of the offices comprises an antiphon with a couple of psalm verses. Winkler identifies it as a processional chant, parallel to the post-vesperal procession to the cross in Egeria (24:7) that has left traces in some Eastern offices, and to the *psallenda* sung during the procession to the baptistry in the Ambrosian rite.[74]

### 2. Iberian Matins:

Matins concluded in the same way as vespers. For the rest, we have seen that it comprised Ps 50 before the canticle, and the *Benedictiones* of Dan 3 at least at festive matins. On the basis of comparative liturgy and what we see in later, hybrid Iberian matins (a fusion of cathedral and monastic elements) I presume that Pss 148–150 were also an integral, fixed part of the service.

And of course with the psalms and canticles there were the usual antiphons, concluding doxology, and collects. The structure would look something like this:

> Ps 50 with antiphon and collect
> Canticle with antiphon and collect
> Psalm (Sundays and feasts: Dan 3) with antiphon
> and collect
> Pss 148–150 with antiphons and collect
> Hymn
> Supplication
> Completuria (final prayer)
> Our Father

---

[73]*Ibid.* 117–118.

[74]"Über die Kathedralvesper," 85 note 19; cf. Pinell, "El oficio hispáno-visigótico," 402–403. For Egeria and the other offices see "station at the cross" in the index.

Petition (embolism of Our Father)
Blessing
[Psallendum]

The similarities between these offices and the cathedral usage of Southern Gaul insofar as we can rebuild it seem clear enough, confirming once again what we have seen about the close contacts among local Churches among the Visigoths, and from the frequent synodal decrees insisting on a unification of liturgical uses.

By way of general conclusion it is apparent that Western cathedral offices in Frankish and Gothic areas were more flexible than their Eastern counterparts in allowing a wider selection of vesperal and lauds psalms beyond the pristine, fixed Ps 140 evensong and Pss 148–150 at morning praise. It is also clear that in the West the cathedral-monastic distinction blurred much earlier than it did in the East, as the breakup of Roman society gave way to a multiplicity of barbarian kingdoms, and the growth of feudal agricultural society, centered as much in countryside as in city, gave an overriding importance to the great Western abbeys that would hold sway over much of church life in the West until the end of the Middle Ages.

# 9

# CATHEDRAL VIGILS

The whole question of vigils remains fraught with pitfalls for the unwary historian of liturgy. Although Baumstark, Marcora, and Jungmann have already covered this ground,[1] there can be no doubt that the topic needs to be reworked. Any extensive treatment would require a book in its own right. Furthermore, apart from the monastic night prayer already treated in previous chapters, vigils in cathedral usage were not so much a part of the *daily* cursus of hours as *occasional* services pertaining more, perhaps, to a study of the liturgical year. Still, a few observations might be in place here, so as to order for the reader some of the evidence already seen, albeit in passing.

It should be clear by now that "vigil(s)" is an analogous term, used for more than one sort of night office, held with greater or lesser frequency depending on just what sort of vigil it was. So the first caveat is to realize that vigils are not one but several things. In the period covered by Part I of this study—roughly the first six Christian centuries—we have seen at least five kinds of common liturgical vigils: two monastic, two cathedral, and one kept in both traditions. They are distinguished by their frequency or time of celebration, if not always by their structure.

[1] A. Baumstark, *Nocturna laus. Typen frühchristlicher Vigilienfeier und ihr Fortleben, vor allem im römischen und monastischen Ritus* (LQF 32, Münster: Aschendorff, 1956); C. Marcora, *La vigilia nella liturgia. Ricerche sulle origini e sui primi sviluppi (sec. I-VI)* (Milan: Pontificia Universitas Gregoriana, 1954); Jungmann, *Pastoral Liturgy*, 105ff.

## Vigils in the
## Pre-Constantinian Church

Before the fourth century the evidence for public vigils held in common is sparse except, of course, for the Easter Vigil, which some see already adumbrated in Matt 25, 1 Pet, and the *Apocalypse.* And there is more than one other NT vigil, as we see in Acts 16:25 and 2 Cor 6:5.

Tertullian (d. after 220) in *To his Wife* II, 4, speaks of "nocturnal assemblies," and Pontius, *De vita et passione Cypriani* 15,[2] refers to the people keeping vigil while Cyprian was in prison before his martyrdom in 258. From the fourth century the witnesses to such martyrs' vigils multiply. Canon 35 of the Synod of Elvira in Spain in 300 excludes women from the vigils at the tombs,[3] a prohibition that will be extended to other vigils and repeated frequently throughout Late Antiquity. This is not without irony, for such vigils at the tombs, and later for the feasts of martyrs that become frequent after the fourth century, especially in Gaul, take their inspiration from the early morning watch of the women at the tomb of Christ. This is what our "wake" is all about, though we have long since forgotten it: it is an act of faith in the resurrection of the dead. We saw the same thing at the death of a monk or nun in Egypt and in Arles. To the best of my knowledge the Apocryphal Acts of the Martyrdom of St. Saturninus of Toulouse (d. ca. 250), a text of around 300, is the earliest document to speak of actual liturgical vigils in honor of the martyrs.[4]

So from the start we are dealing with a multi-faceted phenomenon: daily private prayer at night, testified to by most early writers; the yearly paschal vigil; occasional vigils at the martyrs' tombs.

## Vigils in the
## Church of the Roman Empire

By the end of the fourth century the prayer of Christians at night has evolved into two types of daily monastic vigil, the Egyptian type beginning around cockcrow and leading, in urban monastic usage, into lauds; the Cappadocian variety at midnight, followed by matins only after a break for further rest. Both these vigils have their origins in Christian pri-

---

[2]PL 3, 1554.

[3]Mansi 2, 11.

[4]Th. Ruinart, *Acta primorum martyrum sincera et selecta* (Amsterdam: Wetsten, 1713²) 130; cf. Marcora, *La vigilia,* 61.

vate prayer; the core of both was monastic psalmody "in course," with readings.

In cathedral usage we see first a short weekly resurrection vigil before Sunday Mass in Jerusalem and Antioch. It comprised an incensation in honor of the Myrrhophores, three antiphons in honor of the three days in the tomb, and climaxed in the proclamation of the paschal gospel.

I have already treated all this above in chapters 3–5, since these vigils have been integrated into existing offices to form part of the Liturgy of the Hours in the various traditions. But we have abundant evidence for other, occasional vigils that cannot be fit easily into these categories, yet which are an important testimony to Christian public prayer in Late Antiquity. They were more like the occasional monastic all-night vigil in Bethlehem described in Cassian, *Institutes* III, 8–9 (cf. 4:2).[5] Held on Friday night in honor of the passion, it went from vespers until the fourth cockcrow about two hours before daybreak, and consisted in a unit of three antiphons, three responsories, and three lessons, repeated throughout the night. This is at least a close relative if not the ancestor of the nocturnal *missae* we saw in the rules of Arles in chapter 6, and has parallels in numerous other sources.

## I. ALEXANDRIA

Athanasius of Alexandria (295–373) in his *History of the Arians* 81 and *Defence of his Flight* 24, tells of vigils Thursday night in preparation for Friday Eucharist, an Alexandrine peculiarity. The night service included lections, responsorial psalmody to which the people responded—we learn that Ps 136:1, was one of the responses—and prayers. The text specifies that the people were in church from midnight to dawn, and that there was Eucharist on the morrow, so the service was a true *pannychis* or all-night vigil.

The two fifth-century Byzantine historians Socrates, *Church History* V, 22, and Sozomen, *Church History* VII, 19, allude to the same practice in Egypt though in a somewhat garbled account, it appears: they say that the Egyptians in Alexandria and the Thebaid celebrated an evening agape and Eucharist on the Sabbath. A similiar pre-Eucharistic vigil was kept before Sunday Eucharist by both monks and laity in much of the ancient world.

[5]See above, ch. 5.

## II. CAPPADOCIA

In Cappadocia, Gregory of Nyssa (d. 394) in his *Homily on the Forty Martyrs* describes a vigil he experienced while still a layman. It was held outside in a garden, and the martyrs' relics were honored with psalms.[6] And in his *Life of St. Macrina* 22, Gregory tells of his sister's wake in the year 379:

> While we were busy with these [preparations of the body of Macrina], and the psalmody of the virgins mingled with lamentations filled the place, the news somehow had quickly spread throughout the whole surrounding area and all the neighbors began to hurry there in such numbers that the vestibule could not hold them.
>
> At dawn *(orthros)* after the all-night vigil *(pannychis)* by her [bier], with hymnody as at martyrs' panegyrics, the crowd that had flocked in from the whole surrounding countryside, both men and women, interrupted the psalmody with their grieving.

At this point Gregory takes charge, putting the women with the choir of virgins, the men with the monks, "so that the one psalmody from each [choir] would be rhythmic and harmonious as in choral singing, homogeneously sung in the melody common to all." The wake ended with the procession to the church for the funeral rites.

St. Basil the Great, also a brother of Macrina who died the same year, speaks in his *Homily 14 on Drunkards* 1 of vigils in Lent at which he "witnessed to the Gospel of God's grace," i.e., preached, though he complains, as will Chrysostom, Caesarius of Arles, and others, that his flock was more addicted to other nightly pleasures than to the *pannychis*.[7] Basil's *Homily on Ps 144*, 1, has him preaching on Ps 144 at a vigil in honor of the martyrs, a psalm which he says the people chanted at the service that went from midnight until midday.[8]

In his *Letter 207*, 3, written to the clergy of Neocaesarea in reply to their criticism of his liturgical innovations, Basil gives some details on the contents of these vigils, as we saw in chapter 3. They comprised the usual triad of lections, prayers said kneeling, and various kinds of psalmody. The vigil, a full *pannychis*, concluded with cathedral matins at dawn. Since it is obvious that the laity did not spend all night every night in prayer, the vigil must have been occasional, though we are not told with what frequency it was held.

[6]PG 46, 784–785.
[7]PG 31, 444–445.
[8]PG 29, 484.

III. PALESTINE

In fourth-century Palestinian monasteries, as we saw in Cassian, *Institutes* II, 8-9, there was a vigil Friday night from vespers until the fourth cockcrow. It consisted in the repetition of a liturgical unit comprising three antiphons, three responsorial psalms, and three lessons. This was followed by a period of rest, then matins at daybreak preceded Mass.

For hagiopolite cathedral usage, Egeria in Jerusalem around 381-384 describes not only the Sunday resurrection vigil discussed in chapter 3. She also experienced occasional vigils. Sometimes they were extensions of vespers, like the Easter Vigil (ch. 38); sometimes they were independent of vespers, like the vigils for the Great Tuesday (33) and Maundy Thursday stations in Holy Week (35-36). Here is the description of the vigil held every Friday night during Lent (27:7-8; cf. 29:1):

> . . . on Friday there is a vigil celebrated in the Anastasis from that hour . . . until morning, i.e., from the hour of lucernarium till the morning of the next day, i.e., Saturday, has arrived. And the [Eucharistic] offering is made in the Anastasis earlier [than usual] so that the dismissal takes place before sunrise. Throughout the night they say in turn responsorial psalms, antiphons, and various readings, all of which lasts until morning. . . . That is how they keep each week of Lent.

The fifth-century Armenian lectionary of Jerusalem fills in some details of these vigils.[9] Epiphany, Good Friday, and Easter are all preceded by a long vigil. The Good Friday vigil consists in appending to vespers five *"gobała"* of three psalms each, with responses: Pss 1-3 (Response Ps 2:26); 40-42 (Response 40:9 + 37:22); 58-60 (Response 58:2); 78-80 (Response 87:66 + 88:13); 108-110 (Response 108:2b-3a). After each three-psalm unit there was the customary prayer kneeling, plus a collect. The service concluded with a gospel reading from John 13:16-18:1. On Epiphany and Easter, however, the vigil opens with a responsorial psalm followed by a long series of readings from the Old Testament, concluded by the epistle and gospel of the Mass. Each lesson is followed by a prostration and prayer, indicated at least at Easter.

IV. ANTIOCH

Theodoret of Cyr's *Church History* II, 24 recounts how two laymen of Antioch, Flavian and Diodore, in 347-348 during the episcopate of the

---

[9]See A. Renoux, *Le codex arménien Jérusalem 121*, II: Edition, PO 36, 180-181, 211-215, 269-273, 295-309.

arianizing bishop of Antioch, Leontius the Eunuch (344–358), invented antiphonal psalmody for the night vigils they at first held in private with other fervent Christians:

> They [Flavian and Diodore] were the first to divide choirs of singers in two and teach them to sing the psalms of David alternately. Begun at Antioch, the practice spread everywhere and penetrated to the end of the earth. They now gathered the lovers of the divine word and work at the shrines [tombs] of the martyrs, and spent the whole night with them singing praises to God. When Leontius saw this, he did not think it safe to try to prevent it, for he saw that the people were exceedingly well-disposed toward these excellent men. So . . . he requested that they perform this service in the churches. Though well aware of his evil intent, they set about obeying his behest and readily summoned their adherents to the church, exhorting them to sing praises to the good Lord.

Theodoret is not always reliable, but what he says relates to what we saw in Basil and Cassian concerning the use of antiphonal psalmody at vigils. This sort of vigil at the martyrs' shrines is characteristic of what we shall see in later Western sources: they were celebrated chiefly on the eve of saints' feasts, though the practice does not seem to have caught on in the East.

Chrysostom, too, while still in Antioch before becoming bishop of Constantinople in 397, speaks of night prayer at home, or in common vigils that could include processions, readings, psalms, and preaching.[10] He also knew pre-Eucharistic vigils in honor of the martyrs, as we see in the following passage from his *Homily on the Martyrs:*

> You have turned the night into day by means of holy vigils *(pannychidês)*. Don't change day into night with intemperance and gluttony . . . and lascivious songs. You honored the martyrs by your presence, by hearing [the lessons] . . . honor them also by going home. . . . Think how ridiculous it is after such gatherings, after solemn vigils, after the reading of Sacred Scripture, after participating in the holy mysteries . . . that men and women are seen passing the whole day in the taverns.[11]

For some of Chrysostom's fellow Antiochenes it is clear that vigils were but the start of a cycle of festivities that ended in less noble pursuits. This problem was not unique to Antioch; Caesarius and others make the same complaint.

[10]*Homily after the earthquake* 1, PG 50, 713–714; *In illud: vidi Dominum hom. 1,* 1 and *hom. 4,* 1, PG 56, 98, 120; *Expos. in ps. 133,* 1, PG 55, 386.
[11]PG 60, 663–664.

## v. Constantinople

In the last quarter of the fourth century at Constantinople, Arianism was triumphant and the small Nicene minority, in disarray, appealed to Gregory Nazianzen for help. He accepted the see in 379 only to find all the churches in the hands of the Arians. But he turned a house donated by one of his relatives into a church and soon won a large audience by his eloquent preaching. In 380 the new emperor Theodosius restored the churches to the Orthodox, but objections to Gregory's nomination to the capital see were raised at the Second Ecumenical Council, Constantinople I in 381, and Gregory, who had never wanted anything but a life of solitude anyway, resigned in disgust after a brief reign from 379-381. His famous *Parting Sermon* refers to "all-night stations *(staseis pannychoi)*."[12]

John Chrysostom, Gregory's second successor, who did not last much longer in his see (397-404) before being exiled, waxes eloquent on the consolations of prayer at night in his *Homily 26 on Acts*, 3-4. From what he says it is clear that public, common vigils were only occasional assemblies. But on other nights the people were expected to rise for prayer at home. And even on nights of public vigil the women, forbidden to go out to them, kept watch at home. After recounting examples of night prayer in Acts, Chrysostom romanticizes the Apostolic Church as did Acts itself:

> ... Nothing ever was more splendid than that Church. Let us imitate these, let us emulate them. Not for this was the night made, that we should sleep all through it and be idle. To this the artisans, the porters, and the merchants bear witness: the Church of God rising up in the midst of the night. Rise up also, and behold the choir of the stars, the deep silence, the profound repose . . . .
> 
> Here indeed my discourse is for both men and women. Bend your knees, send forth groans, beseech your master to be merciful. He is moved more by prayers in the night. . . . Let the house be a Church consisting of men and women. For think not because you are the only man, or because she is the only woman there, that this is any hindrance. . . . Where Christ is in the midst, there is a great multitude. Where Christ is, there must angels be, archangels also and other powers. . . . Nothing is weaker than a multitude of unrighteous men, nothing stronger than one man who lives according to the law of God. If you have children, wake them up also, and let your whole household become a Church throughout the night. But if they are young and cannot endure the watching, let them stay for the first or second

[12]*Or. 42, 26, PG 36, 489.*

prayer, and then send them to bed: only stir yourself up. . . . But you will say, "I have worked hard during the day and cannot." This is mere pretext and subterfuge. . . .[13]

He then draws examples from the smith who works the better part of the night amid the sparks and smoke, the women who stay up and keep watch when their menfolk must go out of town or to a vigil which the women could not attend, or the night watchmen who must make their rounds in the rain and cold. He asks much less: that we watch and pray at night, so that tears of repentance might cool our daytime passions as the nighttime dew refreshes the plants burnt by the heat of the day.

But Chrysostom also knew of public vigils in honor of the martyrs as well as on other occasions.[14] The Byzantine historian Socrates (d. after 439) gives us further details. In his *Church History* VI, 8, he tells how John Chrysostom established nocturnal stations to counteract those of the Arians:

> The Arians . . . held their assemblies outside the city. So each week whenever there was a feast—I mean Saturday and Sunday—on which it was customary to hold a synaxis in the churches, they congregated in public squares within the city gates and sang antiphonally odes composed in accord with the Arian belief. And this they did during the greater part of the night. In the morning, chanting the same antiphons, they processed through the center of the city and went outside the gates of the city to their place of assembly. . . . John, concerned lest some of the more simple faithful be drawn away from the Church by such odes, set up some of his own people in opposition to them, so that they too, by devoting themselves to nocturnal hymnody, might obscure the effort of the Arians and confirm his own faithful in the profession of their own faith.

The people took up their bishop's initiative with gusto, bearing in procession silver crosses illumined with lighted tapers designed by Chrysostom and paid for by the Empress Eudoxia. Sozomen's *Church History* VIII, 8, written between 439–450, gives a somewhat more polished if later version of the same events, adding that the custom was continued even after the emperor put a stop to the Arian stations.

Palladius' *Dialogue on the Life of John Chrysostom* 5 also refers to these stational processions at night (*nychterinai litaneiai*), adding that the more negligent of the clergy, more accustomed to sleeping at night than to watching and praying, were not enamored of Chrysostom's initiative.[15]

---

[13]PG 60, 201–204; trans. adapted from NPNF ser. 1, vol. 11, 172–173.
[14]*Hom. nova* 2, PG 63, 467–472; *In Act. hom. 26*, 3–4, PG 60, 202–204, 218.
[15]PG 47, 20.

He also notes that the vigils were for men only: Chrysostom tells their wives to stay at home and pray. This discipline seems to have relaxed, for thirty years later the ill-fated Patriarch Nestorius (428–431) must again forbid women to take part in the night services and sing the hymns and chants.[16]

Are these night stations to be interpreted as vigils? In Constantinople, at least according to later sources such as the tenth-century *Typicon of the Great Church*, the earliest document to give a full picture of Constantinopolitan services throughout the year, "vigils," as elsewhere, can mean several different kinds of services, from the everyday pre-matutinal nocturns of *orthros*; to the *pannychis* comprising vespers, readings *(proanagnôsis)*, and compline; as well as the *paramonê* or solemn vespers with lessons *(anagnôsma)*, the sort of vigil customary at Easter in most traditions.[17] This *paramonê* is the true Constantinopolitan vigil of scriptural lessons, mostly from the Old Testament, celebrated on the eve of Christmas, Theophany (Epiphany), Easter, and, in reduced form with only three readings, on Pentecost and some fifteen or more other festivities depending on the manuscript of the *Typicon*. These vigils sometimes concluded with a Eucharist. But they were not celebrated in conjunction with a stational procession *(litê)*, which in the tenth century still took place at night on some occasions.[18]

Mateos has also distinguished several types of vigils in the East-Syrian tradition, but they are chiefly of a monastic type with psalmody or, on Sundays, included a cathedral vigil of the Antiochene and hagiopolite type seen in the *Apostolic Constitutions* and Egeria.[19] Only at Easter do we see a vesperal vigil, with four readings—indeed in this tradition the Easter Vigil is the only time there are lessons from Scripture in the Liturgy of the Hours.[20]

The tradition of cathedral vigils continued in churches of the Byzantine tradition. During the iconoclast crisis we find some further information on the readings done at them from Stephen the Deacon, of Constantinople, in his *Life of St. Stephen the Younger*, written in 808. Stephen, martyred in 766 during the iconoclast persecution under Con-

---

[16]E. Goeller (ed.), "Ein nestorianisches Bruckstücke zur Kirchengeschichte des 4. und 5. Jahrhunderts," OC 1 (1901) 95.

[17]J. Mateos, *Le typicon de la Grande Eglise. Ms. Sainte-Croix n° 40, X° siécle*, 2 vols. (OCA 165-166, Rome: PIO, 1962-1963) II, 282, 305, 309, 311, 315.

[18]Cf. *Ibid.* II, 304: *litê* II.a.

[19]J. Mateos, "Les differentes espèces de vigiles dans le rite chaldéen," OCP 27 (1961) 46-63. For the *Apost. Const.* and Egeria, see ch. 3 above.

[20]S. Pudichery, *Ramsa. An Analysis and Interpretation of the Chaldean Vespers* (Dhamaram College Studies 9, Bangalore: Dhamaram College, 1972) 115.

stantine V Capronymus (740-775), used to attend night vigils with his mother (the old prohibition against women at vigils had evidently fallen into disuse):

> Nor did he interrupt going by night with his saintly mother to the customary vigils *(agrypnias)* held in memory of the saints. And that honorable young man received such grace that when it was time to be seated for the readings, he stood by the chancel, attentive to the reader, learning what was being read just from hearing it, and repeating it to himself, either a martyrdom, or a life, or the sermon *(didaskalia)* of some Father, especially of the mellifluous Father Chrysostom.[21]

So by that time at least, the vigil lections in the Byzantine tradition included patristic and hagiographic lessons, as well as the Acts of the Martyrs, and, surely, Sacred Scripture.

### VI. MILAN

Ambrose, bishop of Milan from 374 to 397, and others, witness to occasional solemn, public vigils in fourth-century Milan. We hear of them at Easter in Paulinus' *Life of Ambrose* 48, written in 420;[22] for the feast of Saints Peter and Paul in Ambrose's *De virginitate* 19 (124-125), written in 377-378—even if Ambrose complains of the sparse attendance; and for the finding and translation of the relics of Saints Gervase and Protase in Ambrose's *Letter 22*, 2.

Most famous of all are the enforced vigils on the occasion of the troubles with the Empress Justina during Holy Week of 385. Once again, the problem was the Arians. The empress wanted a basilica put at their disposition; Ambrose refused, and so imperial troops surrounded the church and kept Ambrose and the Catholic congregation besieged for three days.[23] In his *Life of Ambrose* 13, Paulinus informs us that it was "in this time that antiphons, hymns, and vigils first began to be celebrated in the Church of Milan," a custom "that remains to this day not only in that Church but indeed throughout almost all the provinces of the West."[24] Arians, antiphons, and vigils seem to be an inseparable trio in all this history, East and West.

Augustine taught rhetoric at Milan from 384-387, and though not yet baptized, he witnessed the events of 385 and recounts them in his *Confessions* IX, 7 (15):

[21]PG 100, 1081.
[22]PL 14, 43.
[23]Ambrose, *Ep. 20*, 24-25, PL 16, 1001-1002.
[24]PL 14, 31.

The Church in Milan had not long before begun to worship with this form of consolation and exhortation, wherein with great fervor the brethren sing together in voice and heart. For it was only a year, or not much more, since Justina, mother of the boy king Valentinian, had persecuted your man Ambrose in favor of her heresy, to which she had been seduced by the Arians. A devout people who were prepared to suffer death together with their bishop, your servant, kept watch in the church. Therein, living in prayer, my mother your hand-maid held a first place amid these cares and watchings. Ourselves, still cold to the warmth of your Spirit, were nevertheless stirred by the astonished and disturbed city. At that time it was established that after the custom of the Eastern Lands, hymns and canticles should be sung so that the people would not become weak through tedium and sorrow. From then up to the present day that custom has been maintained with many, or almost all, of your congregations taking it up throughout other parts of the world.[25]

There were also scriptural lessons in the Milanese vigils. Ambrose's own account of the siege-vigil in *Letter 20*, 13–25 of Easter 385, mentions *lectiones* explicitly, along with responsorial psalmody. From his description it is clear that the lessons included the Book of Job on one night *(Letter 20, 14–17)*, the Prophecy of Jonah on the next *(Letter 20, 25)*. Homilies followed the lessons *(Letter 20, 14ff., 25)*, and Ps 78:1 is referred to as one of the responses at matins *(Letter 20, 20)*.

This is all the information we have about what comprised these vigils: hymns, psalms, antiphons, lessons, preaching, though we can presume prayer as well. Note that both Augustine and Paulinus—but not Ambrose—mention that Ambrose introduced not only the vigils themselves, but also hymns and "antiphons" or psalms executed "in the eastern way *(secundum morem orientalium partium)*." Like Chrysostom at Constantinople, Ambrose used popular hymns as a weapon against the Arians, as he admits in his sermon against the Arian bishop Auxentius:

They [the Arians] say that the people are seduced by my hymns. Nor do I deny it at all. It is a great hymn, more powerful than any other. For what is more powerful than the confession of the Trinity that is celebrated aloud every day by the people . . . ?[26]

But is it true that Ambrose, like Flavian and Diodore at Antioch, and Chrysostom at Constantinople, was the first one to introduce "antiphonal psalmody" at Milan—and hence to the West—as a move against the Arians? This interpretation, though common, has been seriously challenged

[25]*The Confessions of St. Augustine*, trans. J. K. Ryan (New York: Doubleday, 1960) 215 (adapted).

[26]*Sermo contra Auxentium* 34, PL 16, 1017.

by Helmut Leeb, who argues effectively that "antiphonal" here means what we know as responsorial psalmody: the repetition by the people of a fixed response, usually a psalm verse, after each verse of the psalm proclaimed by the psalmist.[27] And indeed, that seems to be all that Ambrose himself claims in *Letter 20*, 20, 24.

But in *Expl. ps. 1*, 9 Ambrose does tell us the pastoral motive for popular participation in the psalmody by means of responses or refrains: it keeps the people from chattering, which is next to impossible, he says, when a single lector is doing the reading.[28]

### VII. ROME AND NORTH AFRICA

Vigils were also known in Rome from before certain feasts: Easter, the Saturday following Pentecost which ended the paschal season, the Saturdays on which fell the fasts of the seventh and tenth month, and the anniversary of certain martyrs.[29] Jerome, in Rome from 382 to 385, tells us in his *Contra vigilantium* that the vigils of Easter, Pentecost, Sts. Peter and Paul, and the Saturdays of the fasts drew large crowds and gave rise to disorders.[30]

Augustine in Africa (387-430) also witnesses to the existence of occasional vigils before Easter, Pentecost, and the feast of St. Cyprian—in short the usual variety before major feasts and the anniversaries of principal martyrs honored by the local Church.[31] The service comprised Scripture lessons, psalmody (apparently responsorial psalmody between the lessons),[32] prayer, and preaching, as well as the endless kneeling for prayer and rising again that characterized vigil services everywhere.[33] We find

[27]H. Leeb, *Die Psalmodie bei Ambrosius* (Wiener Beiträge zur Theologie 18, Vienna: Herder, 1967) ch. 3.

[28]CSEL 64, 8 = PL 14, 925 *(In ps. 1 enarratio 9)*.

[29]Jerome, *Contra vigilantium* I, 9ff., PL 23, 347ff.; *Ep. 107*, PL 22, 875; *Ep. 109*, 3, PL 22, 909; Leo I (440–461), *Serm. 12*, 4; *13*; *15*, 2; *16*, 6; *17*, 4; *18*, 3; *19*, 3; *78*, 4; *81*, 4; *88*, 5; *89*, 6; *90*, 4 (all in PL 54). Cf. V. Monachino, *La cura pastorale a Milano, Cartagine e Roma nel secolo IV* (Rome: Pontifical Gregorian University, 1947) 362-364.

[30]I, 9ff., PL 23, 347ff.

[31]*Serm. 219-223, 266*, PL 38, 1087-1093, 1225; Denis 2, Denis 11, G. Morin (ed.), *Sancti Augustini sermones post Maurinos reperti* (Miscellanea Agostiniana, Testi e studi I, Rome: Tipografia Poliglotta Vaticana, 1930) 11-17, 43-50; Guelferb 4-6, ed. Morin 455-462; Wilmart 4ff., ed. Morin 684-719; *Enarr. 2 in ps. 23, serm. 1*, 5, PL 37, 279; *in ps. 85, serm. 1*, 24, PL 37, 1081, 1099.

[32]*Serm.* Denis 11, ed. Morin, 43-50.

[33]*De cura pro mortuis gerenda* 5 (7), PL 40, 597.

the same thing in chapter 5 of Gerontius' *life of St. Melany the Younger* (d. 439).[34]

VIII. CONCLUSION

From the end of the fourth century we see the multiplication of occasional cathedral vigils for particular needs: to prepare for a feast with its Eucharist, to honor martyrs on their anniversary, to counteract the Arians, to gain strength in time of persecution. The core of these vigils was a series of psalms and lections. So their "model" was not the daily monastic vigil of continuous psalmody, nor the Easter Vigil made up almost exclusively of Scripture readings, but rather the occasional vigil of popular psalmody, lessons, prostrations, and prayers first described by Basil (*Ep. 207*, 3), Egeria (27:7-8: 29:1), and Cassian *(Inst. III, 8-9).*

The correspondence among these three sources is striking:

| *Basil* | *Egeria* | *Cassian* |
|---|---|---|
| Is 26:9ff | | |
| Ps 118 | | |
| antiphonal psalms | responsorial psalms | STANDING: 3 antiphonal psalms |
| prayers | | |
| responsorial psalms | antiphonal psalms | SEATED: 3 responsorial psalms |
| prayers | | |
| | lessons | 3 lessons |

Basil is the only one to mention the invitatory material, and says nothing about readings; Egeria and Cassian do not refer to prostrations and a collect after each psalm or group of psalms. But from all our later evidence for this type of service it appears that these vigils consisted in the repetition of a set liturgical unit of psalmody, lessons, prostrations, collects, though the ordering of elements within the unit differs from place to place. In Caesarius, for example, the prostrations and collect follow each lesson; in other sources they come after each psalm or group of psalms.

But by the time of Augustine's death in 430, the Vandals were at the gates of Hippo and the Western world of the Roman Empire fast becoming Christian was soon to be a memory. It is in the new world of Latin Christianity under the barbarian kingdoms that the occasional cathedral vigil of scriptural lessons, psalmody, preaching, prostrations, and prayers will acquire a consistency and importance it seems not to have achieved, or at least maintained, in most of the East.

[34]D. Gorce (ed.), *Vie de S. Mélanie* (SC 90, Paris: Cerf, 1962) 134.

## Cathedral Vigils in the West at the End of Late Antiquity

Later evidence, all of it from the Latin West, shows that occasional all-night vigils continued to be celebrated in secular churches on the eve of certain feasts. More important, this evidence provides precious information as to the content and spirit of these services. They seem to have followed the same pattern already seen in Egeria, Athanasius, Cassian, Basil, Ambrose, Augustine, and the rules of Arles: psalmody, readings, prostrations, prayer, preaching.

### I. NICETA OF REMESIANA

Niceta (d. 414), Bishop of Remesiana, the present Bela Palanka in Yugoslavia, describes the elements of a vigil in his *On the Usefulness of Hymns*, 12–14, a sermon delivered during a vigil, as he explicitly states at the start (1). This little-known text, full of principles dear to choir directors, secular or monastic, in every age, is worth quoting *in extenso*:[35]

> [12]Can any joy be greater than that of delighting ourselves with psalms and nourishing ourselves with prayer and feeding ourselves with the lessons that are read in between? Like guests at table enjoying a variety of dishes, our souls feast on the rich banquet of lessons and hymns.
>
> [13]Only, brethren, let us please God by singing with attention and a mind wide awake, undistracted by idle talk. . . . That is, we must sing with our intelligences; not only with the spirit (in the sense of the sound of our voice), but also with our mind. We must think about what we are singing, lest we lose the fruit of our effort by distracting talk and extraneous thoughts. The sound and melody of our singing must be suitably religious. It must not be melodramatic, but a revelation of the true Christianity within. It must have nothing theatrical about it, but should move us to sorrow for our sins.
>
> Of course, you must all sing in harmony, without discordant notes. One of you should not linger unreasonably on the notes, while his neighbor is going too fast; nor should one of you sing too low while another is raising his voice. Each one should be asked to contribute his part in humility to the volume of the choir as a whole. No one should sing unbecomingly louder or slower than the rest, as though for vain ostentation or out of human respect. The whole service must

[35]Text in A. E. Burn, *Niceta of Remesiana, His Life and Works* (Cambridge: University Press, 1905); trans. adapted from Niceta of Remesiana, *Writings*, trans. G. G. Walsh (The Fathers of the Church, N. Y.: The Fathers of the Church, Inc., 1949) 74–76.

be carried out in the presence of God, not with a view to pleasing men. In regard to the harmony of voices we have a model and example in the three blessed boys of whom the Prophet Daniel tells us: "Then these three, as with one mouth, praised and glorified and blessed God in the furnace, saying: Blessed are you, O Lord the God of our fathers" [Dan 3: 51–52]. You see that it was for our instruction that we are told that the three boys humbly and holily praised God with one voice. Therefore, let us sing all together, as with one voice, and let all of us modulate our voices in the same way. If one cannot sing in tune with the others, it is better to sing in a low voice rather than to drown out the others. In this way he will take his part in the service without interfering with the community singing. Not everyone, of course, has a flexible and musical voice. St. Cyprian is said to have invited his friend Donatus, whom he knew to be a good singer, to join him in the office: "Let us pass the day in joy, so that not one hour of the feast will be without some heavenly grace. Let the feast be loud with songs, since you have a full memory and a musical voice. Come to this duty regularly. You will feed your beloved friends if you give us something spiritual to listen to. There is something alluring about religious sweetness, and those who sing well have a special grace to attract to religion those who listen to them."[36] And if our voice is without harshness, and in tune with the notes of "well-played cymbals" [Ps 150:5], it will be a joy to ourselves and a source of edification to those who hear us. And "God who makes men of one manner to dwell in his house" [Ps 67:7] will find our united praise agreeable to him.

When we sing, all should sing; when we pray, all should pray. So when the lesson is being read, all should remain silent that all may equally hear. No one should be praying with so loud a voice as to disturb the one who is reading. And if you should happen to come in while the lesson is being read, just adore the Lord and make the sign of the cross, and then give an attentive ear to what is being read.

[14]Obviously, the time to pray is when we are all praying. Of course you may pray privately whenever and as often as you choose. But do not, under the pretext of prayer, miss the lesson. You can always pray whenever you will, but you cannot always have a lesson at hand. Do not imagine that there is little to be gained by listening to the sacred lesson. The fact is that prayer is improved if our mind has been recently fed on reading, and is able to roam among the thoughts of divine things which it has recently heard. The word of the Lord assures us that Mary, the sister of Martha, chose the better part when she sat at the feet of Jesus, listening intently to the word of God without a thought of her sister. We need not wonder, then, if the deacon, in a clear voice like a herald, warns all that whether

[36]*Ep. ad Donatum* 16.

they are praying or bowing the knees, singing hymns, or listening to the lessons, they should all act together. God loves "men of one manner" and, as was said before, "makes them to dwell in his house" [Ps 67:7]. And those who dwell in this house are proclaimed by the psalm to be blessed, because they will praise God forever and ever. Amen.

One can only hope that Niceta had better luck than his successors down through the ages in getting his congregation to march in step. From his admonitions we can get a fairly complete picture of what vigils were like in Remesiana. There were the customary components:

1) congregational chant, undoubtedly psalmody to which the people responded with a response or antiphon, hopefully in tune and in unison, attending without distraction to the meaning of the words being sung (12–13);

2) prostrations and prayers (14), apparently following the readings (12);

3) Scripture lessons, apparently interspersed between the units of psalmody, to which the people were to listen attentively without muttering their private prayers aloud to the distraction of others (13–14);

4) diaconal admonitions (14) to pay attention, to kneel, to rise, to be silent provided the necessary cues and helped maintain a semblance of order and discipline.

Note the warning not to distract others by praying aloud. This will be repeated by Caesarius, and it was obviously something of a liturgical problem in Late Antiquity, for in those days people were not afflicted by the nordic stuffiness and reserve that passes for correct behavior in much of the modern world, and in church they prayed aloud unaffectedly, with sighs and tears. Augustine's De civitate Dei XXII, 8:9 and 13, tells how a crowd of teenagers, with their customary sensitivity, overheard in church the prayers of the old man Florentius of Hippo, and then mocked him afterwards in the street.

## II. Caesarius of Arles

It is especially from Gaul that we have a veritable feast of evidence for occasional vigils in cathedral usage, centered on the proclamation and preaching of the Word of God.

Caesarius, as we saw in chapter 6, strongly insists on the place of God's revealed word in the life of his community, and lections from Scripture as well as preaching had an important place in the cathedral services of

Arles (*Serm 72*, 1; *76*, 3; *118*, 1; *192*, 2, 4). For Caesarius, God's word was a remedy for the evils of this life. In *Sermon 6*, 2 he tells the laity they could well afford to spend three hours on longer nights reading the Scriptures instead of holding interminable suppers or drinking half the night. Many however, are illiterate, he says, and need to be read to if they are to receive this spiritual nourishment: hence the vigils.

But the vigils included more than Scripture readings. The lessons were followed by silent prayer, which helped to interiorize the word listened to attentively. The movement was biblical: God first calls us in his revealed word, then we respond with the words his call brings forth from our hearts. Caesarius has to remind his noisy throng of this dynamic in *Sermon 72*. When they come to church, he admonishes,

> [1] . . . strive to occupy yourselves with prayer or chanting of the psalms rather than idle or worldly gossip. If a person who comes to church wants to engage in useless conversation, it would be better for him not to come, for while he is busy with useless talking he does not pray himself nor does he allow others to pray or listen to the divine lessons. Even if a man of this sort comes to church with but slight sins, he returns home with a greater one. In the very place where he might have secured a remedy for himself and others by psalmody and prayer, he has taken pains to injure himself by idle conversation.
>
> [2] Above all, dearly beloved, as often as we apply ourselves to prayer we should pray in silence and quiet. If a man wants to pray aloud he seems to take the fruit of prayer away from those who are standing near him. Only moans and sighs and groans should be heard. For our prayer ought to be like that of holy Anna the mother of blessed Samuel, of whom it is written that "She prayed, shedding many tears, and only her lips moved, but her voice was not heard at all" (1 Sam 1: 10, 13). . . .
>
> [3] When we pray, dearly beloved, with the Lord's help let us strive as much as we can not to let any extraneous thoughts creep into our minds, lest we have one thing in our hearts and utter another with our lips. Let not our tongues pray to God while our thoughts are busy with different interests and far from the sense of the prayer, for then we would commit a fault in the very place where we might receive a remedy. . . . Therefore, before prostrating yourselves in prayer, each one of you should with God's help remove all useless thoughts from the mind's attention. If our soul is on fire with love for the Holy Spirit it will consume every vice with the fire of compunction and prayer, and dispel all its wandering, fleeting fancies, so that only virtues and holy exercises will find room in our hearts.[37]

[37] The homilies of Caesarius are edited in CCL 103–104; the trans. here is adapted from St. Caesarius of Arles, *Sermons*, vol. 1, trans. by Sr. Mary Magdeleine Mueller, O.S.F.

Caesarius echoes Niceta in his exhortation on the meaning and proper comportment of the faithful at vigils, and he was perfectly aware that these services were something of a workout. He cuts short his homilies on Epiphany (195, 4) and Pentecost (211, 5) because his people are tired "from the labor of the vigils."

From the rules of Caesarius and Aurelian studied in chapter 6 we saw that the passion of the martyrs was read at vigils on their feasts, readings that were sometimes of considerable length. Nor were other non-scriptural lections unknown in Western vigils. In January of 602 Gregory the Great warns the bishop of Ravenna not to let his *Moralia in Job* be read publicly at the vigils because it was not meant for the simple faithful. For them it would be more suitable to read a commentary on the psalms.[38]

### III. GREGORY OF TOURS

Gregory of Tours (d. 594), from whom we have so much precious information concerning the history and uses of the Gallic Church in this period, knew of both private and public nocturnal vigils. His *De cursu stellarum ratio* 36–47 aligns the months and lengths of the days and nights of each month with the amount of psalmody done—privately it seems—at night. For those that wish to keep watch all night, the whole psalter could be done (47).[39]

He also refers in numerous writings to public vigils before Christmas, Easter, and certain saints' days,[40] and in his *History of the Franks* X, 30, he gives the complete calendar of fasts and vigils instituted by St. Perpetuus (d. 490), bishop of Tours.[41] Sixteen annual vigils are mentioned, a full ten of which are in honor of the saints. The vigils of Christmas Epiphany, Easter, and Pentecost are celebrated "in the church," i.e., in the cathedral. Those of St. John the Evangelist, the Resurrection feast on March 27, the Ascension, St. Symphorius, St. Brice, St. Hilary, and two feasts of St. Martin are all celebrated in the basilica dedicated to the latter. St. Peter's Chair is celebrated in St. Peter's, Sts. Peter and Paul in the basilica of the Princes of the Apostles, The *Passio* (Beheading) of John

---

(The Fathers of the Church, New York: The Fathers of the Church, Inc., 1965) 338–340.

[38]*Reg. ep. XII*, 6, MGH, Ep. II/1, 352.

[39]MGH, SRM I, 870–872.

[40]*Hist. Francorum* II, 34; IV, 31; V, 23; VII, 22; X, 31:19, MGH, SRM I, 97–98, 167, 219, 303–304, 448; *De virtutibus S. Iuliani* 24, 35–37, ibid. 575, 578–580; *De virtutibus S. Martini* III, 16, 23, ibid. 636, 638; *De gloria confessorum* 47, 93, ibid. 776, 807.

[41]MGH, SRM I, 444–445.

the Baptist in the cathedral baptistry, St. Litorius in his basilica. This is obviously an embryonic stational system like that of Constantinople: the main dominical feasts are celebrated in the cathedral, whereas the vigils of the sanctoral are distributed among the martyria.[42]

In his account of a meeting of bishops with Gundobad (d. 516), King of Burgundy, concerning the Arian crisis, Gregory gives further details of an all-night vigil at the tomb of St. Justus on the eve of his feast. He mentions, in this order, a reading from Moses (with a citation from Ex 6), then psalms, prophets (Is 6), another psalm, a gospel (Matt 11), and an apostle (Rom 2).[43]

## IV. SIDONIUS APOLLINARIS

From another account of a vigil of the same St. Justus at the same basilica, we get a sense of the popular appeal of these services. Like Christmas in our modern secular culture, they were not only religious celebrations but also occasions of holiday leisure and good fellowship, of fairs, and going out with friends. From this we can also appreciate the pastoral common sense of our forefathers who counteracted popular pagan festivities in the dying Roman Empire with a Christian counterpoise.

The story comes from the pen of St. Sidonius Apollinaris (d. ca. 480-490), a Gallo-Roman patrician and later count *(comes)*, born at Lyons around 432. Both his grandfather, a convert to Christianity, and father had been praetorian prefects of Roman Gaul. Around 450 Sidonius married Papianilla, daughter of Avitus, prefect of Gaul, who was later proclaimed emperor of the western empire by the Goths at Toulouse on November 7, 455. The Gallo-Romans at Arles ratified the choice but the real power of the time, the Germano-Visigothic General Flavius Ricimer, "kingmaker" of the Western Roman Empire from 456-472, defeated him and forced his abdication within the year. As a consolation prize, Avitus was made bishop of Placentia (Piacenza) in Italy.

I tell the story to illustrate the complex and closely intertwined relations between the dying empire and the nascent barbarian kingdoms, and between these two power structures and that of the Gallic Church. For Sidonius himself, a Gallo-Roman to the core, had held high office in the empire and became bishop of the Averni (Auvergne) at Clermont in 469-470, precisely in the period when the West Goths were extending their control over the area. When Rome ceded Auvergne to the Goths in 475,

[42]See J. Baldovin, "La liturgie stationnale à Constantinople," LMD 147 (1981) 89.
[43]PL 71, 1155.

Sidonius was banished from his see for a time, as still happens today when wars change borders, revolutions change governments, and the Church finds itself with a hierarchy no longer acceptable to the new regime. Sidonius was a man of the old Roman order, the last great representative of Roman Christianity in a changing Gaul, a patrician of classical culture and great charm in spite of his lack of theological education.

His descriptions of the stational vigil in *Letter V*, 17: 3–11 to his friend Eriphius of Lyons was written while Sidonius was still a layman:

> We had gathered at the tomb of St. Justus—you were prevented by illness from being present—[where] the anniversary celebration of the procession before daylight was held. There was an enormous number of people of both sexes, too large a crowd for the very spacious basilica to hold even with the expanse of covered porticoes that surrounded it. After the vigil service was over, which the monks and clergy had celebrated together with alternating strains of sweet psalmody *(alternante mulcedine psalmicines)*, everyone withdrew in various directions, but not far, as we wanted to be present at the third hour when mass was to be celebrated by the priests.
>
> Because of the cramped space, the pressure of the crowd, and the [heat of] numerous lights brought in [by the procession], we were absolutely gasping for breath. Moreover, imprisoned as we were under the roof, we were broiled by the heat of what was still almost a summer night, although just beginning to be touched with the coolness of an autumn dawn.
>
> So when groups of various classes were dispersing in different directions, the leading citizens resolved to go in a body to the tomb of Syagrius, which was not quite a full bowshot away. Here some of us sat down under the shadow of a full-grown vine whose overarching foliage made a shady canopy formed by tall stems that drooped over in an interlaced pattern; others of us sat down on the green turf, which was also fragrant with flowers.
>
> Conversation ensued, pleasant, jesting, bantering, and a specially happy feature in it was that there was no mention of officials or of taxes, no talk that invited betrayal, no informer to betray it; certainly everyone could have told freely any story worth relating and worthy in its sentiments. The audience listened in a spirit of eager rivalry; and the story-telling, though tinged with hilarity, was not on that account formless.
>
> By and by, having for some time felt sluggish for want of exertion, we resolved to do something energetic. Thereupon we raised a twofold clamour demanding according to our ages either ball or gaming-board, and these were soon forthcoming. I was the leading champion of the ball; for, as you know, ball no less than book is my constant companion. On the other hand, our most charming and

delightful brother, Domnicius, had seized the dice and was busy shaking them as a sort of trumpet-call summoning the players to the battle of the box. We on our part played with a troop of students, indeed played hard until our limbs deadened by inactive sedentary work could be reinvigorated by the healthful exercise. . . .

Well, when we had sat down the pouring sweat next prompted him to ask for water to bathe his face. . . . While he was drying his cheeks in leisurely fashion he remarked: "I wish you would command to be written for me a quartet of verses in honour of this towel that has done me such service." . . . Without further delay, I next called to my side his secretary, who had his writing tablet ready to hand, and without more ado composed the following epigram: "At dawn, or when the steaming bath invites him, or when his forehead is hot and damp from the chase, with this towel let handsome Philomatius comfort his streaming face, so that all the moisture flows into the absorbent fleece."

Scarcely had our good friend Epiphanius the secretary written the above lines when it was announced that the bishop, at the beckoning of the appointed hour, was proceeding from his lodging, and so we arose. You must treat with indulgence this doggerel you insisted on having. . . .[44]

This languorous approach to vigils, more redolent of a Swinburne than of the homilies of Niceta or Caesarius, is part of the same history and deserves to be cited as counterpoise, lest we be carried away by the wave of nostalgic "early Church" romanticism that can overcome us when we recall those presumably halcyon days. On the other hand, there is no law against liturgy being enjoyable. Chrysostom at Constantinople certainly cannot be accused of indolent laxity—he was run out of town for his moral strictures against the abuses of the day—but he was not above describing the refreshing joys of cathedral prayer in the countryside in terms perfectly intelligible to the harried New York executive with a weekend retreat on Long Island or in New England. Chrysostom is exhorting the country squire to build and maintain a church on his estate for the good of his own soul and those of his dependents. The lengthy passage from *In Act. apost. hom. 18*, 4–5, reads like something from Vergil's *Georgics*, with its aura of bucolic delights. Chrysostom describes the landowner being borne on his litter to his estate church for morning and evening prayer,

[44]Text in MGH, *Auctores antiquissimi* VIII, 89–91; trans. adapted from Sidonius, *Poems and Letters*, with an English trans. by W. B. Anderson, vol. 2 (Cambridge, Mass.: Harvard/London: W. Heinemann, 1965) 227–237. On Sidonius, see C. E. Stevens, *Sidonius Apollinaris and his Age* (Oxford: Clarendon Press, 1933/Westport, Conn.: Greenwood Press, 1979).

and the pleasure of having educated conversation at table with the presbyter, far away from the din and distractions of city life:

> [5]How pleasant to go forth and enter the house of God and know that one built it oneself; to fling himself on his back in his litter, and after the bodily benefit of his pleasant airing, be present both at the evening and the morning hymns; have the priest as a guest at his table; in associating with him enjoy his benediction; see others also coming there. . . . If even without this the country is pleasant because it is so quiet, so free from the distractions of business, what will it not be when this is added to it? The countryside with a church is like the paradise of God. No clamor there, no turmoil, no enemies at variance, no heresies: there you shall see all friends holding the same doctrines in common. The very silence shall lead you to higher views, and receiving you thus prepared by philosophy, the presbyter shall give you an excellent cure. For here [in the city] whatever we may speak, the noise of the market drives it all out; but there, what you hear you will keep fixed in your mind. . . .[45]

## Daily Vigils in the Secular Churches[46]

Although the frequency of these all-night stational vigils may have varied widely from place to place, common sense tells us they could not have been held daily. What, then, of the sixth-century sources that indeed order daily vigils in the secular churches?

In 528 Justinian's Code I, iii, 42: 24 (10), orders all the clergy in each church to chant nocturns (nykterina) as well as matins and vespers daily.[47] And in a text already cited, Ferrandus' Vita Fulgentii 29 (59) tells us that Fulgentius (467–533), bishop of Ruspe in North Africa, "ruled that each week all the clergy and widows, and whoever of the laity was able, to fast Wednesday and Friday, ordering all to be present at the daily vigils, fasts, and morning and evening prayers."[48]

In Rome, the Cautio episcopi of the Liber diurnus 74, a text no later than March 559 when Pope Pelagius I (556–561) refers to it in Letter 44, 1–2, also testifies to daily vigils. In the Cautio, a sort of "oath of office" or contract, a new bishop had to commit himself in detail to live up to the obligations of his office, among which were the following:

---

[45]Trans. adapted from NPNF ser. 1, vol. 11, 119; text in PG 60, 147ff.
[46]Much in this section is owed to de Vogüé, La Règle de S. Benoît V, 453–481.
[47]P. Krüger, Corpus Iuris Civilis, vol. 2 (Berlin: Weidmann, 1900) 28.
[48]PL 65, 147.

I solemnly swear and promise at all times, each day from first cockcrow until morning to celebrate vigils in church with the whole order
of my clergy, so that on the shorter nights, i.e., from Easter until the
equinox of September 24, three readings and three antiphons and three
responsories shall be said; but from this equinox until the other, ver-
nal equinox, and until Easter, four readings with their responsories
and antiphons shall be sung. On Sundays throughout the year,
however, I promise God to accomplish nine readings with their antiphons and responsories.[49]

Note that the term "vigil" is understood in two senses: daily nocturns,
and the "Great Vigil" as de Vogüé calls it, a true *pannychis* or all-night
service celebrated Saturday (or Friday) evenings and on the eve of certain
feasts or days of penance in numerous early sources: Cassian, *Institutes*
III, 8–9; Egeria's diary 27: 7–8; 29:1–2; Caesarius, CV 66, 68–69; Aurelian,
AM 56–57; *The Rule of the Master* 49; *The Rule of Macarius* 15;[50] and
the *Regula cuiusdam patris* 30,[51] of uncertain origin.

No doubt such later references to *daily* vigils in the secular churches
can only mean an office akin to daily monastic nocturns. In Rome, for
example, on the eve of Sundays and feasts these nocturns were lengthened into a vigil by simply adding two more "nocturns" of three psalms
and three lessons, with their three responsories (two for the third nocturn). So we must not be confused by the analogous use of the Latin term
*"uigiliae."* Some sources such as the *Rules* of Caesarius and Aurelian
reserve the term "vigils" for the longer occasional vigil, but most Latin
sources use *"uigiliae"* indiscriminately for both daily monastic-type nocturns and the occasional "Great Vigil." We see this confusion already in
Egeria (24:1, 8; 44:1), Cassian (*Inst.* II, 13:3; 17; III, 4:1; 6; 8:1–4; 9:1–2),
Benedict (RB 8–11), the *Rule of Tarnant* (between 551 and 573) 6;[52] and
doubtless a simple nocturns must be the service imposed "daily" on the
secular clergy by Fulgentius, Justinian, and the *Liber diurnus.*

Indeed, it is obvious that the burden of long monastic vigils was prov-
ing too much even for the monks. The late sixth-century Gallic *Rule of
St. Ferreolus* 13 speaks of daily nocturns (13:7), clearly distinguishing them
from night vigils which are occasional affairs (13:1): "As often as a night
vigil to pray to God is either required by reason of devotion or demanded
because of a feast, let no monk present [in the monastery] presume to absent himself except in case of real illness or necessity."[53]

[49]PL 105, 71.
[50]de Vogüé, *Les règles des saints pères* I, 378; *Early Monastic Rules* 44.
[51]PL 66, 994.
[52]PL 66, 980.
[53]PL 66, 964.

If Gallic rules knew vigils before Saturday as well as Sunday, Italian rules such as the *Rule of the Master* (45, 49) and the sixth-century *Rule of Paul and Stephen* (10:1–3)[54] limit the Great Vigil to Sundays and some feasts. The Master was aware of a crisis in the practice of Great Vigils,[55] and in sixth-century Roman usage the Sunday vigil had been reduced to an extended nocturns of nine antiphons, lessons, and responsories, as we saw in the *Liber diurnus*—three times as long as daily nocturns, but still considerably less than a truly all-night Great Vigil. A similar mitigation was incorporated into his *Rule* by Benedict (RB 9–11), who preferred to let his monks sleep at night and devote the Sunday daylight hours to *lectio* (RB 48: 22–23), rather than having them pray half the night and sleep on Sunday as in the Master (RM 75: 5–7).

Benedict's abandonment of the all-night vigil on the eve of Sunday (RB 11) is one of the major transformations he operated in the tradition received from his monastic forebears such as the Master (RM 49).[56] Some such mitigation can also be seen in Spain and Gaul. The *Rules for Monks* of Isidore of Seville (6:4) and Fructuosus of Braga (3) are content to increase the number of daily *missae*—a unit of three psalms—from five to six in order to have a somewhat longer vigil on Saturdays (Fructuosus), Sundays, and feasts. Fructuosus, however, adds (17) that "the nighttime must be spent for the most part in special prayers and sacred vigils because of the evil spirits which flee the light and deceive the servants of God."[57]

## CONCLUSION

So "vigil(s)" can mean many things:

1) the private night prayer of Christians during the first three centuries;
2) semi-private vigils at the tombs of martyrs during the same period;
3) wakes;
4) the private watches of virgins and ascetics such as Jerome's Roman devotees;

---

[54]*Règles monastiques d'occident,* 351.

[55]de Vogüé, *La Règle de S. Benoît* V, 461-462.

[56]See *ibid.* 474ff. and Mateos, "La vigile cathédrale chez Egérie," 305ff., on the relation between Benedict's third nocturn and the old cathedral resurrection vigil.

[57]PL 83, 876; 87, 1100–1101, 1107.

5) a Sunday resurrection vigil of three psalms or canticles, an incensation, and the proclamation of the paschal gospel, as in Egeria and the *Apostolic Constitutions;*
6) monastic nocturns, a daily office of continuous psalmody and readings in two distinct forms:
    (a) the pre-matins office at cockcrow, as in Cassian and much of the later Western tradition, and
    (b) the *mesonyktikon* or midnight office as in the Cappadocian sources;
7) the eventual adoption of some form of the latter monastic nocturns as a daily service in cathedral usage;
8) the baptismal vigil, originally just the Easter Vigil but later celebrated also on the eve of Christmas, Epiphany, and Pentecost, when they, too, became baptismal days or when their liturgical solemnization was paschalized, depending on the various traditions. This vigil, usually an extension of vespers, comprised an especially solemn paschal lucernarium or light-ritual, followed by numerous Scripture lessons read in the basilica to occupy the people while the bishop was baptizing in the baptistry;
9) vesperal vigils consisting in vespers extended by antiphons and responsories, interspersed with lections, prostrations, and prayers, often terminating in Eucharist on the morrow. This is the sort of vigil we see in Basil, Cassian, Egeria, and numerous other early and later sources. It was an occasional—i.e. not daily—"all-night" vigil in both monastic and cathedral usage. Its use on Saturday nights was widespread; some also celebrated it Friday nights, before great feasts, for stations—i.e. at the shrines of saints, especially martyrs, on their feast day—and in times of special need. I have referred to such vigils as "pre-Eucharistic" since in origin they seem to have been an especially solemn preparation for the celebration of the Eucharist in a period when this was done with limited frequency, at most one or two days a week and on feasts. This vigil was characterized by cathedral psalmody, prayer, and readings, chiefly but not exclusively from the Scriptures. The psalmody was responsorial or antiphonal, with popular participation, and must not be confused with the meditative, continuous psalmody of monastic vigils or nocturns. Great importance was given to the Scripture readings. Prostrations for private prayer,

summed up by a collect, filled out the liturgical unit. Preaching was also customary. It is this type of vigil that eventually takes hold in cathedral usage, especially in the West.

Later we see various combinations of what I have tried to sort out into several basic types, which, if we prescind from nonessential details and from domestic watches such as wakes, can be reduced to four:

1) the baptismal vigil of *Scripture lessons;*
2) the cathedral, Sunday resurrection vigil climaxing in the *proclamation of the paschal gospel;*
3) a monastic-type vigil, really an extended nocturns, in which *continuous psalmody* is the basic element, though there were also lessons, prostrations, and prayers;
4) an occasional vigil of antiphons, responsories, Scripture readings, prostrations, prayers, and preaching, found usually as an *extension of vespers* and *culminating in Eucharist* on the morrow. Of special importance was the *proclamation of the Word* in the lections and homily.

In the later traditions we see various combinations of this material in the liturgical cursus. Elements of the Sunday resurrection vigil can still be identified in several Eastern offices, and Mateos has hypothesized that the same is true in the West.[58] Vigils of the paschal type can still be seen before certain feasts in some traditions, and festive monastic nocturns in the West remains the faithful heir to the extended-nocturns vigil of the monastic tradition. The only sort of vigil that seems to have died out is the one that was most popular in Latin Churches in Late Antiquity: the occasional vigil of psalmody, lessons, preaching, and prayers. But the "Office of Readings" in the new Roman *Liturgy of the Hours,* when celebrated as a vigil, can be considered an attempt to restore something of this ancient, popular Latin night service. And were we not so totally innocent of history, much could be done, at least in the United States, to exploit the pastoral possibilities of the one occasional vigil still commonly observed there, the wake.

[58]Mateos, "La vigile cathédrale chez Egérie."

# 10.

*QUAESTIONES DISPUTATAE:*
THE ORIGINS OF NOCTURNS,
MATINS, AND PRIME

Historians of the liturgy would agree, I think, with most of what I have said in the previous chapters. But there are still other particular issues for which a generally agreed and satisfying solution is yet to be found. Among them is the question of the origins and interrelation of the three canonical hours that precede terce: nocturns (vigils), morning praise (lauds), and prime. This remains *the* outstanding problem in the history of the formation of the Divine Office. Several scholars have dealt with it directly or indirectly in recent years: Baumstark, Bradshaw, Callewaert, Chadwick, Froger, Hanssens, Jungmann, Marcora, Mateos, van der Mensbrugghe, Winkler, to mention the most important.[1]

## The State of the Question

The root problem is that of nocturns and matins, or in more recent Western nomenclature, matins and lauds. Today in almost all traditional

[1]Their works are listed in my article *"Quaestiones disputatae"* from which much of the material in this chapter is resumed. I am grateful to the editors of *Worship* and to The Liturgical Press for permission to use it again here.

rites matins is one composite office comprising a long nocturnal psalmody in sequence *(currente psalterio),* followed by lauds. Some early sources, however, speak of but one hour before prime or terce; others speak of two. And since early monastic witnesses to only one such hour usually say it took place before daybreak, some writers presume that such references are to nocturns, and that lauds are simply the end of this nocturnal psalmody. Others take the exact opposite view, holding that lauds are the original cathedral morning prayer, to which the corresponding and once totally separate monastic vigil was prefixed when monastic and cathedral usages became synthesized in the hybrid office of urban monasticism. Until the publication in 1981 of Paul F. Bradshaw's *Daily Prayer in the Early Church,* recent opinion was running in favor of the latter view.

There are four different but related questions in all this:

1) What was the composition of the original morning office or first synaxis of the day in the pure cathedral usage?
2) What is the origin of the lauds psalms (Pss 148–150), which appear later, in some of the offices in question?
3) What is the relationship between the nocturnal vigil and morning praise, or what the West now calls lauds, both of which, in most extant traditions, now comprise one composite morning office usually called matins?
4) What are the origins of prime?

## The Original Cathedral Morning Office

As we have seen, the earliest witnesses to morning praise, the pure cathedral office at dawn, refer explicitly only to Ps 62/63 as *the* morning psalm. The service ended with the usual intercessions and dismissals. The *Gloria in excelsis* was probably part of this office, too. Can one conclude from this evidence that the earliest cathedral matins had no other proper fixed psalms? It is difficult not to see here a parallel with what the same documents tell us about cathedral vespers: one vesperal psalm (Ps 140); one morning psalm (Ps 62). Ambrose, *Expl. ps.* 1, 9, seems to support this view: "The break of day echoes with a psalm, its close resounds with one *(Diei ortus psalmum resultat, psalmum resonat occasus)."*[2] Is Bradshaw right, then, in concluding that the lauds psalms were not a part of the earliest cathedral matins?[3] I shall return to this question in a moment.

[2]PL 14, 925.
[3]See note 6.

For now, suffice it to say that the evidence does not permit us to conclude with certainty that the earliest cathedral matins had but one psalm. In the first place, the parallel with vespers is weakened by evidence from comparative liturgy: hagiopolite vespers had several vesperal psalms, with no prejudice to the fact that Ps 140 was considered *the* vesperal psalm. Secondly, from the second half of the fourth century, sources with remarkable consistency call matins *"matutini hymni"* or some such plural name.[4] Of course this does not prove there were several matins psalms—but that is the point: the evidence proves nothing one way or the other. Finally, contemporary witnesses to matins in the hybrid offices of urban monasticism indicate other psalms (50, 89) and canticles that are probably of cathedral provenance, and could go back to the earliest cathedral morning prayer. These witnesses will be discussed below.

## The Origins of Lauds

In challenging the long-held assumption that Pss 148–150 were part of the primitive stratum of cathedral morning praise, Bradshaw rehabilitates a thesis formulated in essence by J. Froger thirty years ago.[5] Froger sees Pss 148–150, at least in Eastern offices, not as the pristine core of cathedral morning praise, a core later adopted into their mixed office by the urban monks, but rather as a later addition which the cathedral morning office borrowed from the monastic vigil. Bradshaw adopts basically the same view:

> Cassian's account also throws some illumination on the original place of Pss. 148–150 in the daily office. It has come to be treated as an unquestioned fact that these psalms have always formed the nucleus of the morning office in the cathedral tradition and were derived from the usage of the synagogue. However, like many other such "facts" this rests upon nothing stronger than constant repetition by successive scholars. As we have indicated earlier, the evidence for the use of these psalms in the first-century synagogue liturgy is very flimsy indeed, and claims for their inclusion in the secular morning office in the East in the fourth century rely solely upon supposition. On the other hand, both Cassian and Chrysostom are witnesses to the fact that they formed the conclusion of the monastic night vigil in Syria

<hr />

[4] E. g., Eusebius, *In ps. 64*, 10, PG 23, 640 (cf. Mateos, "Quelques anciens documents," 348); Epiphanius, *Adv. haer.* 3:23, PG 29, 829; Egeria, *Journal* 24:2; Ambrose, *In ps. 118, sermo 19*, 32, PL 15, 1479; and the texts of Chrysostom, Basil, and the *De virginitate* discussed in chapter 5.

[5] J. Froger, "Note pour rectifier l'interpretation de Cassien," 96–102.

and Palestine, and we must not forget that the Egyptian vigil always ended with one of the psalms which had Alleluia marked in its title in the Bible, which would include these psalms. What evidence there is, therefore, points to the original place of the three psalms as being the fixed conclusion of the night vigil, perhaps arising out of the practice of early ascetics who recited the whole Psalter in the course of 24 hours, and so would have reached these psalms at the end of their vigil.

How then did they come to occupy a central position in the morning office in later centuries? This is not hard to explain. We have already seen how in some places, as for example Jerusalem, the monastic vigil led directly into the morning office. This juxtaposition of the two could very easily have led to Pss. 148–150 being thought of as the beginning of the latter rather than the conclusion of the former, and the strong influence exercised by monasticism in the Church would account for their being adopted as the beginning of the morning office even in the cathedral tradition. This was the position which they apparently had throughout Italy in Cassian's day, since he tells us in the above quotation that there "when the morning hymns are ended the 50th [51st] psalm is sung in all the churches," an arrangement which he again mistakenly attributes to the influence of the Bethlehem morning office. There can be little doubt from the context that by "morning hymns" he means Pss. 148–150, and these now form the beginning of the office, with Ps. 51, the original beginning, coming second. A similar arrangement is found in the morning office of the Chaldean rite, which is thought to have remained in many ways closer to the ancient pattern than other Eastern Rites: here Pss. 148–150 precede Ps. 51 on weekdays. In all other rites known to us, however, these psalms form the climax of the morning office, and this seems to have been a further stage of development: we have already seen how in De virginitate Ps. 51 had been drawn back to stand at the head of the whole rite. It would have been perfectly natural for a similar movement to have taken place in the opposite direction so that Pss. 148–150 formed the conclusion not just of the vigil psalmody but of the whole of the hymns and psalms of the combined night and morning offices, and once again the influence of monasticism in the Church as a whole would have ensured that this practice was generally followed.[6]

Let us examine the early evidence for Pss 148–150. "Early" in this instance means the late fourth century, when we see explicit references to the lauds psalms in the office in only two sources: John Chrysostom's *In 1 Tim homily 14*, 3–4, from his Antiochene period; and the famous problem passage of John Cassian's *Institutes* III, 3–6 describing the monastic

[6]*Daily Prayer* 109–110; cf. 82, 103.

offices as he had known them at Bethlehem. Because of the extremely complex problems involved in interpreting this material, I shall summarize first what I have already said in chapters 4–6 regarding the monastic vigil in Antioch and in the difficult texts of Cassian.

## I. CHRYSOSTOM:

Chrysostom's description of the Antiochene monastic office explicitly affirms that Ps 148:1 was said at the end of the monastic vigil, and I argued that the vigil probably was structured as follows:

Invitatory:              Ps 133
                         Is 26:9ff.

Variable monastic psalmody *currente psalterio*

Lauds:                   Pss 148-150

Then after a short rest the monks rose for a brief morning office of cathedral elements comprising:

Ps 62
*Gloria in excelsis*
Intercessions
Concluding prayer(s)

## II. CASSIAN:

Cassian in Palestine around the same time (ca. 382–386) also describes the place of the lauds psalms in the Bethlehem monastic office, and contrasts it with the usage of Gaul. In Bethlehem there was originally but one office before terce, the vigil or nocturns which concluded with Pss 148-150. After this vigil the monks could retire again. Alas, this second period of rest was abused by the monks, who slept from after nocturns right through until terce (*Inst.* III, 5). So a new morning office at sunrise was instituted to make them get up earlier. This new office, like terce and sext, had three psalms (50, 62, 89) with prayers. In Gaul and Italy, however, Pss 148-150 were not a fixed conclusion of nocturns, but part of a separate morning office that followed nocturns after a brief interval. This yields the following patterns:

| | BETHLEHEM | ANTIOCH | PROVENCE |
|---|---|---|---|
| at cockcrow: | *vigil:* | *vigil:* | *vigil:* |
| | | Ps 133 | |
| | | Is 26:9 | |
| | variable psalmody | variable psalmody | variable psalmody |
| | Pss 148–150 | Pss 148–150 | |
| at daybreak: | *novella sollemnitas:* | *morning office:* | *morning office:* |
| | Pss 62, 50, 89 | Pss 50, 62 (?) | Ps 62 |
| | | | Ps 118:117–148 |
| | | | Pss 148–150 |
| | | *Gloria in excelsis* | |
| | | Intercessions | |
| | | Concluding prayer(s) | |

Was this *novella sollemnitas* a Palestinian innovation, as Cassian asserts? The fourth century Antiochene monastic office has an analogous service, and Chrysostom's description above could well go back to his monastic period from 370–376, whereas Cassian did not enter his Bethlehem monastery until 382–383. But these dates are close, and Cassian a generally reliable witness,[7] so I see no reason to doubt his insistence on this point. Perhaps his *"nostro tempore"* of *Institutes* II, 4:1 is to be understood loosely.

Just what was this *novella sollemnitas*? Some have wished to see in it the origins of prime. But in chapter 6 we saw a strikingly similar office in the contemporary *Ordo monasterii* 2, from North Africa ca. 395: "We shall describe how we ought to pray or execute the psalmody: at matins, let three psalms be said: the 62nd, the 5th, and the 89th; at terce . . . [etc.]." Note the similarity between this morning office of three psalms and the *novella sollemnitas* of Cassian. Note also that it is called *matins*, not prime, and that it is followed by terce. Since the text refers later to nocturns, this should warn us not to be hasty in calling the *novella sollemnitas* prime. On the other hand the *Ordo monasterii* cannot be used as an argument in favor of the theory that Pss 148–150 were not an original part of *cathedral* matins. For this is a *monastic* rule, and it is my contention that the lauds psalms in monastic matins are a later influence of *cathedral* morning praise.

A problem passage of *Institutes* III, 4, already cited above in chapter 6, is closely related to all this, and we are now in a position to understand what Cassian means. He says clearly:

[7]See Guy, "Jean Cassien, historian du monachisme égyptien?" 363–372.

1) that in most of the West there is a morning office separated from nocturns by a brief interval of repose;

2) that this office was a recent innovation of Cassian's Bethlehem monastery;

3) that previous to this innovation, that *same* morning office, which in Gaul is *separated from* nocturns by an interval, ended in Bethlehem *at the same time as* the nocturnal vigil.

If we put this together with what we saw in chapter 6 concerning the interpretation of *Institutes* III, 6, it becomes apparent that Cassian considered the lauds psalms *in both Bethlehem and Provence* to be a "matins" or morning office. The case for Provençal usage is clear, because there lauds were an office separate from nocturns in fact as well as theory. In Bethlehem the lauds psalms were at the end of the nocturnal vigil, *but Cassian refers to this final part of the vigil as "this morning office"*—i.e., the *same* as the one celebrated a short time after the end of nocturns in Provence: "For up until that time we find that when *this morning office* (which in the monasteries of Gaul is customarily celebrated after a short interval after the psalms and prayer of nocturns have been finished) was ended [in Bethlehem] together with the daily vigils . . . (Vsque ad illud enim tempus *matutina hac sollemnitate,* quae expletis nocturnis psalmis et orationibus post modicum temporis interuallum solet in Galliae monasteriis celebrari, *cum cotidianis uigiliis pariter consummata . . .*" [emphasis added]).

This view of the lauds psalms as really a distinct office even if appended to nocturns seems confirmed further on in III, 4, when Cassian cites Ps 118: 164 in the context of the new morning office in Bethlehem: *"Seven times a day have I uttered praise to you for the judgments of your justice.* Having added this office and holding these spiritual assemblies seven times a day, we show without doubt that we utter praises to the Lord seven times a day." But only six offices have been mentioned up to this point in the *Institutes:* vigils, the new morning office, terce, sext, none, and vespers. Could the seventh hour be "this morning office"—i.e. lauds appended to the vigil? O. Chadwick thinks so,[8] in spite of the fact that later, in *Institutes* IV, 19:2, Cassian speaks of psalmody just before retiring. Some wish to see in this a reference to compline, and that of course would fill out the complement of seven hours without needing to count lauds as a separate office. Against this Chadwick argues that Cassian did not consider this bedtime psalmody one of the seven hours of prayer because he

[8]"The Origins of Prime," JTS 49 (1948) 179–181.

makes no mention of it in his lengthy and detailed treatment of the Bethlehem cursus. Even more telling is the fact that when he does list the offices
of that cursus in *Institutes* III, 3:11, he refers to vespers "at the end," thereby clearly implying there was no compline: ". . . quod tempus designat
matutinam nostram sollemnitatem, dein tertia, inde sexta, post haec nona,
*ad extremum undecima, in qua lucernaris hora signatur"* (emphasis added).
At any rate Cassian does single out Pss 148-150 for special mention in
the context of the Bethlehem vigil, and though this may be because these
psalms are found in Provençal matins too, it could also be because they
are more than just the last three psalms of the continuous monastic psalmody of the vigil.

   Let us examine this final point more closely. Bradshaw's argument rests,
in part, on the supposition that the Bethlehem monks read the entire psalter
nightly in the course of the nocturnal vigil. This is highly improbable.
We know very little about the *pensum* of psalms in this early period. As
we saw in chapter 5, the *De virginitate* orders as many psalms as is physi-
cally possible, and Callinicus' *Life of St. Hypatius* 26, tells us that Hypatius
(d. 446) said a hundred psalms and prayers every twenty-four hours.[9] Cassian, however, so detailed in his descriptions of Bethlehem usage, says
nothing about doing the whole psalter every night at the vigil, although
such a crippling *pensum* would certainly have attracted his admiring attention. Not even his Egyptian heroes went to such excess in their psalmody, and Cassian explicitly refers to the Bethlehem usage as a *mitigation*
of the Egyptian cursus (*Inst.* III, 1).

   There was, however, an all-night vigil in Bethlehem Friday night, from
vespers until the fourth cockcrow about two hours before daybreak, in
honor of the passion (*Inst.* III, 8-9), as we saw also in Jerusalem in the
diary of Egeria 27:7. We know from later sources that the Palestinian
monks observed a Saturday night *agrypnia*, and we have a detailed description of this vigil in the account of a visit paid by Abbots John and
Sophronius to the anchorite Abbot Nilus of Sinai, a Greek source of the
late sixth or early seventh century.[10] According to this source the entire
psalter, divided like the Irish psalters[11] into three "stations" *(staseis)* of

---

   [9] G.J.M. Bartelink (ed.), Callinicos, *Vie d'Hypatios* (SC 177, Paris: Cerf, 1971) 180-182.
On the whole question of the recitation of the entire psalter within a set period of time,
see Baumstark, *Nocturna laus* 156-166, and de Vogüé, *La Règle de S. Benoît* V, 545ff.
   [10] Critical edition in A. Longo, "Il testo integrale della *Narrazione degli abati Giovanni
e Sofronio* attraverso le *Hermêneiai* di Nicone," *Rivista di studi bizantini e neoellenici* 12-13
(1965-1966) 223-267 (the text concerning the *agrypnia* is on pp. 251-252). See also the introduction, pp. 230ff., and J. Mateos, "La psalmodie variable dans l'office byzantin," Societas academica Dacoromana, *Acta philosophica et theologica* 2 (Rome, 1964) 336ff.
   [11] See above, p. 115.

fifty psalms each, was read, interrupted as in Cassian (*Inst.* III, 8:4) by lessons from the New Testament. But the narrative also informs us that this continuous psalmody was integrated into matins in such a way that the customary fixed psalms of that office, *including the* Ainoi *or lauds psalms*, retain their traditional place independent of the monastic canon of 150 psalms said *currente psalterio*. This can be seen in the following outline. Those familiar with the Byzantine office, derived from the Palestinian Sabaitic office, will recognize immediately the similarities between this outline and present-day Byzantine orthros. The text refers to the *hexapsalmos* without specifying which psalms it comprised. I presume it to mean the *hexapsalmos* of orthros, not the one in compline, and indicate today's usage in parentheses.

| | | |
|---|---|---|
| *Hexapsalmos:* | | (Pss 3, 37, 62, 87, 102, 142) |
| | | |
| Our Father | | |
| Psalmody: | *Stasis* I: | Pss 1–50 |
| | | Our Father |
| | | *Kyrie eleison* 50 times |
| | | Lesson from James |
| | *Stasis* II: | Pss 51–100 |
| | | Our Father |
| | | *Kyrie eleison* 50 times |
| | | Lesson from 1 or 2 Peter |
| | *Stasis* III: | Pss 101–150 |
| | | Our Father |
| | | *Kyrie eleison* 50 times |
| | | Lesson from 1, 2 or 3 John |

Nine Biblical Canticles, with Our Father and *Kyrie eleison* after the 3rd and 6th

| | |
|---|---|
| The *Ainoi:* | Pss 148–150 |
| *Gloria in excelsis* | |
| Creed | |
| Our Father | |
| *Kyrie eleison* 300 times | |
| Concluding Prayer | |

Although this vigil clearly represents a later stage of the Palestinian office than the one described by Cassian, and the liturgical material of the narrative is not necessarily, at least in its entirety, as old as the rest of the account, it hardly lends support to Bradshaw's view that the psalms of lauds are simply the end of the continuous monastic psalmody. Furthermore, I know of no evidence that the Palestinians recited the whole psalter at their nocturns on weekdays. So I find gratuitous the hypothesis that the custom of chanting Pss 148–150 at morning praise arose from an ancient monastic practice of reciting the entire psalter every night.

But even if we accepted Bradshaw's assumption that the entire psalter was done nightly at the vigil, how does one explain why both Cassian and Chrysostom single out the lauds psalms for special comment, if they were just the final psalms of the continuous psalter? And how does one explain the rapidity with which these last three psalms of the continuous monastic nocturnal psalmody were detached from the vigil and joined to the morning office in all traditions, cathedral and monastic, Eastern and Western?

Actually, the Antiochene and Palestinian evidence gives only part of the picture. As we have seen in Cassian, there was also another Western pattern, *equally ancient,* found in the monasteries of Provence and, seemingly, in the secular churches of Italy. In this tradition the lauds psalms are not appended to the monastic vigil but constitute a separate morning office, a system we see by the sixth century in cathedral and monastic matins throughout the West. Does this open the possibility of another explanation of the origins of the lauds psalms in matins? Bradshaw would say that the original core of cathedral matins was Ps 62, and that Pss 148–150 came in later.[12] That may be true, but did it come about as a result of the influence of a monastic vigil that always ended with these psalms? Others would conclude that Pss 148–150 are simply the lauds of cathedral morning praise that have been tacked onto the end of monastic nocturns in urban monasteries that were in contact with the cathedral churches.

Two strong arguments support the first viewpoint:

1) In both our earliest witnesses to Pss 148–150 in a morning office, Cassian in Bethlehem and Chrysostom in Antioch, they are found attached to the end of the monastic vigil.
2) The earliest witnesses to the two cathedral offices from the same period all speak of Ps 140 as the core of cathedral vespers and Ps 62 as that of cathedral matins, without a whisper concerning Pss 148–150 as part of morning prayer.

[12]*Daily Prayer* 82–83.

There are also arguments in favor of the other view, which considers Pss 148–150 original to cathedral morning prayer and sees their presence in monastic vigils as the result of cathedral influence on the monastic office.

1) In the West, the testimony of Cassian for Gaul and Italy, at the beginning of the fifth century.

2) The overwhelming weight, from the sixth century on, of all Western sources known to me with one exception, the *Ordo monasterii*. All these sources have Pss 148–150 at the end of morning prayer, not in the vigil.

3) Earlier Eastern sources such as Basil, Egeria, the Cappadocian *De virginitate* attributed to Athanasius, though they do not mention the lauds psalms explicitly, do refer to "morning hymns" or use some analogous expression that cannot be said to exclude the presence of Pss 148–150—especially

4) in the light of the presence today of these psalms at the end of matins in every Eastern Rite except the pure Egyptian monastic *Horologion*. This Eastern picture does not become clear until a bit later, but when it does, one finds this pattern in which the lauds psalms are part of a separate morning office in every tradition.

So it is not completely gratuitous to theorize 1) that the lauds psalms are an ancient element of cathedral morning prayer, and 2) that the presence of Pss 148–150 at the end of the vigil in some *mixed* urban monastic usages we have seen, but *not* in the purely monastic Egyptian *Horologion*,[13] could indicate a cathedral influence on monastic nocturns rather than vice-versa.

But if this is not implausible then how does one explain the original relation, if any, of lauds to nocturns?

## The Relationship between Nocturns and Lauds

It is intriguing that the "received theory" concerning the original core of cathedral vespers and morning prayer is based in the early evidence on a split vote. The East—but not the West—provides ample and clear early evidence for Ps 140 as the central psalm of cathedral vespers. In the

[13]The Coptic midnight office has Pss (LXX) 3, 6, 12, 69, 85, 90, 116–133, 136–137, 140–141, 145–147. Matins has Pss 1–6, 8, 11–12, 14–15, 18, to which have been added in modern

best study on vespers, G. Winkler has meticulously examined all the early evidence. In the West, as I have noted above, it is limited to an occasional hint; in the East it is almost overwhelming.[14] Conversely, beginning with Cassian's early fifth-century testimony, and abounding with witnesses from the start of the sixth century, the West—but not the East—is practically unanimous in placing the psalms of lauds at the heart of cathedral morning prayer. So in the case of morning prayer it is the earlier, Eastern evidence that is ambiguous. That is why the relationship between nocturns and lauds remains a problem in the history of the formation of the Liturgy of the Hours. Although I am not so sanguine as to pretend that I can unknot here this tangled skein, I shall suggest what I think the solution might look like were we able to trace each thread of evidence back through its multifarious intertwinings to its point of origin.

As we saw in chapter 4, originally the *pure monastic* rule of prayer was simply the evangelical "pray always," which came to be interpreted in Egypt as pray at every hour, twelve a day and twelve at night. This "rule of the angel" is probably the primitive basis for dividing the continuous psalmody of the later two daily synaxes into groups of twelve It is at this stage that we pick up Cassian in Lower Egypt: two daily synaxes, upon rising in the wee hours of the morning and in the late afternoon before retiring, with twelve psalms and two readings at each.

The *pure cathedral* usage in the late fourth-century sources contemporaneous to Cassian also had two common synaxes: morning praise or matins at daybreak, and vespers or evensong at dusk. But as we have already seen, the fact that these two cathedral synaxes were a bit later than their monastic parallels does not mean that we are dealing with different "hours" of the office. It simply reflects the fact that the monks rose earlier. Both traditions are inheritors of exactly the same ancient custom of beginning and ending the day with prayer. So what we have in *both* cases is the fourth-century formalizing of the ancient, private prayer at the beginning and end of the day. The monks rose earlier and prayed longer, so what was *matins* and vespers in cathedral usage was *vigils* and vespers for the monks. In other words we have parallel sets of two offices and *not* a three-office structure of nocturns, matins, vespers.

Finally, in the same period in *urban monasticism*—i.e. monasteries in or near towns in closer contact with cathedral usages—of Bethlehem, An-

---

usage Pss 24, 26, 62, 66, 69, 112, 142. Terce follows matins. See O.H.E. Burmester, *The Egyptian or Coptic Church* (Publications de la Société d'archéologie copte: textes et documents, Cairo: Printing Office of the French Institute of Oriental Archaeology, 1967) 100, 105–106.

[14]Winkler, "Über die Kathedralvesper," 53–102.

tioch, Cappadocia, Gaul, we find evidence of mixed traditions containing both monastic and cathedral elements in the offices. These hybrid offices fall into not one but several patterns, depending on how the synthesis came about in each area. In other words when urban monks in different regions began to develop composite offices incorporating elements of both the monastic and cathedral traditions, *they did so in different ways:*

1)   Some *started with the monastic usage* as the basis, and *added cathedral elements:*

    a)   In Bethlehem and Antioch the monks added Pss 148–150 of cathedral morning praise to the end of their monastic vigil, celebrating the two services without interruption. Later, to get up at sunrise the monks who had retired again after this office, the Bethlehem monks create *another* morning office, made up apparently of other elements of cathedral morning praise: Pss 50, 62, 89. Thus they absorbed elements of cathedral matins in two phases. The first step could have been to append the lauds psalms of cathedral matins to the end of the corresponding monastic office that opened the day. Later, when need was felt for another morning service to get the monks up from their post-vigil repose, since the monks already had the tradition of saying Pss 148–150 at the end of their original morning office, they left them there and formed the new office from other elements of cathedral matins. This fits in well, I think, with Cassian's language in *Institutes* III, 3 and 6, where, as we have seen, he refers to *both* the new office and the lauds psalms at the end of vigils as *matins.*

    b)   In Gaul the monks finished their monastic vigil, then after a brief interval celebrated a second, morning office containing the psalms of lauds borrowed, I believe, from cathedral usage.

    c)   We saw a similar pattern in the Western monastic rules of the Master, Benedict, Columban, Caesarius and Aurelian. The late fourth-century *Ordo monasterii*, when compared to later Western monastic offices, shows us this very process underway. It has only three fixed psalms in the morning office, whereas slightly later rules from Italy such as the *Rule of the Master* (34–35, 39) and the *Rule of St. Benedict* (12–13) conclude matins with canticles and the psalms of lauds.

2)    Others *started with cathedral usage* and *monasticized it:*
   a)    At daybreak, the hour of cathedral morning praise, Cappadocian ascetics had matins, comprising Ps 50 or 62 plus "hymns and odes." To this they added a monastic *mesonyktikon* or midnight office. This I would interpret as a mixed system rooted primarily in the cathedral usage with its full and separate morning prayer at dawn, to which the ascetics later added a monastic vigil. So what we have here is a monasticized cathedral office, rather than a cathedralized monastic office as in the first case. This, I believe, is what we saw in the writings of St. Basil and in the *De virginitate.*

Which system is earlier? Cassian arrived in Bethlehem around 385, and settled in Gaul around 415. So the Provençal-Roman usage is witnessed to only thirty years after we first hear of the Bethlehem office. And although Cassian described the Bethlehem *novella sollemnitas* as new, he does not put the Gallican usage in the same category, as he undoubtedly would have since the history of the monastic office is his major concern. So it is not illegitimate to conclude that the Gallican use of Pss 148–150 in a morning office *separate* and *distinct* from the vigil is just about as old as the Palestinian monastic usage. And since we find this latter usage of Pss 148–150 at the end of the morning office absolutely everywhere in *all* cathedral and in some hybrid cathedral-monastic offices, but *not* in the purely monastic night or morning synaxes of Egypt, the weight of comparative liturgy seems to favor the theory that these lauds psalms are original to the cathedral usage, from which they entered the monastic office in various ways, depending on the tradition. Perhaps the North African monk Arnobius the Younger (ca. 470) is referring to this cathedral usage when in his *Commentary on Ps 148* he says that Ps 148 is sung throughout the whole world at dawn.[15]

Of course these two suggested patterns do not exhaust the possibilities. There could have been others, and indeed, the *Ordo monasterii* might well reflect an earlier influence of cathedral matins on monastic usage before that office had incorporated Pss 148–150 as a fixed finale.

---

[15]PL 53, 566, cited above in chapter 8 at note 11.

## One Office or Two?

From what I have said it is clear that I prefer Mateos' view that the current psalmody of our present composite matins office is a nocturnal monastic vigil originally separate and distinct from the morning praise or lauds to which it is now prefixed in most extant offices.[16] Whether these two offices were originally always *celebrated* separately cannot be answered *per modum unius*. One cannot argue from the earlier *agrypnia* of the anchorites of Sinai referred to above. Such an all-night vigil by its very nature ran through the night until it joined and ended with morning praise. Certainly in the *Rule of St. Benedict* (8) they were separate. In the earlier *Rule of the Master* (33) the two offices are celebrated together in the spring and summer when the nights are short, but it is clear that the legislator considers them two distinct offices. Indeed, he returns to the question three times in order to justify the practice of doing them one after the other without a break:

> [33]In spring and summer . . . the brothers are to begin the nocturns at cockcrow because of the shortness of the nights, and as soon as they have finished the set number of psalms they are to append Matins with its full number of psalms. We have prescribed that nocturns in these short nights are to begin after cockcrow and are to be joined with Matins so that the brothers do not go back to bed after the nocturns, become drowsy and, overpowered by sweet morning sleep, not only miss Matins but be put to shame by saying even Prime late. Furthermore, we have said to join the nocturns with Matins after cockcrow so that the brothers, now refreshed by a long sleep, may go through both offices attentively, then after paying the divine debt of Matins the brothers who so wish need have no qualms about going back to bed until Prime. . . . So the shortness of nighttime relative to daytime requires, because of the weakness of human nature, that the psalmody of the Divine Office be curtailed and the daytime Office be joined to that of the night. . . . These nocturns in summertime, as we have said above, are to begin right after cockcrow, and as soon as they are finished they are to be followed by Matins because of the shortness of the nights.[17]

Other documents enumerate vigils and matins as two offices, but do not tell us just how they were celebrated.[18]

---

[16]*Lelya-Ṣapra, passim;* "Les matines chaldéennes, maronites et syriennes," 54–55, 58ff., 61ff., 68; "L'invitatoire," 353–356; "Un office de minuit chez les chaldéens?" 101–113; "Les differentes espèces de vigiles," 48ff.; "Quelques problèmes de l'orthros byzantin," 22–31.

[17]Eberle, *The Rule of the Master* 194–197.

[18]For example Caesarius, CM 20–21, CV 66; 69; Aurelian, AM 56:11–22; AV 41–42.

As for the East, where there is considerably less evidence for the peri-od of Late Antiquity, I think the same pattern can be discerned in some sources already cited (Basil, *De virginitate*, Chrysostom) as well as in the slightly later Callinicus (366–446), *Vita S. Hypatii* 26.[19] Even later, a text of St. Theodore Studites describing the monastic office of Constantino-ple at the end of the eighth century could be interpreted in the same way.[20] But I would agree with J. Leroy that by the time of the ninth-century Stu-dite *Hypotyposis*, which dates from the years immediately following St. Theodore's death in 826, orthros in the Studite usage of Constantinople is one composite office of nocturns and matins, much as it still is to-day.[21] This is confirmed by Pseudo-Chrysostom, *In ps. 118*, 4, which also dates from the period of Iconoclasm if not later.[22] But the insertion of the resurrection vigil between nocturns and matins on Sundays and feasts at the "All-night Vigil" in Byzantine monasteries and in Muscovite cathedral usage still betrays the original separateness of these two offices.

What of the present Byzantine night office, called *mesonyktikon*, that now comes between compline and orthros in the Byzantine cursus? Doesn't this show that the psalmody at the beginning of orthros is not the origi-nal night office but just a prelude to lauds? Against this is the fact that when the "All-night Vigil" is celebrated, *mesonyktikon* is simply omitted and vespers is followed immediately by the psalmody of orthros. This would be unthinkable if *mesonyktikon* were the original psalmody of the night in the Byzantine cursus. So I think *mesonyktikon* is a later office added to fill the gap in the cursus caused by the fusion of the original nocturns with orthros.

## The Origins of Prime

The first unambiguous references to prime are in Latin sources of the sixth century beginning with Caesarius of Arles, CV 69 (ca. 534); then in Aurelian of Arles, AM 28; the rules of the Master (RM 34–35, 41) and Benedict (RB 16). Leroy has demonstrated its existence in the Byzantine monastic office before the end of the eighth century, and there is reason to believe it was not an innovation of that period but a usage that had come in earlier.[23] Can one pinpoint its origins more precisely? Froger is

[19] See note 9.

[20] *Magnae catecheseos sermo 6*, A. Mai, *Nova patrum bibliotheca* IX. 2, 17. But see J. Leroy, "Le cursus monastique chez S. Théodore Studite," EL 68 (1954) 10.

[21] Leroy, "Le cursus monastique," 16ff.

[22] PG 55, 705.

[23] "Le cursus monastique," 6ff.

surely right in considering Cassian's *novella sollemnitas* matins, not prime,[24] since that is what Cassian himself called it, and he considered it the equivalent of morning praise in the monasteries of Gaul. It is also called matins in the contemporary *Ordo monasterii* cited above in chapter 6. But words are words and things are things, and the fact that Cassian did not consider this new office "prime" nor call it by that name does not of course prove that the remote origins of prime cannot be seen in this *novella sollemnitas*. Against this, however, is the fact that we have no evidence for prime anywhere else in the East until centuries later. Furthermore, Sabaitic prime in the present-day Byzantine Office, which represents what has come down to us from Palestinian monastic usage, has Pss 5, 89, 100, not Pss 62, 50 and 89 of Cassian's new office. And in fact the latter psalms of Cassian's new Palestinian matins, like the parallel Pss 62, 5, 89 of matins in the *Ordo monasterii* 2, are found much more often in later offices of lauds, as Froger pointed out.[25] So Froger's arguments against the once common thesis that in Cassian's *novella sollemnitas* we have the origins of prime still stand.

## Conclusion

The question of the origins and history of the first three hours of the office has presented us with a classic problem of comparative liturgy:

1)   A set of similarities that demonstrate either a common origin in the Urtradition, or later borrowing and mutual influence among traditions;

2)   and at the same time a set of variations that must be explained in a way that does not contradict what we affirm regarding no. 1.

### I. The data:

The facts are clear enough:

1)   In both cathedral and monastic usage there was originally one office to open the day: matins or nocturns respectively.

[24]J. Froger, *Les origines du prime* (Bibliotheca EL 19, Rome: Edizioni liturgiche, 1946) and "Note pour rectifier l'interpretation de Cassien."

[25]"Note pour rectifier l'interpretation de Cassien," 101; *Les origines du prime* 43–44.

2)    In cathedral usage where select psalmody was the basis of the offices, *the* morning psalm was Ps 62.

3)    The basis of the monastic office was psalmody *currente psalterio.*

4)    Pss 148–150 are found at the end of monastic nocturns in Bethlehem and Antioch according to Cassian and Chrysostom.

5)    But in Gaul and Italy according to Cassian, and everywhere else from the sixth century on, Pss 148–150 are the fixed part of the morning office in all cathedral and hybrid offices, though not in the purely monastic Egyptian *Horologion.*

6)    In almost all extant rites this morning office has a long monastic psalmody prefixed to it.

7)    From the sixth century on this morning office is followed in the cursus by prime.

## II. INTERPRETATION

There is no dispute concerning these facts. But how to interpret them? Bradshaw argues from (2) and (4) that the original *Sitz im Gottesdienst* of the lauds psalms is the monastic vigil, not cathedral matins. Pss 148–150 are just the normal end of the nocturnal psalmody, when all the psalms were recited in sequence. From there they went to cathedral matins and the hybrid offices (5).

It is here that I disagree with Bradshaw. The earliest cathedral matins may not have included the lauds psalms, but I believe that the office of cathedral matins is their native habitat in the Divine Office. In other words, I believe the present place of Pss 148–150 as a fixed element of the ordinary of matins to be the original one, and that the monastic vigil of Cassian and Chrysostom borrowed them from there, for these reasons:

1)    There is no evidence whatever that the whole psalter was read every night at the monastic vigil. And even if it were, this would not prove that Pss 148–150 were not also, and perhaps earlier, a part of cathedral matins, as in the Saturday vigil described in the account of the meeting with Nilus of Sinai.

2)    Cassian does not consider Pss 148–150 just the last of the 150 psalms. He singles them out as a distinct unit and calls them a distinct morning office *even*

in Bethlehem where they were appended to
nocturns.

3) Pss 148–150 are at the end of matins, not nocturns,
in all extant rites.

4) Apart from Cassian in Bethlehem and Chrysostom
in Antioch, all early descriptions of urban monastic or later cathedral and hybrid offices (Basil, *De
virginitate*, Cassian for Gaul and Italy, the Master,
Benedict, Caesarius and Aurelian of Arles, Gaul of
Clermont . . .) show there was more to matins than
Ps 62, and this "more"—especially in the light of
later unanimous evidence from comparative liturgy
—could well have included Pss 148–150.

Of course (3) and (4) are also explained by Bradshaw's hypothesis,
though less adequately, I believe, because of the time element. Is it likely
that within a century Pss 148–150 went from the monastic vigil to cathedral
and hybrid matins absolutely everywhere in Christendom? This is of course
possible, but I find it unlikely that the evolution would have been so
universally uniform as to have left no trace anywhere—not even in the
pure Egyptian office—of the supposed original place of Pss 148–150 in
the daily monastic vigil (1). And Bradshaw's theory gives no adequate
explanation of (2).

So I prefer to see Cassian and Chrysostom as describing an originally
monastic office that has absorbed cathedral elements such as Pss 148–150.
Such a system starts with nocturns as its pristine first service of the day
and appends lauds to it. Others, such as Basil, seem to have started with
cathedral matins that included Pss 148–150, and then added to the cursus
a separate monastic night office. It is this pattern—two separate offices,
one monastic (nocturns), and one cathedral (matins or lauds)—that is at
the basis of all extant offices apart from the Egyptian tradition.

As for prime, it is a later addition. Cassian's *novella sollemnitas* is
neither prime nor, properly speaking, matins, but a sort of "second matins" formed from cathedral elements in circumstances peculiar to Cassian's Bethlehem community at the end of the fourth century. *So the mere
fact that Cassian is the earliest surviving witness to the material we have
been studying does not mean that the office he describes is the prototype
of all later developments.* But in the absence of conflicting contemporaneous witnesses all historical reconstructions of this material, including this
one, must remain tentative when not downright temerarious.

# 11

## CONCLUSION: MONASTIC AND CATHEDRAL STRUCTURES

From what we have seen, some general conclusions can be drawn concerning the nature and ideal forms of monastic and cathedral hours.

### Monastic Offices

Monastic offices had no special relation to the time of day when they were celebrated, but were simply a stimulus to the monk's uninterrupted prayer. They consisted in continuous psalmody according to the numbering of the psalter. Each psalm or unit of psalmody was followed by a prostration for private prayer and concluded with a collect. Scripture readings concluded the synaxis. In some traditions monastic vigils were simply a drawn out version of the same basic structure.

### Cathedral Offices

The cathedral hours of morning praise and evensong developed the symbolism of the rising sun and evening lamp as images of Christ, the

211

light of the world. Unlike monastic offices, they were clearly related to the time of celebration. Psalms, chants, symbols were chosen to suit the hour. Thus evensong opened with a lucernarium or ritualization of the evening lamp at the coming of darkness, symbol of Christ illuminating the sin-darkened world. The lamplighting was often accompanied by a Hymn of Light, such as the ancient *Phôs hilaron*. Then followed the evening Ps 140/141, with an offering of incense, symbol of our praise rising to the throne of God as in Ps 140:2. This opening was more or less standard, as were the concluding intercessions and dismissal, and the whole structure was sprinkled with collects at the cardinal points. Between these two fixed points one often finds other elements such as other psalms, a canticle or responsory, and perhaps a lesson. So the basic structure of vespers was somewhat as follows:

> Lamplighting rite
> Hymn of Light with opening collect
> Ps 140/141 with incensation and collect
> [other psalms
> Responsory
> Lesson
> Canticle]
> Intercessions and collect
> Concluding prayer "of inclination" (blessing)
> Dismissal

Morning praise opened with a penitential (Ps 50/51) or matutinal (Ps 62/63) psalm and ended with an Old Testament canticle, the psalms of lauds (Pss 148–150), the *Gloria in excelsis* on Sundays and feasts, and the usual concluding intercessions and prayers. Other elements such as variable psalms, a hymn in praise of the morning light, a lesson, will be found depending on the tradition. So the basic skeleton looked something like this:

> Opening psalm (50/51 or 62/63) with collect
> [Variable psalm(s)
> Lesson]
> OT canticle
> Pss 148–150 with collect
> Hymn of Light
> *Gloria in excelsis*
> Intercessions and collect
> Concluding prayer "of inclination" (blessing)
> Dismissal

Cathedral vigils had three basic forms:

1) the weekly resurrection vigil of three antiphons, incensation, and the proclamation of the paschal gospel;

2) occasional vigils consisting in the repetition of a liturgical unit comprising—though not necessarily in this order—cathedral psalmody (responsories and antiphons), lessons, prostrations for prayer followed by collects, and, often, preaching;

3) the vigil of readings as at Easter and some other feasts.

This second type of vigil was like an accordion: it could be longer or shorter to suit the occasion. It is found usually as an extension of vespers, but could also go all through the night from vespers to matins, or be celebrated independently of other offices.

Let us now see how these basic structures have been combined to form the offices of our still extant traditions.

# PART II

# The Divine Office in
# the Christian East

# Introduction

Let us now see what has become of this creation of Late Antiquity in the Christian East. Because of the vastness of the topic—a full cursus of canonical hours in seven distinct traditions—I shall limit my remarks to the principal hours at the beginning (nocturns-matins-lauds) and end (vespers) of the day in the several traditions.

At one end of the spectrum we have the Armenian and East-Syrian or Assyro-Chaldean offices, which have best retained their pristine cathedral character unalloyed. At the other extreme is the Coptic tradition, strongly monastic in its history and hence in its liturgy, which has kept its monastic and cathedral offices juxtaposed but not synthesized. Other traditions, especially the Byzantine, are more hybrid, the product of the fusion of monastic and cathedral usages effected during the period of evolution prior to their codification in the more or less fixed form that we know today.

I shall treat the several rites in the order given above, except for the Syrian traditions, which I treat together because of their close affinity, and the Ethiopian tradition, which I discuss after the Coptic for the same reason.

# 12

# THE ARMENIAN OFFICE

## History

The Armenian Rite, in some ways related to the Byzantine, is by no means just a variant or branch of that neighboring tradition, as some once thought. The historical cradle of Christian Armenia lies around Lake Van, just east of Greek Cappadocia and north of Syriac Osrhoene and Adiabene, and the earliest Christian influence in the third to fifth centuries flowed in from both streams. The evangelization of Armenia is traditionally attributed to St. Gregory the Illuminator (ca. 231–325) who was consecrated bishop by Leontius of Caesarea in Cappadocia around 302. Cappadocian Greek influence was predominant in this period, but there had been Syriac Christian influence even earlier. And from the fifth to the seventh century, when an indigenous Armenian Christian tradition was in the Golden Age of its formation, there was strong liturgical influence from Jerusalem. There followed a period of Byzantinization from the ninth to the thirteenth century, when Constantinopolitan political and ecclesiastical influence was especially strong. And finally during the Crusades, from the twelfth through the fourteenth centuries, the Latin presence in Asia Minor also left its traces on the liturgical uses of Armenia.

Our earliest witness to the Armenian office is Catholicos Yovhannes Ōjneçʻi (ca. 650–728), who wrote a commentary on the offices and left further evidence in his *Oratio synodalis* 10 and 13-15, and other frag-ments.[1] There is also a commentary by his contemporary Step‘annos Siwneç‘i (ca. 680-735),[2] and a later one, in the tenth century, by Xosrov Anjewaç‘i.[3] F. C. Conybeare in his old but still invaluable *Rituale Armeno-rum* also gives information on some manuscripts of the Armenian hours,[4] and at least two translations of the office are available, in Latin and English.[5]

## The Offices

The present Armenian office has seven hours—but not the exact same seven we are used to:

| | |
|---|---|
| The night hour (nocturns) | gišerayin žam |
| The morning hour (matins) | aṙawōtean žam |
| The sunrise hour (prime) | arewagali žam |
| The midday hour (typica) | čašu žam |
| The evening hour (vespers) | erekoyean žam |
| The hour of peace | xałałakan žam |
| The hour of rest (compline) | hangstean žam |

[1] "De officiis ecclesiae," Armenian text and Latin trans. in J.B. Aucher (ed.), *Domini Jo-hannis Ozniensis philosophi Armeniorum Catholici opera* (Venice: Mechitarist Press, 1834) 180-223; see also "Fragmenta," *ibid.* 236-249; "Oratio synodalis," *ibid.* 41ff. There is a La-tin version also in "John of Odsun on the Breviary," F. C. Conybeare, *Rituale Armenorum, being the administration of the sacraments and the breviary rites of the Armenian Church . . .*(Oxford: Clarendon Press, 1905) 488-502. A. Raes, "Note sur les anciennes ma-tines byzantines et arméniennes," OCP 19 (1953) 207ff., comments on matins in John of Odsun.

[2] S. Amatowni (ed.), "The Commentary on the Divine Office by Step‘annos the Philos-opher of Siwnik" (in Armenian), *Ararat* (1915) 225-239, 361-364, 485-496, 634-639; (1916) 129-141, 406-412, 694-703.

[3] Armenian text: *The Book which is called the Commentary on the Prayers* (Constan-tinople, 1730); summary in Conybeare, *Rituale Armenorum* 502-507.

[4] Conybeare, *Rituale Armenorum* 443-488.

[5] *The Book of Hours or the Order of Common Prayers of the Armenian Apostolic Or-thodox Church* (Evanston: Ouzoomian House, 1964), an incomplete translation; *Breviari-um Armenium sive dispositio communium Armeniacae Ecclesiae precum a sanctis Isaaco patriarcha, Mesrobio doctore, Kindio atque a Joanne Mantagunensi habita* (Venice: Mechitarist Press, 1908).

1. NOCTURNS

The night office is structured as follows:

| | |
|---|---|
| *Opening prayers:* | Doxology |
| | Our Father |
| *Invitatory:* | Doxology (Ps 50:17) |
| | Pss 3, 87, 102, 142 |
| | Chant |
| | Biddings |
| | Chant |
| | Collect |
| *Psalmody:* | Doxology |
| | Variable Psalms |
| | [Office of the dead—later addition] |
| | OT canticle |
| | Anthem of the canticle |
| *Conclusion:* | Intercesssions |
| | Collect |
| | Concluding chants and prayers |

This is the only Armenian service that has continuous monastic psalmody. According to the reconstruction of these offices by G. Winkler,[6] the whole psalter, exclusive of the lauds psalms, was divided into eight canons, each with its corresponding Old Testament canticle. The daily psalmody of this office comprised one canon with its canticle. Formerly, each canon had seven subsections of the psalter, of which only the seventh has survived. And the canticles have been replaced by hymns.

Note that the invitatory psalms (3, 87, 102, 142) include four of the six psalms of the present Byzantine *hexapsalmos* at the beginning of Sabaitic orthros. The original invitatory is undoubtedly Ps 3, found also as an invitatory to the nocturnal psalmody in the Chaldean, Tikritan, Byzantine Sabaitic, and old Constantinopolitan rites, as well as in the Latin monastic office.[7]

[6]G Winkler, "The Armenian Night Office, I," *Journal of the Society for Armenian Studies* 1 (1984) 93–113; II, *Revue des études arméniennes* 17 (1983) 471–551. I am most grateful to Prof. Winkler for allowing me to see the typescript of her article, the source of my information on Armenian nocturns and matins, before it went to press.

[7]Mateos, "Office de minuit et office du matin chez s. Athanase," 176–178; cf. Winkler, "The Armenian Night Office, I," 105–108.

II. MATINS

Today the morning office has the following structure:

Our Father
Introit: Ps 89:14–17
Doxology
*(original beginning of Sunday Cathedral Vigil
    according to Winkler:)*
OT Canticles: Dan 3:26–45 + troparion
                Dan 3:52–88 + troparion
Biddings
NT Canticle: *Magnificat* + troparion-*Benedictus-Nunc dimittis*
Litany and collect

---

*(Cathedral Vigil on Sundays:)*
Ps 112:1–3
Ps 43:26, 24
Ps 145:10, 1
Gospel of the Myrrhophores
Refrain of the gospel
Biddings

---

Ps 50 + troparion
Biddings
Pss 148–50 + troparion
*Gloria in excelsis*
*Kataxioson (Dignare Domine . . .)*
Refrain of the resurrection of Christ
Intercesssions: Litany and collect
                Angel of peace petitions
                and collect
                Prayer of Blessing
Trisagion

To this original conclusion of the office has been appended:

Bidding
Responsory
Gospel of healing
Anthem of the gospel

Bidding
Blessing

## iii. Vespers

Armenian vespers is a purely cathedral service, with no monastic psalmody:

| | |
|---|---|
| Our Father | |
| *Invitatory:* | Ps 54:17–18 |
| | Ps 85 |
| *Fixed vesperal psalms:* | Pss 139, 140, 141 |
| *Lucernarium:* | Prayer of blessing of the light |
| | Hymn of light (*Phôs hilaron* on Sundays) |
| | Prayer of thanksgiving for the light |
| | Biddings |
| | Responsory 1 |
| | Responsory 2: *Dirigatur* (Ps 140:2) |
| *Intercessions:* | Litany |
| | Angel of peace petitions |
| | Collect |
| | Prayer of blessing |

And as at matins, other material has been appended to this conclusion:

Trisagion
Biddings
Ps 121 + troparion
Biddings
Collect
Psalms of dismissal (2 or 3)
Biddings
Collect of dismissal
Our Father
Dismissal

Gabriele Winkler[8] has interpreted Armenian vespers as a juxtaposition of two traditions, the early Armenian vespers comprising:

---

[8]"Über die Kathedralvesper," 78–80.

Ps 54

*Lucernarium:* Prayer, hymn, thanksgiving

*Dirigatur* responsory

Intercessions

To this structure, she hypothesizes, elements from the Old Constantinopolitan office were prefixed:

Ps 85

Ps 140, later expanded by the addition of Pss 139
    and 141

This finds support in the commentary of Catholicos Yovhannes Ōjneçʻi (ca. 700), which says that Ps 85 was introduced by Catholicos Nerses,[9] either Nerses II (ca. 548) or the Nerses who was Catholicos in 641–661.[10] But this solution is weakened by the fact that Sabaitic vespers also had the normal vesperal psalms plus, it seems the *Kateuthynthêtô*— i.e., the *Dirigatur:* Ps 140 done responsorially as in the present Byzantine Liturgy of the Presanctified—according to the account of that service in the narrative of the visit of Abbots John and Sophronius to the anchorite Nilus of Sinai, a document of the sixth or seventh century already referred to in the preceding chapter apropros of the *agrypnia* in Palestine.[11]

## Present Usage

Today in Armenian parish worship, vespers, once celebrated every day, is usually done only on Saturday evening, though many parishes still celebrate daily the night and morning offices together in the morning. In addition, during Lent, parishes in the same town take turns celebrating the Peace and Rest (compline) Services[12] and the Sunrise Service (prime), one parish doing them each day of the week. This at least is the usage in the Patriarchate of Constantinople.[13]

[9]*Ibid.* 79; text in Conybeare, *Rituale Armenorum* 497.

[10]Winkler, "Über die Kathedralvesper," 79.

[11]Longo, "Il testo integrale della *Narrazione degli abati Giovanni e Sofronio,*" 253.

[12]*Breviarium Armenium* 239–290.

[13]Information from my student Rev. Khajag Barsamian, to whom I am also grateful for helpful bibliographical information concerning Armenian sources.

# 13

## THE ASSYRO-CHALDEAN OFFICE

The East-Syrian or Assyro-Chaldean Liturgy of the Hours, like the Armenian, has remained largely cathedral in character. Though today's office does bear some traces of monastic influence in the lesser hours, the three catheral hours of matins, vespers, and the festal cathedral vigil have retained their cathedral purity unalloyed. Indeed, in today's Assyro-Chaldean breviary these are the only extant hours outside of Lent, except for subba'a or compline or certain saints' days and feasts apart from Sunday.

### History

The Assyro-Chaldean Rite, used today by the members of the "Church of the East" who call themselves "Assyrians," as well as by the Chaldean and Malabar Catholics, is the ancient usage of the Mesopotamian Church in the Persian Empire, with its ecclesiastical center in the Catholicosate of Seleucia-Ctesiphon on the Tigris River, about fifty kilometers down river south of Baghdad in present-day Iraq.

The Synod of Seleucia-Ctesiphon in 410, the earliest known instance of an entire Church attempting to unify and fix its liturgical customs, decreed in canon 13 that the liturgical usage of the Church of Seleucia be observed by all, but the canon does not mention the Divine Office specifically.[1] Further, canon 15 of the Synod held under Catholicos George I

[1]. J.-B. Chabot, *Synodicon orientale ou recueil des synodes nestoriens* (Paris: Imprimerie nationale, 1902) 266–267.

225

at Darin in 676 ordered the laity to come to morning and evening prayer
in church. It was not enough to do the prayers at home, nor even
in one's own private chapel. And while at the offices they must participate, not just be there, and must stay until the end of the service. And
on feasts they must not abandon the common synaxes to go off and
celebrate the feast in some monastery.[2] Some aspects of this legislation
sound astonishingly contemporary, showing once again that pastoral
problems have a way of cropping up repeatedly in more or less the same
form. Especially interesting is the insistence on the communitarian aspect
of the prayer of hours: they are obligatory for everybody, and it is not
enough to do them in private, nor is it sufficient to do them in common
apart from the local ecclesial gathering. This was also the original sense
of the Catholic canonical obligation to hear Mass on Sundays—the obligation could not be fulfilled except by assisting at Mass in at least a semi-
public oratory, for the obligation was to assist at the *public* worship of
God, not just to "hear Mass."

Very little is known about the early shape of the Assyro-Chaldean Di-
vine Office, though it still contains compositions attributed to such early
Syrian Fathers as Ephrem (d. 373) and his contemporary Jacob, bishop
of Nisibis, Catholicos Simeon bar Sabba'ê (d. ca. 341–344), Marutha of
Maipharkat (d. ca. 420), Narsai (d. 502), and Babai the Great (d. 628).[3]
According to Bar Hebraeus (1225–1286), *Chronicon* II, 11, it was the same
Patriarch Simeon bar Sabba'ê who arranged the daily office into two
"choirs" or "weeks."[4] This refers to the earliest stratum of the organization of the weekday propers for the cathedral offices, an arrangement still
in use today. Assyro-Chaldean ferial offices have twelve propers divided
into two "weeks" depending on whether they follow an even or uneven
Sunday in the calendar numbering.[5] Each week has six sets of propers,
one for each day, Monday through Saturday, for the offices of lelya, sapra
and ramša (nocturns, matins, vespers). Two choirs alternate the privilege
of intoning the services, the First Choir on Monday, Wednesday and Friday of uneven weeks, the Second Choir on Tuesday, Thursday, and Saturday, with the order reversed for even weeks.

These propers have been incorporated into today's breviary from the
*Book of Before and After,* of which an edition was published by the Assyrians in Mosul in 1923. This liturgical book takes it name from the

---

[2]Ibid. 488.

[3]S. Pudichery, *Ramsa* 2ff.

[4]Gregorius Bar Hebraeus, *Chronicon ecclesiasticum,* ed. J. B. Abbeloos, T. J. Lamy (Louvain: Peeters/Paris: Maisonneuve, 1877) vol. 3, 33–34.

[5]See Mateos, *Lelya/Ṣapra* 32–36, 465–467.

variable "šurraya (alleluia psalm) before" and the " 'onita (anthem or antiphon) before" and the parallel pieces "after"—i.e., before and after the cathedral psalmody of vespers (Ps 140, etc.).[6]

But the most significant historical event in the formation of this Divine Office was undoubtedly the reform instigated by Catholicos Išo 'yahb III in 650-651 at the Upper Monastery or Convent of Mar Gabriel on the right bank of the Tigris in Mosul.[7] Today the Church called Tāhira (The Pure One) of the Chaldeans, which I was able to visit in December 1956 during my years as a missionary in Iraq, is all that is left of this large monastery that played so important a role in the history of the Assyro-Chaldean Rite. In this reform the patriarch established norms for the cathedral office that fixed it in more or less the shape in which it has come down to us. But the patriarch left the monks free to organize their nightly vigils according to their own customs. The monks celebrated the cathedral hours, too, but in doing so they respected their integrity according to Išo 'yahb's reform, and so they have remained. It is the usage of this Upper Monastery, then, that has been preserved until today in the Assyro-Chaldean Liturgy of the Hours.

The East-Syrian monks also had the three day hours and compline, and these, too, eventually entered the Assyro-Chaldean cursus. But they have largely disappeared except for terce and sext on Lenten ferias, and some extant remnants during the rest of the year: compline on some feasts, the residue of terce in the marmita or psalmody at the opening of Mass, and of none in the initial psalmody of vespers.[8] These hours had already disappeared by the time of the ninth-century anonymous *Commentary on the Ecclesiastical Offices* attributed to George of Arbela.[9]

[6]These ferial propers have been translated into English by A.J. Maclean, *East–Syrian Daily Offices* (London: Rivington, Percival & Co., 1894); German trans. in J. Molitor, *Chaldäisches Brevier. Ordinarium des ostsyrischen Stundengebets* (Düsseldorf: Patmos-Verlag, 1961). An English version of the paschal propers can be found in V. Pathikulangara, *Resurrection, Life and Renewal. A Theological Study of the Liturgical Celebrations of the Great Saturday and the Sunday of Resurrection in the Chaldeo-Indian Church* (Bangalore, Kottayam: Dhamaram Publications, 1982) 315–411.

[7]Mateos, *Lelya-Ṣapra* 27; *id.*, "L'office divin chez les chaldéens," Msgr. Cassien, B. Botte (eds.), *La prière des heures* (Lex orandi 35, Paris: Cerf, 1963) 255ff. On the Upper Monastery and its liturgical role, see A. Rücker, "Das 'Obere Kloster' bei Mossul und seine Bedeutung für die Geschichte der ostsyrischen Liturgie," *Oriens Christianus* 20 = ser. 3 vol. 7 (1932) 180–187.

[8]Mateos, "L'office divin chez les chaldéens," 258–260.

[9]R.H. Connolly (ed.), *Anonymi auctoris Expositio officiorum ecclesiae Georgio Arbelensi vulgo adscripta accedit Abrahae bar Lipheh Interpretatio officiorum* (CSCO, scr. syri, series 2, tomes 91–92, Rome/Paris/Leipzig, 1911-1915). These two commentaries will be cited hereafter as *Expositio* or *Interpretatio*, with reference to the Latin trans. in CSCO vols. 91–92. The present reference is to *Expositio* 91:107.

Later developments do not affect the basic structure of the offices, but consist rather in the addition of occasional services, in the effects of the developing calendar of feasts and commemorations on the proper, and in the addition of new ecclesiastical compositions. Among the latter one should mention especially those of Patriarch Elias III (d. 1190), alias Abu Halim, who composed a large number of the prayers in the *Abu Halim*, a liturgical book that still bears his nickname.[10] Other prayers, the oldest of which are attributed to Paul of Anbar (d. 740–741) and his contemporary Sallitā of Reš-'ayna, are in the same anthology. Another liturgical book, the *Warda* (Rose), also bears an author's name. George Warda (d. before 1300) was a prolific writer of 'onyata or antiphons which were later gathered into the *Warda* along with those of his contemporary Šlemon, metropolitan of Basra, as well as those of Catholicos Yahballaha II (1190–1222) and others.

Lesser changes and the introduction of some Latin feasts were ordered under the Chaldean Catholic patriarchs Mar Joseph II (1696–1713) and Mar Joseph VI Audo (1848–1878), and at the Synod of Baghdad under Mar Joseph VII Ghanima in May, 1957, an event witnessed by the present writer who at the time was teaching at Baghdad College where the synod was held. An earlier synod on June 7–21, 1853, at the Monastery of Rabban Hormizd in Alqoš north of Mosul decreed some abbreviations in the offices and a purging of what were considered "Nestorianisms." These changes were put into effect in the three-volume breviary of the Chaldean Vincentian (Lazarist) Paul Bedjan (1838–1925), from Khosrova in Persia: *Breviarium iuxta ritum Syrorum Orientalium id est Chaldaeorum*, published in Paris in 1886–1887. Reprinted in Rome in 1938 with some corrections by J.-M. Vosté, and E. Rassam, an updating of the calendar, and a new Preface by Eugène Cardinal Tisserant, this is the office still in common use among Chaldeans and some Assyrians, though the use of manuscripts has by no means died out in the villages and monasteries of the North. The publication of Bedjan's breviary provoked a wave of protest from Chaldean Catholic Patriarch Elias XIV Abbo-Alyonan (1879–1894) and the Chaldeans in Mosul because of changes they viewed as arbitrary.[11] But whatever its defects regarding particular texts, it remains faithful to the structure of the offices as found in the ancient manuscript tradition;[12] and the gathering into three convenient volumes of material previously scattered throughout several books—and those available only in manuscript—was a great advance still appreciated today.

[10]On these later additions see Mateos, *Lelya-Sapra* 12–14; Pudichery, *Ramsa* 4–5.

[11]On the history of Bedjan's breviary see J.-M. Vosté, "Paul Bedjan, lazariste persan," OCP 11 (1945) 45–102, esp. 57–67; Mateos, *Lelya-Sapra* 3–37 describes its contents.

[12]Mateos, *Lelya-Sapra* 3.

## The Liturgical Disposition of the Church

To understand the ancient ceremonial of the Assyro-Chaldean offices one must recall that until the fourteenth century, East-Syrian churches were equipped with a bema or large enclosed platform in the middle of the nave.[13] This enclosure contained the bishop's throne at its western end, facing east toward the sanctuary. There were also benches for the concelebrating priests—or at least so it seems—and at the east end, two pulpits for the scriptural readings. In the center of the platform there was a small altar meant to hold the gospel and cross, and called "Golgotha," which it meant to symbolize. This whole structure was connected to the sanctuary by a narrow pathway, the šqaqona.

The East-Syrian liturgical commentators, especially Gabriel Qatraya bar Lipah (ca. 615), Abraham bar Lipah (seventh century), and Pseudo-George of Arbela (ninth century), have provided us with a description of the liturgy and office sufficiently detailed to give a fairly complete picture of the use of the bema in the Assyro-Chaldean Rite.[14] It is evident from the layout of the church—nave divided by a north-south barrier into two sections for the men and women, and obstructed in the middle by a large bema—that a processional introit through a door in the west wall and down the center of the nave to the sanctuary is out of the question. In fact, there was usually no entrance at all in the west wall. Nor does it appear that the clergy ordinarily made any processional entrance into the church. The description of the eucharistic liturgy begins with the clergy already in the sanctuary, and the introit procession does not go from nave to sanctuary, but in the reverse direction, from the sanctuary to the bema in the nave.[15]

Because of the peculiar shape of this Assyro-Chaldean introit procession that went not into but out from the sanctuary to the bema in the nave, the disappearance of the bema after the fourteenth century inevitably led to the suppression of the introit. But the ancient liturgical structure showed a fine sense of ceremonial clarity eminently suited to cathedral offices. Liturgically the eucharistic table has nothing whatever to do with

[13]On the bema and its liturgical use, see R. Taft, "Some Notes on the Bema in the East and West Syrian Traditions," OCP 34 (1968) 326-359; id., "On the Use of the Bema in the East-Syrian Liturgy," *Eastern Churches Review* 3 (1970) 30-39. Some of the following material is resumed from the latter article, with the permission of the editors.

[14]Qatraya's commentary remains unpublished except for a Latin trans. of chs. 1-2 on the Eucharist in S. Y. Hermiz Jammo, *La structure de la messe chaldéenne du début jusqu'à l'anaphore. Étude historique* (OCA 207, Rome: PIO, 1979) 29-48. For the commentaries of Ps.-George and bar Lipah, see note 9 above.

[15]*Expositio* 92:7ff.

the Liturgy of the Word or other offices such as the hours, and the use of the sanctuary and altar only for the anaphora shows a grasp of the nature of liturgy that is sadly lacking in the present muddled state of most rites.

On the basis of this principle that the altar is the place proper to the anaphora, we can expect to find a broad use of the bema in Assyro-Chaldean cathedral offices. All three cathedral services in this tradition are rich in ceremonial as befits their popular character, and this ceremonial is centered on the bema and the comings and goings to and from it. Without the bema, almost all the popular ceremonial of these offices is destroyed.

## The Offices

### 1. NOCTURNS (LELYA)

There are several types of monastic vigils in the Assyro-Chaldean office, depending on the day or feast.[16] On ferial days the monks rise for a nocturnal office at midnight, followed by another period of rest before matins. This night office has the classic structure of a monastic vigil:

> *Invitatory:*        Ps 3:6–9 and Ps 113
> or Ps 118:62–64
> or Ps 118:57–58 and Ps 91
> *Continuous monastic psalmody:* 7 hullale (sections of the
> psalter)
> 'Onyata d-mawtba (poetic strophes)
> Select psalm with refrain
> Hymn
> Litany

The Assyro-Chaldean liturgical psalter is divided into sixty marmyata, each marmita having ideally three psalms. These marmyata are in turn gathered into twenty-one hullale of three marmyata each, so that seven hullale are a third of the psalter. The name "mawtba" for the poetry following the psalms has the same meaning and function as the Byzantine *kathismata*, literally "sessions": they provide a time to sit and rest after the long psalmody, which in these traditions, unlike the Egyptian, was said standing.

---

[16]See Mateos, "Les differentes espèces de vigiles dans le rite chaldéen," 46–63; *id.*, "L'office divin chez les chaldéens," 261–263.

On days when there is compline this nocturns or lelya follows compline immediately and there is no rest beforehand. And on Sundays, instead of returning to bed after nocturns or lelya the monks add two more sections of the psalter, then proceed directly to the cathedral vigil (qale d-šahra), matins (ṣapra), and Sunday Eucharist. Finally, on the eve of three feasts, Christmas, Epiphany, and Good Friday, there is a vigil that lasts through the whole night.

## ii. The Cathedral Vigil

The cathedral vigil or qale d-šahra, celebrated in the narthex of the church since the disappearance of the bema, formerly comprised:[17]

> Opening of sanctuary doors and veil
> Procession of bishop to the bema
> 3 marmyata (originally composed of OT canticles)
>     followed by prayers, all at bema
> Procession from bema to sanctuary and chant of 'onita
> Šubbaha (psalm with refrain)
> Tešbohta (= *gloria*, a poetic composition)
> Litany and prayer

There are remarkable similarities between this vigil and the Sunday resurrection vigil of Jerusalem described in Egeria's *Journal* 24:9–11, discussed in chapter 3:

| *Egeria:* | *Assyro-Chaldean vigil:* |
|---|---|
| Entrance of bishop | Entrance of bishop to bema |
| Three "psalms" and prayers | Three canticles and prayers |
| *Commemoratio omnium* | |
| Gospel | |
| Procession to the cross | Procession to sanctuary |
|     with hymn |     with 'onita |
| Psalm | Psalm with refrain |
|  | Tešbohta |
| Prayer | Litany and prayer |

The procession to the sanctuary in the qale d-šahra is an adaptation of the procession from the Holy Sepulcher to Calvary in Egeria (24:11).[18] It should be noted, however, that its original meaning as a procession to the cross (Golgotha) has been lost, and is even contradicted by the tradi-

---

[17]*Expositio* 91:230–231; 92:122–123.
[18]Mateos, *Lelya-Ṣapra* 431; *id.*, "La vigile cathédrale chez Egerie," 307.

tional Assyro-Chaldean symbolism of the church in which the bema altar represents Golgotha, and the rite of the bema represents the earthly life of the Lord accomplished in Jerusalem. The ministers process into the sanctuary to indicate that the ascension has been accomplished, for the sanctuary represents heaven.[19]

### III. MATINS (ṢAPRA)[20]

Matins or tešmešta d-ṣapra at dawn has a pure cathedral shape. I give here only a general outline that does not include all possible variants:

> *Fixed morning psalms with refrains:* Pss 99, 90,
> 103:1–16a, 112, 92
> *Lauds psalms:* Pss 148, (149 on ferias only), 150, 116
> Collect
> 'Onita d-ṣapra (incense antiphon of matins) or
> Laku Mara Hymn (on ferial days)
> Nuhra (festal hymns of light)
> *Benedicite* (festal) or *Miserere* (ferial)
> *Gloria in excelsis* (festal) or tešbohta (hymn)
> Trisagion and Our Father
> Trisagion prayer
> Prayer of blessing

At the beginning of the office the bishop and clergy were in the sanctuary for the chanting of the first psalms with their refrains, usually referring to the theme of light.[21] Ps 99 is a psalm of entrance, suited to open the service: "Praise the Lord all the earth . . . come into his presence with exultation . . . enter into his gates with thanksgiving." The others are all psalms of praise, some of which were chosen because of their reference to light or sunrise:

> Ps 103:2, "You have clothed yourself with light as with a garment."
> Ps 112:3, "From the rising of the sun to the setting, the name of the Lord be praised."

During the chanting of Ps 112 all the lamps were lighted and the bishop and clergy approached the doors of the sanctuary, where the bishop him-

---

[19]*Expositio* 91:224, 231.

[20]*Ibid.* 91:213, 224–225; *Interpretatio* 92:168; Mateos, "Les matines chaldéennes, maronites et syriennes," 52–54; id., *Lelya-Sapra* 392–393.

[21]J. Mateos, "L'office paroissial du matin et du soir dans le rite chaldéen," LMD 64 (1960) 70ff.

self solemnly intoned Ps 92, and while it was being chanted the bishop and his accompanying retinue of clergy exited in solemn procession to the bema, where they remained standing while the lauds psalms were chanted, concluded by the short Ps 116 often used as a concluding doxology in Eastern cathedral psalmody. These lauds psalms once had refrains which are now preserved only on Lenten ferias. The omission of Ps 149 on Sundays and feasts is an Assyro-Chaldean peculiarity. According to the ninth-century anonymous *Commentary on the Ecclesiastical Offices* it came to be omitted on days when the authorities attended services because of verse 8: "to bind their kings with chains and their nobles with iron fetters."[22]

The refrain of Ps 116, "O Christ light, to you we give glory!" is also the theme of the collect that concludes the psalmody:

> To you O Christ, true light, splendor of the glory of the Father, who have revealed yourself and shone in the world to renew and save our nature by the first fruits [assumed] from us, we raise up praise, honor, thanksgiving and adoration, at all times, Lord of all. . . .[23]

During the 'onita d-ṣapra or morning antiphon there is a solemn incensation, and then the hymns of light resume the theme of Christ, light of the world, underlining especially its relation to the eschatological dawn to come at the parousia. The traditional final blessing or Prayer of Inclination has been preserved only in Lent; the other final prayers have been added at a later date.[24]

It may seem odd that Ps 62, the "classic" cathedral matins psalm, is missing from this service. But as Mateos shows,[25] the Pšiṭta version of this psalm makes no references to the *orthrizo* of LXX Ps 62:1, and translates the LXX "in the mornings" *(en tois orthrois)* of verse 6 as "in the nights." As for Ps 90, traditional psalm of compline and sext in other traditions, its presence here in matins is an Assyro-Chaldean peculiarity.

IV. Vespers (ramša)[26]

In ramša or vespers, too, we see a pure cathedral service, if we prescind from the remains of none that have become attached to the beginning of vespers:

[22]*Ibid.* 71 note 13, and *Expositio* 91:173.
[23]Mateos, "L'office paroissial du matin et du soir dans le rite chaldéen," 71.
[24]Mateos, *Lelya-Ṣapra* 78–81.
[25]Mateos, "L'office divin chez les chaldéens," 265–266.
[26]Mateos, "L'office paroissial du matin et du soir dans le rite chaldéen," 76ff. Pudichery, *Ramsa* chs. 2–3.

Marmita (psalmody: remnant of none)
ʿOnita of incense
Laku Mara Hymn and its collect
Šurraya da-qdam (alleluia psalm before the vesperal
    psalmody)
ʿOnita da-qdam (antiphon before the vesperal
    psalmody)
*Fixed vesperal cathedral psalms:* Pss 140, 141,
    118:105–112, 116
Šurraya d-batar (alleluia psalm after the vesperal
    psalmody)
ʿOnita d-batar (antiphon after the vesperal psalmody)
*Intercessions:* karozuta (litany)
                 angel of peace petitions
Trisagion and its collect
Prayer of blessing

*Stational procession:*

(On feasts of the Lord and memori-
    als: suyyake = Pss 93–98)
ʿOnita d-basiliqe (antiphon of the procession)
Šurraya (alleluia psalm)
Our Father
Final prayers

This is the outline of festive ramša. Ferial vespers omit the ʿonyata da-qdam
and d-batar, and conclude as follows:

Trisagion and collect
ʿOnita d-ramša (antiphon of the evening)
Šurraya (alleluia psalm)
Procession, with ʿonita d-sahde (antiphon of the
    martyrs)
Subbaʿa (compline)
Final prayers

Formerly, the beginning of ramša was similar to the first part of the
Liturgy of the Word.[27] The office now opens with one or two marmyata,
subsections of the psalter with ideally three psalms each, which are the

---

[27]See *Interpretatio* 92:163ff.; *Expositio* 91:157–212 *passim*, esp. 157ff., 164 ff., 199ff.;
S. Y. H. Jammo, "L'office du soir chaldéen au temps de Gabriel Qatraya," OS 12 (1967)
187–210.

remains of none. So ramša proper really began, like Mass and matins, with the raising of the outer sanctuary veil. Then the 'onita of incense was intoned:

> Like the fragrance of precious spices
>   and like the perfume of sweet-smelling incense,
> Accept, O Lord, the supplication and the prayer of
>   your worshipers.

The theme is obviously resumed from Ps 140:2, "Let my prayer rise like incense before you, the lifting up of my hands like the evening sacrifice." This antiphon was repeated, intercalated between the verses of Ps 83, until the procession had arrived at the bema and the bishop was seated at his throne there. Ps 83, a psalm of love and longing for God's temple, was ideally suited for such an introit procession:

> How lovely is your dwelling place
>   Lord God of hosts.
> My soul is longing and yearning,
>   is yearning for the courts of the Lord. . . .
> They are happy who dwell in your house,
>   forever singing your praise. . . .
> One day within your courts
>   is better than a thousand elsewhere. . . .

In the time of Gabriel Qatraya bar Lipah (ca. 615) this was followed by the lucernarium when the evening lamp on the qestroma or platform before the sanctuary door was lighted, as in Egeria (24:4), with flame brought from the ever-burning lamp within the sanctuary, and a prayer was said to Christ, light of the world.[28] Then came the prayer of incense and the incensation, the Laku Mara Hymn, the vesperal psalms and accompanying ecclesiastical poetry.

The Laku Mara Hymn, named for its incipit, "To you, Lord," and its collect, like the 'onita of incense just cited, reveal one of the most beautiful traits of the Assyro-Chaldean Rite: hymns and prayers of pure praise, in which we ask for nothing more than the privilege of glorifying God.

> *Hymn:*
> Lord of all, we confess you!
>   Jesus Christ, we glorify you!
> For you raise our bodies,
>   You save our souls!

---

[28]The symbolism of this rite had been obscured by the time of the ninth-century *Expositio*, when it had already evolved into a solemn procession to the bema with candles, incense, etc., like the introit of the eucharistic liturgy. See Jammo, "L'office du soir chaldéen," 188ff., 206.

*Collect:*

You, O my Lord, are in truth the raiser of our bodies, you the good savior of our souls. You, O my Lord, we are bound to confess and adore and glorify at all times, Lord of all, Father, Son and Holy Spirit, forever!

Ps 140 is of course the classic vesperal psalm. Ps 141, which begins in the same way, also follows Ps 140 in Byzantine Sabaitic vespers. As we saw in chapter 3, multiple vesperal psalms were a trait of hagiopolite evensong: Egeria (24:4) refers to more than one psalm, whereas only one cathedral psalm is found in the early Antiochene vespers. Ps 118:105-112 was chosen because of verse 105: "Your law is a lamp for my feet and a light for my path," as well as for the penitential spirit of subsequent verses—in other words because of its suitability to express the two traditional themes of cathedral evensong: light, and penance or forgiveness for failings.

The service concluded with the customary intercessions and final benediction or Prayer of Inclination, all at the bema. Then the veil of the sanctuary was closed, indicating the true end of ramša. The stational service that follows, similar to the one after the Prayer of Inclination original final blessing of Byzantine festive vespers, took place only on Sundays and is not an integral part of vespers.[29]

The striking parallels between the order of ramša and the beginning of the Liturgy of the Word in the Mass, as both are described in the commentary of Gabriel Qatraya bar Lipah (ca. 615), have been pointed out by Jammo:[30]

| *Ramša:* | *Liturgy of the Word:* |
|---|---|
| Marmita | Marmita |
| *Pax nobiscum* | *Pax nobiscum* |
| Opening of veil | Opening of veil |
| Procession with candle and incense | Procession with two candles, incense, and cross |
| Prayer *Lux quae apparuisti in terra* (text lost) | |
| Prayer *Et cum redolet nobis* | Prayer *Et cum redolet nobis* (festive) |
| . . . *Et propter* | *Et propter* (ferial) |

[29]For the other ceremonies that have been appended to this office see *ibid.* 193ff., 200, 208ff., and Mateos, "L'office paroissial du matin et du soir dans le rite chaldéen," 87–88.

[30]"L'office du soir chaldéen," 203ff.

Laku Mara Hymn           Laku Mara Hymn
Collect *Domine, tu es vere*    Collect *Domine, tu es vere*

Mateos[31] has summed up the "cathedral" qualities of these offices celebrated on the bema in the midst of the community: brevity, variety, popular participation, and a highly successful equilibrium of their constitutive
elements: praise (psalms, canticles, chants), ceremonial (incense, light,
processions), prayer (litanies, collects). The orientation is christological
more than Trinitarian, and praise and thanksgiving predominate over the
more monastic penitential theme.

## Present Usage

The ancient Church of the East remains the only one in Christendom,
at least as far as I know, that has retained in parish worship the daily
celebration of the integral cathedral cursus. The Chaldean Catholics still
celebrate in their parishes the full cycle of offices as found in Bedjan's
breviary. In South India among the Thomas Christians of the Malabar
Rite, the parish office has died out but is being restored in the diocese
of Kanjirapilly, where ṣapra (matins) is now said with the people before
Mass.[32]

---

[31]"L'office paroissial du matin et du soir dans le rite chaldéen," 75–76.

[32]For this information I am indebted to my student Rev. John Moolan, Malabarese Catholic
priest of the diocese of Trichur. On the office in the Malabar Rite, see V. Pathikulangara,
"Divine Office in Malabar Liturgy," EL 88 (1974) 131–141.

# 14

## THE WEST-SYRIAN AND
## MARONITE TRADITIONS

The West-Syrian or Syro-Antiochene Rite is the tradition of the Syrian Orthodox in the Patriarchate of Antioch and in India, as well as of the Syrian and Malankarese Catholics. W. F. Macomber has explained the complex relationship between the three Syriac liturgical families.[1] Three principal liturgical centers had a major influence in the origins of these rites: Antioch, Jerusalem, and Edessa. Of these, only Edessa was a center of Syriac language and culture; the other two were Greek cities, though not without Syriac-speaking minorities.

The rite of Mesopotamia that developed into the Chaldean tradition is of Syriac origin and so its roots can probably be traced back to Edessa.

The West-Syrian Rite is a synthesis of native Syriac elements, especially hymns and other choral pieces, with material translated from Greek liturgical texts of Antiochene and hagiopolite provenance. This synthesis was the work of Syriac, non-Chalcedonian monastic communities in the Syriac-speaking hinterlands of Syria, Palestine, and parts of Mesopotamia, beyond the Greek cities of the Mediterranean littoral. These Syriac-speaking Christians were organized into an independent Church under

---

[1]"A Theory on the Origins of the Syrian, Maronite and Chaldean Rites," OCP 39 (1973) 235–242.

Jacob Baradai (d. 578), which is the reason they are sometimes called "Jacobites."

The Maronite Rite, once considered just a latinized variant of the Syro-Antiochene tradition, has been shown by Macomber to be an independent synthesis that probably can be traced back to Syriac-speaking Chalcedonian communities which in Syria, though not in Palestine, managed to establish themselves independently of the Greek-speaking coastline and to preserve their ancient Syriac usages. Later, most of these Syriac-speaking Chalcedonians were Byzantinized, but the ancient Syrian rites and traditions were preserved and developed by monks who had taken refuge in the mountains of Lebanon at the beginning of the eighth century, thus laying the foundations for the independent Maronite Church. This Church came into contact with the Crusaders in the Middle Ages and underwent progressive Latin influence. Later this latinization was accentuated under Patriarch Joseph Rizzi at the end of the sixteenth century. But the Office was not tarnished by this, and the Mass has recently been restored.

## The Offices

The Maronite and Syrian traditions both have a full complement of the customary seven canonical hours: nocturns, matins, terce, sext, none, vespers, and compline. Matins or ṣafro has absorbed the remains of the cathedral vigil. In nocturns or lilyo, the replacement of the continuous nocturnal psalmody by ecclesiastical poetry, and the doubling of matins created by the juxtaposition in the same service of monastic and cathedral usages, have created special problems that need not concern us here.[2] I shall limit myself to a summary of the cathedral offices of matins and vespers.

### 1. MATINS (ṢAFRO)[3]

The following schema reveals the affinity of the morning office in the two related traditions. The various Syriac pieces—nuhro, sogito, bo'uto, qolo—are all strophic chants, ecclesiastical poetry in one form or another, in spite of the literal meaning of their names, which at times betrays the

[2]See Mateos, "Les matines chaldéennes, maronites et syriennes," 55–65.

[3]See Mateos, " 'Sedre' et prières connexes dans quelques anciennes collections," OCP 28 (1962) 239–287; id., "Trois recueils anciens de prooemia syriens," OCP 33 (1967) 457–482; A. Cody, "L'office divin chez les Syriens Jacobites," POC 19 (1969) 293–319; J. Tabet, L'Office commun maronite ch. 2.

original liturgical unit they have replaced. The bo'uto at the end of the offices, which means "supplication," is a paradigmatic instance.

| Maronite: | West-Syrian (Sundays): |
|---|---|

Remnants of the cathedral vigil

| Magnificat | Ps 50 |
| Ps 62 | Ps 62 |
| Ps 90 (festive) | Ps 18 |
| | Canticle of Is 42:10–13; 45:8 |

Cathedral Matins

| Ps 50 (festive) | |
| Nuhro (Hymn of St. Ephrem) | |
| Benedicite | Magnificat |

Fixed psalms of lauds: 148, 149, 150, 116

| Sogito | Beatitudes |
| Ḥussoyo (prooemion and sedro) | |
| Mazmuro (lessons: festive) | |
| Bo'uto | Qolo, bo'uto |
| | Hullolo (alleluia psalm) |
| | Gospel |

## II. Maronite Ramšo (vespers)[4]

Maronite vespers today comprises:

Opening prayers

[Monastic synaxis:]
  Prayer (before the psalmody)
  (formerly: variable monastic psalmody)
  Alleluia (after the psalmody)

[Cathedral vespers:]
  Invitatory: Prayer
    Ps 50 with refrains
  Fixed cathedral psalmody: Pss 140, 141, 118:105–112,
    116

⁴Tabet, L'office commun maronite ch. 3, and P. Gemayel, "La structure des vêpres maronites," OS 9 (1964) 105–134; J. Mateos, "Le ramšo maronite," in id., De officio matutino et vespertino in ritibus orientalibus (pro manuscripto, Rome: S. Anselmo, 1968–1969) 60–69.

Sogito (metrical poetry)
Rite of incense: Imposition of incense
                 Prooemion of the prayer of incense
                 Sedro or prayer of incense
                 Incensation
                 Qolo or incense chant
                 'Etro or prayer for acceptance of the
                   offering of incense
Mazmuro: Responsory
         Readings
         Hullolo (alleluia after the readings)
Conclusion: Bo'uto ("supplication:" now metrical
            strophes)
            Huttomo (blessing)

The first part of the office contains debris of the former monastic evening synaxis of continuous psalmody. Cathedral evensong opens with Ps
50 as invitatory. The Maronite Rite is the only one that uses Ps 50 for
this purpose in vespers as well as matins, but the penitential character
of cathedral evening prayer in the Fathers of the Church makes this entirely appropriate. Then come the vesperal psalms with their themes of
prayer, incense, and light. The sogito or poetry after the vesperal psalms
resumes the theme of light in Ps 118:105, "Your law is a lamp for my feet
and a light for my path":

> Light your lamps, brethren, because he has arrived, the bride-
> groom who was to come. . . . In the day of judgment he will
> open to them [the just] the paradise of light . . . (Sunday).
>
> Illumine our hearts, Lord, and make our steps walk in the
> path of your Law. In the evening, when the light recedes, be
> for us a sun, and we shall be illumined by you . . . (Monday).[5]

As is customary in services of the Syrian and Maronite traditions, the
offering of incense is highly developed, and interpreted as a symbol of
our prayers as in Ps 140:2, as well as an atonement for sin as in Num
16:46: "And Moses said to Aaron, 'take your censer, and put fire therein,
and lay incense on it, and carry it quickly to the congregation, and make
atonement for them; for wrath has gone forth from the Lord. . . .'" This
oblationary-expiatory emphasis of the rite of incense is characteristic of
the Syro-Antiochene and Maronite rites. Finally, the name bo'uto" (supplication) betrays here, too, the traditional structure of the end of the offices,

[5]Gemayel, "La structure des vêpres maronites," 116.

which, as in other rites, concluded with intercessions for the needs of the Church, the people, and the whole world.

### III. WEST-SYRIAN RAMŠO (VESPERS)

Solemn vespers in the Syro-Antiochene usage appears as follows:[6]

> Opening prayers
> Prayer of the day
> Variable invitatory psalm with strophes
> *Fixed cathedral psalmody:* Pss 140, 141, 118:105–112,
>    116, with 'enyone (intercalated strophes)
> Ḥussoyo ("expiation"): Prooemion and sedro with
>    solemn incensation
> Qolo 1
> 'Etro
> Qolo 2
> Bo'uto
> Hullolo (alleluia verse)
> Gospel
> Korozuto (litany) in Syrian Catholic usage
> Ma'nito (responsory) or tešmešto (*gloria* chant) in
>    Syrian Orthodox usage
> Final prayers
> Huttomo (final blessing)

## Present Usage

### I. THE SYRIAN ORTHODOX IN JERUSALEM

Today among the Syrian Orthodox in Jerusalem the offices are grouped into two synaxes: none, vespers, and compline at 4:00 P.M. in winter and one hour earlier in summer; nocturns (lilyo) and matins (ṣafro) are chanted with terce and sext at 6:30 A.M. At both synaxes the huttomo or final prayer of benediction and dismissal is said only at the end of the entire series of offices.[7]

---

[6]Cody, "L'office divin chez les Syriens Jacobites," 11–13. For an outline of ferial vespers see *ibid.* 9–11.
[7]*Ibid.* 14.

## II. IN KERALA

In the Syro-Malankara Catholic Church of South India the office is still celebrated in the parishes. In the Syrian Orthodox Church of India,[8] if the priest resides in a parish house near the church, the offices are done daily at 6:00 A.M. and 6:00 P.M. Otherwise the common parish celebration is limited to none, vespers, and compline at 6:00 P.M. on Saturday, followed at 5:00 A.M. on Sunday by lilyo, then about 8:00 A.M. by ṣafro, terce, sext, and Eucharist. Those unable to attend church read these offices together at home. In monastic communities the hours are spread throughout the day rather than grouped together in this fashion.

## III. KURISUMALA ASHRAM[9]

One such monastic community in the Syro-Malankara Catholic Church in Kerala has effected in recent years a renewal of the West-Syrian Liturgy of the Hours adapted to the Indian context. Much is written in the West today about monastic renewal on Mt. Athos or in the Coptic Orthodox Church of Egypt, but for thirty years there has been underway another movement, less known, perhaps, but undoubtedly one of the most radical and far-reaching monastic experiments of our time. In 1950 the French missionary priest Abbé Jules Monchanin (d. 1957), known as Swami Paramarubyananda, and the Benedictine Fr. Henri Le Saux or Swami Abhishiktananda, settled in huts on the banks of the river Kavery near Tiruchirapalli. Thus began Saccidananda Ashram or Shantivanam as it is popularly known, the pioneer attempt in modern India to live a Christian life of monastic contemplation according to the model of a Hindu Ashram. In 1953 they were joined by the Trappist Fr. Francis Mahieu, monk of Our Lady of Scourmont in Belgium. In 1958, at the invitation of the Malankara Catholics of Kerala, Fr. Francis, now known as Francis Acharya—the name given to a spiritual guide, like the Russian title "starets"—founded Kurisumala Ashram on a wildly beautiful mountain in the hill country of the Western Ghats on the Trivandrum-Cape Camorin road in Kerala, in the diocese of Tiruvalla. He was joined in this enterprise by Dom Bede Griffiths, monk of Prinknash in England.

[8]For this information I am grateful to my student Rev. Mathai Mattathil of the Syrian Orthodox Church of India.

[9]On Kurisumala see Francis Acharya, *Kurisumala Ashram. Chronique de douze années* (Bloise: Editions N.-D. de la Trinité, 1972); *id.* (ed.), *Kurisumala. A Symposium on Ashram Life* (Vagamon: Kurisumala Ashram, 1974); Bede Griffiths, *Christian Ashram. Essays towards a Hindu-Christian Dialogue* (London: Darton, Longmann & Todd, 1966).

The monastery was to be of the Syro-Malankara Rite, but the ideal of the two founders was to create a new type of monastic life, rooted not only in the Eastern Christian tradition of South India, but also incorporating the monastic and contemplative values of non-Christian India. The dynamism and growth of this foundation have been astonishing. But what is of special interest to us here is the Acharya's efforts at adapting the profoundly contemplative Syro-Antiochene Liturgy of the Hours.[10]

Basically the changes respect the structure of the offices while suppressing the frequent duplication of liturgical units such as qolo or prooemion and sedro. In addition, the qolo texts of the weekly cycle have been enriched with new material, some adjustments have been made in the calendar, a lucernarium added to vespers, and Indian texts from non-Christian sources have been introduced experimentally into the hours.[11] These are called "Seeds of the Word." At weekday vespers these texts, chosen because the religious experience they express is similar to what one finds in the Bible, are woven into the first qolo. At ferial ṣafro the "seeds" replace the strophes of the morning psalmody, and are chosen not because of similarities with the Judeo-Christian tradition, but to express charisms proper to Indian religious culture.

So the revised offices appear as follows. At ramšo a light ritual with *Phôs hilaron* has been prefixed to the service, "Seeds of the Word" have been added to the first qolo, and qolo 1–2 have been joined and somewhat abbreviated. This both tightens and simplifies the structure. In addition, the 'enyone (strophes) of Ps 50 and of the vesperal psalms have been expurgated of anti-Jewish expressions, and the hullolo (alleluia verse) and korozuto (litany) have been expanded.

In lilyo the repetitions of the commemoration of the saints, and of prooemion with sedro (prayer of incense), are reduced, and the *Gloria in excelsis*, originally the chant of festive morning prayer, as we have seen, is used only on Sundays and feasts. In festive lilyo a time for meditation

---

[10]To date the following three volumes in English have appeared, all published by Kurisumala Ashram: *The Book of Common Prayer of the Syrian Church*, trans. by Bede Griffiths (n.d.); Francis Acharya, *Prayer with the Harp of the Spirit*, vol. 1: *A Weekly Celebration of the Economy of Salvation* (1980; 2d revised ed. 1983); vol. 2: *The Crown of the Year*, part I (1982); vol. 3, part II (1985). Bede Griffiths' work is a straight translation of the daily common and propers; the Acharya's first volume gives his revision of that same cycle, vol. 2 contains the propers for Advent to Epiphany, vol. 3 for Lent and Easter. I am deeply grateful to the Acharya for sending me copies of his precious volumes. They can be obtained from Kurisumala Ashram, Vagamon 685 503, Kerala, India.

[11]These additions are found only in the weekly cycle in vol. 1 of *Prayer with the Harp of the Spirit*.

is added at the end of the first two "watches," replacing the repetition of qolo, the poetic madrosho (didactic poetry) and the boʻuto (supplication).

At ferial ṣafro, in addition to the "Seeds of the Word" replacing the strophes of the psalmody, a selection has been made of qolo texts to reduce repetitions. More surprising is the suppression of the *Magnificat* and Pss 148–150 if lauds have been celebrated at lilyo. It is true, as we saw above in this chapter, that the Syrian offices have a double matins, but it would have been better either to leave the lauds psalms in ṣafro, suppressing them at lilyo—or on days when lilyo and ṣafro are done as one, to simply suppress the second ṣafro entirely.

But I do not wish to quibble. With the exception of that last point, the changes do no violence to the structure, nature, or genius of these offices, nor to the Eastern liturgical spirit. Eastern liturgical books, especially of the Divine Office, are not rigid *editiones typicae* but anthologies of material to be used with a certain freedom, though always within the limits of the lived tradition. This is especially true in monastic usage. Eastern monasteries have always been jealous of their particular liturgical uses as set down in their customaries or preserved in the living oral tradition, and one can only applaud the prudent flexibility of the Acharya of Kurisumala in adapting the ancient Syrian offices to the concrete needs of a living, vibrant monastic life in the mountains of India's lush southwest coast.

## IV. THE MARONITES

Among the Maronites[12] the office was for long reduced to the *Shimto* or ordinary, with no use made of the prescribed readings or of the anthology of festive propers in the *Phenqito.* After Vatican Council II an Arabic translation of the revised monastic office was prepared, beginning in 1973, at the Université Saint-Esprit in Kaslik, Lebanon, under the direction of the monks of the Lebanese Maronite Order. This office has a reduced cursus of nocturns, lauds, sext, vespers, and compline, with seasonal propers and readings daily at ṣafro and ramšo. Though not yet enjoying official approval of the Maronite hierarchy, use of this office is permitted experimentally and it has had widespread success in monasteries, seminaries, and other religious communities.

As for the parishes, it is impossible to generalize. In some parishes served by monks, the laity pray reformed vespers in Arabic together with the monks. Several parishes still do the offices of Holy Week in Syriac.

---

[12] I am grateful to my student, the Maronite monk Rev. Joseph Hage, for this information.

In some parishes in the care of the diocesan clergy there have also been attempts to pray the renewed Arabic office with the people. The full cursus of the traditional office, in Syriac, is still prayed at the proper hours (0400, 0900, 1200, 1500, 1800, 2100, 2400) in Maronite hermitages of Lebanon where solitary voices once again raise to God the ceaseless prayer of the anchorite as in days of old, to the unending glory of his Holy Name.

The Maronite community in the United States has in recent years shown extraordinary dynamism under the leadership of its ordinary, Archbishop Francis M. Zayek. A vigorous community and Eucharistic life is already operative in the parishes, and one can now hope for a restoration of the Liturgy of the Hours: since 1982 three volumes of the hours, with seasonal propers, and adapted for use in the U.S.A., have appeared in English as *The Prayer of the Faithful according to the Maronite Liturgical Year.*[13] Both the title and the archbishop's *Foreword* make it quite clear that the Maronite Office was not meant to be just a private prayerbook for clergy and religious.

[13]*The Prayer of the Faithful according to the Maronite Liturgical Year,* translated and adapted for use in the Diocese of St. Maron, U.S.A., from *Prière croyant selon l'année liturgique maronite,* ed. by Boutros Gemayel, vol. 1: *Sundays of the Church, Season of Announcement & Birth of our Lord, Season of Epiphany;* vol. 2: *Season of Great Lent, Passion Week, Season of Resurrection;* vol. 3: *Season of Resurrection, Season after Pentecost, Season of the Holy Cross* (Brooklyn: Diocese of St. Maron, 1982, 1984, 1985).

# 15

## THE COPTIC OFFICE[1]

As one would expect, the Eastern office that has retained the purest monastic form is that of the Coptic Church of Egypt.

### History

The liturgical significance of native Coptic monasticism goes back to the early centuries of the Coptic Orthodox Church. The monastic centers of Lower Egypt, though largely Coptic, were not without strong Greek influence—one need recall only Evagrius of Pontus (345–399), one of the great luminaries of Kellia. But the true cradle of native Coptic ecclesiastical culture was in Upper Egypt, in the White Monastery near Achmin, not far from the present city of Sohag. Under its second abbot Shenoute (ca. 383–451) it became a center of Sahidic literature, the "classical" language of Coptic writing.[2]

---

[1]Much of this material is resumed from my article "Praise in the Desert" already cited in chapter 4. Once again, I am grateful to the editors of *Worship* and to The Liturgical Press, Collegeville, Minn., for permission to use this material again here.

[2]On the early development of Christianity in Egypt, see C. H. Roberts, *Manuscript, Society and Belief in Early Christian Egypt* (London: Oxford University Press, 1979). The classical study on the origins of Coptic Christianity remains J. Leipoldt, *Schenute von Atripe und die Entstehung des national ägyptischen Christentums* (TU 25, Leipzig: J. C. Hinrichs, 1903).

The present liturgical language, Bohairic, is the dialect of Lower Egypt, and its rise to prominence is connected to a change in the fortunes of the still active Monastery of St. Macarius in Scetis the same year that Shenoute died. For it is to the Council of Chalcedon (451), the watershed event in the history of Egyptian Christianity, that one can trace the overriding role of the Monastery of St. Macarius in the development of the Coptic Church and its liturgy.[3] In the aftermath of the council, the non-Chalcedonians underwent fierce persecution and were driven from their churches. The patriarchate, forced to leave Alexandria, took refuge in the Monastery of St. Macarius, which became perforce the center of the Coptic Church, thereafter providing twenty-nine of its patriarchs, more than any other monastery.

More important, perhaps, this banishment from Alexandria emancipated indigenous Egyptian Christianity from the tutelage of its hellenic overlords of the Mediterranean littoral and the Nile Delta. There had always been two Egypts, that of the native Egyptian up the Nile, and that of the foreigner in the Delta and along the coast.[4] From the conquest of Egypt and founding of Alexandria by Alexander the Great in B.C. 332–331 until the Byzantine epoch at the time of Chalcedon the situation had remained the same: a ruling class of hellenophones in the cities, especially in Alexandria and other coastal towns and in the Delta; an indigenous mass of native Egyptians or Copts ("Copt" is the "gypt" of Egypt) concentrated chiefly along the Nile in Upper Egypt.

Egyptian Christianity began in Alexandria and was Greek. By the third century, however, there were numerous converts among the Copts, and the Scriptures and liturgy were already in the native tongue. But it was not until the rise of monasticism that the Coptic Church solidified as a native counterbalance to the cosmopolitan, theologically sophisticated, hellenic Church of Alexandria, whose speculative, spiritualizing intellectualism stood in marked contrast to the popular, traditionalistic piety of the South, a largely oral culture transmitted through sayings, proverbs, ritual, rather than through theological treatises. This monastic culture—concrete, popular, ascetic—created the liturgy and offices of the Coptic

---

See also W. H. Worrell, *A Short Account of the Copts* (Ann Arbor: University of Michigan Press, 1945). On the works of Shenoute see CSCO 41–42, 73, 96, 108, 129. His *vita* has recently been translated: Besa, *The Life of Shenoute*, trans., introd., notes by D. N. Bell (CS 73, Kalamazoo: Cistercian Publications, 1983).

[3] For this story consult Evelyn-White, *The Monasteries* part 2; O. F. A. Meinardus, *Monks and Monasteries of the Egyptian Desert* (Cairo: American University of Cairo Press, 1961).

[4] H. H. Ayrout, "Regards sur le christianisme en Égypte hier et aujourd'hui," POC 15 (1965) 3–42, esp. 11ff.

Church. It is a highly penitential, contemplative rite, long, solemn, even monotonous, with much less speculative poetry, symbolic splendor and sumptuous ceremonial than, for example, the Byzantine tradition.

Today's Coptic Rite is basically the usage of Scetis somewhat modified by later reforms. Patriarch Gabriel II Ibn Turayk (1131–1145) reduced the number of anaphoras to the present three, and Gabriel V (1409–1427) composed a *Liturgical Order* to unify the divergent usages of Egypt. These regulations still govern the Coptic Rite today.[5]

The basic structure of the office of Scetis described by Cassian is still clearly visible in the hours of the present Coptic *Horologion*, though in monasteries the weekday hours are now done in common, and the cursus has been filled out with the other canonical hours that ultimately became a fixed part of the official daily prayer cycle in most traditions.

When the weekday synaxes came to be celebrated in common we do not know for sure. The Coptic *Life of Abba John Khamé*, who lived sometime between 700 and 850, seems to witness to the practice at that time:

> And he established for them canons and holy laws, and set up for them a meeting-place where they should meet together in the middle of the night and should sing psalmody and spiritual songs until the light dawn. And he bade them moreover one and all that they should pray each one apart.[6]

But it is extremely difficult to conclude anything certain and generally applicable from such occasional references, which can be found in an earlier period, too,[7] since the documents rarely specify exactly what sort of assembly—occasional or regular, Sunday or daily—is being described.

As for the additional hours of prime, terce, sext, none, and compline, in chapter 5 we saw them in fourth-century monastic usage outside Egypt, but Cassian (*Inst.* III, 2) says the Egyptians resisted these hours, and apparently they did not acquire *droits du cité* in Egyptian monasticism until much later. Evelyn-White cites a text of the *Life of Abba John Khamé* ordering—according to Evelyn-White's interpretation—prayer at every canonical hour.[8] This is put forward as evidence that the Little Hours were introduced into Scetis by Agathon the stylite, who was there for ten years, not later than 672–682, before mounting his column. But that is not how the Coptic text reads. It says, rather, that Abba Teroti taught John "the

---

[5]See Malak Hanna, "Le rôle de la divine liturgie eucharistique dans la vie de l'Église copte hier et aujourd'hui," POC 23 (1973) 266–283.

[6]M. H. Davis (ed.), *The Life of Abba John Khamé*, PO 14, 352–353.

[7]For example the synaxis described in the additions of Rufinus to *The History of the Monks in Egypt* XXIII (see Russell, *The Lives of the Desert Fathers* 153–154).

[8]Evelyn-White, *The Monasteries* part 2, 281–282.

canon of the holy *Synaxis* of the hours, that he should pray every hour, according to the commandment of our father Abba Agathon, the stylite. . . ."[9] That is not a reference to the Little Hours at all, but rather a throwback to the much older tradition of praying at every hour of the twenty-four, twelve per day and twelve per night. As we saw in chapter 4 this was just another way of stating the evangelical command to "pray always." This was the original Egyptian tradition, and seems also to have been the primitive sense of the "rule of the angel." Palladius' *Lausiac History* 32:6 (cf. 7:5) refers to prayer at the ninth hour in addition to the two traditional synaxes,[10] and Shenoute's *Monastic Precepts* speak of "those who are the first at church in the morning, in the evening, at midday, and at the requisite hour."[11] But such texts cannot simply be taken as evidence for the day hours without further ado. The history of this development remains to be written, and the whole question would require a separate study beyond the scope of this brief summary. For the present, I can only say I know of no secure evidence for the day hours in the Coptic tradition before the Sahidic manuscript *Pierpont Morgan M 574* from Fayyum at the end of the ninth century, edited and thoroughly analyzed by H. Quecke.[12]

# The Offices

## I. THE MONASTIC HOROLOGION

The present Coptic *Horologion* has eight hours: morning prayer, terce, sext, none, eleventh hour (vespers), and compline, plus two hours that are apparently later additions: the "Prayer of the Veil," and a midnight hour comprising three nocturns. Both of these additional hours repeat psalmody already distributed throughout the other six hours. The Prayer of the Veil, a doubling of compline, appears first in Abu'l-Barakat ibn Kabar around 1320, exists only in Arabic sources (a sure sign of its late origin), and is composed of elements from the other hours. It is used only in monasteries.[13]

[9]Davis (ed.), PO 14, 377.

[10]On these texts see Veilleux, *La liturgie* 331–332.

[11]E. Amélineau (ed.), *Oeuvres de Schenoudi.* Texte copte et trad. française (Paris, 1914) vol. 2, 233, cited in O. H. E. Burmester, "The Canonical Hours of the Coptic Church," OCP 2 (1936) 82.

[12]Quecke, *Untersuchungen* 117ff. (see p. 87 for the date of the ms.).

[13]See Burmester, "The Canonical Hours" 89–100. For the text of Abu'l Barakat see L. Villecourt, "Les observances liturgiques et al disciple du jeûne dans l'eglise copte (ch. XVI-

With the exception of these two later additions, the structure of all these hours is the same:[14]

> Fixed initial prayers
> Twelve psalms (ideally)
> Gospel lesson
> Troparia (poetic refrains)
> *Kyrie eleison* (41 or 50 times)
> Trisagion
> Our Father
> Dismissal Prayer of Absolution
> Final Prayer

Variety among the hours is minimal. Morning prayer has the Great Doxology (*Gloria in excelsis*), as one would expect, and the creed. Other hours also have certain minor peculiarities, but the basic structure is the same. So apart from the later addition of seven further psalms to the original twelve at morning prayer, and some variety in the final prayers, this is the structure of all the traditional hours from morning prayer to compline. The refrains or troparia are a later addition of Palestinian origin,[15] and if we prescind from them we see an office that is almost pure Cassian.

## II. CATHEDRAL REMNANTS

But in addition to this monastic psalmody we find other services, the Offering of Incense morning and evening, and the threefold Psalmodia of the night, the morning, and the evening, which contain elements apparently of cathedral provenance.

The Offering of Incense is as follows, with the variable or proper parts in italics:[16]

---

XIX de la *Lampe des ténèbres*)." *Le Muséon* 36 (1923) 249-292; 37 (1924) 201-282; 38 (1925) 261-320.

[14]See Burmester, "The Canonical Hours," 89-100; *id., The Egyptian or Coptic Church* 96-107; Quecke, *Untersuchungen* 20ff.

[15]On the question of their origin see A. Baumstark, "Palästinensisches Erbe im byzantinischen und koptischen Horologion," *Studi bizantini e neoellenici* 6 (1940) 463-469; Quecke, *Untersuchungen* 47-52; *id.*, "Neue griechische Parallelen zum koptischen Horologion," *Le Muséon* 77 (1964) 285-294; Burmester, "The Canonical Hours," 84-49. Many of the same texts are found in Greek in the present Byzantine horologion—but that is of Palestinian, not Byzantine provenance.

[16]On the Offering of Incense, see Quecke, *Untersuchungen* 2-13; Burmester, *The Egyptian or Coptic Church* 35-45. The text can be found in John, Marquis of Bute, *The Coptic Liturgy, The Coptic Morning Service for the Lord's Day* (Christian Liturgies, London: Cope

Fixed introductory prayers
*Invitatory*
Praise of Mary
*Supplications to the saints*
*Prayer of Incense*
Incensation of the altar, with short intercessions
*Great Intercession*
Incensation
Trisagion
Our Father
Praise of Mary
*Doxologies* (poetic refrains)
Creed
Incensation with prayers
Blessing with candles and cross
Solemn Kyrie eleison (litany)
(*OT lessons* and litanies at Morning Offering of
   Incense on certain fast days)
Prayer of the Gospel
*Psalm verse*
Alleluia
*Gospel lesson*
Incensation and short intercessions
Prayer of Absolution to the Son
(*Reading of the synaxary* at Morning Offering of
   Incense)
Veneration of cross and gospel
*Final blessing*

This office contains what seems to be the debris of older cathedral services. Even more significant in this regard is the so-called Psalmodia, which refers not to biblical psalmody but the sung office,[17] a term akin to the Greek *asmatikos* or old sung cathedral office of Hagia Sophia in Byzan-

---

and Fewick, 1908); *id., The Coptic Morning Service for the Lord's Day*, translated into English by John, Marquess of Bute, K.T., with the original Coptic of those parts said aloud (London, 1882). Some parts are also translated in Burmester, *The Egyptian or Coptic Church*, appendix.

[17]In the Pachomian usage "psalmody" was characteristic of the Sunday office. See the Pachomian *Precepts* 15–18 (Veilleux, *Pachomian Koinonia* vol. 2, 147–148) and Veilleux, *La Liturgie* 314.

tine parlance.[18] This Psalmodia has never been subjected to thorough scholarly analysis, and poses numerous problems,[19] but the cathedral elements in its structure are particularly evident in the Psalmodia of the Evening and in the Psalmodia of the Night. The former is rarely celebrated today, but when done it comes between compline (and the Prayer of the Veil in monasteries) and the Evening Offering of Incense. It has the following elements (the variable proper parts are italicized):[20]

Psalmodia of the Evening:
> Fixed initial prayers
> Ps 116
> Hos (ode) 4: Pss. 148–150 with alleluia
> *Psali (poetic refrains) of season or feast and day*
> *Theotokia (Marian hymns) of the day*
> *Lobsh (crown) of the Theotokia*
> *Hymn from the Difnar (antiphonary)*
> *Conclusion of the Theotokia*

The much longer Psalmodia of the Night, sung between nocturns and the morning office, comprises:[21]

Psalmodia of the Night:
> Fixed initial prayers
> Invitatory versicles (chiefly psalmic)
> (Resurrectional praises on Sundays and in
>   Paschaltide)
> Hos (ode) 1) Ex 15:1–21 with Psali (poetic com-
>   mentary on the ode)
>   2) Ps 135 with Psali
>   3) Dan 3:52–88 with Psali of the paschal
>     mystery and Psali of the ode (on the
>     three youths in the furnace)
> Litany of the saints
> *Doxologies of the feast or day*

[18]I list numerous studies on this office in R. Taft, "The Byzantine Office in the *Prayerbook* of New Skete: Evaluation of a Proposed Reform," OCP 48 (1982) 361ff.

[19]See the discussion in Quecke, *Untersuchungen* 52–80.

[20]C. Ballin, *L'office copte. L'office des heures, l'offrande de l'incens, la psalmodie annuelle* (unpublished licentiate thesis, Rome: PIO, 1979) 73; Burmester, *The Egyptian or Coptic Church* 108–111; Italian trans. of the text in M. Brogi, *La santa salmodia annuale della chiesa copta* (Studia orientalia christiana. Aegyptiaca, Cairo: Edizioni del Centro francescano di Studi orientali cristiani, 1962).

[21]Ballin, *L'office copte* 90–94.

Hos (ode) 4: Pss 148–150 with alleluia after each
verse
*Psali of the feast or day*
*Theotokia*
*Lobsch (crown) of the Theotokia*
*Hymn of the day from the Difnar (antiphonary),*
*with its Tarh (response)*
*Conclusion of the Theotokia*
Creed
Concluding litany
Sanctus
Our Father
Dismissal Prayer of Absolution

The Psalmodia of the Morning, which follows the morning office of the *Horologion*, is made up of only a couple of poetic pieces and can hardly be called an office at all.[22] The Psalmodia of the Evening and of the Night seem to be the remnants, in the first case, of cathedral lauds, and in the second, of lauds again, this time preceded by elements of the old Sunday Resurrection Vigil as reconstructed by Mateos.[23]

As for cathedral vespers in the Egyptian tradition, evidence of it can still be found in Ethiopian vespers, which is of Egyptian provenance at least in part; Winkler has identified the residue of an old cathedral vespers in the Coptic Evening Offering of Incense;[24] and Ugo Zanetti has recently found in a fourteenth-century manuscript at the Monastery of St. Macarius in the Wadi an-Natrun a Byzantine-type cathedral evensong or "Prayer of the Eleventh Hour according to the Use of Cairo." Other manuscripts at St. Macarius have the psalter distributed in the Byzantine manner, including the invitatory Ps 103 and the select vesperal psalms of Byzantine Sabaitic cathedral vespers: Pss 140, 141, 129, 116.[25]

## Present Usage

When describing the liturgical customs of a living and developing Christian community it is always temerarious to generalize. That is especially true of communities undergoing a renaissance, like the Coptic Orthodox

---

[22]Burmester, *The Egyptian or Coptic Church* 111.

[23]Ballin, *L'office copte* 95ff. On the cathedral vigil, see ch. 3.

[24]Winkler, "Über die Kathedralvesper," 81–83, and see the next chapter.

[25]"Horologion copte et vêpres byzantines," *Le Muséon* 102 (1989) 237–254. I am most grateful to Fr. Zanetti for his unfailingly kind and informative assistance during my "liturgical study-pilgrimage" to Egypt in the early fall of 1981 (see the following note).

Church of Egypt, which in the past generation has experienced a remarkable spiritual and monastic renewal. So I shall limit myself to describing those customs of which I have had personal experience.[26]

## 1. The Monastic Cursus of Scetis Today

At the huge Coptic Orthodox Monastery of Dayr Abu Maqar (St. Macarius) in the Wadi an-Natrun—Scetis of old—the daily monastic office is accomplished for the most part in two synaxes. When the bell rings at 3:00 A.M. the monks rise to pray in their cells until the morning synaxis, which lasts from about 4:30 to 6:30 and includes nocturns, Psalmodia of the Night, matins, terce and sext, all done in sequence without interruption. The bell is rung a second time before matins, to summon those who have preferred to prolong their solitary prayer.

The offices are performed standing, except for the prostrations that accompany the prayers; one can sit cross-legged on the floor if the standing becomes too much (there are no pews in Coptic monastic churches, though one finds them commonly in secular churches today). Unlike the secular churches, which are generally basilical in form, the monastic churches are more square, and when one takes a substantial strip all along the east wall for the enclosed triple sanctuary (haikal), the remaining area outside the haikal is wider than it is long, and the monks stand single file, facing the haikal with their backs to the grill separating the choir from the nave. There are no special places except for the senior priest present, who always presides. Before the rank of monks there is a long lectern to hold the books needed for the Psalmodia, which is still done in Coptic except for some parts that are taken in Arabic. The hours of the *Horologion*, done entirely in Arabic and absolutely invariable every day including even the lessons, are done entirely from memory, without books. So the church is lit only by one or two tapers except at the Psalmodia, when lanterns are lighted to permit reading.

The office opens with the presiding priest pronouncing the initial phrases of the opening prayers, which each monk then recites to himself. Since twelve psalms per hour is a considerable *pensum*, the psalmody is now done in the following manner: a precentor goes down the line whispering the incipit of a psalm to each monk, making as many runs as necessary to distribute all at once, in their prescribed order, the assigned psalms of the hour. Then everyone simultaneously recites by heart his assigned

---

[26]See R. Taft, "A Pilgrimage to the Origins of Religious Life: the Fathers of the Desert Today," *The American Benedictine Review* 36 (1985) 113-142.

psalm(s) in silence. Needless to say, such a practice is a later abuse designed to relax the burden of excessively long synaxes. After the psalmody, the assigned reader, standing facing the sanctuary a bit to the right of the closed doors of the haikal screen, recites the gospel lesson in a low voice (since it is invariable, everyone knows it by heart). This, too, is a later corruption. The present invariable readings are from the printed Arabic editions, which provide at most a selection of only two or three lessons per hour.[27] The lesson is followed by the Psali or poetic refrains, done by a soloist from his place. Then the *Gloria patri* is chanted by all, and the hour is concluded with the *Kyrie eleison*, Trisagion, Our Father, and final prayers.

Such an office is more a meditation in common than a liturgical service. As such, it is faithful to the pristine orientation of the pure monastic hours. But this is not true of the Psalmodia, a sung office chanted in Coptic in a swiftly moving, strongly punctuated, almost staccato rhythm, the presider keeping time all the while with small cymbals.

Weekday evenings from 6:00 to 6:30 the monks chant vespers, compline and the Prayer of the Veil. None is done in the refectory before the noon meal, the only common repast at St. Macarius.

At the end of each synaxis all the monks except the presiding priest line up facing him, their backs to the sanctuary wall, while he says the final prayers of intercession, then one by one they approach him and one another for the "peace," the juniors placing the palm of their right hand in that of the senior (or if they are priests, taking his hand in both of theirs). Then each one kisses his own hand and places it over his breast—a common greeting of respect in Egypt even apart from such formal circumstances. The monks also give the *pax* to one another (or only to the presider if the office has begun) on entering church before the synaxis, though with less formality.

On Saturday the evening synaxis begins at 4:00 P.M. because the Evening Offering of Incense and Evening Psalmodia, not done on ordinary days, are celebrated in preparation for Sundays or feasts. And on the morrow everyone is in church again at 2:00 A.M. for the usual daily offices, followed at 4:30 by the Morning Offering of Incense, generally done only on Eucharistic days, and at 5:30 by the Eucharistic liturgy.

At the monastery of Dayr al-Baramus, northernmost of the four active Coptic Orthodox monasteries in the Wadi an-Natrun today, and the oldest, the daily cursus begins at 4:00 A.M. with the Psalmodia of the Evening and of the Night, the morning office of the monastic *Horologion*, and the Psalmodia of the Morning, followed at about 6:00 by the Morning

---

[27]Burmester, "The Canonical Hours," 90 note 2; 93 note 6; 95 note 1; 99 note 3.

Offering of Incense and the Eucharist, which is celebrated daily at Baramus and some other "renewed" monasteries. At 11:00 A.M. the monks go
about their tasks and devotions, returning to church from 5:00–5:30 P.M.
for vespers, compline, and the Prayer of the Veil. This combined service
is short because the psalms are distributed as at St. Macarius. On Saturday evening and the eve of feasts, the Evening Offering of Incense is also
celebrated. I have no information on the Little Hours at Baramus. Perhaps
some of them are included in the two common synaxes, as at St. Macarius,
with the others recited in private.

In parish worship it is customary to celebrate the Evening Offering
of Incense on the eve of any day when Eucharist is to be celebrated. In
the morning, Eucharist is always preceded by the Morning Offering of
Incense. And during the month of Khoiak, a sort of Coptic Advent in
preparation for the celebrations of the Nativity cycle, the very popular
proper office called the Psalmodia of Khoiak, made up chiefly of ecclesiastical poetry in praise of the Mother of God, is celebrated in parishes in
the presence of huge crowds.

# 16

# THE ETHIOPIAN RITE

There are almost no scientifically reliable studies available on the origins and development of the Ethiopian Rite, so there is little secure data to offer by way of historical background. Nor are we much better informed concerning the Ethiopian Divine Office: published texts and studies are rare and often inadequate. Notable exceptions are Velat's partial edition and study of the cathedral office;[1] and van Lantschoot's Latin version and commentary, and Turaev's edition of the Ge'ez text with Russian translation plus commentary, of the Ethiopian *Horologion* derived from Coptic usage.[2] In addition, one of my graduate students at the Pontifical Oriental Institute in Rome, the Ethiopian Capuchin priest Father Habtemichael Kidane, son of an Ethiopian Orthodox priest, is preparing his doctoral dissertation on the Divine Office of the Ethiopian Church. His recently

[1] B. Velat, *Ṣoma deggua*, PO 32/3-4, *id, Etudes sur le me'erāf. Commun de l'office divin éthiopien. Introduction, traduction française, commentaire liturgique et musicale*, PO 33.

[2] S. Congregazione "Pro Ecclesia Orientali" Prot. n. 293/1937: *Horologion Aethiopicum iuxta recensionem Alexandrinam Copticam* (Vatican: Typis polyglottis Vaticanis 1940), prepared by Arnold van Lantschoot and published for private use by the Oriental Congregation (not available commercially); B. Turaev, *Chasoslov efiopskoj tserkvi. Izdal i perevël na osnovanii neskol'skikh rukopisej B. Turaev* (Memoires de l'Académie impériale des sciences de St.-Pétersbourg, VIIIᵉ série, Classe historico-philologique, vol. 1 no. 7, St. Petersburg, 1897).

completed licentiate thesis, a study propaedeutic to the dissertation, has provided me with much valuable information for the preparation of this chapter.[3] Finally, Professor Peter Jeffery of the University of Delaware has been kind enough to place at my disposal the first draft of his paper on Ethiopian chant that contains valuable information on the office.[4]

Like the Coptic Rite, the Ethiopian tradition has parallel cathedral and monastic hours that remain separate, and have not been fused into one office as in other liturgical families.

## The Cathedral Services[5]

Native Ethiopian cathedral hours are a sung office like the Byzantine *asmatikos*, celebrated solemnly by the dabtara or "masters" in the larger churches on days of special solemnity. This cathedral office comprises the three chief hours of vespers, nocturns, and matins, except at certain times of the year such as Lent when one also finds the third, sixth, and ninth hours, as well as some special occasional offices.

These services are all sung by the dabtara or professional cantors in the complex chant of their tradition. The qumet or sacred chant of the Ethiopian Church has three modes:[6]

a) ge'ez, a simple tone for ferial and penitential days
b) 'ezel for feasts and funerals
c) ārārāy.

The chant is executed "āquāquām" (from *quoma*, to stand), that is, standing keeping time with the maquomeyā or choir cane held in the right hands and accompanying the chant with bodily movements to the beat of drums and the shaking of sistrums. There are twenty four varieties of āquāquām. The rhythmic sway of the chanting dabtara has been compared to the trees of a forest slowly waving in unison in the breeze. These movements are the famous "liturgical dance" of the Ethiopians that has so fascinated Westerners in our century.

---

[3]Habtemichael Kidane, *L'ufficio divino della Chiesa Etiopica* (unpublished licentiate thesis, Rome: PIO, 1984).

[4]P. Jeffery, "The Living Tradition of Ethiopic Chant" (unpublished manuscript).

[5]Kidane, *L'ufficio divino della Chiesa Etiopica* 81ff. See also Velat, *Etudes sur le me'erāf* PO 33 *passim.*

[6]Kidane, *L'ufficio divino della Chiesa Etiopica* 38ff., 47ff.

I. WĀZĒMĀ OR SOLEMN VESPERS[7]

An Ethiopian festive celebration opens in the early afternoon of the vigil with the chanting of vespers, a service of four or five hours duration. Here is the structure of festive vespers:

Fixed opening prayer
Wāzēmā (proper hymn)
Ps 23
Baḥāmestu (proper antiphon)
Qenē wāzēmā (vesper hymn) 1
Prayer for rain
Ps 92
Baḥāmestu (proper antiphon)
Qenē wāzēmā (vesper hymn) 2
Prayer for the sovereign
Ps 140
Baḥāmestu (proper antiphon)
Liṭon (prayer of evening thanks)
Epistle lessons
Yetebārak (canticle of Dan 3:52-56)
Yetebārak (antiphon of the canticle)
2 or 3 qenē (hymns)
Mesbāk (alleluia psalm)
Gospel
Kidān (prayer of evening)
Ps 101 with salast (antiphon)
Ps 84 with salām (antiphon)
"Christ Lord have mercy on us" (3 times)
Final prayer
Creed
Our Father

On ferias the two variable psalms of the initial psalmody are part of the continuous psalter, as can be seen from a glance at the table of psalms and canticles of the Lenten ferial office.[8] But on festive days these two variable psalms plus Ps 50 are replaced by Pss 23, 92, 140—the last of which, at least, is a standard element of cathedral evensong in the tradition.

[7]*Ibid.* 88ff; Velat, *Etudes sur le me'erāf*, PO 33, 128-129; Winkler, "Über die Kathedralvesper," 82-83.
[8]See the schema in Velat, *Etudes sur le me'erāf*, PO 33, 140a.

## II. MAWADDES OR SUNDAY NOCTURNS[9]

After a period of repose, vespers is followed by the night office or mawaddes at first cockcrow, matins (lauds) or ṣebehāta nagh, and the Eucharist, all done without interruption.[10]

Mawaddes consists of a series of units of psalmody, prayers, and other elements, in which both monastic and cathedral material are intermingled. Here is the ordinary structure of mawaddes for non-penitential times:

> Fixed opening prayer
> Qeddus (Trisagion)
> Kidān (prayer of the night)
> Mesbāk (alleluia psalm)
> Supplication of the night
> Mesbāk (alleluia psalm)
> Liṭon (litany)
> Prayer for the sick
> Pss 62, 63, 65
> Prayer for travellers
> Pss 39–41 with arbā'et (antiphon)
> Prayer for rain
> Pss 42–44
> Prayer for crops
> Pss 46–47
> Prayer for the river waters
> Pss 48–49 with baḥāmestu (antiphon)
> Ps 50 with arbā'et (antiphon)
> Prayer for the king
> Prayer for the sovereign
> Pss 117, 91 with baḥāmestu (antiphon)
> Ps 92
> Prayer for peace

## III. SEBEHĀTA NAGH (MATINS)[11]

Sebehāta nagh, our matins or lauds, is found in several forms: ordinary or ferial, for minor solemnities; festive, for major feasts; for the season "of flowers" dedicated to the Mother of God; for Holy Week; for Holy

---

[9]Kidane, L'ufficio divino della Chiesa Etiopica 92ff.
[10]Ibid. 88.
[11]Ibid. 94ff.

Saturday. At sebehāta nagh two choirs of dabtara chant the psalms alternately, intercalated with proper antiphons and interspersed with prayers, litanies, doxologies, hymns, invocations, and intercessions.

The basic structure of festive sebehāta nagh is:

> Angargāri (antiphon)
> Esema la-ālam (antiphon)
> Liṭon (litany)
> Za-āmelākeyā (Pss 62, 64, 91, 5)
> Qenē za-āmelākeyā (hymn with Ps 62)
> Prayer for the sick
> *Nunc dimittis*
> Qenē za-sellase or za-ye'eze (hymn with *Nunc
>   dimittis*)
> Prayer for travellers
> 'Ezel (chant)
> Canticle of Dan 3:52–56
> Qenē (hymn)
> Ẏetebārak (antiphon of Dan 3)
> Canticle of Dan 3:57–90
> Sebehāta nagh (antiphon of sabbehewo or lauds)
> Sabbehewo (lauds: Pss 148–150)
> Prayer for the king
> Abun (antiphon)
> Mawāse'et (hymn or antiphon)
> Esema la-ālam or qenewāt (antiphon)
> Ps 101 with salast (antiphon)
> Ps 84 with salām (antiphon)
> "Christ Lord have mercy on us" (3 times)
> Final prayer
> Creed
> Our Father

The cathedral elements such as Pss 148–150 and the canticle of Dan 3 are immediately apparent in this service.

## IV. KESTAT ZA-ĀRYĀM[12]

Another service of the sung office, kestat za-āryām, is celebrated only on the thirty greatest feasts of the Marian and sanctoral cycles, including

[12]*Ibid.* 99ff.

the Finding of the Holy Cross, which in the Ethiopian tradition is not considered a christological solemnity. This office is the longest Ethiopian hour and the richest in ecclesiastical, i.e., non-biblical, compositions. It replaces the other morning offices on feasts when it is celebrated, and includes psalms plus the entire corpus of Old and New Testament canticles[13] with antiphons, along with numerous invocations, readings from the Senkessār (synaxarium), from *The Book of Miracles of Mary*, from the Gospels, *The Praises of Mary*, and various prayers reserved to the priest.

## The Saʿātāt or Ethiopian Hours

In addition to the cathedral services, the Ethiopians also have not one but several other cursus of daily prayers preserved in office books called saʿātāta or *horologia*.[14] Not only are these distinct offices separate from the cathedral services, but what is completely novel and peculiar to Ethiopia is that there are not one but four independent and competing types of Ethiopian horologion, as identified by Jeffery:[15]

1) the saʿātāt za-Gebs or "Horologion of the Copts"
2) the saʿātāt of Abba Giyorgis Saglawi
3) a saʿātāt that includes the entire psalter in the daily *pensum*
4) the cursus of prayers found in *Codex Vatican Ethiopic 21*.

### I. THE SAʿĀTĀT ZA-GEBS

One would expect to find an Ethopian office akin to that of the neighboring Copts, and indeed the saʿātāt za-Gebs or "Horologion of the Copts" is a translation of the Coptic *Horologion* with the addition of Byzantine elements. This cursus has the traditional sevenfold cycle of offices before the addition of prime: nocturns, matins, terce, sext, none, vespers, compline.

When this Coptic-type office was introduced, and what use was made of it in relation to the other manuscript office traditions, we have no idea. For we know little of the relationship between these two African Christian traditions before 1270, when there was a definite "Copticizing" movement under the aegis of the Ethiopian monk and theologian Tekle

---

[13]There are fifteen of them in the Ethiopian Office; see *ibid.* 61–62.
[14]Jeffery, "Ethiopic Chant," 25.
[15]*Ibid.* 25–29.

Haymanot.[16] At any rate it is clear that at some time or other the hours of the Coptic monastic *Horologion* were translated into Ge'ez, the Ethiopian liturgical language, and incorporated into the Ethiopian office.[17] The same is true of the Coptic Psalmodia of the Night.

### 1. The night office:

The Ethiopian nocturnal service in these hours is simply an adaptation of the Coptic Psalmodia of the Night. But in the Ethiopic redaction of this service it is interesting to note that lauds or the "Fourth Hos" (canticle), Pss 148–150, are preceded in the manuscripts by the title: "In the Name of the Holy Trinity. Prayer at Cockcrow."[18] This confirms what we saw in the previous chapter concerning the composite nature of the Coptic Psalmodia of the Night as an office of cathedral lauds to which a cathedral vigil with three canticles has been prefixed.

In the Ethiopian tradition this matins or "cockcrow" hour concludes with material not found in present Coptic usage, including three gospels with eschatological themes of watching and vigilance in expectation of the parousia. Here is an outline of this additional material:[19]

> NT canticles: *Magnificat-Benedictus-Nunc dimittis*
> (Luke 7:46–55, 68–79; 2:29–32)
> OT canticle of Hezekiah (Is 38:10–20)
> *Gloria in excelsis*
> *Dignare domine (Kataxioson)*
> Ps 91:2–3
> Trisagion
> Our Father
> Creed with its prooemion
> Prayer and blessing before the gospel
> Gospel: Luke 11:5–13
> Troparia
> *Kyrie eleison* 51 times
> Absolution
> Prayer
> Psali

[16]Ephraim Isaac, "An Obscure Component in Ethiopian Church History: an Examination of Various Theories pertaining to the Problem of the Origins and Nature of Ethiopian Christianity," *Le Muséon* 85 (1972) 246ff., 249ff.

[17]Ge'ez text with Russian trans. in Turaev, *Chasoslov* 2–127; Latin version in van Lantschoot, *Horologion* 159–175.

[18]Turaev, *Chasoslov* 138–139; van Lantschoot, *Horologion* 68.

[19]Turaev, *Chasoslov* 72–87; van Lantschoot, *Horologion* 159–175.

Prayer and blessing before the gospel
Gospel: Mark 13:32-37
Gospel: Matt 25:14-30
*Kyrie eleison* 3 times
Invocation of the Trinity
Prayer of blessing of St. Basil
Invocation of the King of Peace
*Deacon:* intercession for the Church
Concluding doxology

### 2. The eleventh hour (vespers):[20]

Even more cathedral elements not found in Coptic usage are interspersed after the monastic psalmody and gospel lesson of the eleventh hour (vespers) in the Ethiopic recension of the Coptic *Horologion.* These elements peculiar to the Ethiopic recension are italicized in the following outline:

Initial prayers
Monastic psalmody (12 psalms): Pss 116–117,
   119–128
Gospel lesson
*Ps 129:7-8 with refrain*
*Ps 116:1, refrain; verse 2, refrain; glory . . . both*
   *now . . .; refrain*
*Phôs hilaron*
Kataxioson (after Nunc dimittis in the Coptic
   recension)
*Ps 91:1 with refrain*
*Ps 122:1 with refrain*
Troparia
Nunc dimittis
*Ps 140:1, refrain; verse 2, refrain*
Trisagion
Evening thanks

Then the Coptic *Horologion* resumes with the customary concluding prayers: O Holy Trinity, Our Father, etc.[21] Until much further work is done on this poorly-known, little-studied liturgical tradition, we cannot know whence, when or how these elements, some of them clearly of

[20]Turaev, *Chasoslov* 72-87; van Lantschoot, *Horologion* 40ff.
[21]See Burmester, *The Egyptian or Coptic Church* 104.

Byzantine-Sabaitic provenance, entered Ethiopian usage. Were they once part of the Coptic Rite too? As I said in the previous chapter, Ugo Zanetti has uncovered at Dayr Abu Maqar manuscripts of a hitherto unknown variety of Coptic vespers entitled "according to the usage of Cairo" which in fact is little more than a Coptic redaction of Byzantine-Sabaitic vespers.[22] But until all this material is sifted and studied in relation to the whole history and development of these sister traditions, whatever I might say about all this would be sheer speculation.

## II. THE SAʿĀTĀT OF ABBA GIYORGIS SAGLAWI[23]

Abba Giyorgis, nicknamed Baʿāla Saʿātāt, "Composer of the Book of Hours," was a liturgical reformer from the small town of Sagla in Amhara who died around 1426. He composed the office that bears his name.[24] This saʿātāt has replaced the hours of Coptic provenance as the common horologion of the Ethiopian Orthodox Church, contrary to what I recently affirmed concerning the continued use of the former in Ethiopia.[25]

This second type of saʿātāt, apparently the only one still in common use, comprises nocturns and an eleventh and twelfth hour. Nocturns and vespers or the eleventh hour are little more than a series of four Scripture lessons, with a responsorial psalm before the last, always a gospel, at nocturns. This lection unit is enclosed in a framework of opening prayers and concluding intercessions, hymns, orations, canticles, etc. The twelfth hour is a devotional office in praise of Mary.

Thus the Ethiopians can lay claim to having transformed the hours into a Liturgy of the Word centered on Scripture lections a century before Luther.

These hours are celebrated only in church, but they do not require the participation of the dabtara or trained cantors needed for the sung office, and so they are celebrated daily in churches and monasteries throughout the land.

[22]See note 25 in the previous chapter.

[23]Kidane, *L'ufficio divino della Chiesa Etiopica* 106ff.; Jeffery, "Ethiopic Chant," 29.

[24]On Abba Giyorgis and his saʿātāt see Taddesse Tamrat, *Church and State in Ethiopia 1270-1527* (Oxford: Clarendon Press, 1972) 222ff.; Getatchew Haile, "*Fekkare Haymanot* or the Faith of *Abba* Giyorgis Säglawi," *Le Muséon* 94 (1981) 236-237; *id.*, "Writings of *Abba* Giyorgis Säglawi from Two Unedited Miracles of Mary," OCP 48 (1982) 65-91, esp. 65-66, 71, 81, 85.

[25]R. Taft, *The Liturgy of the Hours in the Christian East: Origins, Meaning, Place in the Life of the Church* (Cochin: K.C.M. Press, 1984) 192.

### III. THE SAʿĀTĀT OF THE PSALTER[26]

Another Ethiopian saʿātāt has the customary seven hours of the office, with no psalms at compline (newam) or the midnight office (lelit), but with thirty psalms and three canticles in each of the other five hours, so that the entire Ethiopian psalter including fifteen biblical canticles is recited each day.

### IV. THE SAʿĀTĀT OF *Codex Vaticanus Aethiopicus 21*[27]

The fifteenth-century manuscript office in *Codex Vatican Ethiopic 21* gives a cursus with not only the usual midnight, morning, and evening prayers, but with prayer for each of the twelve daylight hours, a practice seen also in the Iberian monastic usage described by Fructuosus of Braga.[28]

In this cursus the morning and day hours are just a series of non-biblical prayers without psalmody, canticles, or lessons. But the midnight hour and vespers have four and five biblical readings respectively, and vespers includes the light ritual with its dialogue and prayer of blessing from *Apostolic Tradition* 25:[29]

1. **The midnight hour:**[30]

> Opening Prayer
> Lessons: Eph 6:10–24
>         2 Pet 3:8–14
>         Acts 12:6–11
>         Mark 13:32–36
> Prayer to Christ
> Prayer of Imposition of Hands
> Profession of faith

[26]Jeffery, "Ethiopic Chant," 28; mss. *Vat. Aeth. 15*, in S. Grébaut, E. Tisserant, *Codices Aethiopici Vaticani et Borgiani*, pars prior (Vatican: Bibliotheca Vaticana, 1935) 45–48; EMML 2097, in Getatchew Haile and W. F. Macomber, *A Catalogue of Ethiopian Manuscripts Microfilmed for the Ethiopian Manuscript Microfilm Library, Addis Ababa, and for the Hill Monastic Manuscript Library, Collegeville* (Collegeville, Minn.: Hill Monastic Manuscript Library, St. John's Abbey and University, 1976-) vol. 6; both cited in Jeffery note 111. in Jeffery note 111.

[27]Jeffery, "Ethiopic Chant," 29. The ms. is described in Grébaut and Tisserant, *Codices Aethiopici Vaticani* I, 85–105. A translation can be found in S. Salaville, "La prière de toutes les heures dans la littérature éthiopienne," *id.*, *Studia orientalia liturgico-theologica* (Rome: EL, 1940) 170–185.

[28]See above, chapter 6, p. 119.

[29]Cited above, chapter 2, pp. 26–27.

[30]Grébaut and Tisserant, *Codices Aethiopici Vaticani* I, 86.

**2. Vespers:**[31]

> Vesperal "Prayer of Ephrem"
> Lucernarium from *ApTrad* 25
> 3 vesperal prayers
> Lessons: Zech 14:5–9
>          Eph 2:19–22
>          Jas 4:7–12
>          Acts 10:34–38
>          Luke 23:50–56
> Prayer of Imposition of Hands
> Creed with anathemas
> Final prayer

## Present Usage[32]

Today in the Ethiopian Orthodox Church the full office is celebrated only in monasteries. In parish usage on the eve of Eucharistic days (Sundays and feasts) vespers is celebrated in the evening, followed at about 1:00 A.M. by nocturns, matins (lauds), and the Eucharistic liturgy, all done in succession without interruption. But of course only the dabtara and other clergy, exceedingly numerous in the Ethiopian Orthodox Church, are present for the whole length of the offices.

[31]*Ibid.* 103–105.
[32]Personal communication from Habtemichael Kidane.

# 17

# THE BYZANTINE OFFICE

## History

We are accustomed—and not without reason—to viewing the Byzantine Rite as the liturgical tradition formed in the capital city of Constantinople, the "New Rome" founded by Constantine on the site of the town of Byzantium in 324. But like the Roman Rite and, indeed, most great cultural traditions, the Byzantine Rite is a mongrel. Its Eucharistic liturgy is the outcome of the liturgical synthesis formed in the cathedral liturgy of Constantinople at the beginning of the eighth century.[1] But the old cathedral office of Hagia Sophia, the "Great Church," fell into disuse some time after the fall of the city to the Latins during the Fourth Crusade in 1204, and was gradually replaced by the monastic office.[2]

So it is to the monasteries of Constantinople, and beyond them to those of Palestine, that we must look for the origins of the "Sabaitic" office

---

[1] See R. Taft, "How Liturgies Grow: the Evolution of the Byzantine Divine Liturgy," OCP 43 (1977) 355-378; *id.*, "The Liturgy of the Great Church: an Initial Synthesis of Structure and Interpretation on the Eve of Iconoclasm," *Dumbarton Oaks Papers* 34-35 (1980-1981) 45-75.

[2] On the old cathedral office of Constantinople see the bibliography in Taft, "The Byzantine Office in the *Prayerbook* of New Skete," 361 nn. 48-60, 80-81, 104.

presently in use in the Churches that follow the Byzantine Rite.[3] We have already studied in chapters 3 and 5 the description of the early hagiopolite cathedral offices in the diary of Egeria, and the Palestinian monastic office as described in the writings of Cassian. But it is not until later, around the end of the sixth or beginning of the seventh century, that we have our next reasonably detailed description of a Palestinian office in the account of the visit of Abbots John and Sophronius to the anchorite Abbot Nilus of Sinai.[4] I described this *agrypnia* or all-night vigil in chapter 10. It comprised the *hexapsalmos* (see schema 2 below) followed by the entire liturgical psalter: all 150 psalms plus the nine biblical canticles, with prayers and lessons. To this were appended elements of cathedral lauds:

> The *Ainoi:* Pss 148–150
> *Gloria in excelsis*
> Creed
> Our Father
> *Kyrie eleison* 300 times
> Concluding prayer

Vespers in the same document consists in:

> *Gloria patri*
> "Blessed is the man" (Ps 1:1)
> "O Lord I have cried" (Ps 140:1) without
>   troparia (refrains)
> *Phôs hilaron*
> *Kataxioson*
> *Nunc dimittis*
> "And the rest"

This is basically today's Byzantine vespers (see schema 1 below) minus the ecclesiastical poetry, the responsorial psalm, the prayers and litanies

---

[3]For the history of this Sabaitic office and its gradual introduction into the Byzantine Rite, see the complete bibliography in *ibid.* 358–370. The best general studies are: M. Arranz, "Les grandes étapes de la liturgie byzantine: Palestine-Byzance-Russie," *Liturgie de l'église particulière, liturgie de l'église universelle* ( BELS 7, Rome: Edizioni liturgiche, 1976) 43–72; id., "L'office divin en orient," *Dictionnaire de spiritualité* 11, 707–720; N. Egender, "Introduction," *La prière des heures: Hôrologion* (La prière des églises de rite byzantin 1, Chevetogne: Editions de Chevetogne, 1975) 25–56; C. Hannick, "Le texte de l'Oktoechos," *Dimanche: office selon les huit tons: Oktôêchos* (La prière des églises de rite byzantin 3, Chevetogne: Editions de Chevetogne, 1968) 37–60; R. Taft, "Mount Athos: A Late Chapter in the History of the 'Byzantine Rite,'" *Dumbarton Oaks Papers* 42 (1988) 179–194. The following summary of the history of the Byzantine office is based principally on these sources.

[4]Longo, "Il testo integrale della *Narrazione degli abati Giovanni e Sofronio,*" 251ff.

from the euchology, and the stational procession now appended after the final blessing of vespers.

The document also gives an account of the discussion that followed Nilus' description of these offices of the Palestinian anchorite.[5] His interlocutors John and Sophronius expressed their astonishment at the absence of ecclesiastical poetry and other elements apart from such traditional fixed pieces as the *Gloria in excelsis* at matins and the *Phôs hilaron* at evensong. They mention specifically the following missing items they had expected to find: 1) at vespers: the refrains or troparia with Ps 140; the *Kateuthynthêtô* or Ps 140:2 responsory, as in today's Presanctified Vespers; 2) at nocturns: the invitatory responsory "The Lord is God" (Ps 117:27a, 26a) and the *kathismata anastasima* or poetic refrains after the psalmody; and 3) at matins: the refrains with the biblical canticles; the responsory "Let everything that breathes" (Ps 150:6) before the gospel; and the troparion after the *Gloria in excelsis*. To their surprise Nilus replied that all this was suitable for the clergy, i.e., for the cathedral office, but not for monks.

This discussion shows that all these elements were part of the daily cycle at that time. Nilus was quite correct in seeing them as an innovation, for the first element in the formation of this Palestinian hybrid monastic office was indeed the daily cycle of the Palestinian *Horologion* that he describes. And we have not only Nilus' description but also three ninth-century manuscripts of just such an horologion: Sinai Greek 863 edited by J. Mateos,[6] the unedited *Sinai Greek 864*, and the Syriac *Horologion* edited by M. Black from *Berlin MS. Or. Oct. 1019.*[7]

Such conservatives as Nilus were not able to prevent the inexorable incursion of ecclesiastical poetry into even the monastic offices in the next step in their evolution, the formation of the dominical and paschal propers—i.e., the movable cycle. An early hagiopolite stage in the development of this ecclesiastical poetry can be seen in the fact that, for matins and vespers, the fifth-to-eighth-century manuscripts of the Georgian lectionary of Jerusalem contain the texts of several proper poetic chants not found in the earlier fifth-century Armenian recension of the Jerusalem lectionary.[8] Helmut Leeb has studied this material in relation to the

---

[5]*Ibid.* 252ff., 264–265.

[6]"Un horologion inédit de Saint-Sabas."

[7]*A Christian Palestinian Syriac Horologion (Berlin MS. Or. Oct. 1019)* (Texts and Studies, new series, 1, Cambridge: At the University Press, 1967).

[8]The respective lectionary mss. are edited by A. Renoux, *Le codex arménien Jérusalem 121*, PO 36/2 (cf. PO 35/1); M. Tarchnišvili, *Le grand lectionnaire de l'église de Jérusalem (V^e–VIII^e siècle)*, CSCO 188–189, 204–205, scr. iberici 9–10, 13–14.

history of the Byzantine Divine Office.[9]

Here is how it seems to have entered the monastic usage of Palestine and, ultimately, of the whole Byzantine Church. After the Persians destroyed the Holy City in 614, the monks of St. Sabas Monastery in the wilderness picked up the pieces and restored monastic life. As often happens after violent destruction, a remarkably creative period followed, and a new monastic office was produced via a massive infusion of ecclesiastical poetry into the former staid and sober monastic psalmody described by Nilus.

This Palestinian monastic office was then adopted by the monasteries of Constantinople in the restoration following the first wave of Iconoclasm (726–775), when a new monastic synthesis was in formation under the leadership of the great Byzantine monastic reformer St. Theodore Studites (d. 826). One interesting aspect of this synthesis was the adaptation to a basically Palestinian structure of the prayers and litanies of the Constantinopolitan offices of vespers and matins found in the *Euchologion* of the capital. In these Studite monasteries the composition of new ecclesiastical poetry continued apace, and St. Theodore himself gave a large place to the new compositions in his adaptation of the Palestinian monastic offices. It is from this poetry that the Byzantine Sunday and Lenten-paschal anthologies, the *Oktoichos, Triodion,* and *Pentekostarion,* were later formed. The first Studite *Typika* or liturgical ordos to govern their use were composed in the ninth or tenth century.

This hybrid urban monastic office spread to the Byzantine monasteries of Mount Athos, Georgia, Rus', and Southern Italy. Meanwhile in Palestine, at St. Sabas, the monks had retained a more sober usage, and it is their new *Typikon,* called "of St. Sabas" or "of Jerusalem," that is the ancestor of our present Byzantine office. This Sabaitic synthesis, for which we have evidence from the twelfth century, can be found in Constantinople a century later. It, too, reached Mount Athos and had taken over even in Rus by the end of the fourteenth century. The spread of the hesychast movement favored the diffusion of this more sober, more "monastic" rite, and it is this usage that is codified in the rubrics of the *diataxis* or "ceremonial" of Philotheus Kokkinos[10] which are still in force today.

---

[9]*Die Gesänge im Gemeindegottesdienst von Jerusalem (vom 5. bis 8. Jahrhundert)* (Wiener Beiträge zur Theologie 28, Vienna: Herder, 1970).

[10]PG 154, 745–766. Philotheus was Higoumen of the Great Lavra on Mt. Athos before becoming Bishop of Heraclea in 1347 and Patriarch of Constantinople twice from 1353 to 1354, 1364–1376.

Some time after the fall of Constantinople to the Latins in 1204 the monastic office replaced the more elaborate cathedral rite even in the secular churches of the capital, and it is this monastic synthesis of Palestino-Constantinopolitan monastic uses with the euchology of Constantinople that is our "Byzantine Office" today.

## The Offices

The complex structure of this rite can be seen in the following schemata, where the composite nature of the offices is immediately apparent from the outlines on pages 278 to 282.

### I. VESPERS:

Vespers in this tradition is basically a hagiopolite cathedral lucernarium with Constantinopolitan prayers and litanies, to which a monastic synaxis of continuous psalmody has been prefixed.[11] The presidential prayers now bunched at the beginning of both vespers and matins were of course meant to be distributed throughout the office, each in its proper place. The numerous "dangling doxologies" or *ekphoneseis* unattached to any prayer that are scattered throughout these services usually indicate the original place of one of these collects.

### II. ORTHROS[12]

In its present form orthros or matins is really a conflation of four distinct offices. First there is the so-called Royal Office, a brief service for the sovereign celebrated, apparently, in imperial monastic foundations. This is really a separate service, extraneous to the structure of matins. Because monks are fond of adding but only rarely subtract material from their offices, it has become permanently prefixed to Byzantine matins, though in fact it is often omitted in parochial worship. The second part of orthros is a monastic nocturns of continuous psalmody. On Sundays and feasts a cathedral vigil of the type described in Egeria and the *Apostolic Constitutions* has been inserted to form the third part of this composite service. The fourth part, cathedral morning praise, begins with Ps 50, and

---

[11]See J. Mateos, "La synaxe monastique des vêpres byzantines," OCP 36 (1970) 248–272.

[12]On orthros see Mateos, "Quelques problèmes de l'orthros byzantin."

---

### Schema 1

#### VESPERS

#### I. MONASTIC VESPERS

*Fixed opening*

Initial blessing and prayers

*Monastic psalmody*

Invitatory Psalm 103
Seven vesperal prayers said
  silently by priest during
  Ps 103
Great synapte
Psalmody

#### II. CATHEDRAL VESPERS

*Lucernarium*

Vesperal psalmody and offering of incense

Psalms 140, 141, 129, 116,
  with intercalcated
  strophes
Incensation

*Introit*

*At Great Vespers:*

Entrance with thurible
Introit Prayer
Hymn of Light: *Phôs hilaron*

*Responsory and readings*

Prokeimenon
*On the vigil of some feasts:*
Three readings from the OT
  or the epistles

---

(*Lenten ferias:* two OT lessons
with prokeimenon before
each)

*Intercessions*

Ektene
Kataxioson
Great synapte with aiteseis
Peace to all
Prayer of Inclination
*On the vigil of some feasts:*
rogation (litê)

*Aposticha and concluding prayers*

Aposticha
Nunc dimittis
Concluding prayers and
troparia
Dismissal (apolysis)

**Schema 2**

**MATINS**

Daily:                                                    Festal:

I. Royal Office

Fixed opening prayers
Pss 19, 20
Trisagion
Our Father
Troparia
Ektene

II. Nocturns

*Invitatory*

Hexapsalmos: Pss 3, 37, 62,
87, 102, 142

|  (Daily:) | (Festal:) |
|---|---|

Twelve prayers of matins,
said by priest during the
hexapsalmos

Great synapte

| | |
|---|---|
| Verses from Ps 117<br>*(in Lent*: Is 26) | Verses from Ps 117 |
| Troparion<br>*(in Lent*: Trinitarian troparia) | Troparion |
| *M o n a s t i c   p s a l m o d y* | *M o n a s t i c   p s a l m o d y*<br>(often omitted in parishes) |
| Psalmody, with sessional hymns<br>and small synapte after each<br>stasis | Psalmody: two staseis, with<br>small synapte after each |

III. CATHEDRAL VIGIL

*P s a l m s   a n d   h y m n s*

Ps 118 or
Polyeleos:
  (Pss 134–135; *add in
  Lent:* Ps 136)
(*On feasts in Slavic and
  Rumanian usage:* icon
  enthroned; megalynarion)
Incensation
Eulogitaria *(Sunday)*
Small synapte
Hypakoe *(Sunday)* or Sessional
  hymns
Gradual hymns (anabathmoi)

*R e s p o n s o r y*

Prokeimenon
"Let us pray to the Lord!"
Ekphonesis
"Let everything that breathes
  praise the Lord!"

|                          |                          |
|--------------------------|--------------------------|
| (Daily:)                 | (Festal:)                |

*Gospel*

Gospel of the resurrection
*(Sunday)* or of the feast
*(Sunday*: Resurrection troparia;
gospel enthroned)

IV. MORNING OFFICE

*Invitatory*

Ps 50

Troparia

*(Lent*: intercessions)     Intercessions

*Canon*

Odes 1–3
Small synapte
Odes 4–6
Small synapte
Kontakion
Ikos
*(Greek usage:* Synaxarion)
Odes 7–9: Magnificat
Incensation
Small Synapte

*Lauds*

| (Daily) | (Festal) |
|---------|----------|
| Exaposteilarion | Exaposteilarion *(Sunday:* "Holy is the Lord our God!") |
| *(Lent:* Photogogikon) | |
| Pss 148–150 | Pss 148–150 with intercalated strophes |
| "Glory to you who have shown us the light!" | "Glory to you who have shown us the light!" |
| Doxology | Great Doxology |
| Kataxioson | Kataxioson |

|  (Daily:) | (Festal:) |
|---|---|
|  | Trisagion |
|  | Troparion/apolytikion |

*Intercessions and dismissal*

|  | Ektene |
|---|---|
| Synapte with aiteseis | Synapte with aiteseis |
| Prayer of Inclination | Prayer of Inclination |
|  | Apolysis |

*Aposticha and*
*Concluding Prayers*

Aposticha
Trisagion
"Most Holy Trinity . . ."
Our Father
Troparion
Theotokion
Ektene
Apolysis

concludes, as we would expect, with lauds, intercessions, a blessing, and the dismissal, followed, on ferias, by a brief appendix.

But between the invitatory (Ps 50) and lauds there are nine poetic odes[13] that now make up the bulk of the service. These odes, called the "canon," have for the most part supplanted the corresponding nine biblical canticles of the Byzantine liturgical psalter except in the Lenten-paschal season, where the original three-canticle structure has been preserved, in accord with Baumstark's law that more solemn liturgical times have a tendency to be conservative and retain old forms.[14]

---

[13]Only eight are used outside of Lent, since the second ode is suppressed during the rest of the year. On the reasons for this, see L. Bernhard, "Der Ausfall der 2. Ode im byzantinischen Neunodenkanon," T. Michels (ed.), *Heuresis*. Festschrift für A. Rohracher (Salzburg: Otto Müller Verlag, 1969) 91-101.

[14]A. Baumstark, "Das Gesetz der Erhaltung des Alten in liturgisch hochwertiger Zeit," *Jahrbuch für Liturgiewissenschaft* 7 (1927) 1-23; *id., Comparative Liturgy* (Westminster Md.: Newman, 1958) 27ff.

At other times only the *Magnificat* has been retained. Originally the practice of doing all nine canticles daily was customary only in the monastic *agrypnia*, as we saw in the vigil described by the anchorite Abbot Nilus of Sinai, above in chapter 10. Normally the nine canticles were distributed throughout the week, two per day, one variable and one fixed (the ninth: *Magnificat/Benedictus*), with three on Sunday, as follows:[15]

| DAY | CANTICLE |
|---|---|
| Monday: | 2, 9 |
| Tuesday: | 3, 9 |
| Wednesday: | 4, 9 |
| Thursday: | 5, 9 |
| Friday: | 6, 9 |
| Saturday: | 7, 9 |
| Sunday: | 1 (cathedral vigil) |
| | 8, 9 |

In 1976 the Monks of New Skete, a monastery in Cambridge, New York, published a reformed Byzantine Office which, though not without defects, is a move in the right direction toward correcting some of the inconsistencies in present Byzantine usage of the Liturgy of the Hours.[16]

## Present Usage

Today the Byzantine Sabaitic office is the most widely used Liturgy of the Hours in the Christian East. Nor is its use confined to monasteries. The celebration of morning praise and evensong has remained an integral part of parish worship at least on weekends and feast days in much of the Byzantine East. The following testimony of an anonymous Greek Orthodox layman concerning the practice in Greece is an example:

> Pastoral activity in the parishes consists above all in the celebration of the liturgy. The care of souls is principally celebrating the liturgy. That is also the source of piety. In the morning there is *orthros* (matins and lauds) in the church, followed immediately by the Eucharistic celebration, which, however, is not celebrated every weekday. In the evening there is vespers, *hesperinos.* Thus the Liturgy of the Hours has kept its role in the daily life of the parish. The celebration of the liturgy is carried out with great reverence. . . . Each service is a chant

---

[15]Mateos, "Quelques problèmes de l'orthros byzantin," 31–32.

[16]For a critique of this reform see Taft, "The Byzantine Office in the *Prayerbook* of New Skete."

alternated between the priest and cantors. . . . The singers are men from the parish, where boys follow in the footsteps of their fathers and learn the Byzantine usages from childhood. Only the head cantor of each parish has some professional formation and is paid. It goes without saying that daily the cantors are present in their places for 7:00 A.M. orthros and 6:00 P.M. vespers, even in the smallest village. . . . The people learn the liturgical chants from childhood, without the help of books, and can sing them spontaneously at any moment.[17]

But to get a real sense of the meaning of these services in the life of the local Church, the aura of transcendent splendor that overcomes the participant in this glorious tradition, one must simply live it. One of the most splendid and moving liturgical services in Christendom is the *vsenoshchnoe bdenie* or "all-night vigil" as practiced in parishes of the Russian tradition.[18] This vigil is a service comprising solemn vespers, the Sunday resurrection vigil, matins, and lauds, which in monasteries was drawn out through the night with long monastic psalmody. In parish worship this vigil is either split up, with vespers on Saturday evening and the rest before Sunday morning Mass, or, as in the Russian usage, it is celebrated as a unit Saturday evening, but without the long monastic psalmody. In this abbreviated parochial form it lasts at least an hour and a half, and is a service of unparalleled beauty.

It opens in a flood of light and incense, as the doors of the brilliantly illumined sanctuary are opened before the darkened church, and the celebrant proclaims in solemn chant: "Glory to the holy, consubstantial, life-giving, and undivided Trinity, always, now and ever, and unto ages of ages!" No Byzantine service begins without a blessing or glorification of the Holy Trinity, the ultimate aim of all worship. Then the deacon and priest call the congregation to prayer with verses adapted from Psalm 94:6:

> Come let us adore our God and King!
> Come let us adore Christ our God and King!
> Come let us adore and fall down before the same Lord
>     Jesus Christ our God and King!
> Yes, come let us worship and bow down to him!

[17]"Tendenzen im Leben der orthodoxen Kirche Griechenlands," *Der christliche Osten* 37 (1982) 16–17.

[18]On this service see M. Arranz, "N. D. Uspensky: The Office of the All-Night Vigil in the Greek Church and in the Russian Church," *St. Vladimir's Theological Quarterly* 24 (1980) 83–113, 169–195 (French original in OCP 42, 1976, 117–155, 402–425). The following description is adapted from R. Taft, "Sunday in the Eastern Tradition," M. Searle (ed.), *Sunday Morning: a Time for Worship* (Collegeville: The Liturgical Press, 1982) 52ff.

After this the deacon, lighting the way with a huge candle, symbol of Christ who lights up our path, leads the celebrant through the whole church incensing—really incensing, with clouds of smoke, not just a few perfunctory swings of the thurible from the distant sanctuary.

Meanwhile, the choir is chanting the invitatory psalm of vespers, Psalm 103, a psalm of creation. In the East, liturgy is not just a service. It is also the place of theophany. In the Sunday vigil, as in the Bible, the very first theophany is creation. In chanting the invitatory psalm, special emphasis is given to the christological theme of darkness and light, which forms the fundamental symbolism of the cathedral office. The psalm verses expressing this theme are repeated twice:

> The sun knows when to set; you bring darkness and
>      it is night.
> How manifold are your works, O Lord! In wisdom,
>      you wrought them all!

This light theme is resumed immediately in the central rite of evensong, the lucernarium, which opens with Psalm 140, the heart of all Christian vesperal psalmody:

> O Lord I cry to you: hear me, hear me O Lord!
> O Lord I cry to you, hear me!
> Let my prayer rise like incense before you,
>      the lifting up of my hands
>      like the evening sacrifice.

While clouds of incense once again fill the church, sign of our prayers rising to the throne of God, as the psalm says, every candle in the church is lit, and the choir chants the proper refrains with which the psalmody is farced, refrains showing how the mystery of light that transforms creation is fulfilled in the dying and rising of Christ. Here are some of the variable refrains from the Sunday service in the third tone:[19]

> Everything has been enlightened by your resurrection, O Lord, and paradise has been opened again; all creation, extolling you, offers to you the perpetual hymn of praise.

> We, who unworthily stay in your pure house, intone the evening hymn, crying from the depths: "O Christ our God, who have enlightened the world with your resurrection, free your people from your enemies, you who love humankind."

> O Christ, who through your passion have darkened the sun, and with the light of your resurrection have illumined the universe: accept our

---

[19]English trans. adapted from A. Nadson, *The Order of Vespers in the Byzantine Rite* (London: Darton, Longman and Todd, 1965) 42–43.

evening hymn of praise, O you who love humankind.

Your life-giving resurrection, O Lord, has illumined the whole world, and your own creation, which had been corrupted, has been called back. Therefore, freed from the curse of Adam, we cry: "O Lord almighty, glory to you."

You underwent death, O Christ, so that you might free our race from death; and having risen from the dead on the third day, you raised with you those that acknowledge you as God, and you have illumined the world. O Lord, glory to you.

During the chanting of the final refrain, the priest and deacon, bearing the smoking censer, walk in procession through the church. On coming to the doors of the sanctuary, they intone the age-old Hymn of Light, the *Phôs hilaron,* which for over sixteen centuries, day after day, without variation or change, has proclaimed that the light of the world is not the sun of creation by day, nor the evening lamp by night, but the eternal Son of God, "the true light that enlightens everyone," in the words of the prologue of St. John's Gospel (1:9). I must confess that I find consolation in the company I am in when I intone this immortal hymn. St. Basil the Great (d. 379), who quotes it in *On the Holy Spirit* 29 (73), says it was already so old that no one remembers who composed it, and Egeria surely heard it in Jerusalem around the same time. A literal vision of the original Greek text reads:

> O joyous light of the holy glory of the immortal Father,
>     heavenly, holy, blessed Jesus Christ!
> As we come to the setting of the sun and behold the
>     evening light,
> We praise you Father, Son and Holy Spirit, God!
> It is fitting at all times that you be praised with
>     auspicious voices, O Son of God, giver of life.
> That is why the whole world glorifies you!

The collect at the end of the vesperal intercessions resumes the themes of the service:

> O great and exalted God! You alone are immortal and dwell in unapproachable light! In your wisdom, you created the entire universe: You separated light from darkness, giving the sun charge of the day, and the moon and stars, the night. At this very hour, you permit us, sinful as we are, to approach you with our evening hymns of praise and glory. In your love for us, direct our prayers as incense in your sight, and accept them as a delightful fragrance. Throughout this present evening and the night that is to come, fill us with your peace.

Clothe us in the armor of light. Rescue us from the terror of night. . . . Give us that sleep which you designed to soothe our weakness. . . . As we lie in bed this night, fill us with compunction, and enable us to keep your name in mind. Then, gladdened by your joy and enlightened by your precepts, may we rise to glorify your goodness, imploring your great tenderness of heart not only for our own sins, but for those of all your people. And for the sake of the Theotokos, touch all our lives with your mercy. For you are good and full of love for us, O God, and we give you glory, Father, Son, and Holy Spirit: now and forever, and unto ages of ages, amen.[20]

In spite of its great solemnity, this is liturgy at its most basic, taking the ordinary but universal fears and needs of human life and turning them into theophany, signs of God. The fear of darkness is a basic fear; the light that dispels it is a need felt by all. "God is light," says the First Letter of John (1:15), and this light shines in our world through the transfigured face of Jesus Christ.

In the Sunday vigil this theme serves as symbolic matrix to express the unity of the Sunday mystery—the Passover of Christ—and its sacramental symbols: baptism, which in the Early Church was called *phôtismos* or "illumination," and Eucharist.

It is a theme that pervades all of Byzantine spirituality and mysticism. The life of the Spirit is an illumination by this divine light; to see God by this light is to live in him. St. Irenaeus wrote:

To see the light is to be in the light and participate in its clarity; likewise to see God is to be in him and participate in his life-giving splendor; thus those who see God participate in his life (*Adv. haer.* IV, 20:5).

And in a moving passage of his Sermon on the Transfiguration, Anastasius of Sinai (d. ca. 700) has our transfigured Lord say:

It is thus that the just shall shine at the resurrection. It is thus that they shall be glorified; into my condition they shall be transfigured, to this form, to this image, to this imprint, to this light and to this beatitude they shall be configured, and they shall reign with me, the Son of God.[21]

It is this symbolism that marks the rhythm of the hours in the Byzantine Office, evoking in the faithful a nostalgia for the divine vision which they are allowed to glimpse symbolically here on earth. It is a symbolism

[20] *A Prayerbook* (Cambridge, N.Y.: New Skete, 1976) 198–199.
[21] A. Guillou, "Homélie inédite d'Anastase le sinaite sur la transfiguration (étude et texte critique)," *Mélanges d'archéologie et d'histoire* 67 (1955) 252.

fulfilled in the Eucharist, as we hear in the refrain chanted after Communion: "We have seen the true light! We have received the heavenly Spirit!" There is nothing specifically Eastern or Byzantine about all of this—except that in the East it is still a living reality.

In the Sunday vigil, vespers is followed by matins, the resurrection vigil, and lauds. The invitatory of matins, Psalm 117 in the Septuagint Greek, resumes once again the theme of light and applies it to Christ:

> The Lord God is our light! Blessed is he who comes in the name of the Lord!
>
> *Verse:* Give thanks to the Lord, for he is good! Everlasting is his love!
>
> *Verse:* They surrounded me, they encircled me, but in the Lord's name I overcome them!
>
> *Verse:* No, I will not die; I will live, and declare the works of the Lord!
>
> *Verse:* The stone rejected by the builders has become the cornerstone; this is the Lord's doing, a marvel in our eyes.[22]

In parish worship the monastic psalmody of matins is generally omitted, and one passes immediately to the three psalms of the third nocturn, which on Saturday night is transformed into the psalmody of the resurrection vigil described by Egeria (24:9–11) and the *Apostolic Constitutions* (II, 59:2–4). The elements of this service are:

1) Three psalms in remembrance of the three days in the tomb;
2) An incensation in remembrance of the aromatic spices brought by the women to anoint the body of the Lord, thus inaugurating the first watch before the tomb, model of all Christian resurrection vigils, including what we call a "wake;"
3) A solemn proclamation of the gospel of the resurrection, in remembrance of the angel who stood at the rolled-back stone of the tomb announcing, "He is risen!"

In the Byzantine tradition the present vigil opens with the solemn chanting of select verses from Psalms 134, 135, and 118, accompanied by refrains of the myrrh-bearing women, those who went to the tomb to anoint the body of the Lord and thus became the first witnesses to the resurrection. As soon as the choir intones "Praise the name of the Lord" from Psalm 134, the doors of the sanctuary are opened, all the lights and candles in

[22]*Prayerbook* 69.

the church are lit, and the celebrant, preceded once more by the deacon and his candle, incenses again the whole church. The refrains of the myrrh-bearers give the sense of this service:

> By the tomb stood an angel radiant in light, and thus did he speak to the myrrh-bearing women: "Let not your sorrow mingle tears with precious ointment. You see the tomb before you; look for yourselves. He is not here; he has risen!"
>
> With the first rays of dawn they had set out for the tomb, sobbing and lamenting as they walked along. But when they reached the tomb, they were startled by an angel who said: "The time for tears and sorrow is now over. Go! Tell his friends that he has risen!"
>
> Your women friends had come with ointment, Lord, hoping to anoint your bruised and battered body cold in death. But the angel stood before them, saying: "Why seek the living among the dead? He is God! He has risen from the grave."[23]

There follow the responsory and the solemn chanting of the gospel of the resurrection, after which the gospel book is solemnly borne in procession to the center of the church and enthroned there, while the choir sings the resurrection hymn professing faith that, having heard the paschal gospel, we, too, have seen and tasted the glory of God:

> Having seen Christ's resurrection, let us adore the holy Lord Jesus Christ, who is alone without sin. We worship your cross, O Christ, we sing and tell the glory of your holy resurrection. For you are our God, we know of no other than you, we call on your name. Come all you faithful, let us worship Christ's holy resurrection. For behold, through the cross has joy come to all the world. As we continually bless the Lord, we sing of his resurrection, for he has endured the cross and destroyed death by death.

After the intercessions, one of the eight Canons of the Resurrection is chanted according to the Sunday tone, while the faithful come up to venerate the gospel, be anointed with aromatic oil, and receive a piece of blessed bread, signs of the fortitude needed in the true vigil, the vigil of life.

The same themes of light and paschal triumph are found throughout the rich poetry of lauds, especially in the odes of the canon, a series of refrains composed according to the themes of the biblical canticles. There is not the space to describe all this, but the same realities are proclaimed: darkness and light; the darkness of sin overcome by the illumination of the Risen Christ.

[23]*Prayerbook* 110–111.

Equally important liturgically is that these realities are not just affirmed *pro forma*, in a ho-hum sort of way. They are shouted and chanted and hymned. They are woven into a scenario of poetry and procession, movement and rest, darkness and light, smoke and symbol and song, so that the casual visitor is often a bit overwhelmed, and would be moved to say, "Why, they really believe all that!" And, indeed, they do. The Vatican II Constitution on the Sacred Liturgy (no. 2) calls the liturgy "the outstanding means by which the faithful can express in their lives and manifest to others the mystery of Christ and the real nature of the true Church." A concrete example of what this means can be seen on any Sunday in the Byzantine tradition. One of my favorite anecdotes comes from the eastern marches of Poland between the two world wars. A Polish Catholic picked up in his carriage a poor Orthodox peasant-priest who was trudging along the dirt road on foot, and engaged him in spiritual discourse, somewhat in the polemic tones of those pre-ecumenical times. What was important, the Latin said, was the conversion of sinners, confession, catechism, prayer. The Orthodox were too involved in ritual, which is secondary to the real ministry of the Church. The Orthodox priest replied with great dignity:

> Among you it is indeed only an accessory. Among us Orthodox (and at these words he blessed himself) it is not so. The liturgy is our common prayer, it initiates our faithful into the mystery of Christ better than all your catechism. It passes before our eyes the life of our Christ, the Russian Christ, and that can be understood only in common, at our holy rites, in the mystery of our icons. When one sins, one sins alone. But to understand the mystery of the Risen Christ, neither your books nor your sermons are of any help. For that, one must have lived with the Orthodox Church the Joyous Night (of Easter). And he blessed himself again.[24]

The story refers to the Easter vigil, but this same liturgical spirit characterizes every Sunday vigil, and indeed all worship, in the Byzantine East. Throughout all the vicissitudes of its history, the Christian East has preserved a continuity of faith and worship, rooted in the resurrection and hope of the world to come, that has sustained its faithful during the dark ages of oppression. Political circumstances have often deprived the Eastern Churches of the need or possibility of developing the more active apostolic activities that are so integral to church life and organization in the West. But as long as the mysteries can be celebrated, the Church

[24]C. Bourgeois, "Chez les paysans de la Podlachie et du nord de la Pologne. Mai 1924–décembre 1925," *Etudes* 191 (1927) 585.

lives, held together not by organization nor authority nor education, but by communion year after year in the regular cycle of the offices of the Church. Isn't that what liturgy is all about?

# PART III

The Liturgy of the Hours
in the Western Traditions

# Introduction

The chapters in this section, as in the previous one, will focus on the main hours, here in the classic Western liturgical traditions. But the peculiar vagaries of Western liturgical history demand some departure from the pattern set in part II: from several standpoints what became of the Liturgy of the Hours in the West is not the rule but its exception. In the Roman Rite, and that is far and away the liturgical tradition with the largest body of adherents, the Divine Office is by and large a private affair, a prayerbook, the breviary, something one "reads" alone. From everything we have seen up to this point, it should be perfectly obvious to everyone that this is the last thing the Liturgy of the Hours was intended to be. But that is what it became, and despite the results of over half a century of liturgical studies,[1] that is what it has remained. How all this happened is summarized briefly in chapter 18 and the first part of chapter 19, as the necessary backdrop to the later history and to the sixteenth century and modern reforms of the Liturgy of the Hours in the West.

---

[1] See Thaddäus A. Schnitker, *Publica oratio. Laudes matutinae und Vesper als Gemeindegottesdienste in diesem Jahrhundert. Eine liturgiehistorische und liturgietheologische Untersuchung* (Dissertation, Münster, 1977) 5-33 for the results of pre-Vatican II studies and proposals on the Divine Office. The remainder of the thesis deals with what became of it all.

# 18

# FROM LITURGY TO PRAYERBOOK:
# THE OFFICE BECOMES THE BREVIARY
# IN THE WEST

## The Breakup of the System of Cathedral Liturgy[1]

In Late Antiquity, Christian communities in cities of the Western Roman Empire—even in those with several church buildings and numerous clergy—were organized as one unit under the direction of the bishop. There was nothing like the modern system of parish churches, each with its own clergy responsible for the care of a number of souls residing within clearly defined boundaries. It was the bishop who presided at services in the cathedral, with the rest of the clergy—presbyters, deacons, and minor clerics—assisting him in the celebration of the sacraments and other liturgical services, and in his other pastoral duties. Even small towns had a fair number of clergy, and the burdens of pastoral care were not particularly onerous. They consisted chiefly in celebrating the offices daily, and on weekends

[1]Cf. H. G. J. Beck, *The Pastoral Care of Souls in South-East France during the Sixth Century* (Analecta Gregoriana 51, Rome: Gregorian University, 1950) 66–79; G. W. O. Addleshaw, *The Early Parochial System and the Divine Office* (Alcuin Club Prayer Book Revision Pamphlets 15, London: Mowbray, n. d.); P. Salmon, *The Breviary through the Centuries* (Collegeville: The Liturgical Press, 1962) 6ff.

and feasts, solemn vigils and Mass; in baptizing, instructing, ministering
to the sick, supervising those in public penance—in a word, mostly what
today we call "liturgy." With clergy numerous and the population small,
clerics had more than enough time to chant daily morning praise and evensong in common in the cathedral. This system of church organization lasted
in cathedral cities in some parts of Western Europe until the tenth or
eleventh century.

In addition to the cathedral with its cure of souls in the hands of the
"canonical clergy" (*clerici canonici*), so called because they were listed in
the "canon" or clergy roll of the diocese, a network of monasteries and
convents was spread throughout town and country. Of course there were
also country chapels beyond the towns, but initially these were served,
as in the East, by presbyters sent out from the cathedral by the bishop.
Only the cathedral had a baptistry, and all major feasts were celebrated
only at this main church. Even in larger cities like Rome, where there were
numerous suburban churches, the unity of the one Eucharistic and ecclesial community was maintained by such practices as the *fermentum* or
carrying a particle of the Eucharist from the one Sunday papal or
"cathedral" Mass to the outlying communities as a sign of their communion in the one Eucharist of the *basilica senior*, the episcopal church.

Eventually such country chapels and suburban churches came to be
served by their own clergy. These churches were called minsters in Anglo-
Saxon England, baptismal churches (*plebes baptismales*) in Gaul, or simply *plebes* in Italy, from which we have the Italian *pieve*, still used for
parish churches in some parts of Central Italy and which, like minster
in England, is at the origin of many place names.

Historians refer to these churches as "first foundation" parishes, to distinguish them from the later breakup of urban dioceses into parishes "of
the second foundation" by the middle of the twelfth century. Unlike the
latter, which were served by one presbyter, "first foundation" parishes
were organized just like the cathedral churches, except that the superior
was not a bishop but a prelate called chorbishop (from the Greek *chora*,
a rural habitation), provost, custos, archpriest, or abbot, depending on
the area in question.[2] There, too, the body of clergy shared a quasi-
common life and celebrated the offices in common.

Obviously, the ultimate breakdown of this system had dire consequences
for the public celebration of the Liturgy of the Hours. With the whole
burden of pastoral and liturgical care on the shoulders of one presbyter,

---

[2]Chorbishop (*chorepiscopus*) was also a Latin title. See Isidore of Seville, *De eccl. officiis*
II, 6, PL 83, 786–787.

and the continual encroachment of the full cursus of monastic offices as part of the daily obligation of the parish clergy, it became impossible to accomplish the office publicly in church and get much else done in the course of the day. The intelligent solution would have been to return the parochial celebration of the hours to its original cathedral dimensions, but intelligence has been only rarely an operative force in the development of liturgy.

Various solutions were tried to lessen the burden: celebrating the offices in rotation, for example, one day in one church, one day in another, and even doing the hours in shifts by the clergy of the church whose turn it was. Another, more ominous solution, was to recite the hours in private. These are among the principal factors in the late medieval degeneration of the Liturgy of the Hours as *liturgy* in the West.

## Monasticization and Privatization of the Office

Pierre Salmon has detailed how the full daily cursus of hours, once distributed among the various churches in the early Middle Ages, eventually comes to be celebrated in its entirety in each Church as part of the general monasticization of the Western hours in areas such as Rome and Southern Gaul.[3] There was also a progressive monasticization of the clergy.[4] The reform of the clergy under St. Chrodegang, bishop of Metz (d. 766), after the model of the monastic communities he had observed serving the great Roman basilicas, is but one example of the movement under Pepin and Charlemagne to have clerics live "canonically," i.e., in common and praying the hours together, which from the eighth century becomes considered a daily obligation on all the clergy.

*The Rule of Chrodegang*, chapter 4, adds an innovation that will also have far-reaching effects: whoever cannot be in church for the hours in common must say them in private.[5] This was an unheard of novelty for the secular clergy, though it was common practice in monastic circles, and by the tenth century it becomes common legislation for the clergy in Western canonical sources. It is not by accident that our first portable breviaries, a single collection in one volume of all the necessary elements

---

[3] *The Breviary* ch. 2. On the monasticization of the western cathedral office, see ch. 8 above.

[4] Salmon, *The Breviary* 8ff., and especially S. J. P. van Dijk and J. Hazelden Walker, *The Origins of the Modern Roman Liturgy. The Liturgy of the Papal Court and the Franciscan Order in the Thirteenth Century* (Westminster Md.: Newman / London: Darton, Longmann & Todd, 1960) 16ff.

[5] Salmon, *The Breviary* 9–13.

for the recitation of the offices previously distributed throughout several anthologies (psalter, antiphonary, responsorial, homiliary, evangelary), appear in monastic circles in the eleventh century.

## The Friars and the University

Two thirteenth-century developments contribute further to the spread of this creeping privatization: the friars and the medieval university. With the advent of the friars, a class of religious without stable abode appears in the West. Often on the march, swept across the face of Europe by their apostolic tours, the friars had to do their offices wherever they happened to be. And the numerous clerical students at the universities, though obliged to the public hours at the church of their benefice (the one they were paid to serve in), could not both study and fulfill this obligation at the same time. As usual the moralists and canonists came to the rescue, providing the necessary loopholes in what had become an impossible situation. The first formal justification of private recitation of the hours is found in Hostiensis (d. 1271), *Lectures on the Five Books of the Decretals.*[6] Just as the pope and his curia sometimes dispense themselves from the choral office because of the pressure of work, he argues, other clerics can dispense themselves, too, for a sound reason, as long as they make up the missed hours in private. Communal prayer, once the *only* way, is now reduced to the *better* way to pray the hours. And what was once an obligation of the entire Christian community *in solidum*, and a special duty of the cleric only because he was paid to serve a specific community in its celebration, has now become an individual, personal obligation of the clergy as such.

## Canons, Chapters, and Private Recitation

By the fifteenth century, private recitation of the office has become a common practice among the parish clergy, and the obligation of common celebration, once incumbent on all, gradually devolves upon a remnant of professional choir beneficiaries, the "canons" or "cathedral chapter." But it took at least another century for this evolution to come to term. Right up through the Council of Trent (1545–1563), I know not a single synodal decree that obliges private recitation of the office. More

---

[6] *Ibid.* 14.

important, there is not a single decree that approves such recitation as the norm. Up until the sixteenth century, official Church legislation, at least, continues to view private recitation of the office as an exception, permissible only when necessary.[7]

Trent itself in Session XXI, *Decreta reformationis*, canon 4, refers to the public office in parishes but never to private recitation. In spite of the official line, however, by this time the early and medieval notion of the public office in common as the only one normative for all had died under the pressure of new forms of spirituality and apostolic and religious life. Already in the fourteenth century the *devotio moderna* moves away from medieval, regular, external observances toward a more spontaneous, interior, personal piety. We have entered the age of the "devout life" in reaction to the excessive externalism of medieval religious practices, and devout souls favor a more "interior" life in place of the "distractions" of common, choral prayer.

## Religious without Choral Office: The Jesuits and After

It is into this world that the Jesuits were born, approved as an order in 1540 from its original nucleus of reformed secular priests that had gathered around Ignatius Loyola during his studies in Paris from 1528 to 1535. As is well known, the Jesuits eschewed office in choir. This was not, however, from any distaste or disrespect for the Church's public prayer. The evidence for Ignatius' personal devotion to the public hours and his daily attendance at them during the "pilgrim years" is beyond challenge.[8] His sole purpose in obstinately refusing to let his men assume the *obligation* of daily, common office in choir was exactly the same as his reason for refusing to accept the permanent cure of souls: both require fixed residence and the obligation to be in certain places at certain times, and that would hinder the mobility and freedom Ignatius wished for the apostolic endeavours he envisaged as the vocation of his men (*Constitutions* 324, 586, 588–9).[9]

But this does not mean that devotion to the public office is in some way contrary to the Ignatian spirit, as is sometimes implied. The *Constitutions* explicitly state that Jesuits who "experience devotion in them," ac-

[7]*Ibid.* 17ff.

[8]See P. Dudon, *St. Ignatius of Loyola* (Milwaukee: Bruce, 1949) 59.

[9]St. Ignatius of Loyola, *The Constitutions of the Society of Jesus*, trans. with an introd. and commentary by G. E. Ganss (St. Louis: Institute of Jesuit Sources, 1970). References to the *Constitutions* according to the official numbering is given in parentheses in the text.

cording to the vocabulary of those days of pietism, will find plenty of opportunity to assist at them (586). In this regulation we discern the essence of the Ignatian spirit. Jesuit work and piety was directed *ad extra*, and Ignatius resolutely refused to legislate *anything* that would interfere with or restrict in any way the Jesuit apostolic obligation to serve where necessary. All else was subordinate to this: prayer, dress, penance—and liturgy. No Jesuit should ever be able to refuse a mission, a service of his neighbor, a ministry, a work of mercy, with the excuse that he had to be at vespers. The office could be celebrated in Jesuit houses and churches (586). What was rejected was the *obligation* to celebrate them *regularly* (586). Far from being opposed to the hours, Ignatius made the Little Office of the Blessed Virgin, along with two daily examinations of conscience, the contents of the daily hour of prayer he ruled for Jesuit students during their course of training (342–43).

But contrary to what is generally supposed, the abolition of choral office in religious life was not a Jesuit invention. Of the new, sixteenth century orders of clerks regular founded just before or after the Jesuits— Theatines (1524), Barnabites (1533), Somaschi (1534), Jesuits (1540), Clerks Regular of the Mother of God (1574), Camillians (1582), Clerics Regular Minor (1588)—only the first two retained the canonical obligation of the office in choir, though in fact a simplified choral recitation of the office was generally practiced out of devotion or by prescription in the constitutions.[10] Here as elsewhere, the Jesuits are given far too much credit for originality. These orders, like the Jesuits, also had no distinctive religious habit, and several had a "fourth vow" for this or that purpose as one of the basics of their tradition.

So Jesuits in these and other matters were not so much innovators as preeminently men of their times, with the dynamism and organization to adopt the new methods and popularize them throughout the Latin Church. But the needs were not of their making. They had already been percolating in developments that three centuries earlier had led to the friars' movement, religious orders devoted not just to the spiritual advancement of their members, like the monks, but also to learning, teaching, preaching, writing. If monks did some of these things too, that was not the purpose of the monastic foundations.

The beginnings of this shift in religious life go back to the twelfth century, when what David Knowles describes as a "new urban, plebeian, mer-

---

[10]Cf. F. Andreu, "Chierici regolari," *Dizionario degli istituti di perfezione*, vol. 2 (Rome: Ed. Paoline, 1975) 907; T. H. Clancy, *An Introduction to Jesuit Life. The Constitution and its History through 435 Years* (St. Louis: Institute of Jesuit Sources, 1979) 17–18.

cantile" world was in gestation, a world whose needs were not being met by the existing orders of monks and canons.[11]

> Towards the end of the twelfth century a sense of lassitude and disintegration was creeping into the higher circles of church life. The monastic revival had spent its force. . . .
>
> Meanwhile in the second half of the twelfth century an entirely new religious climate was developing in the towns of northern Italy and the valleys of the Rhine and Rhône, which were the first districts to profit by the new wealth and trade and the first to expand the weaving industry, which brought about the first industrial revolution in medieval Europe. In these centers of population, unaffected by the orders of monks and canons and imperfectly served by an ignorant and often degraded clergy, a new type of fervent lay piety made its appearance, containing almost from birth the germs of all the characteristics later associated with early Protestantism and Nonconformity: a distrust of sacerdotalism and sacramentalism, insistence on the reading of Scripture in the vernacular, zeal for preaching and hearing sermons, a love of association and "meetings" for prayer, and the organization of charity. Of these the best-known and most permanent, if we exclude the frankly heterodox Albigenses, were the Waldenses of Lyons, who spread into Lombardy and south Germany, and the Humiliati of Milan and north Italy. Some of these became quasi-religious orders within the Church. . . . For our purpose the interest of all these is the part they played in the pre-history of the friars, and we note in them: first the need of the urban population, both proletariat and bourgeoisie, for the devout life; secondly, the appeal of poverty and the communal life; and thirdly, the urge for moral exhortation and a study of the life of Christ, rather than liturgical prayer. It will be seen at once that the principal "notes" of the friars' movement, preaching, mendicancy, and the invitation to the "third" or "penitential" order of lay people, correspond exactly to these needs. The rift, especially in Italy and Provence, between the official, moneyed Church, whether of high ecclesiastics or great religious corporations, and the masses of the people, whether well-to-do townspeople or illiterate peasantry, was growing yearly wider, and the threats to the sacerdotal and sacramental system foreshadowed a cleavage such as did in fact take place three hundred years later.[12]

It was the friars and later the *devotio moderna* that began and fostered the shift away from a spiritual life of ritual observances, often overburdened and sterile even to the monks, as they themselves abundantly testi-

[11]D. Knowles, *From Pachomius to Ignatius. A Study in the Constitutional History of Religious Orders* (Oxford: Clarendon Press, 1966) 42.

[12]*Ibid.* 42–43.

fy. One example will suffice: at their chapter of 1277 the Black Monks of England lament that

> . . . because of the length of the Office which causes disgust and ex-
> tinguishes devotion, study, once the glory of the Order, has become
> obsolete. . . . Therefore, many people distinguished for dignity,
> knowledge and morals keep away from the Order and contemptu-
> ously refuse to enter it.[13]

Little wonder, then, that fertile ground was ready for a more affective, subjective, interior devotional life focused on the person of Jesus and finding expression in meditation and a proliferation of "devotions," rather than in the more traditional monastic practices of *lectio divina*, the study of the Fathers, and the office in choir.[14]

That the friars were ultimately unable to solve the problem is seen in later developments culminating in the Protestant Reformation and the Catholic Tridentine Reform, movements which contemporary historians such as Jean Delumeaux show to have much more in common than might appear at first sight.[15] Ignatian views on prayer are part of this reaction against medieval externalism and ritualistic sacramentalism that the sixteenth century Catholic reform movement shared with the Protestant reformers. That explains the popularity of early Jesuit books of piety among Protestants.[16] For both, prayer was not something, like the office, accomplished in set forms and at set times.

Ignatius has often been accused by those ignorant of his writings and spirit of setting down restrictive, straight-jacket methods of prayer. Nothing is further from the truth. No founder of a religious order or congregation in history more resolutely refused to make any legislation whatever concerning the prayer of his formed religious, beyond the general norm of constant union with God (*Constitutions* 342–45, 582): ". . . in what pertains to prayer, meditation, . . . fasts, vigils, and other austerities or penances, it does not seem expedient to give them any other rule than that which discreet charity dictates to them . . ." (582). Ignatius' *Spiritual Exercises* contain numerous methods of prayer, but their very number shows them to be merely a selection of possibilities to be used insofar as they are helpful. Ignatius' constantly repeated norm in all such matters

[13]W. A. Pantin, *Documents Illustrating Activities of the General and Provincial Chapters of the English Black Monks* (The Royal Historical Society, Camden Third Series XLV, London, 1931) 64ff., cited here from van Dijk and Walker, *Origins* 24.

[14]Clancy, *Introduction to Jesuit Life* 13ff., 28ff.

[15]J. Delumeaux, *Catholicism between Luther and Voltaire: a New View of the Counter-Reformation* (London: Burns and Oates, 1977).

[16]Clancy, *Introduction to Jesuit Life* 127–128, 148.

is to stress whatever is conducive to the end sought, under the direction of the spiritual guide or superior, and always avoiding excess in austerities.

The formula that best sums up Ignatius' teaching on prayer is his expression, "finding God in all things." As such, Ignatian prayer was more akin to that of the early Egyptian anchorites, who eschewed a cursus of common hours of prayer because of the evangelical command to pray always. And so they prayed while they worked and worked while they prayed. All Ignatius did was make the work apostolic: far from having no "office," that of the Jesuit is whatever mission he does under obedience, with purity of intention and in union with God. For it is his vocation to find God not in psalms and lections, in prostrations and vigils, but in whatever the will of God calls him to. Hence Ignatius had a very New-Testament view of "liturgy" in its literal sense of service. When he says that Jesuits vow "to go anywhere His Holiness will order . . . for the sake of matters pertaining to the worship of God and the welfare of the Christian religion" (*General Examen*, 7), he could not be more Pauline. For both Ignatius and Paul, the true Christian "worship of God" is much more than that we do in church.[17]

My purpose in all this is not to write an *apologia pro domo mea*, but simply to set the record straight by putting the Ignatian vision into its historical context. This is important, I think, for Jesuits and most later Latin Catholic congregations that have imitated them in abolishing office in choir for the sake of the apostolate. Ignatius saw the acute apostolic needs of the Church disintegrating before his very eyes. He also saw that the monks of the day, with their offices, much as he loved them, were doing nothing to stem the tide. And so he drew his conclusions.

In deciding to reduce the burden of liturgy in favor of apostolic mobility, Ignatius showed himself a man of great vision. What shows how historically conditioned the actual practice of such legitimate spiritual insights must always be, is his decision to gain time and mobility by eliminating the daily common office. It would not have crossed a sixteenth-century Latin Catholic's mind to eliminate daily "private" Masses instead, but in the light of liturgical history that would have been the far more traditional option. So Ignatius' choice was totally Latin, totally medieval. Before the Western Middle Ages no one would have dreamt of preferring daily private Mass to the common hours on weekdays.[18] If such an affirmation leaves the reader perplexed, that only shows that we, too, are the victims of our own clichés. There is just as much (indeed, more) extant historical evidence for the obligation of daily morning and evening prayer, in com-

[17]See chapter 18.
[18]See Taft, "The Frequency of the Eucharist," and *id., Beyond East and West* ch. 5.

mon and incumbent on all, laity as well as clergy and religious, as there
is for the obligation of Sunday Mass. That doesn't change until the Middle Ages, and even then it changes only in the West. But of course Ignatius and his contemporaries did not have a clue about any of this.

What Ignatius and founders who took inspiration from him would do
today is, of course, another matter. Many things in present-day religious
life—academic tenure and the limiting demands of professional speciali-
zation, for instance—unavoidably place far greater restrictions on apostolic
mobility than common prayer would. And Jesuits today see no problem
in accepting the cure of souls in parishes, though Ignatius, as we saw above,
excluded that for exactly the same reasons that he excluded choir. More
importantly, from what we have seen it should be clear that the question
can no longer be posed in terms of "choir," a medieval concept. The real
issue is whether, in the light of what we know of the history of the hours,
any Christian can be considered permanently dispensed from the age-old
obligation of praising God in common at the beginning and end of each
day.

Seventeenth-century priestly piety, especially in France, only furthers
the same trend toward interiorization among the diocesan clergy. By this
time the breviary has become the private prayerbook of the priest, and
scholars of the epoch such as Thomassin even try to show that the obligation of private recitation goes back to the Middle Ages and even to the
first five centuries![19]

These developments, seminal in the whole history of Western *attitudes*
to the hours and the attendant, privatized clerical spirituality of which
Latin clergy by and large are still victims, also had their effect on the development of the Roman Breviary into its Tridentine form. We already
spoke of the pope and his curia, and of the friars. They had faced much
the same problem the Jesuits were to face in a later period, but the time
had not then been ripe for so radical a solution as that of Ignatius. And
it was not until the Liturgical Movement of our times, and the historical
studies on the nature of the Liturgy of the Hours issuing from it, that we
have come to see that the real solution is to be found neither in the liturgical privatism of sixteenth-century pietism, nor in the nineteenth-
century romanticism of the Benedictine revival à la Guéranger, but rather,
perhaps, in a renewed understanding of what this sort of common prayer
is all about in the first place. But myths die hard, as references in otherwise truly excellent contemporary books to the office as originally something for monks continue to show.[20]

[19]Salmon, *The Breviary* 22.
[20]E.g., Clancy, *Introduction to Jesuit Life* 19.

# 19

# THE ROMAN OFFICE

## From Benedict to the Friars

Not much has changed in the basic skeleton of the Roman Office from the time of St. Benedict: its structure has remained substantially the same from the sixth century until Vatican II. Tradition has it that Pope St. Gregory I, the Great (590–604), the first pope from among the monks, reformed the Roman Office, but if so we have no idea what he did. One thing is sure, however. He used early Benedictine monasticism as an instrument in his missions to Northern Europe and Britain, and with them went the northward spread of Roman usages.[1] In 596 St. Augustine of Canterbury brought Roman office books to Britain, and the Council of Cloveshoe in 747 decreed that offices be celebrated according to the use of the Roman Church. From Britain, Roman uses passed to Germany with St. Boniface (d. 755) and companions. Pepin the Short (751–768) suppressed Gallic offices in his empire in favor of the Roman liturgy. So by the eighth century the Roman Rite had begun to take hold all over the West outside of the Iberian peninsula, and eventually Gregory VII (1073–1085) imposed the Roman Office even there.

But of course this does not imply a uniformity of liturgical uses everywhere. Some Churches such as Milan clung to their own practices, and

---

[1] Van Dijk and Walker, *Origins* 18ff.

others adopted the Roman framework to their own needs. Indeed, Abelard in 1140 claims that even in Rome it was only in the Lateran Basilica that the old Roman Rite was observed.[2] What he means is that monastic communities serving the Roman basilicas each had its own local practices, as was true everywhere in the pre-Tridentine West, is still true most everywhere in the East, and is becoming true once again in the post-Vatican II Roman tradition. For if available documents show a basic continuity of framework from the earliest evidence through Amalar of Metz's (d. 850) *Liber officialis* IV, 1–12, and *De ordine antiphonarum* 1–7,[3] to the reforms of Pius V and Pius X, it is nonetheless true that this framework was simply the skeleton for the antiphons, collects, etc., that were selected from anthologies such as the antiphonaries and collectaries, according to norms contained in the local calendars and customaries.

The later history, which I do not have the space to detail here, included rearrangements in the distribution of the psalms, the multiplication of sanctoral propers to the detriment of the *proprium de tempore,* and the piling up of votive offices and offices for the dead until the apogee of Gothic extremes is reached in the twelfth and thirteenth centuries, when *monachus propter chorum* was the rule, and the offices occupied almost every waking moment of the choir-monk.[4] As van Dijk and Walker put it, "Medieval monastic life suffered from sheer liturgical exhaustion, from overnutrition and consequent spiritual indigestion."[5] That one could have too much of a good thing had not yet become a recognized liturgical principle. Already in the eleventh and especially twelfth centuries, groans at the insupportable burden of the overcharged office were becoming more frequent, and the decline of Cluny after the death of Peter the Venerable in 1156, and the rise of the Cistercian movement with its return to pristine Benedictine simplicity, are signs that something was about to give.[6]

## The Curial Office and the Friars Minor

It is at this point that the papal palace and the Friars Minor enter the stage, in a history that has been reconstructed masterfully by S. J. P. van Dijk and Joan Hazelden Walker.[7] Because the pope and his court also had

[2] *Ep.* 10, PL 178, 340.

[3] J.-M. Hanssens (ed.), *Amalarii episcopi opera liturgica omnia,* 3 vols. (ST 138–140, Vatican City: Bibliotheca Apostolica Vaticana, 1948–1950); here, II 403–457; III, 19–37.

[4] Van Dijk and Walker, *Origins* 20ff.

[5] *Ibid.* 21.

[6] *Ibid.* 22ff.

[7] *Ibid.,* on which I depend in the summary history to follow.

to do a day's work, they "always shortened and often altered (*semper breviabant et saepe alterabant*) the Office," as the conservative dean of Tongres, Ralph van der Beke (Radulph de Rivo, d. 1403) grumbled in *propositio 22* of his *De canonum observantia liber.* He adds that "In Rome I saw an ordinal of that Office. It was compiled in the days of Innocent III; and the Friars Minor follow this shortened office. Hence they entitle their books as 'according to the use of the Roman Curia.' "[8] That, in a nutshell, summarizes the history of the Roman Breviary from the thirteenth century until Trent. Ralph harrumphed about it all, but at the time, the reform of Innocent III (d. 1216) was greeted with sighs of relief. The Franciscan Friar Salimbene de Adam of Parma (d. after 1287) wrote in his garrulous chronicle:[9]

> Innocent III improved the ecclesiastical Office by correction and rearrangements, adding things of his own and suppressing those of others. For all that, it is not yet really in order, as many people feel. There is still much that could be safely omitted, since it is more wearisome than devotional, as well for those who have to say the Office as for those who assist.

Note that final bit of medieval clericalism, a clear statement of the demise of any notion of a cathedral office as part of the duties of the People of God. Then Ralph gives some examples of needed changes, concluding, "In brief, there are many things in the ecclesiastical Office that could be put right. And it would be worth while, for it is full of roughness, although this is not always recognized."

It is in this thirteenth century, then, that the Roman Liturgy of Hours begins to be metamorphosed into the "breviary." The crucial step in the process was the adopting by the Friars Minor of Innocent III's ordinal regulating the office of the curia. Later, around 1250, the great Minister General Haymo of Faversham revised the curial-type ordinal to regulate the Franciscan usage of existing office books, and it was this revised usage that the friars spread throughout the length and breadth of Latin Christendom.

Of course the curia and the friars did not invent the breviary, as was once thought. The original breviaries, as van Dijk and Walker have shown, were not portable office books or books designed for private recitation of the office, but simply attempts to synthesize into one volume the various elements of the office scattered throughout several books—psalter, antiphonary, responsorial, homiliary, legendary (lives of the saints),

[8]Cited *ibid.* 3.

[9]*Ibid.* 1, from *Cronica,* MGH, *Scriptores* XXXII, 31. For Innocent III's reform, see van Dijk and Walker, *Origins* 95ff.

library (Scripture lessons)—with the ordinal to tell what went where and when.[10] Such breviaries, or anthologies of enough selected pieces to say a coherent office, were in use in the papal curia before Innocent III's reform. And even after that reform and its Franciscan adaptations, those who used the new, handy, portable breviaries adapted them in their own way. The stability of Western Catholic liturgy between Trent and Vatican II must not be read back into this earlier period, for it is not until after Trent that this liturgical unity and stability to which pre-Vatican II Latin Catholics were accustomed began to take hold.

## The Age of Reform

The sixteenth century was an age of reform. By that time there is abundant evidence of the sterility of the Latin choral office, and it is no surprise that most of the new religious orders abandoned choir. Even the monks were fed up. Blessed Paul Giustiniani (1476–1528), a contemporary of Ignatius Loyola, reformer of the Camaldolese hermits, and founder of the Congregation of Camaldolese Hermits of Monte Corona, speaks of liturgy in terms remarkably reminiscent of the Jesuit *Constitutions*, with their insistence on a liturgy marked by simplicity and austerity in reaction against the prevalent Renaissance pomp of the day: "We do not sing, except very rarely. . . . You must not take pleasure in the pomp of processions."[11]

Prior to Trent there were various attempts at breviary reform, some of them admittedly more humanist than spiritual in inspiration. Christian Latin was little more than doggerel for the Renaissance humanist, churchman or not, and more than one cultured clerical humanist shared this disdain for many of the hymns and other elements of the breviary (problems of liturgical language were not created by the International Commission on English in the Liturgy; they go back to the first time someone decided to translate the predominantly Greek primitive liturgies into some other tongue). Other sixteenth-century Catholic reformers, more spiritually motivated, wished to expurgate apocryphal and legendary hagiographic material, trim away the excessive votive offices, give more space to Scripture lections, and restore the *proprium de tempore* to the pristine centrality it had before giving way to the encroachments of an overgrown sanctoral cycle. A third group, more pietist than liturgical, desired a breviary more suitable for private recitation with spiritual profit.

[10]Cf. van Dijk and Walker, *Origins* 26ff.
[11]Cited in J. Leclercq, *Alone with God* (London: Catholic Book Club, 1962) 111.

I. THE BREVIARY OF QUIÑONES[12]

Only two of these numerous sixteenth century breviary reform projects need delay us here: that of the Spanish Franciscan Cardinal Francisco de los Angeles de Quiñones in 1535, and that of Pius V which superceded Quiñones' after Trent, in 1568. Quiñones' breviary was one of several revisions commissioned by Clement VII. Designed for private recitation, its first edition (1535) distributed the whole psalter weekly, without repetitions, three psalms per hour; increased the length of the Scripture readings "in course"; suppressed legends, votive offices, as well as such choral elements as antiphons, responses, chapters, intercessions, and many hymns; and reduced matins to one nocturn with three lessons. The result was a short, homogeneous, simple, easy-to-use breviary, with a large amount of Sacred Scripture. Its disadvantage was the opposition it provoked among those who thought it too radical a departure from tradition.

The first edition, printed with Paul III's approval in 1535, spread like wildfire: it went through eleven printings the first year. A revised edition, with the antiphons restored in some places, appeared the following year (1536), also with Paul III's approval allowing secular priests to use it if they wished. Popularly known as *The Breviary of the Holy Cross* because Quiñones was the Cardinal of Santa Croce, just down the street from where I am typing this manuscript, in the thirty-two years it was in use it went through over a hundred editions, a clear enough indication of how badly it was needed.

II. THE BREVIARY OF PIUS V

The Tridentine breviary of Pius V (1568) represented a return to the principles of Cardinal Giampietro Carafa, who had revoked the papal approval of Quiñones' breviary during his brief pontificate as Paul IV (1555–1559), though the approval was renewed by his successor Pius IV (1559–1565). The new breviary was to be a restoration of the Roman Office, not a new creation, and so the choral elements were restored, though the legendary and votive material expunged by Quiñones was left out, and the offices were shortened and simplified. This breviary of Pius V, if we except the later proliferation of local neo-Gallican breviaries in seventeenth–nineteenth century France, superceded all Latin offices that could not claim a tradition going back at least two centuries.

[12]On Quiñones see P. Salmon, *L'office divin au Moyen Age. Histoire de la formation du bréviaire du IXe au XVIe siècle* (Lex orandi 43, Paris: Cerf, 1967) 178–184; Jungmann, *Pastoral Liturgy* 200–214.

## Modern Reforms

### 1. Pius X

Apart from minor adjustments in the course of the intervening centuries, especially in the lessons,[13] the next Roman breviary reform was that of Pius X in 1911. The basic problem of Pius V's office was its return to the pre-Quiñones situation in which the sanctoral was predominant, with the inevitable result that the small number of psalms in the common of the saints was repeated *ad nauseam*.[14] Pius X attempted to integrate the sanctoral and temporal cycles instead of having the former replace the latter on most days.

More important, he redistributed the psalter. The traditional Roman system was to divide the psalter between nocturns (matins) and vespers, the former containing Pss 1–108, the latter Pss 109–150, distributed in these two hours throughout one week. We already saw how Benedict had modified this by omitting from matins or vespers those psalms (for example, Pss 148–150 of lauds) that already had a fixed place in the cursus. Quiñones had opted for a distribution of the psalter based not on the biblical order of psalms but on the suitability and length of the individual psalm, three per hour, two short and one long, with the result that each hour had approximately the same length. Pius V returned to a slightly modified traditional Roman system which was not abandoned until Pius X. The latter reduced matins (nocturns) from the traditional twelve to nine psalms, and for the first time in the history of Christian morning praise in East or West, the psalms of lauds, Pss 148–150, were not said daily, but one psalm of praise was assigned to each day of the week, beginning with Saturday: Pss. 148, 116, 134, 145, 146, 147, 150. Furthermore Pss 50 and 62 were abandoned as fixed psalms at lauds, as were the traditional canticles except for Lent and vigils.[15] For anyone with a sense of the history of the office, this was a shocking departure from almost universal Christian tradition, and that is how things remained until Vatican II.

The disappearance of another cathedral element from the Pius X office, this time in vespers, is also worth noting. Before Pius X's reform, vespers in the Roman breviary had the following structure:[16]

---

[13]Cf. Righetti, *Storia liturgica* vol. 2, 677ff.
[14]Jungmann, *Pastoral Liturgy* 202.
[15]Righetti, *Storia liturgica* vol. 2, 690, gives a table with Pius X's psalter distribution.
[16]See Winkler, "Über die Kathedralvesper," 97.

Invitatory: Ps 69
Current Psalmody: 5 psalms
Lesson
Hymn
Versicle: Ps 140:2 (daily except Saturday)
*Magnificat*

Now we know that the *Magnificat* is a later, Benedictine addition, and that in Amalar of Metz (d. 850), *Liber officialis* IV, 7:17–19, the incensation at vespers was in conjunction not with the *Magnificat*, as today, but with the versicle of Ps 140:2, "Let my prayer rise like incense before you, the lifting up of my hands like the evening sacrifice."[17]

Throughout these various reforms until Pius X the problem of the Roman Office was not so much its structure, for its basic skeleton had hardly changed from our earliest evidence until the work of Pius X's commission was promulgated in 1911 and became obligatory in 1913 for all who had formerly been bound to Pius V's breviary. Far more serious than any structural defect was the constant tendency of the overgrown sanctoral to strangle the more important temporal cycle, and Pius X's reform did manage to prune that growth once more and restore Sunday to some of its pristine primacy.

## ii. Vatican II

The 1971 reform of the Roman Office that issued from Vatican II was even more radical than that of Pius X. Again the basic structure of the Roman hours was more or less respected with these exceptions: in line with contemporary renewed interest in the proclamation of God's word, a Scripture lesson was added to each hour, followed by a short response and a gospel canticle; collects were provided for each psalm; the hymn was moved up to the beginning of the offices from its traditional position after the lesson and response. I would judge all these structural changes admirable. The hymn now opens the hour and expresses its theme at the start, and the centrality of Sacred Scripture surely needs no defense.

In addition, the number of hours in the cursus has been reduced from eight (or seven if we count nocturns and lauds as one) to five by the suppression of prime and the reduction of the remaining day hours to one. Vigils or nocturns are replaced by an "Office of Readings" that can be read at any hour or celebrated as a vigil.

[17]*Ibid.* 100–101; for Amalar, ed. Hanssens (note 3 above) II, 435.

Great changes also appear in the psalter. In a break with the long-standing tradition of the weekly psalter, the *pensum* of psalmody is reduced by three-quarters and the psalter is now distributed over four weeks rather than one. Furthermore, the monastic principle of continuous psalmody is abandoned in favor of the "cathedral" principle of selecting psalms adapted to the hour, as Quiñones had done. The reform commission also had the courage to omit some psalms or psalm verses as "unsuitable," and many more biblical canticles are included in the psalmody than previously. Indeed, the traditional Roman repertoire, not only of canticles, but also of hymns and lections, has been greatly expanded.

Finally, a certain amount of flexibility of choice is left to the discretion of those using the office, and the relation of ordinary and proper has been greatly simplified, no longer requiring the almost Talmudic lore once needed to make one's way through the old Roman Breviary on certain days.

The structure of morning and evening prayer in the new office is as follows:

| *Matins* | | *Vespers* |
|---|---|---|
| | Opening verse | |
| Ps 94 | | |
| | Hymn | |
| | *Psalmody* | |
| Morning psalm | | 2 psalms |
| OT canticle | | NT canticle |
| Psalm of praise | | |
| | Scripture lessons | |
| | Short response | |
| | Gospel canticle | |
| Benedictus | | Magnificat |
| | *Prayers* | |
| Prayers of offering and praise | | Intercessions |
| | Concluding collect | |
| | Blessing | |

But the problem with the new Roman *Liturgy of the Hours* is not structural. The renewed structure represents in many respects a courageous break with the past. Problems—of language, length, a too-full monastic cursus, too many psalms in one week—were faced with imagination and resoluteness. But many believe that the unwillingness to make a more radical break with not just the forms, but with the mentality of this past, has marred the recent reform of the Roman Office.[18]

In the post-Vatican II discussions on the hours more than one informed voice was raised urging the case for a popular "cathedral" office suitable for public celebration in the parishes.[19] But from Annibale Bugnini's account of the deliberations of the commission for the reform of the office, three things are clear:[20]

1) the overriding concern was to produce a prayerbook for clergy and religious;

2) it was simply presumed this prayer would be done, for the most part, in private. Celebration "with the people," as they called it, was envisioned and even desired, but the whole tenor and vocabulary of the discussions show that this was the exception and not the point of departure for understanding the hours;

3) the historical basis underlying much of the discussion was gravely deficient, based as it was almost exclusively on post-medieval Latin tradition.

These same defects of clericalism, privatization, and ignorance of early and Eastern tradition can be seen also in the discussions of Eucharistic concelebration, and indeed are endemic to much of the Western liturgical enterprise. Liturgiology, like philology, is a comparative discipline. The liturgiologist who knows only one tradition is like a philologist who knows only one language.

In the debates on the office one sees this problem surface, for instance, in criticisms that the office is too "monastic."[21] What is meant is that the office has elements designed for common use—as if this were a characteristic of monastic rather than secular usage! Similarly, objections against the introduction of general intercessions at the end of lauds and vespers show a total unawareness of the large place such petitions held in early cathedral usage.[22]

[18]See for example W. Storey, "The Liturgy of the Hours: Cathedral versus Monastery," J. Gallen (ed.), *Christians at Prayer* (Liturgical Studies, Notre Dame and London: University of Notre Dame Press, 1977) 61–82.

[19]Among them Herman Schmidt S. J. and Juan Mateos S. J., consultors of the Consilium ad exsequendam *Constitutionem de Sacra Liturgia*. Mateos' articles "The Origins of the Divine Office," *Worship* 41 (1967) 477–485, and "The Morning and Evening Office," *Worship* 42 (1968) 31–47, were originally written in Latin as *vota* submitted to the Consilium.

[20]A. Bugnini, *La riforma liturgica (1948–1975)* (BELS 30, Rome: Edizioni liturgiche, 1983) 482–557, esp. 482–483, 503.

[21]*Ibid.* 503.

[22]*Ibid.* 543 note 62.

Under these conditions it is not surprising that the new *Liturgy of the Hours* bears a monastic stamp. Such an office, more a contemplative prayer than a popular devotional service, may be eminently suitable for the private prayer of clergy and religious. But this skirts the real issue, which is whether the Liturgy of the Hours should be a prayerbook for the clergy, or something more.

But I do not wish to play Cassandra. A compromise, by definition, cannot satisfy all expectations, and committees rarely produce anything but a compromise. The same is true of the new Roman *Liturgy of the Hours.* Its basic shape, in accord with fourteen centuries of Roman tradition, has retained a monastic stamp. Anyone who knows anything about church history could hardly have expected anything else.

Yet all is not lost. Flexibility is one of the hallmarks of post-Vatican II Roman Catholic Worship, and there is nothing to prevent communities from doing today what communities did in the fourth and fifth centuries: develop popular forms of morning and evening prayer suitable for common parish celebration. Of course we could not call this the "official" Roman Office, but it is difficult to see what possible difference that could make. This is precisely what is being done in more than one place in this country. The highly successful popular offices in *Praise God in Song* by William G. Storey and John Allyn Melloh are a case in point.[23]

But perhaps so radical a departure from the official *Liturgy of the Hours* is not necessary. The desire for a truly public celebration of this liturgy, and what is more important, its underlying theology, find pride of place in the *General Instruction on the Liturgy of the Hours* of February 2, 1971.[24] All one needs is a little imagination. Taking a page from the new U.S. *Lutheran Book of Worship,* or Episcopal *Book of Common Prayer,*[25] some communities have found that a lucernarium can easily be used to open "official" vespers, and this is certainly in accord with the spirit of the *General Instruction.* Furthermore, that same document provides for such a variety of hymnody and types of psalmody that the real problem is not so much the limitations of the office itself, as the incompetence of those unable to celebrate it properly and the indifference of those who fail to celebrate it at all. Behind this, of course lies the more fundamental issue of Western liturgical privatization and Eucharistic excess. But I have already addressed these problems in chapter 18.

[23]John Allyn Melloh and William G. Storey, *Praise God in Song* (Chicago: G.I.A. Publications, Inc., 1979).

[24]*The Liturgy of the Hours. The General Instruction on the Liturgy of the Hours,* with a Commentary by A. M. Roguet (Collegeville: The Liturgical Press, 1971).

[25]See the following chapter.

What the future will bring is not for the historian to predict. Daily Eucharist is here to stay. I think the attempt to convince those who want it that they really shouldn't is plain foolishness. But in the days before television, Vatican II, and mugging, the devout also attended Benediction on Sunday night and novena devotions at least once a week. As Carl Dehne has shown in his superb article on Catholic private devotions, these services filled a real need and were the true successors to the cathedral office in the West.[26] Perhaps it is time for Western Catholics to ask themselves once again whether a liturgical tradition that for all practical purposes is limited to the Eucharist is really offering a balanced diet.

Is a restoration of parish hours a viable possibility? That is for the pastoral liturgist to decide. All the historian can do is remove obstacles to understanding produced by a misreading of the past. But where the pastoral liturgists have assumed their responsibilities in this matter their efforts have not been without success.[27]

[26]"Roman Catholic Popular Devotions," Gallen, *Christians at Prayer* 83–99.

[27]For example at the University of Notre Dame (Indiana, U.S.A.) where *Praise God in Song* (above at note 23) and the Vatican II *Liturgy of the Hours* are celebrated with great effectiveness. On this and other attempts to restore the public cathedral celebration of the Divine Office in the U.S. and elsewhere see the writings of Schnitker, Bartolomiello, Quentin, and Rheinhart cited in section 10 of the Bibliography below.

# 20

# THE HOURS IN THE CHURCHES
# OF THE REFORMATION

The sixteenth-century Protestant reformers on the continent and in England had exactly the same problems with the medieval Roman Office as their Catholic contemporaries like Quiñones. The offices were too complicated, the overgrown sanctoral strangled the temporal cycle and disrupted the continuous psalmody, not enough Scripture was read, the legends of the saints were often absurd and a hindrance to the use of more Scripture. The difference between the Protestant reformers and Quiñones is that the former had the sense to realize that the office was for everyone, not just for the clergy. So they did not abolish the hours, but put them into the vernacular.

## Luther[1]

Luther, like his Catholic contemporaries, found the overstuffed, heavily sanctoral and votive medieval offices, full of legends, to be suffocating. So he proceeded to reform them. More confident than knowledgeable in matters liturgical, he thought that daily matins and vespers were basically

[1]J. Neil Alexander, "Luther's Reform of the Daily Office," Worship 57 (1983) 348–360.

services for proclaiming God's word.[2] He could not have been more wrong. Morning praise and evensong historically can in no way be considered services of the Word—though of course one is free to think they ought to be. At any rate, Luther proceeded to reform the hours on that basis. He retained the basic Roman skeleton of matins and vespers, but gave more space to Scripture lessons and insisted on preaching. These two hours were envisaged as common daily services, for Luther was opposed to weekday Masses.[3]

## Strasbourg

In Strasbourg, too, the Reformed Church of Bucer and others preserved a vernacular, daily morning and evening prayer that maintained the basic structure of the Roman hours, but dropped the antiphons and inserted after the psalmody a *lectio continua* of the Bible, from the New Testament in the morning and from the Old Testament in the evening, followed by a sermon.[4]

## The Lutheran Book of Worship[5]

The new 1978 *Lutheran Book of Worship*, prepared under the sure guidance of distinguished American Lutheran liturgist Eugene L. Brand, contains the hours of Morning Prayer (matins), Evening Prayer (vespers), and Prayer at the Close of the Day (compline). Matins and vespers are structured as in the following table. Silence for meditation, then a collect, follows each psalm or canticle as in ancient monastic usage. After each lesson there is also silence, then, if desired, a responsory.

| Matins: | Vespers: |
|---|---|
| "O Lord, open my lips . . ." | Light service (optional): Procession with candle |
| Doxology | Proclamation and response |

[2]H. T. Lehmann (ed.), *Luther's Works*, vol. 53: U. S. Leupold (ed.), *Liturgy and Hymns* (Philadelphia: Fortress, 1965) 38.
[3]*Ibid.* 37–38.
[4]H. O. Old, "Daily Prayer in the Reformed Church of Strasbourg, 1525–1530," *Worship* 52 (1978) 121–138.
[5]*Lutheran Book of Worship* (Minneapolis: Augsburg Publishing House, 1978).

*(Matins:)*          *(Vespers:)*

Phós hilaron
Lighting of candles
   during hymn
Thanksgiving for the

Invitatory Ps 94 (95)    Vesperal Ps 140 (141)

2nd psalm

(other psalms and an    (other psalms and a NT
   OT canticle may be      canticle may be added)
   added)

Hymn
1-2 lections

Benedictus      Magnificat
   or Te deum
Prayer of the day      Litany
   or other prayers

Our Father
Benediction
Concluding Hymn
(optional)

If there is to be a sermon, the benediction is omitted and the service continues:

Offering (collection)
Hymn
Sermon
Prayer
Benediction

At matins the paschal blessing and *Te deum* may replace the benediction.

The Light Service of vespers, with Ps 140 (141) and its collect, is an excellent example of what can be done to take a traditionally structured Western evening office and "cathedralize" it.[6] The service may begin with a procession in which a large lighted candle is carried to its stand before the congregation. Then the proclamation of the evening light is intoned by the leader *(L)*:

L. Jesus Christ is the Light of the World.
   Rx: The light no darkness can overcome.
L. Stay with us, Lord, for it is evening.
   Rx: And the day is almost over.
L. Let your light scatter the darkness.
   Rx: And illumine your church.

[6]*Ibid.* 142ff.

Then the *Phôs hilaron* is sung. During the hymn, other candles are lighted from the large one, if it has been used in the entrance rite. The Thanksgiving for the Light follows:

L. The Lord be with you.
Rx: And also with you.
L. Let us give thanks to the Lord our God.
Rx: It is right to give him thanks and praise.
L. Blessed are you, O Lord, our God, king of the universe, who led your people Israel by a pillar of cloud by day and a pillar of fire by night: Enlighten our darkness by the Light of your Christ; may his Word be a lamp to our feet and a light to our path; for you are merciful, and you love your whole creation, and we, your creatures, glorify you, Father, Son, and Holy Spirit.
Rx: Amen.

There follows the traditional cathedral vesperal psalm, Ps 140 (141). Verses 1–4a, 8, with verse 2 as the traditional antiphon, are chanted in the Roman manner with the antiphon repeated at the head of the psalm and following the doxology. The psalm unit is concluded by its collect, which sets the tone of the service:

Ant. Let my prayer rise before you as incense;
    the lifting up of my hands as the evening sacrifice.

V. O Lord, I call to you, come to me quickly;
    hear my voice when I cry to you.
Let my prayer rise before you as incense;
    the lifting up of my hands as the evening sacrifice.
Set a watch before my mouth, O Lord,
    and guard the door of my lips.
But my eyes are turned to you, Lord God;
    in you I take refuge. Strip me not of my life.
Glory to the Father and to the Son,
    and to the Holy Spirit;
as it was in the beginning, is now,
    and will be forever. Amen.

Ant. Let my prayer rise before you as incense;
    the lifting up of my hands as the evening sacrifice.

(Silence for meditation)

Leader: Let the incense of our repentant prayer ascend before you, O Lord, and let your loving kindness descend upon us, that with purified minds we may sing your praises with the Church on earth and the whole heavenly host, and may glorify you forever and ever.

Congregation: Amen.

## The Book of Common Prayer[7]

Easily the most important of all sixteenth-century reformed offices is that of the Anglican *Book of Common Prayer*. To its great merit the Anglican communion alone of all Western Christian Churches has preserved to some extent at least the daily services of morning praise and evensong as a living part of parish worship. As Louis Bouyer said in his *Liturgical Piety*, a book that has had such enormous positive influence in initiating Catholics to the meaning and value of liturgical prayer, morning and evensong in the *Book of Common Prayer*

> . . . is a Divine Office which is not a devotion of specialists but a truly public Office of the whole Christian people . . . we must admit frankly that the Offices of Morning Prayer and of Evensong, as they are performed even today in St. Paul's, Westminster Abbey, York Minster, or Canterbury Cathedral, are not only one of the most impressive, but also one of the purest forms of Christian common prayer to be found anywhere in the world.[8]

Archbishop Cranmer, like his continental contemporaries from whom he derived some of the inspiration for his reform of the hours, adopted solutions similar to those we have seen already. The raw material Cranmer worked with was the Sarum use then current in England, but his principles were largely Quiñonian. *The Preface* of the 1549 *Book of Common Prayer* is largely a paraphrase of Quiñones' preface, and Cranmer also borrowed the basic structure of Quiñones' offices and the principles of that reform: cut back the sanctoral, eliminate the legends, use more Sacred Scripture. The psalter and Scripture lessons were to be read in continuous sequence *(lectio continua)*. For the reformers, the purpose of the offices was to edify by means of the pure Word of God, and for some reason they all seem to have seen the *lectio continua* as more faithful to that aim, though one would be hard put to substantiate that principle historically from the tradition of cathedral liturgy. Non-scriptural lessons, at any rate, were excluded, as were antiphons, responds, and invitatories, which interrupt the text as found in the Bible. The two offices of matins and evensong had the same structure:

> Our Father
> Opening verse ("O Lord, open my lips . . .")
> and doxology

[7]E. C. Ratcliff, "The Choir Offices," W. K. Lowther Clarke and C. Harris (eds.), *Liturgy and Worship. A Companion to the Prayer Books of the Anglican Communion* (London: SPCK, 1954) 266ff.

[8]*Liturgical Piety* (Liturgical Studies, Notre Dame: University of Notre Dame Press, 1955) 47.

(At matins: Ps 94[95])
Psalms
OT lesson
Canticle
NT lesson
Canticle
Lord have mercy on us . . .
Creed
Our Father
Suffrages
3 collects

At matins the canticles are the *Te deum* or *Benedicite* (Dan 3), and the *Benedictus* of Luke 1:68–79; at vespers, the *Magnificat* and *Nunc dimittis*. In both offices elements have been added from other traditional hours that were suppressed: some of the concluding material in matins is taken from prime (the Athanasian Creed on feasts, prayers, third collect), and some at vespers is from compline (*Nunc dimittis*, creed, third collect). The second collect is from the Office of the Blessed Virgin Mary.

## The New Episcopal Prayerbook

Later prayerbook revisions do not affect the substance of these services until we come to the reform of 1977. In that year the *Proposed Book of Common Prayer*, now approved usage in the U.S.A., restored compline with its traditional Canticle of Simeon which the 1549 Prayerbook had transferred to vespers. A new noonday prayer is also provided. But the basic structure of morning and evening prayer remain as in the Prayerbook tradition, except for greater flexibility, the insertion of versicle, response, and doxology for the psalms, and, at vespers, the addition of *Phôs hilaron* or some other suitable evening hymn. In addition, a lucernarium is provided with the intention of restoring some cathedral elements to the tradition. This brief office may be used to introduce evensong, as in the *Lutheran Book of Worship*, in which case it would rejoin that service at the *Phôs hilaron*. So morning and evening prayer look as follows (optional elements are italicized):

*Matins:*                                    *Vespers:*

Opening verses
*Confession of sin*
Invitatory

*(Matins:)*                                    *(Vespers:)*

Ps 94 (95)                                     Invitatory verses
  or 99 (100)

                                    *Phôs hilaron* or other
                                    hymn

Appointed psalm(s)
Lesson 1 (usually
OT)
Silent prayer
Canticle
Lesson 2 (NT)
Silent prayer
Canticle
Apostles' Creed
Our Father
Suffrages
3 collects
*Thanksgiving prayer*
Dismissal
Grace

The lucernarium is structured as follows:

An Order of Worship in the Evening
    I. *The Service of Light:*
        Greeting: "Light and peace in Jesus Christ
           our Lord . . ."
        Short reading
        Collect for Light
        *Phôs hilaron* or other Hymn of Light
    II. *If this service is used independently, as a complete*
        *service, it may continue:*
        Psalmody
        Lesson (unless there has been one already)
        Magnificat or other canticle
        Intercessions
        Our Father
        Blessing
        Dismissal
        Sign of Peace

One can only congratulate the American Lutheran and Episcopal Churches for restoring these cathedral elements to evening prayer. It is ironic, however, to see the balance thus shifted. For recent Western office reforms have not only cathedralized the long defective Western tradition of vespers. They have at the same time weakened the age-old, strong tradition of cathedral elements in Western lauds.

# PART IV

# What It All Means

# Introduction

What I have said thus far has been, in intention at least, an objective interpretation of the history and present shape of the Liturgy of the Hours in the traditions of Eastern and Western Christianity. What follows in this final section is more experiential, the fruit of reflection on my own experience chanting the Liturgy of the Hours day by day, solemnly and in common, according to the Russian usage of the Byzantine Rite. That experience, however, has been measured against years of studying the Divine Office in the tradition of the Church, both Eastern and Western, across its entire history. So it is a personal reflection—but not, I trust, an arbitrarily subjective one.

# 21

## TOWARD A THEOLOGY OF THE LITURGY OF THE HOURS

Surprisingly, in spite of its importance in the liturgical life of the Church, especially in religious and clerical life, there has been relatively little written of late on the theology or spirituality of the Divine Office.[1] But since the appearance in 1945 of Dom Gregory Dix's classic *The Shape of the Liturgy*[2] it has been customary to fit the office under the heading of "sanctification of time," as a "liturgy of time" distinct from the "eschatological" Eucharist. Furthermore, Dix sees the office as something new, part of the fourth-century revolution in the spirit of worship.

Here is Dix's argument.[3] In the pre-Nicene Church, faith and worship informed the whole inner life of the believer, but because secular life was pagan, liturgy and daily life were distinct and even opposed. Worship was countercultural, world-renouncing, exclusive, not all-inclusive as it was to become later in monasticism.

The monastic movement swept the fourth-century world, bringing in its train a new emphasis on personal edification in Christian worship. This

---

[1] There is one work on the theology of the recently reformed Roman *Liturgia horarum:* D. de Reynal, *Théólogie de la Liturgie des heures* (Beauchesne religions, Paris: Beauchesne, 1978).

[2] Dix, *The Shape of the Liturgy.*

[3] *Ibid.* 323–332. References to quotations from these pages will be indicated in the text.

element, though present from the beginning, "had hitherto found only restricted expression in christian corporate worship and none at all in the eucharistic rite" (323). Hippolytus' *Apostolic Tradition* presents a regime of prayer "recognizably semi-monastic in character," which "represents the purely *personal* aspect of devotion, and stands quite apart . . . from the corporate worship of the *ecclesia*" (324). There were of course "private meetings," agape suppers for instance, for edification, but these were not corporate assemblies. ". . . The corporate worship of the pre-Nicene christians in its official and organised forms, the synaxis and the eucharist, was overwhelmingly a 'world-renouncing' cultus, which deliberately and rigidly rejected the whole idea of sanctifying and expressing towards God the life of human society in general . . ." (326).

Such is the scenario drawn by Dix, all of which was to change in the fourth century when the pre-Nicene system of *private* prayer, developed by the monks into a large part of their *public* worship, leads to the introduction of services of praise into the public worship of secular churches. The older worship stressed the corporate action of the Church. The new offices, though done in common, are intended chiefly to express and evoke the devotion of the individual worshiper.

So for Dix the cathedral office is "a direct result of the monastic-ascetic movement" (328). The monks gave the Church the office and with it the idea that the whole of life was consummated in worship, instead of seeing worship as "the contradiction of daily life, like the pre-Nicene church" (332).

Another novelty is that these services, unlike the Eucharist, were open to all. True, catechumens and others were also dismissed at the office, before the final Prayers of the Faithful, "but the element of prayer in the secular office was never a large one, and the bulk of the office . . . was always open to all" (331).

I trust that the historical sources already adduced suffice to show how totally wrong Dix is in almost every aspect of this interpretation. The prayer we saw, for example, in the *Apostolic Tradition* is not "semi-monastic" but in direct continuity with a tradition of daily Christian private prayer that goes back to the beginnings of the Church. All later development is simply an expansion and formalizing of this earlier tradition. What happened in the fourth century was but one more step in the process. The monks prayed at the same hours as in the earlier system. If they were cenobites they did this in common because *koinobion* means common life: they did *everything* together. And when the secular churches came above ground they developed some of the private prayer times into public services because "to assemble" was what it meant to be "church."

It is enough to read again the early Fathers on the cathedral hours to see how unfounded is Dix's notion that the cathedral offices were more expressions of individual piety than a corporate action of the Church. The *Apostolic Constitutions* II, 59, one of our earliest witnesses to the cathedral office, is quite explicit on just this point:

> When you teach, bishop, command and exhort the people to frequent the church regularly, morning and evening every day, and not to forsake it at all, but to assemble continually, and not diminish the Church by absenting themselves and making the Body of Christ lack a member. For it is not only said for the benefit of the priests, but let each of the laity hear what was said by the Lord as spoken to himself: "He who is not with me is against me, and he who does not gather with me scatters" (Matt 12:30). Do not scatter yourselves by not gathering together, you who are members of Christ. . . . Do not be neglectful of yourselves nor rob the savior of his members nor divide his body nor scatter his members, nor prefer the needs of this life to the Word of God, but assemble each day morning and evening, singing psalms and praying in the Lord's houses, in the morning saying Ps 62, and in the evening Ps 140.
>
> But especially on the Sabbath and the Lord's Day of the resurrection of the Lord, meet even more diligently, sending up praise to God. . . . Otherwise how will one defend himself before God, one who does not assemble on that day . . . on which is accomplished the reading of the prophets and the proclamation of the gospel and the offering of the sacrifice and the gift of the holy food?

The conclusion alone, which refers indiscriminately to the daily office and Sunday Eucharist, is proof enough that there is no basis for distinguishing as Dix does between the Mass as a "corporate action of the Church" and fourth-century "offices of devotion."

In the first place, moves in the direction of non-Eucharistic morning and evening assemblies are seen well before the post-Nicene, Constantinian era. Furthermore, to look upon the pre-Nicene agape and other non-Eucharistic Christian assemblies as "private" is to introduce anachronistic categories and distinctions that find no support whatever in the sources of this early period. The same can be said for the notion that the new offices were "inclusive" whereas the Eucharist was "exclusive." Catechumens and others were dismissed from fourth-century cathedral offices in exactly the same way and for exactly the same reason and at exactly the same point in the prayers as they were at the Liturgy of the Word. And both had the same number of "prayers," which were not at all inconsiderable, as we saw in the *Apostolic Constitutions* VIII, 35–39 (cf. 6–9), where they seem almost endless.[4] Such dismissals had nothing to do with whether a service was Eucharistic or not, but with who could or could not participate in certain acts of the priestly people of God. As for the novel *spirit* of these services, being directed at edification, there is no difference whatever between this and the spirit of Christian life and worship in the New Testament itself, as we shall see.

But since Dix, a whole theology of the hours as a "sanctification of time" distinct from the "eschatalogical" Eucharist on the Lord's Day has developed. The inevitable conclusion is that Eucharist should ideally be celebrated only on Sundays—as if the cathedral hours of morning praise and evensong were not also an integral part of the celebration of the Lord's Day!

Earlier theories took the opposite tack, considering the Eucharist the "summit of the Divine Office," as if the daily celebration of the Eucharist had some intimate connection with the daily hours of prayer, like a jewel in its setting.[5]

I must frankly confess I see no warrant for any of this in the sources, which from the beginning are reasonably clear on the meaning of Christian life and liturgy, and, within that context, on the meaning of the Liturgy of the Hours. For the hours take their meaning not from the Eucharist, nor from Christian daily life as opposed to an otherworldly eschatological expectation, nor from the natural cycle of morning and evening, nor from personal devotion and edification as distinct from the work of the community. Rather, they take their meaning from that which alone gives meaning to all of these things: the paschal mystery of salvation in Christ Jesus. This is the basis of any theology of Christian worship that takes, as it surely must, the New Testament as its starting point.

## Worship in the New Testament

A fundamental principle of New Testament theology is that all salvation history is recapitulated and "personalized" in Jesus.[6] Nothing is clearer than the fact that everything in sacred history—event, object, sacred place, theophany, cult—has quite simply been assumed into the person of the Incarnate Christ. He is God's eternal Word (John 1:1, 14); his new crea-

---

[4]See ch. 3 at note 30.

[5]On this see J. Dubois, "Office des heures et messe dans la tradition monastique," LMD 135 (1978) 62ff.; de Vogüé, *La Règle de s. Benôit* VII, 240ff. (English trans. in CS 54, 159 ff.); Taft, "The Frequency of the Eucharist," 17–18.

[6]In the following pages I resume some material from my article "The Liturgical Year: Studies, Prospects, Reflections," *Worship* 55 (1981) 14ff.

tion (2 Cor 5:17; Gal 6:15; Rom 8:19ff.; Rev 21—22) and the new Adam (1 Cor 15:45; Rom 5:14); the new Pasch and its lamb (1 Cor 5:7; John 1:29, 36; 19:36; 1 Pet 1:19; Rev 5ff.); the new covenant (Matt 26:28; Mark 14:24; Luke 22:20; Heb 8—13), the new circumcision (Col 2:11-12), and the heavenly manna (John 6:30-58; Rev 2:17); God's temple (John 2:19-27), the new sacrifice, and its priest (Eph 5:2; Heb 2:17—3:2; 4:14—10:14); the fulfillment of the Sabbath rest (Col 2:16-17; Matt 11:28—12:8; Heb 3:7—4:11) and the Messianic Age that was to come (Luke 4:16-21; Acts 2:14-36). Neither the list nor the references are exhaustive. He is quite simply "all in all" (Col 3:11), "the alpha and the omega, the first and the last, the beginning and the end" (Rev 1:8; 21:6; 22:13). All that went before is fulfilled in him: "For the law has but a shadow of the good things to come instead of the true form of these realities" (Heb 10:1); and that includes cultic realities: "Let no one pass judgment on you in questions of food and drink or with regard to a festival or a new moon or a sabbath. These are only a shadow of what is to come; but the substance belongs to Christ" (Col 2:16-17).

This is seminal for any theology of Christian worship. The Old Testament temple and altar with their rituals and sacrifices are replaced not by a new set of rituals and shrines, but by the self-giving of a person, the very Son of God. Henceforth, true worship pleasing to the Father is none other than the saving life, death and resurrection of Christ. And our worship is this same sacrificial existence in us. Paul tells us, "Just as surely as we have borne the image of the man of dust, we shall also bear the image of the man of heaven" (1 Cor 15:49; cf. Phil 2:7-11; 3:20-21; Eph 4:22-24), the Risen Christ, "image of the invisible God, the first-born of all creation" (Col 1:15; cf. 2 Cor 4:4), who conforms us to his image through the gift of his Spirit (2 Cor 3:15; Rom 8:11ff., 29). For St. Paul, "to live is Christ" (Phil 1:21), and to be saved is to be conformed to Christ by dying to self and rising to new life in him (2 Cor 4:10ff.; 13:4; Rom 6:3ff.; Col 2:12-13, 20; 3:1-3; Gal 2:20; Eph 2:1ff.; Phil 2:5ff.; 3:10-11, 18-21) who, as the "last Adam" (1 Cor 15:45), is the definitive form of redeemed human nature (1 Cor 15:21-22; Rom 5:12-21; Col 3:9-11; Eph 4:22-24). Until this pattern is so repeated in each of us that Christ is indeed "all in all" (Col 3:11), we shall not yet have "filled up what is lacking in Christ's afflictions for the sake of his body, that is, the church" (Col 1:24). For we know "the power of his resurrection" only if we "share his sufferings, becoming like him in his death" (Phil 3:10).

Far from being a fourth-century innovation, edification and personal sanctification and the intimate relation of liturgy to everyday life are the essence of the New Testament message concerning the new cult.

Indeed, for St. Paul liturgy *is* Christian life. Never once does he use cultic nomenclature (liturgy, sacrifice, priest, offering) for anything but a life of self-giving, lived after the pattern of Christ.[7] When he does speak of what we call liturgy, as in 1 Cor 10—14, Eph 4, or Gal 3:27-28, he makes it clear that its purpose is to build up the Body of Christ into that new temple and liturgy and priesthood, in which sanctuary and offerer and offered are one. For it is in the liturgy of the Church, in the ministry of word and sacrament, that the biblical pattern of recapitulation of all in Christ is returned to the collectivity, and applied to the community of faith that will live in him.

To borrow a term from the biblical scholars, the liturgy is the on-going *Sitz im Leben* of Christ's saving pattern in every age, and what we do in the liturgy is exactly what the New Testament itself did with Christ: it applied him and what he was and is to the present. For the *Sitz im Leben* of the Gospels is the historical setting not of the original event, but of its telling during the early years of the primitive Church. Do not both New Testament and liturgy tell us this holy history again and again as a perpetual anamnesis? Note that this is not kerygma, as it is often mistakenly called. Kerygma is the preaching of the Good News in order to awaken the response of faith in the new message. But the kerygma written down and proclaimed in the liturgical assembly to recall us to our commitment to the Good News already heard and accepted in faith, even though "we know them and are established in the truth" (2 Pet 1:12), is anamnesis, and that is what we do in liturgy. We make anamnesis, memorial, of this dynamic saving power in our lives, to make it penetrate ever more into the depths of our being, for the building up of the Body of Christ.

> That which was from the beginning, which we have heard, which we have seen with our eyes, which we have looked upon and touched with our hands, concerning the word of life—the life was made manifest and we saw it, and testify to it, and proclaim to you the eternal life which was with the Father and was made manifest to us—that which we have seen and heard we proclaim also to you, so that you may have communion with us; and our communion is with the Father and with his Son Jesus Christ. And we are writing this that our joy may be complete (1 John 1:1-4).

It seems to me, then, that the eschatalogical expectation vs. sanctification of life dichotomy arose long before the fourth century, *pace* Dix, and was solved by the Apostolic Church. But it was not solved by abandoning New Testament eschatology, which sees Christ as inaugurating

[7]See for example Rom 10:9; 12:1; 15:16; Phil 2:17; 4:18; 2 Tim 4:6; also Heb 13:11-16.

the age of salvation. What was abandoned was the mistaken belief that this implied an imminent parousia. But that does not modify the main point of Christian eschatology, that the endtime is not in the future but *now*. And it is operative now, though not exclusively, through the anamnesis in word and sacrament of the dynamic present reality of Emmanuel, "God-with-us," through the power of his Spirit in every age.

In the Gospels the transition to this new age of salvation history is portrayed in the accounts of the post-resurrection appearances of Jesus.[8] They introduce us to a new mode of his presence, a presence that is real and experienced, yet quite different from the former presence before his passover. When he appears he is not recognized immediately (Luke 24:16, 37; John 2:14, 7, 12). There is a strange aura about him; the disciples are uncertain, afraid; Jesus must reassure them (Luke 24:36ff.). At Emmaus they recognize him only in the breaking of the bread—and then he vanishes (Luke 24:16, 30-31, 35). Like his presence among us now, his presence to the disciples is accessible only through faith.

What these post-resurrection accounts seem to be telling us is that Jesus is with us, but not as he was before.[9] He is with us and not with us, real presence and real absence. He is the one whom "heaven must receive until the time for establishing all that God spoke by the mouth of his holy prophets from of old" (Acts 3:21), but who also said "I am with you always, until the close of the age" (Matt 28:20). It is simply this reality that we live in the liturgy, believing from Matt 18:20 that "where two or three are gathered in my name, there am I in the midst of them," yet celebrating the Lord's Supper to "proclaim the Lord's death until he comes" (1 Cor 11:26) in the spirit of the early Christians, with their liturgical cry of hope: "Marana-tha! Amen. Come Lord Jesus!" (Rev 22:20).

So the Jesus of the Apostolic Church is not the historical Jesus of the past, but the Heavenly Priest interceding for us constantly before the throne of the Father (Rom 8:34; Heb 9:11—28), and actively directing the life of his Church (Rev 1:17—3:22 and *passim*).[10] The vision of the People who produced these documents was not directed backwards, to the "good old days" when Jesus was with them on earth. We see such nostalgia only after Jesus' death, before the resurrection appearances give birth to Christian faith.

The Church did keep a record of the historical events, but they were reinterpreted in the light of the resurrection, and were meant to assist Chris-

[8]D. N. Stanley, *A Modern Scriptural Approach to the Spiritual Exercises* (Chicago: Loyola University Press, 1967) 278ff.

[9]*Ibid.* 280ff.

[10]*Ibid.* 284–285.

tians to grasp the significance of Jesus in their lives.[11] That this was the chief interest of the New Testament Church, the contemporary, active, Risen Christ present in the Church through his Spirit, can be seen in the earliest writings, the epistles of St. Paul, which say next to nothing about the historical details of Jesus' life.

It is this consciousness of Jesus as the Lord not of the past but of contemporary history that is the aim of all Christian spirituality and liturgical anamnesis. Christian vision is rooted in the gradually acquired realization of the Apostolic Church that the parousia was not imminent, and that the eschatological, definitive victory won by Christ must be repeated in each one of us, until the end of time. And since Christ is both model and source of this struggle, the New Testament presents both his victory and his cult of the Father as ours: just as we have died and risen with him (Rom 6:3-11; 2 Cor 4:10ff.; Gal 2:20; Col 2:12-13, 20; 3:1-3; Eph 2:5-6), so, too, it is we who have become a new creation (2 Cor 5:17; Eph 4:22-24), a new circumcision (Phil 3:3), a new temple (1 Cor 3:16-17; 6:19; 2 Cor 6:16; Eph 2:19-22), a new sacrifice (Eph 5:2), and a new priesthood (1 Pet 2:5-9; Rev 1:6; 5:10; 20:6). This is why we meditate on the pattern of his life, proclaim it, preach it, celebrate it: to make it ever more deeply our own. This is why the Apostolic Church left us a book and a rite, word and sacrament, so that what Christ did and was, we may do and be, in him. For this reason, sacred history is never finished: it continues in us.

## The Newness of Christian Ritual

I think it fair to say that this New Testament vision of cult is something startlingly, radically new. Of course human beings have always gathered to express themselves in ritual, so when Christians do so they are not inventing something new.[12] What is new is the vision they are expressing.

Ritual itself is simply a set of conventions, an organized pattern of signs and gestures which members of a community use to interpret and enact for themselves, and to express and transmit to others, their relation to reality.[13] It is a way of saying what we as a group are, in the full sense

[11]Ibid. 285.

[12]I resume here some material from my article, "Thanksgiving for the Light—Toward a Theology of Vespers," Diakonia 13 (1978) 27-50.

[13]I follow here some of the ideas of V. Turner, "Ritual, Tribal, Catholic," Worship 50 (1976) 504-526.

of that *are*, with our past that made us what we are, our present in which we live what we are, and the future we hope to be. Ritual, then, is ideology and experience in action, the celebration or interpretation-through-action of our human experience and how we view it.

Human societies have used ritual especially to express their religious outlook, their universal system for relating to the ultimate questions of life. A religion is different from a personal philosophy of life in that it is a *shared* perspective, a common outlook on reality. As such it depends on *history*, on the group's collective remembrance of things past, of events that have been transformed in the collective memory of the community into key symbolic episodes determinative of the community's being and self-understanding.

This is the basis of ritual behavior. For it is through the interpretation of its past that a community relates to the present and copes with the future. In the process of ritual representation, past constitutive events are made present in ritual time, in order to communicate their force to new generations of the social group, providing thus a community of identity throughout history.

In primitive, natural religious systems the past was seen as cyclic, as an ever-repeating pattern of natural seasons. Rituals were celebrations of this cycle of autumn, winter, spring, harvest—of natural death and rebirth. But even at this primitive stage men and women came to see these natural rhythms as symbols of higher realities, of death and resurrection, of the perdurance of human existence beyond natural death.

So even natural religious ritual is not just an interpretation of experience, but implies a reaching for the beyond, for an ultimate meaning in the cycle of life that seemed to be an ever-recurring circle closed by death. The discovery of history was a breakthrough in this process: life was seen to have a pattern that extended beyond the closed cycles of nature, of life and death. Time acquired a new meaning, and human ritual was transformed from a way of interpreting *nature* into a way of interpreting *history*.

Thus, events in the past came to acquire a universal symbolic value in the mind of the community; in fact, these events were so fundamental that they actually created and constituted the community's very identity. By celebrating these events ritually, the community made them present again, and mediated to its members their formative power. Of course these were usually events of salvation, of escape from calamity and death, and it was but one further step for them to become transformed in the collective memory of the group into symbols of God's care and eternal salvation.

This is what happened with Israel. What makes Israelite liturgy different from other rituals is revelation. The Jews did not have to *imagine* that their escape from Egypt was a sign of God's saving Providence: he *told* them so. When they celebrated this Exodus ritually in the Passover meal, they knew they were celebrating more than the universalization of a past event in the historical imagination of their poets and prophets. The covenant with God which they reaffirmed ritually was a permanent and hence ever present reality because God had said so.

Here we encounter a basic difference between Judeo-Christian worship and other cults. Biblical worship is not an attempt to contact the divine, to mediate to us the power of God's intervention in past saving events. It is the other way around. It is a worship of the already saved. We do not reach for God to appease him; he has bent down to us.

With Christian liturgy we take another step in our understanding of ritual. As in the Old Testament, we, too, celebrate a saving event. For us, too, the meaning of this event has been revealed. But that is where the parallel ends. For Old Testament ritual looked forward to a promised fulfillment; it was not only an actualization of the covenant, but the pledge of a yet unrealized messianic future. In Christianity, what all other rituals strain to achieve has, we believe, already been fufilled once and for all by Christ. Reconciliation with the Father has been accomplished eternally in the mystery of his Son (2 Cor 5:18-19; Rom 5:10-11). The gap is bridged forever through God's initiative.

So Christian worship is not how we seek to contact God; it is a celebration of how God has touched us, has united us to himself and is ever present to us and dwelling in us. It is not a reaching out for a distant reality but a joyful celebration of a salvation that is just as real and active in the ritual celebration as it was in the historical event. It is ritual perfected by divine realism; ritual in which the symbolic action is not a memorial of the past, but a participation in the eternally present salvific Pasch of Christ.

Christian liturgy, therefore, publicly feasts the mystery of our salvation already accomplished in Christ, thanking and glorifying God for it so that it might be intensified in us and communicated to others for the building up of the Church, to the perpetual glory of God's Holy Name.


## Liturgy: A Work of the Church

So liturgy is an activity of the Church. It is one of the ways the Church responds in praise, surrender, thanksgiving, to the call of God's revealing, saving word and deed. This eternal doxology is a response *to* something, and it is important to note that this divine action itself is not extrinsic to the liturgy but an integral part of it. Liturgy is not just our response; it is also the eternally repeated call. It is both God's unending saving activity and our prayerful response to it in faith and commitment throughout the ages.

Liturgy, then, is much more than an individual expression of faith and devotion, and infinitely more than a subjective expression of "where we're at," or "where we're coming from," as contemporary American slang puts it. It is first and foremost an activity of God in Christ. Christ saves through the ages in the activity of the body of which he is the head. He does this in the word that calls us to conversion to him and union with him, and to reconciliation with one another in him. He creates and nourishes and heals and restores this life in the water and oil and food of sacrament, and joins his prayer to ours to glorify the Father for those gifts. And all this is liturgy.

Liturgy then is the common work of Christ and his Church. This is its glory. It is also what makes possible the extraordinary claims the Church has made about the nature of Christian worship. Our prayers are worthless, but in the liturgy Christ himself prays in us. For the liturgy is the efficacious sign of Christ's saving presence in his Church. His saving offering is eternally active and present before the throne of the Father. By our celebration of the divine mysteries, we are drawn into the saving action of Christ and our personal self-offering is transformed into an act of the Body of Christ through the worship of the body with its head. What men and women have vainly striven for throughout history in natural ritual— contact with the divine—is transformed from image to reality in Christ.

Of course, Christ, through the Spirit, does all these things apart from the liturgy, too—all this calling and healing and nourishing and saving and praying in us and with us. Then what is so special about the liturgy? Certainly not its efficaciousness, for God is always efficacious in all he does. The obstacles come from us. What is special about the liturgy is that it is a *visible* activity of the *whole* Church. Indeed, in a certain sense Church is Church only in liturgy, for a gathering in its fullest sense is a gathering only when it is gathered! Liturgy therefore is different from private prayer and other means and vehicles of grace and salvation in that it is a "symbol," a symbolic movement both expressing what we are and calling us to be it more fully. It is a celebration of the fact that we have been saved in Christ, and in the very celebration that same saving mystery of Christ is offered to us again in anamnesis for our unendingly renewed acceptance, and as everlasting motive for our song of joyful thanks and praise:

"He who is mighty has done great things for me—holy is his name!" (Luke 1:49).

We do all this together because we *are* a "together," and not just individuals. Christian salvation is by its very nature "Church," a "gathering," a one Body of Christ, and if we do not express this, then we are not what we proclaim to be. Redemption in the New Testament is a coming together, a solidarity in the face of the evil of this world. It necessarily leads to community because only in common can new human values be effectively released and implemented. Christ came not just to save individuals, but to change the course of history by creating the leaven of a new group, a new People of God, paradigm of what all peoples must one day be. In the Acts of the Apostles the life of this group is sustained in *gatherings*, and its basic dynamic is toward unity: that they may be one in Jesus, that they may love one another as Jesus has loved them and as the Father loves Jesus, is the will and prayer of Jesus in the Last Discourse in John's Gospel (15:9ff., 17:20ff.). This is the remedy for hate and divisiveness and enmity, the products of egoism that is the root of all evil.

Unless seen in this broader context of the whole of life, what the community does in its synaxes does not make much sense, for liturgy is not an end in itself. It is only the means and expression of a life together in Christ. It is that which is primary: a common life of mutual support and generosity, of putting self second so that others can be first. Prayer in common is one of the means to this unity, part of the group's cement, as well as its joyful celebration of the fact that inchoatively, if not perfectly, this unity exists already.

So it is towards *life* that worship is always directed. We see this in 1 Cor 11–14 and Matt 5:23–24. We see it in the *Didache* 14:1–2: "And on the Lord's day of the Lord, after you have gathered, break bread and offer the Eucharist, . . . . But let no one who has a quarrel with his neighbor join you until he is reconciled, lest your sacrifice be defiled." A few years later, around 111–113 A.D., we see it in the garbled account of a Christian assembly in the letter of the pagan governor Pliny to the emperor Trajan, during the time of persecutions in the Roman Empire. Pliny had interrogated Christians concerning their private gatherings, which had brought them under suspicion after Trajan's edict forbidding *hetaeriae* or secret meetings. Pliny obviously did not comprehend the information he had received from them. But he did understand that these Christian assemblies involved commitment to a covenant with stringent ethical implications:

> They insisted, however, that their whole fault or error consisted in the fact that they were accustomed to gather before daylight on a fixed

day to sing a hymn to Christ as God and to bind themselves mutually, by means of a religious vow, not to any crime, but rather not to commit any theft or robbery or adultery, nor to go back on their word, nor to refuse to return a loan when it is demanded back. (Plinius Minor, *Ep.* 10, 96:7).

We see it in the questions asked the *baptizandi* in Hippolytus, *Apostolic Tradition* 20:

And when those who are to receive baptism are chosen, let their life be examined: did they live good lives when they were catechumens? Did they visit the sick? Have they done every kind of good work? And when those who sponsored them bear witness to each: "He has," let them hear the gospel.

In short, the touchstone of our liturgy is whether or not it is being lived out in our lives. Is the symbolic moment symbolizing what we really are? Is our shared celebration of life a sign that we truly live in this way?

In taking this perspective we are doing precisely what we saw the New Testament do with the mystery that is Christ: we recall it, make anamnesis of it, as a medium for encountering this mystery anew, so that we might see it as it is, the model and source of what we must be. But its purpose is not merely didactic. Its blazing light serves not only to illumine our deficiencies. It also burns away our darkness and draws us into its divine light.

Liturgy then has precisely the same dynamic as the New Testament, and also contains my response to it. To appropriate an expression of Mark Searle, just as the Bible is the saving Word of God in the words of human beings, so the liturgy is the saving deeds of God in the actions of men and women. And both have the same end: that we might respond to the call, and live it. Indeed, in a sense liturgy is more inclusive than the Scriptures, for it comprises both the saving Word *and* the saving actions of God, and our response to both. But just as the Word and deeds of God are seen here in sacramental form, but are present to us at every moment, symbolized but not exhausted in the ritual movement, so, too, my ritual response is but the symbolic movement of what must be the response of my every moment, with God's help.

For liturgy is a present encounter. Salvation is now. The death and resurrection of Jesus are past events only in their historicity, that is, with respect to us. But they are eternally present in God, who has entered our history but is not entrapped in it, and they have brought the presence of God among us to fulfillment in Jesus, and that enduring reality we encounter at every moment of our lives. The past memorialized is the efficacious saving event of salvation now, re-presented in symbol. In the Risen

Lord, creation is at last seen as what it was meant to be, and Christ is Adam, that is, all humankind.

So the Jesus we recall is the fulfillment of all that went before. But this fulfillment of the past is directed at the future. For just as Christ has become everything and fulfilled all, so for us to be fulfilled, we must become him. And we can do this only by letting him conform us to himself, to his pattern, the model of the new creation. It is this remaking of us into a new humanity that is the true worship of the New Law. The old cult and priesthood have been replaced by the self-offering of the Son of God, and our worship is to repeat this same pattern in our own lives, a pattern we celebrate in symbol when we gather to remember what he was and what we are to be.

To express this spiritual identity, St. Paul uses several compound verbs that begin with the preposition *syn* (with): I suffer with Christ, am crucified with Christ, die with Christ, am buried with Christ, am raised and live with Christ, am carried off to heaven and sit at the right hand of the Father with Christ (Rom 6:3–11; Gal 2:20; 2 Cor 1:5; 4:7ff.; Col 2:20; Eph 2:5–6).[14] This is one of Paul's ways of underscoring the necessity of personal participation in redemption. We must "put on Christ" (Gal 13:27), and assimilate him, somehow experience with God's grace the principal events by which Christ has saved us and repeat them in the pattern of my own life. For by undergoing them he has transformed the basic human experiences into a new creation. How do we experience these events? In him, by so entering into the mystery of his life so that each can affirm with Paul: "I have been crucified with Christ; it is no longer I who live, but Christ who lives in me" (Gal 2:20).

This is what Christian life, our true liturgy, is all about. Our common worship is a living metaphor of this same saving reality, not only representing and re-presenting it to us constantly in symbol to evoke our response in faith and deed, but actively effecting it in us through the work of the Holy Spirit, in order to build up the Body of Christ into a new temple and liturgy and priesthood in which offerer and offered are one.

This is what I mean when I say that all liturgy is anamnesis. It is not just a psychological reminiscence, not just a remembering, but an active and self-fulfilling prophecy in which by the power of God we become what we celebrate, while at the same time thanking and glorifying him for that great gift.

2 Pet 1:12–16 says:

> Therefore I intend always to *remind* you of these things, though you
> know them and are established in the truth that you have. I think

[14]Stanley, *A Modern Scriptural Approach* 210–211.

it is right . . . to arouse you by way of *reminder*. . . . And I will
see to it that after my departure you may be able at any time to *recall*
these things. For we did not follow cleverly devised myths when we
made known to you the power and coming of our Lord Jesus Christ,
but we were eye-witnesses of his majesty.

Liturgy also reminds us of the powerful deeds of God in Christ. And being reminded we remember, and remembering we celebrate, and celebrating we become what we do. The dancer dancing is the dance.


## Liturgy and Spirituality

Christian life, according to the several New Testament metaphors for
it, is a process of conversion into Christ.[15] He is the *Ursakrament* which
we have seen the New Testament present as the personalization of all that
went before, and the recapitulation and completion and model and fore-
taste of all that will ever be. As such, he is not just the mystery of the
Father's love for us, "the image of the unseen God" (Col 1:15); he is also
the revelation of what we are to be (1 Cor 15:49; 2 Cor 3:18; Rom 8:29).
His life is the story of entering sinful humanity and returning it to the
Father through the cross, a return that was accepted and crowned in
Christ's deliverance and exaltation (Phil 2:5ff.). And this same story, as
we have seen, is also presented as the story of everyone, the archetype
of our experience of returning to God through a life of death to self, lived
after the pattern Christ showed us: "He died for all, that those who live
might live no longer for themselves but for him who for their sake died
and was raised" (2 Cor 5:15).

In the New Testament, the very process of its composition reveals the
growing realization of this fact: that our final passage to the Father through
death and resurrection was to be preceded by a life of death to sin and
new life in Christ. The whole point of the New Testament reflection on
Christ's life is to make it speak to this new awareness: that the new age
was to be not a quick end but a new, holy history. As Abbot Patrick Re-
gan has said, the eschaton is not a time or a thing, it is a person, the new
Adam, Jesus Christ (1 Cor 5:20ff., 42ff.). And the new creation is a life
lived in him (2 Cor 5:13-19)—or rather, his life in us (Gal 2:20).[16]

[15]See M. Searle, "The Journey of Conversion," *Worship* 54 (1980) 48-49, and his "Liturgy as Metaphor," *Worship* 55 (1981) 111ff.

[16]"Pneumatological and Eschatological Aspects of Liturgical Celebration," *Worship* 51 (1977)
347.

Liturgy, therefore, has the same purpose as the gospel: to present this new reality in "anamnesis" as a continual sign to us not of a past history, but of the present reality of our lives in him. "Behold *now* is the acceptable time; behold, *now* is the day of salvation" (2 Cor 6:2). The liturgy of the Church presents us with a multi-dimensional celebration of this basic reality, but the reality is always the same. What we celebrate is the fact that Jesus lived, died, and rose for our salvation, and that we have died to sin and risen to new life in him, in expectation of the final fulfillment. Baptism celebrates the initiation of this gift in us. Eucharist nourishes it, and celebrates it as a community of life now, and as a sign that the final days have already begun, when we shall eat and drink at God's table in the kingdom.

This common celebration of our salvation in Christ is the most perfect expression and realization of the spirituality of the Church. There are many "schools" of spirituality, but they are legitimate only insofar as they are rooted in the worship of the Church. The purpose of the spiritual life is to "put on Christ," so that, as St. Paul says, "It is no longer I who live, but Christ who lives in me" (Gal 2:20). And this life is created, fed and renewed in the liturgy. Baptized into the mystery of his death and resurrection, we rise in him, having "put on Christ." Henceforth he dwells in us, prays in us, proclaims to us the word of his new covenant, seals it with his sacrifice, feeds us with his body and blood, draws us to penance and conversion, glorifies the Father in us. In proclamation and preaching he explains to us his mystery; in rite and song he celebrates it with us; in sacramental grace he gives us the strength to live it.

The mystery that is Christ is the center of Christian life and it is this mystery and nothing else that the Church renews in the liturgy so that we might be drawn into it. When we leave the assembly to return to our other tasks, we have only to assimilate what we have experienced and realize the mystery in our lives: in a word, to become other Christs. For the purpose of the liturgy is to generate in our lives what the Church realizes for us in its public worship. The spiritual life is just another word for a personal relationship with God, and the liturgy is nothing less than the common expression of the Church's personal relationship with God.

In such a liturgical spirituality the Church's public worship and the spiritual life of the individual are one. All the supposed tension in spirituality between public and private, objective and subjective, liturgical and personal, is an illusion, a false dichotomy. For in her public worship it is precisely this work of spiritual formation that the Church carries on.

# The Divine Office as Liturgy

So liturgy is simply a celebration of the Christian life—or the "spiritual life," if you will—and the same is true of the Liturgy of the Hours. It is no more, no less than a common celebration of what we are, or rather of what we have become and are ever becoming in Christ. And we do it in common because all Christian life is a shared life, a group life. Throughout history social groups have always gathered to express in rite and feast their common vision of what they are, because this is one of the ways of *being* it. A group that does nothing as a group is not a group.

But if what we are as a group is the Body of Christ, and if the eternally present Christ is an everlasting hymn of praise and glory before the throne of the Father, it is our vocation to enter into this salvific event; to live that Christ-life of priestly praise and glory. And so the Church, as his Mystical Body, associates herself with the eternal priestly prayer of her head. In so doing, she truly participates in the salvific praise of Christ, according to the theology of the Vatican II *Constitution on the Sacred Liturgy* 83–85:

> Christ Jesus, high priest of the new and eternal covenant, taking human nature, introduced into this earthly exile that hymn which is sung throughout all ages in the halls of heaven. He joins the entire community of mankind to Himself, associating it with His own singing of this canticle of divine praise. For He continues His priestly work through the agency of His Church, which is ceaselessly engaged in praising the Lord and interceding for the salvation of the whole world. This she does not only by celebrating the Eucharist, but also in other ways, especially by praying the divine Office. . . . It is truly the voice of the bride addressing her bridegroom; it is the very prayer which Christ Himself, together with His body, addresses to the Father. Hence all who perform this service are not only fulfilling a duty of the Church, but also are sharing in the greatest honor accorded to Christ's spouse, for by offering these praises to God they are standing before God's throne in the name of the Church, their Mother.[17]

# The Spirit of the Cathedral Office

Traditionally, morning praise and evensong with Eucharist have been the principal ways in which the Church exercises this *leitourgia*. Per se there is no special mystical significance about morning and evening as times

[17]W. M. Abbott (trans.), *The Documents of Vatican II* (New York: The America Press, 1966) 163–164.

of prayer. They are the beginning and end of the day, and so it was perfectly natural to select them as the "symbolic moments" in which we express what ought to be the quality of the whole day. As seen in chapter 3, the cathedral offices by the beginning of the fifth century had fleshed out the bare bones of psalmody and prayer with rites and symbols that revealed the morning and evening hours as sacraments of the mystery of Christ. In this sense the early cathedral office can be called a "sanctification of time" in that time is "sacramentalized" into a symbol of the time that transcends time.

In the liturgical mystery, time becomes transformed into event, an epiphany of the kingdom of God. All of creation is a cosmic sacrament of our saving God, and the Church's use of such symbolism in the office is but a step in the restoration of all things in Christ (Eph 1:10). For the Christian everything, including the morning and evening, the day and the night, the sun and its setting, can be a means of communication with God: "The heavens declare the glory of God and the firmament proclaims his handiwork" (Ps 18:1).

## "GOD IS LIGHT" (1 JOHN 1:15)

The basic natural symbol from which this ritual elaboration springs is, of course, light, a theme that can be traced back to the Old Testament and beyond, to the prominent use of sun imagery in the paganism of the Mediterranean world.

> Behind the imagery of the light and the sun in the religions of the Near East was the attempt to find meaning and hope for human life in the daily victory of light over darkness: the dawn was the harbinger of divine rescue and of eternal salvation. Indeed, the power of the light to bring hope is much older and deeper than mere human history. In responding as they did to the power of light, the religions of the Near East gave liturgical expression to the yearnings and the stirrings of the protoplasm, the nameless need in the very stuff of life to be sustained by light.[18]

In spite of the power of the imagery of sun and light in Hellenistic Judaism (Philo), it does not seem to have especially affected the ritual of Jewish morning and evening prayer. The Yotzer benediction of the Shema recited at these hours in the synagogue does refer to light and darkness in the context of creation, but its symbolic application does not seem to have been ritualized: "Blessed are you, Lord our God, King of the universe,

[18]J. Pelikan, *The Light of the World. A Basic Image in Early Christian Thought* (New York: Harper & Brothers, 1962) 13.

who form the light and create the darkness, who make peace and create all things (Is 45:7), who illumine the earth and those that dwell on it with mercy, and from your goodness renew daily the work of creation. . . ."[19]

Christians at any rate were quick to apply this symbolism to Christ: it is a constant New Testament theme, especially in the Johannine literature:

> In him was life, and the life was the light of men. The light shines in the darkness, and the darkness has not overcome it. There was a man sent from God, whose name was John. He came for testimony, to bear witness to the light, that all might believe through him. He was not the light, but came to bear witness to the light. The true light that enlightens every man was coming into the world (John 1:4-9).
>
> I am the light of the world; he who follows me will not walk in darkness, but will have the light of life (John 8:12; cf. 9:5).
>
> He who sees me sees him who sent me. I have come as light into the world, that whoever believes in me may not remain in darkness (John 12:45-46; cf. 12:35-36).

In Christ, this illumination has already been accomplished:

> . . . (give) thanks to the Father, who has qualified us to share in the inheritance of the saints of light. He has delivered us from the dominion of darkness and transferred us to the kingdom of his beloved Son, in whom we have redemption, the forgiveness of sins (Col 1:12-13; cf. 1 Thess 5:5; Heb 6:4; 10:32).

Eph 5 and 1 John stress that this illumination has a moral and communitarian dimension:

> . . . God is light and in him is no darkness at all. If we say we have fellowship with him while we walk in darkness, we lie and do not live according to the truth; but if we walk in the light, as he is in the light, we have fellowship with one another, and the blood of Jesus his son cleanses us from all sin (1 John 1:5-7).
>
> Yet I am writing you a new commandment, which is true in him and in you, because the darkness is passing away and the light is already shining. He who says he is in the light and hates his brother abides in the darkness still. He who loves his brother abides in the light, and in it there is no cause for stumbling. But he who hates his brother is in the darkness and walks in the darkness, and does not know where he is going, because the darkness has blinded his eyes (1 John 2:8-11).

---

[19]See W. O. E. Oesterly, *The Jewish Background of the Christian Liturgy* (Gloucester: Peter Smith, 1965) 48. Of course Jewish tradition offers parallels in the ritual of the Hannukah lights, and the ritual lighting of the Sabbath lights Friday evening and of the Havdalah lamp at the completion of the Sabbath. But I know of no parallel in the *daily* domestic or synagogue rituals of the Jews in the first Christian centuries.

But perhaps the most pregnantly beautiful passage for our purposes is the description in the Apocalypse of the light of the Lamb in the City of God, the New Jerusalem. The visionary is describing the Heavenly City:

> And I saw no temple in the city, for its temple is the Lord God the Almighty and the Lamb. And the city has no need of sun or moon to shine upon it, for the glory of God is its light, and its lamp is the Lamb. By its light shall the nations walk; and the kings of the earth shall bring their glory into it, and its gates shall never be shut by day— and there shall be no night there . . . (Rev 21:22-26).

The passage is a deliberate fulfillment of the prophecy of Isaiah (60:1-3, 11, 19-20) in the prophet's vision of the same heavenly abode:

> Arise, shine; for your light has come
>   and the glory of the Lord has risen upon you.
> For behold, darkness shall cover the earth . . .
>   but the Lord will arise upon you,
>   and his glory will be seen upon you.
> And the nations shall come to your light,
>   and kings to the brightness of your rising. . . .
> Your gates shall be open continually;
>   day and night they shall not be shut. . . .
> The sun shall be no more your light by day,
>   nor for brightness shall the moon give light to
>   you by night;
> but the Lord will be your everlasting light,
>   and your God will be your glory.
> Your sun shall no more go down,
>   nor your moon withdraw
>   itself;
> for the Lord will be your everlasting light,
>   and your days of mourning shall be ended. . . .

It was not long before this symbolism passed into the poetry and hymnody of Christian worship. A venerable hymn is cited in part in Eph 5:14. Clement of Alexandria (d. 215), *Protrepticus* 9, 84:2, gives the full text:

> Awake, O sleeper, and arise from the dead,
> and Christ shall give you light,
>   the sun of the resurrection,
>   begotten before the morning star (Ps 109),
>   who gives life by his own very rays.

This light Christ gives is salvation, and it is received in baptism. Heb 6:4-6, in a passage strikingly reminiscent of the three stages of initiation, speaks of "those who have . . . been enlightened, who have tasted the heavenly gift, and have become partakers of the Holy Spirit and have tasted the goodness of the word of God and the power of the age to come. . . ." And in the early Church, baptism was called *"phôtismos"* or *"phôtisma,"* illumination; those to be baptised were *"illuminandi, phô-tizomenoi."*

It is not surprising, then, that Christians prayed facing East, as we saw in chapter 2, seeing in the rising sun a symbol of the Risen Christ, light of the world. For Malachi 4:2 prophecied, "the sun of righteousness shall rise, with healing in its wings," and Zechariah proclaimed that in Jesus "the day shall dawn upon us from on high to give light to those who sit in darkness and the shadow of death, to guide our feet into the way of peace" (Luke 1:78-79). Nor is it remarkable that in the evening office, celebrated at the setting of the sun and the onset of darkness, the hour of lamplighting, Christians were drawn to see the evening lamp as a symbol of Christ the light of the world, the lamp of the Heavenly City where there is no darkness or night but only day, and to render thanks to God for it.

As we saw in numerous texts cited in previous chapters, this "sacramentalizing" of sunrise and sunset, with its evening lamp, is by no means a fourth-century novelty. Already in the last decade of the first century, Clement of Rome (1 Clem. 24:1–3) relates the natural succession of light and darkness to the resurrection of the just at the parousia, and around 250 Cyprian's treatise *On the Lord's Prayer* 35–36 first applies the resurrection theme to early Christian prayer times:

> . . . One must also pray in the morning, that the resurrection of the Lord may be celebrated by morning prayer. . . . Likewise at sunset and the passing of the day it is necessary to pray. For since Christ is the true sun and the true day, when we pray and ask, as the sun and the day of the world recede, that the light may come upon us again, we pray for the coming of Christ, which provides us with the grace of eternal light. For in the psalms the Holy Spirit declares that Christ is called the day . . . "This is the day that the Lord has made; let us exult and rejoice in it" (Ps 117:24). Likewise the prophet Malachy testifies that he is called the sun, when he says: "But unto you that fear the name of the Lord the sun of justice shall arise, and in his wings there is healing" (Mal 3:20).

From what follows it is evident that Cyprian looked on these times as signs of what every Christian "time" must be:

> But if in the Holy Scriptures Christ is the true sun and the true day, no hour is excepted in which God should be adored frequently and always, so that we who are in Christ, that is, in the true sun and day,

should be insistent throughout the whole day in our petitions, and should pray. And when by the laws of nature the return of night, recurring in its turn, follows, for those that pray there can be no harm from the nocturnal darkness, because for the sons of light, even in the night there is day. For when is one without light who has light in the heart? Or when does one not have the sun and the day, for whom Christ is sun and day?

So let us who are always in Christ, that is in the light, not cease praying even at night. . . . Let us, beloved brethren, who are always in the light of the Lord . . . count the night as day. Let us believe that we walk always in the light. Let us not be hindered by the darkness which we have escaped, let there be no loss of prayers in the night hours. . . . Let us, who by God's indulgence are recreated spiritually and reborn, imitate what we are destined to be. Let us who in the kingdom are to have only day with no intervening night, be as vigilant at night as in the light [of day]. Let us who are to pray always and render thanks to God, not cease here also to pray and give thanks.

## Morning Praise

These symbols have remained an integral part of the fabric of Christian daily prayer. Dietrich Bonhoeffer, a twentieth-century martyr whom no one could accuse of being cut off from modern culture and the agonies of contemporary history, speaks of common Christian morning prayer in terms with which the Cyprians and the Clements, the Basils and the Benedicts, would have been completely at ease:

The Old Testament day begins at evening and ends with the going down of the sun. It is the time of expectation. The day of the New Testament Church begins with the break of day and ends with the dawning light of the next morning. It is the time of fulfillment, the resurrection of the Lord. At night, Christ was born, a light in darkness; noonday turned to night when Christ suffered and died on the Cross. But in the dawn of Easter morning Christ rose in victory from the grave. . . . Christ is the "Sun of righteousness," risen upon the expectant congregation (Mal 4:2), and they that love him shall "be as the sun when he goeth forth in his might" (Judg 5:31). The early morning belongs to the Church of the risen Christ. At the break of light it remembers the morning on which death and sin lay prostrate in defeat and new life and salvation were given to mankind.

What do we today, who no longer have any fear or awe of night, know of the great joy that our forefathers and the early Christians felt every morning at the return of light? If we were to learn again something of the praise and adoration that is due the triune God at break of day, God the Father and Creator, who has preserved our life through dark night and wakened us to a new day, God the Son and Saviour, who conquered death and hell for us and dwells in our midst as Victor, God the Holy Spirit, who pours the bright gleam of God's Word into our hearts at the dawn of day, driving away all darkness and sin and teaching us to pray aright—then we would also begin to sense something of the joy that comes when night is past and brethren who dwell together in unity come together early in the morning for common praise of their God, common hearing of the Word, and common prayer. Morning does not belong to the individual, it belongs to the Church of the triune God, to the Christian family, to the brotherhood. . . .

Common life under the Word begins with common worship at the beginning of the day. . . . The deep stillness of morning is broken first by the prayer and song of the fellowship. . . .

For Christians, the beginning of the day should not be burdened and oppressed with besetting concerns for the day's work. At the threshold of the new day stands the Lord who made it. All the darkness and distraction of the dreams of night retreat before the clear light of Jesus Christ and his wakening Word. All unrest, all impurity, all care and anxiety flee before him. Therefore, at the beginning of the day let all distraction and empty talk be silenced and let the first thought and first word belong to him to whom our whole life belongs. "Awake thou that sleepest, and arise from the dead, and Christ shall give thee light" (Eph 5:14).[20]

And so at the start of the day we do as Jesus did (Mark 1:35), we begin the day with prayer. In morning praise we renew our commitment to Christ by consecrating the day through thanks and praise. And the hour provides our symbols. The rising sun, one of the ongoing marvels of God's creation, a source of life and food, warmth and light, leads spontaneously to praise and thanks, and to prayer for protection throughout the day. And since we celebrate what we are, and our core reality is that we have been saved by the saving death and resurrection of Jesus, the rising sun calls to mind that true Sun of Justice in whose rising we receive the light of salvation. Another part of our celebration is the exercise of our priestly intercession for the whole world, for as Christ's body we share in his responsibilities, too.

As we saw in chapters 3–4, Basil (*Longer Rules* 37:3), Chrysostom (*Commentary on Ps 140; Baptismal Catecheses* VIII, 17), and the *Apostolic Constitutions* (VIII, 38–39) all make it clear that morning praise served

---

[20]D. Bonhoeffer, *Life Together* (San Francisco: Harper & Row, 1954) 40–43. I am grateful to my colleague John Allyn Melloh for this reference.

to consecrate the day to the works of God, to thank him for benefits received, especially the benefit of redemption in the rising of his Son, to rekindle our desire for him as a remedy against sin during the beginning day, and to ask continued help. In *Conference* 21:26 Cassian has Abbot Theonas exhort the monks at length on the same themes:[21]

> But what shall I say of the first fruits which surely are given by all who serve Christ faithfully? For when people waking from sleep and arising with renewed activity after their rest, before they take in any impulse or thought in their heart, or admit any recollection or consideration of business, consecrate their first and earliest thoughts as divine offerings, what are they doing indeed but rendering the first fruits of their produce through the High Priest Jesus Christ for the enjoyment of this life and a figure of the daily resurrection? And also when roused from sleep in the same way they offer to God a sacrifice of joy and invoke him with the first motion of their tongue and celebrate his name and praise, and throwing open, as the first thing [they do], the door of their lips to sing hymns to him, they offer to God the offices of their mouth; and to him also in the same way they bring the earliest offerings of their hands and steps, when they rise from bed and stand in prayer and before they use the services of their limbs for their own purposes, take to themselves nothing of their services, but advance their steps for his glory, and set them in his praise, and so render the first fruits of all their movements by stretching forth the hands, bending the knees, and prostrating the whole body. For in no other way can we fulfill what we sing in the psalm: "I anticipated the dawning of the day and cried out," and "My eyes have anticipated the break of day, that I might meditate on your words," and "In the morning shall my prayer come before you" (Pss 118:147–148; 87:14), unless after our rest in sleep when, as we said above, we are restored as from darkness and death to this light, we have the courage not to begin by taking for our own use any of all the services both of mind and body. . . . And many even of those who live in the world observe this kind of devotion with the utmost care, as they rise before it is light, or very early, and do not engage at all in the ordinary and necessary business of this world before hastening to church and striving to consecrate in the sight of God the first fruits of all their actions and doings.

---

[21]Trans. adapted from NPNF series 2, vol. 11, 513–514. Note in this passage how the ancients looked on sleep as a sort of death. On this see H. Bacht, "Agrypnia. Die Motive des Schlafentzugs im frühen Mönchtum," G. Pflug, B. Eckert, H. Friesenhahn (eds.), *Bibliothek-Buch-Geschichte.* Festschrift für K. Köster (Frankfurt/M: Vittorio Klostermann, 1977) 357–360.

EVENSONG

In the evening, after the day's work is done, we turn once more to
God in prayer. The passing of day reminds us of the darkness of Christ's
passion and death, and of the passing nature of all earthly creation. But
the gift of light reminds us again of Christ the light of the world. With
vespers we close the day, much as compline does in the later urban monastic offices. And as in morning prayer, the service of evensong closes
with intercessions for the needs of all humankind, and then in the collect
and final blessing we thank God for the graces of the day, above all for
the grace of the Risen Christ. We ask pardon for the sins of the day and
request protection during the coming night, for we are exhorted, "Do not
let the sun go down on your anger and give no opportunity to the devil
. . . let all bitterness and wrath and anger be put away from you, with
all malice, and be kind to one another, tenderhearted, forgiving one
another, as God in Christ forgave you"—and the motivation is clear: "for
we are members of one another" (Eph 4:25–32).

In *Longer Rules* 37:4 Basil emphasizes thanksgiving and confession of
the faults of the day as the purpose of the evening hour:

> And when the day is finished, thanksgiving should be offered for what
> has been given us during the day or for what we have done rightly,
> and confession made for what we have failed to do—an offence com-
> mitted, be it voluntary or involuntary, or perhaps unnoticed, either
> in word or deed or in the very heart—propitiating God in our prayers
> for all our failings. For the examination of past actions is a great
> help against falling into similar faults again.

The collect that concludes evensong in the *Apostolic Constitutions* VIII,
37 expresses a like spirit:

> O God . . . who has made the day for the works of light and the
> night for the refreshment of our infirmity . . . mercifully accept now
> this, our evening thanksgiving. You who have brought us through
> the length of the day and to the beginning of the night, preserve us
> by your Christ. Grant us a peaceful evening and a night free from
> sin, and give us everlasting life by your Christ. . . .

The second basic element of the rite of vespers in every tradition is
thanksgiving for the light, in which the Church uses the lamplighting at
sunset to remind us of the Johannine vision of the Lamb who is the eternal lamp of the Heavenly Jerusalem, the sun that never sets. We saw this already at the beginning of the second century in the domestic rite alluded
to by Tertullian in his *Apology* 39:18 and described in the *Apostolic Tra-*

*dition* 25, with its thanksgiving prayer at the bringing in of the evening lamp:

> We give you thanks, Lord, through your Son Jesus Christ our Lord, through whom you have shone upon us and revealed to us the inextinguishable light. So when we have completed the length of the day and have come to the beginning of the night, and have satisfied ourselves with the light of day which you created for our satisfying; and since now through your grace we do not lack the light of evening, we praise and glorify you through your Son Jesus Christ our Lord, through whom be glory and power and honour to you with the holy Spirit, both now and always and to the ages of ages. Amen.

Chrysostom in Antioch does not mention a lucernarium, but he insists more than once on the theme of penance and reconciliation at evensong:

> . . . let each one go to his affairs with fear and trembling, and so pass the daytime as one who is obliged to return here in the evening to give the master an account of the entire day and ask pardon for failures. For it is impossible even if we are ten thousand times watchful to avoid being liable for all sorts of faults. . . . And that is why every evening we must ask the master's pardon for all these faults. . . . Then we must pass the time of night with sobriety and thus be ready to present oneself once again at the morning praise . . . (*Baptismal Catecheses* VIII, 17–18).[22]

Indeed, repentance is the reason why the Fathers chose Ps 140 for vespers, according to Chrysostom's *Commentary on Ps 140*, 1: "They ordered it to be said as a salutary medicine and forgiveness of sins, so that whatever has dirtied us throughout the whole length of the day . . . we get rid of it in the evening through this spiritual song. For it is indeed a medicine that destroys all those things."[23]

For Chrysostom, then, vespers is basically a penitential service and, we might add, an efficacious one, for the forgiveness humbly requested is, in fact, granted. In the Eastern traditions the oblation of incense that accompanies this vesperal psalm (inspired undoubtedly by verse 2: "Let my prayer rise like incense before you, the lifting up of my hands like the evening sacrifice.") has a penitential meaning referring to our self-offering of repentance rising with our prayers and uplifted hands.

[22]Ed. Wenger (SC 50) 256–257.
[23]PG 55, 427.

## ESCHATOLOGICAL PRAYER

The request for protection during the darkness of night has eschato-logical overtones. We know not the day nor the hour (Matt 24:36; 25:13); death comes like a thief in the night (1 Thess 5:2; 2 Pet 3:10; Rev 3:3; 16:15); the bridegroom comes at night and we must be found waiting, lamps in hand (Matt 25:1-13). This is a standard theme of night prayer; so is the cosmic theme of those at vigil joining their voices to those of the angels and all creation in praise of God, as in the *Benedicite* of Daniel, while the world sleeps.

Canon 27 of the *Canons of Hippolytus* from Egypt around 336-340 expresses this eschatological theme, showing how it forms the bridge unit-ing evening and morning prayer, which, once again, like all liturgy, are simply moments expressive of the ceaseless hymn of praise that is Chris-tian life:

> Let each one take care to pray with great vigilance in the middle of the night, for our fathers have said that at that hour all creation is assiduous in the service of praising God, all the angelic hosts and the souls of the just bless God. For the Lord testifies to this saying, "In the middle of the night there was a cry: Behold, the bridegroom has come, go out to meet him" (Matt 25:6). At cockcrow, again, is a time when there are prayers in the churches, for the Lord says, "Watch, for you do not know at what time the Master will come, in the eve-ning, or in the middle of the night, or at cockcrow, or in the morning" (Mark 13:35), which means we must praise God at every hour. And when a man sleeps on his bed, he must pray to God in his heart.[24]

It should be clear from these texts that the earliest tradition of non-Eucharistic public prayer had nothing to do with theories of the "sancti-fication of time," with *kairos* and *chronos*, with a liturgy of "time" or "history" as distinct from the "eschatological" Eucharist. Rather, the morn-ing office dedicates the new day to God, and the evening office at the close of day leads us to reflect on the hours just passed, with thanksgiving for the good they have brought and sorrow for the evil we have done.

Note the limpid simplicity of the early Church's liturgical theology reflected in the basic structure and spirit of morning praise and evensong. Like all prayer in both the Old and New Testaments, they are a glorifica-tion of God that wells up from the joyful proclamation of his saving deeds: "The almighty has done great things for me! Holy is his name!" (Luke 1:49). This is the core of biblical prayer: remembrance, praise, and thanksgiving—and these can then flow into petition for the continuance

[24]PO 31, 397.

of this saving care in our present time of need. Remembrance, anamnesis, is also at the heart of all ritual celebration, for celebrations are celebrations *of* something: through symbol and gesture and text we render present—proclaim—once again the reality we feast.

In the early liturgical tradition this reality is one unique event, the paschal mystery in its totality, the mystery of Christ and of our salvation in him. This is the meaning of baptism; it is the meaning of Eucharist; it is the meaning of the Office as well. The anamnesis of the Christ-event is the wellspring of all Christian prayer. This is still reflected in the proper of the Byzantine Office found in the daily cycle of the *Oktoechos:* the texts are all focused squarely on the paschal mystery of salvation. Here for example are some of the refrains of the Byzantine Office for Saturday vespers, tone 3:

Everything has been enlightened by your Resurrection, O Lord, and Paradise has been opened again; all creation, extolling you, offers to you the perpetual hymn of praise.

We bow down in worship before your precious Cross, O Christ, and we praise and glorify your Resurrection: for it is by your wounds that we have been healed.

We praise the Savior, incarnate of a Virgin: for he was crucified for us and rose on the third day, giving us the great mercy.

The Christ, having descended among those who were in Hell, proclaimed, saying: "Take courage, I have conquered. I am the Resurrection and I shall lead you away, after having destroyed the gates of death."

We, who unworthily stay in your pure house, intone the evening hymn, crying from the depths: "O Christ our God, who have enlightened the world with your Resurrection, free your people from your enemies, you who love humankind."

O Christ, who through your Passion have darkened the sun, and with the light of your Resurrection have illumined the universe: accept our evening hymn of praise, O you who love humankind.

Your life-giving Resurrection, O Lord, has illumined the whole world, and your own creation, which had been corrupted, has been called back. Therefore, freed from the curse of Adam, we cry: "O Lord almighty, glory to you."

You underwent death, O Christ, so that you might free our race from death; and having risen from the dead on the third day, you raised with you those that acknowledge you as God, and you have illumined the world. O Lord, glory to you.[25]

[25]Trans. adapted from A. Nadson, *The Order of Vespers in the Byzantine Rite* 42–43.

It is incorrect, then, to view the Divine Office as primarily "historical" rather than "eschatological." Theologically the coming of Christ is one indivisible event, though it can intersect with human history at different points in time. The eschaton, the final fulfillment of history, has already occurred in Christ. The time of the kingdom, the beginning of the final days, is already begun. In *all* true Christian worship the basic emphasis must *always* be on this eschatological element; on salvation history, yes, but as one indivisible, eternally present reality which is the Kingdom of God in its fulness in the Passover of Christ.

Hence the Liturgy of the Hours, like all Christian liturgy, is an eschatological proclamation of the salvation received in Christ, and a glorification and thanksgiving to God for that gift. In this original and primitive sense the Liturgy of the Hours—indeed, all liturgy—is beyond time. For the Christian there is really no sacred space, no sacred persons or times: all are redeemed in Christ, for whom only God is holy, and those to whom he has given his sanctification, his saints, i.e., his people.

The later development of the Christian calendar and its proper introduced into the offices historical commemorations of individual events in salvation history. But that must not be allowed to obscure the original purity of the meaning of primitive Christian morning and evening prayer, which was not an "historical commemoration" nor a "liturgy of time" as opposed to the "eschatological, beyond-time" service of the Eucharist. Both were and are a praise of the same God for the same reason: Christ.

Christians by faith had the supreme joy of knowing that they lived a new life in Christ, a life of love shared with all of the same faith. What could have been more normal then, than for those who were able to gather at daybreak to turn the first thoughts of the day to this mystery of their salvation and to praise and glorify God for it? And at the close of day they came together once again to ask forgiveness for the failings of the day and to praise God once more for his mighty deeds. In this way the natural rhythm of time was turned into a hymn of praise to God and a proclamation before the world of faith in his salvation in Christ.

## The Office as a Celebration of Our Life in Christ

The Liturgy of the Hours, then, is a sanctification of life by turning to God at the beginning and end of each of its days to do what all liturgy always does—to celebrate and manifest in ritual moments what is and must be the constant stance of our every minute of the day: our unceasing priestly offering, in Christ, of self, to the praise and glory of the Father in thanks for his saving gift in Christ.

For Christian ritual is distinguished not only by its eschatological fulfillment and its sacramental realism; it is also distinct in that it is but the external expression of what is present within us. Salvation is an interior reality implying a whole way of life. So true Christian ritual is the opposite of magical rituals, which concentrate on the working of *things*. Christian ritual is *personalistic*: the purpose of Eucharist is not to change bread and wine, but to change you and me. And so our liturgy must be an expression of the covenant in our hearts, a celebration of what we are. Otherwise it is an empty show.

Hence in the liturgy there is a constant dialectic between celebration and life. For if we do not live what we celebrate, our liturgy is a meaningless expression of what we are not. As we saw in the New Testament, especially in St. Paul, the true cult of the Christian is interior. It is the life of self-oblation in charity, a life, like Christ's, that is lived in loving service—in short, a life of self-giving. Paul tells the Corinthians that their Eucharist is in fact no Eucharist at all because the mystery of communion, that is, unity in Christ, which Eucharist expresses was not lived in their lives (1 Cor 11:17-34).

That mystery is a mystery of self-offering, a giving of self for others, in obedience to the will of the Father, who has shown us, in Christ, that this is the only life worthy of human persons. This is what St. Paul means in Rom 12:1: "I implore you by God's mercy to offer your very selves to him: a living sacrifice, consecrated and fit for his acceptance; *this is your authentic worship.*"

In the present dispensation there is of course only one acceptable sacrifice, that of Christ. But his offering needs to be filled up. We must fill up what is wanting in the sacrifice of Christ (see Col 1:24). This does not mean that Christ's salvific work was defective. Rather, it remains incomplete until all men and women have freely entered into Christ's offering, making their lives, too, a Christian oblation. This offering is pleasing in the sight of God only because Christ has made us his body, so that our offering is joined to his and transformed by it.

We make this offering in every act of our Christian lives. We do it when our faith is expressed in charity, as in Heb 13:15-16: "Through Jesus . . . let us continually offer up to God the sacrifice of praise, that is the tribute of lips which acknowledge his name, and never forget to show kindness and to share what you have with others; *for such are the sacrifices which God approves.*" We also offer liturgy when we proclaim our faith. In Phil 2:17 Paul speaks of "that liturgical sacrifice which is your faith." In Rom 1:9 he says "I worship God with my person, proclaiming the gospel of his Son," and in 15:16, "My priestly service is the announcing of the good news of God."

This is why we are all priests: as Christians it is of the very essence of our lives to *offer*. And all we have to offer is ourselves, in witness to our faith, professing it before others and living it through love. 1 Pet 2:2 says: "You are a chosen race, a royal priesthood, a dedicated nation, a people claimed by God for his own, to proclaim the triumphs of him who has called you out of darkness into his marvelous light."

Hence for the New Testament there is no separation between liturgy and life. Our Christian life *is* our liturgy. That is why the New Testament uses liturgical and priestly vocabulary for two things only: 1) for Christ and his offering; 2) for all of us and the offering of our lives. For the Christian, then, worship, sacrifice, liturgy, are a life of faith and fraternal love— i.e., surrender to God and service of others. And these two, faith and charity, are really one. For by faith we see the world as the place where God's love is active and given to each person in a unique way, and hence we see each one as lovable. To say "yes" to God and "no" to people is impossible for the Christian. "If anyone says, 'I love God', and hates his brother, he is a liar" (1 John 4:20). Worship, then, is not a department of life; it is life itself.

All true Christian liturgy is a celebration of that reality. Thus the offices at the beginning and end of the day are but ritual moments symbolic of the whole of time. As such they are a proclamation of faith to the world and partake of our mission to witness to Christ and his salvation. They are also a praise and thanksgiving for this gift of salvation in Christ. Lastly, they are our priestly prayer, as God's priestly people, for our needs and those of the entire world.

## The Spirit of the Monastic Office

The *Apostolic Constitutions* II, 59 cited at the beginning of this chapter exhorts the congregation to be present regularly at the offices of morning prayer and evensong as well as at the Sunday vigil and Eucharist. It states explicitly that this exhortation is directed not just to the clergy but to the laity as well.

This passage is important to counteract a common misconception, often expressed in modern documents on the office: the notion that certain categories and groups in the Church are "deputed" to pray the office in the Church's name. When presbyters and deacons are ordained today in the Roman Rite they are asked to pray the hours for the Church. I think it important to understand such later notions within the context of the early tradition. One can and must pray *for* everyone, including the Church and her needs and intentions. But no one can pray *in place of* anyone else, like some living prayer wheel that spins on vicariously while the world goes about its business. Some can be called to assume freely the obligations of a life more totally dedicated to prayer in common, but not in the sense that they are "official pray-ers" for others who thereby can consider themselves freed from the evangelical command to pray. The burden of common prayer is incumbent on all.

Many post-Vatican II Latin Catholic clergy consider the canonical obligation to recite the breviary the result of a later, Tridentine legalism ill-suited to our "modern" mentality. The truth of the matter is somewhat different. The privatization of the office into a breviary-become-clerical-prayerbook is certainly not traditional, for traditionally the Liturgy of the Hours is something a *group celebrates*, not something an *individual reads*. The narrowing of this further into a grave canonical obligation was still a later development in the Latin Church, in a period when her life found expression in the multiplication of canonical legislation. But it is not at all untraditional that attendance in common at the main cathedral hours be considered obligatory. The novelty is to think that *only* the clergy is obliged. In the early Church it was just as much an obligation of the priest's wife or grandmother as of the priest himself. What is untraditional, therefore, is not the *obligation* of the office, but its *clericalization*. As with so much else in the history of the Church, what was once the property of the entire People of God has degenerated into a clerical residue, only reminiscent of what it was meant to be.

But what of the monastic hours? Does this not contradict what we have so often heard concerning the purpose of the obligation of choir? Surely the monastic orders are deputed to offer the official cult in the name of the whole Church?

According to Dom Adalbert de Vogüé, in chapter 8 of his classic commentary on the *Rule of St. Benedict* concerning the meaning of the Divine Office, no early monk at his prayers had any idea of "performing an act in the name of the Church."[26] This purely Latin notion is largely the result of urban monasticism in the West from the fifth–sixth centuries, when monastic communities served major city sanctuaries such as the great Roman basilicas, and were responsible for the cult. This eventually results in the Cluniac *"monachus propter chorum"* ideology, and

[26]*La Règle de s. Benôit* VII, 193ff. (English trans. CS 54, 139).

passed into the Benedictine revival literature of modern times, as in the following citation from Delatte's 1913 commentary on the Benedictine Rule:

> The proper and distinctive work of the Benedictine, his lot in life, his mission, is the liturgy. He makes his profession in order to be in the Church a society of divine praise, one who glorifies God according to the forms instituted by the Church, she who knows how to glorify the Lord. . . .[27]

But the earliest monks had no such "liturgical mystique," which owes more to the neo-Gothic religious revival of nineteenth-century romanticism than to the Fathers of the Church. The meaning of the word "monk" is an enemy of such distinctions. For the early monk, life was one continual prayer, with no compartmentalization of life into "liturgical" prayer and other kinds of prayer and work. The one rule was the absolute primacy of the spiritual in the everyday lives of these men. The monastic movement began in the second half of the third century with the "solitaries," but the original meaning of *monachos* is not living alone, but living without a wife. Its motivation is the need for a "unified" heart: "Teach me your way, O Lord, that I may walk in your truth; *unite my heart* to fear your name. I give thanks to you . . . with my whole heart" (Ps 86:11–12).

According to 1 Cor 7:32, the married person is "divided" *(memeristai)* by family cares; the monk is dedicated to God's service "undividedly," with no other aim or task in life.[28] "Single-mindedness" is the characteristic of the monk, and the aim of this unilateral existence was the life with God, a life lived through unceasing prayer. So the monks prayed while they worked and worked while they prayed. Wherever they were, refectory, oratory, workshop, cell, the differences were only accidental. What they sought ultimately was what modern spiritual writers would call a *state of prayer*,[29] a degree of spiritual perfection known to the hesychast movement in the Byzantine East, in which one's every breath, one's very existence is a continuous prayer not subject to fragmentation into successive acts, nor to interruption by external activities.

Necessary activities such as eating forced the early monk to interrupt his *offices*, his psalmody, his prostrations; but he *never* interrupted his *prayer!* So the rule was not, as today, to fix a *minimum* number of hours for prayer, and give the rest of the time to other occupations, but to fix

---

[27]Cited *ibid.* 196 (English trans. CS 54, 134); cf. the similar opinions cited on p. 197.

[28]A. Guillaumont, "Perspectives actuelles sur les origines du monachisme," *id., Aux origines du monachisme chrétien* 218–223.

[29]See Hausherr, "Comment priaient les pères," 39ff.

a *maximum* amount of time to be grudgingly accorded to such physical necessities as sleep, and give the rest to prayer. God is all, and demands not part of our time but all of it. The *monachos* was the unilateral, the undistracted one, with a one-track mind, tuned in to God alone.

Indeed in a certain sense one can say that the early anchorites lived liturgy rather than celebrating it. Life seems to have replaced liturgy except for the weekend services which they had in common with all Christians. The rest of the time their whole life was a living prayer. Only later does the monastic office get detached from the rest of life and become an "obligation," a *pensum* to be got through whenever one can.

Later, too, is the notion of the monastic office as a "public cult." It is evident from the documents cited in chapter 4 that originally monastic psalmody was God's Word to us, as de Vogüé has pointed out.[30] The monks' psalms were not chants of praise in the mouth of the Church, as in cathedral prayer, but God's Word on which to meditate before turning to him with prayerful response. Only later is the monastic psalmody seen as the Church's prayer to God, our message to him, thus approaching the cathedral notion of morning praise and evensong. We see this shift already in the pre-Benedictine *Rule of the Master* 47. Of course the two ideas are not opposed, for God is indeed glorified in the liturgy by us— but only insofar as we are sanctified by his grace, for our glorification of him is his gift to us, not ours to him. But this shift of accent is worth noting, for we thus arrive at a cultic notion of monastic psalmody that is simply not found in monastic texts of the late fourth and early fifth century. The earliest monastic prayer expressed a spirituality different from that which animated cathedral hours. The whole of cenobitic life was a communion, and hence also a communion in prayer, but the early cenobites had no notion whatever of participating in an "official" prayer of the Church.

So there is originally a slightly different orientation in the two spiritualities of the Prayer of Hours. But they eventually come together in urban monasticism, so that today I think it is legitimate to say that the differences are more in style than in substance, more in the structure and aim of the offices than in their theologies. The vocation of all Christians, not just monks, is to be a living prayer, and long-standing tradition has also taught monks that their praise of God is part of the official *leitourgia* of the Church. By vocation they are privileged to give more frequent common symbolic expression to what, ideally, must be the rhythm of the whole of every Christian life: a prayerful, continuous communion with the living God and with one another in him.

[30]*La Règle de s. Benôit* VII, 209–221 (English trans. CS 54, 139–149).

This theology of the monastic office is expressed in the *Preface* of the post-Vatican II *Thesaurus liturgiae horarum monasticae* issued by the confederation of Benedictine congregations in 1976. The "Dei" of *Opus Dei,* as I. Hausherr has shown, is an objective as well as subjective genitive: a work of God in us before it is a work we do in response to his call.[31] Hence the monks' prayer is *contemplative praise,* for the monastic hours repeatedly commemorate the motive for our praise in God's great works, and the monk contemplates it and glorifies him for it: "The almighty has done great things for me—holy is his name!" in the words of Mary's *Magnificat* (Luke 1:49) that we have already used to sum up the whole dynamic of liturgical anamnesis and thankful praise.

[31]"Opus Dei," *Monastic Studies* 11 (1975) 195ff.

# 22

# THE LITURGY OF THE HOURS AS THE
# CHURCH'S SCHOOL OF PRAYER

The Divine Office is said to have a superior value over other forms of prayer because it is approved by the Church, and that is perfectly true. As the prayer of the Church it is the prayer of Christ himself, the full Christ, head and members, and this fact alone gives a transforming value to our prayer that it cannot have when done alone. For it is in our common prayer that the Church is most fully and visibly Church: ". . . at your meetings let there be one prayer, one supplication, one mind, one hope in love, in the blameless joy that is Jesus Christ. . . . Come together all of you as to one temple of God and to one altar, to one Jesus Christ . . .," Ignatius of Antioch exhorts in his *Letter to the Magnesians* 6-7.

But that does not answer the question why the Church has blessed precisely *this* form of prayer as her daily prayer *par excellence.* Undoubtedly many reasons could be advanced to prove the excellence of the office, but three stand out in my mind: the Divine Office is biblical, objective, traditional prayer.

## I. TRADITIONAL

We can dispense quickly with the last quality, for we have already seen abundant proof of it. The Liturgy of the Hours is traditional—and by that I do not mean "conservative" or "traditionalistic"—in that it has stood the test of time in every Church in Christendom that can with any historical seriousness lay claim to an ancient liturgical tradition. It is a form of prayer shared by Catholics Roman and Eastern, Orthodox Eastern and Oriental, Anglicans, Episcopalians, Lutherans, and others, in one form or another, from the early centuries right up until our own day. That is a very respectable track record, one that the Church could not ignore and remain true to its heritage.

## II. BIBLICAL

More important, even if the Divine Office evolved only gradually during the early Christian centuries, the pattern of this prayer goes back to the New Testament itself. When the early Christian community gathered for prayer, it remembered God's mighty deeds and glorified him for them. It prayed especially for the accomplishment of his holy will (Col 1:13-14; 4:2; Phil 1:3-11). It committed itself again to the covenant with God in Christ. It prayed "marana-tha," and "Thy kingdom come," for the fulfillment of the end of the ages. All these elements are still operative in the Liturgy of the Hours.

## III. OBJECTIVE

The final characteristic, objectivity, is really the result of the first two. The aim of Christian life is to enter ever more fully into the mystery of Jesus Christ, the New Adam, paradigm of the re-created humankind. As a memorial of this mystery, the Liturgy of the Hours is a true and efficacious encounter with the Father through Jesus in the Spirit, as long as our hearts remain open to respond in faith to this ecclesial sign of the unending divine call echoing through the ages in the rites of the Church.

Because of this objectivity, the office is the Church's own school of prayer, a novitiate in which she teaches her age-old ways of how to glorify God in Christ as Church, together as one body, in union with and after the example of her head. No other form of prayer is so rooted in the mysteries of salvation history as they are unfolded day by day in the Church's annual cycle. Through this constant diet of Sacred Scripture not only does God speak his Word to us, not only do we contemplate over and over again the central mysteries of salvation, but our own lives are gradually attuned to this rhythm, and we meditate again and again on this history of Israel, recapitulated in Jesus, that is also the saga of our own spiritual odyssey. The march of Israel across the horizon of history is a metaphor for the spiritual pilgrimage of us all.

Furthermore, our own response to this prophetic word in our lives is also revealed. In the psalms we answer God in his very own prayers. This gives the Divine Office a concentration on the essential rather than the peripheral; it gives it a balance insofar as its rhythms are set by the Church and not by our own subjectivity. How much penance, how much festivity, how much contrition, how much praise, how much petition and how much thanks should our prayer contain? It is all right there in the age-old pedagogy of the Church's offices. How much devotion to the Mother of God, how much fasting, how much attention to the saints, how much to the mysteries of Jesus' earthly life? The Divine Office with its seasonal and festive propers has it all.

This gives a balanced and objective comprehensiveness to the Church's prayer that is a sure remedy for the one-sided excess and exaggerations of a subjective devotionalism that puts all its emphasis on only those aspects of the life of prayer that happen to have personal appeal to the individual at some given moment, often for less than ideal reasons. St. Gertrude prayed *"ut devotio ipsius concordet cum officiis ecclesiae,"* that her piety might be in agreement with the offices of the Church. That is the sure guide that one is on the right path. For an objective ecclesial piety is not all penitential, not all Eucharistic nor all Marian nor all devotion to the passion. It is not *just* christological nor *just* Trinitarian. It is a balanced synthesis of all of this.[1]

Hence prayer according to the common offices of the Church is an unending school of prayer that constantly pulls us out of whatever bourgeois sentimentalism and inverted egoism there may be in our "private" devotions, and draws us inexhorably into the objective spiritual values of a life lived according to the mystery that is Christ. What St. Benedict says in his "Prologue" to the *Rule* about the monastery as a school for the service of the Lord can be applied equally to the Liturgy of the Hours, for the "Prologue" is nothing but a meditation on verses of Sacred Scripture and psalmody heard in the offices day in and day out. Niceta (d. after 414), bishop of Remesiana (Bela Palanka in Yugoslavia), discussing the usefulness of vigils in his treatise *On the Vigils of the Servants of God* 8, expounds a similar doctrine:

[1]Of course it would be ecclesiolatry to pretend that the Church has always maintained this proper balance in her liturgical uses, for she, too, lives within history. But from what I know of private attempts, past and present, at liturgical reform, I still prefer the inadequacies of Christ's Church to the fancies of individuals. The former have the advantage of being shared, and that is what liturgy is all about. And if the latter are right the Church will eventually come to see it.

I must turn now to the next point, as I promised, and say a word about their usefulness—although this can be better learned by experience than expressed in words. It would seem that we must ourselves "taste," as the Scripture has it, "how sweet is the Lord" (Ps 33:9). Only one who has tasted, understands and feels how great a weight is taken from our heart, what sloth is shaken from our minds when we watch, what light floods the soul of one who watches and prays, what a grace and presence fills every member with joy. By watching, all fear is cast out and confidence is born, the flesh is weakened, vices waste away and charity is strengthened, folly disappears and prudence takes its place, the mind is sharpened, error is blunted, the Devil, instigator of our sins, is wounded by the sword of the Spirit. Is there anything we need more than we do such advantages, any profit greater than such gains, anything sweeter than this joy or more blessed than this happiness? I need only call to witness the Prophet who in the beginning of his psalms describes the happy man and indicates his supreme felicity in this verse: "If he meditates on the law of the Lord day and night" (Ps 1:2).[2]

In this way the hours provide us with a framework that molds and feeds and moderates our private prayer, and which our private prayer in turn makes more interior and personal and intense. Any aspect of human life, if it is to be fruitful, demands framework and consistency. Those who accomplish the most work are usually those that keep to a schedule, that lead a reasonably regular life. The same is true in the spiritual life. Those who pray at the same time every day are the ones who pray every day. Otherwise things of the spirit often get lost in the shuffle of our other more mundane but seemingly more pressing daily obligations.

Furthermore, the hours have a great consoling and strengthening power for anyone with a sense of human history, a sense of the solidarity of humankind down through the ages, a sense of that much neglected article of the creed, the communion of saints. When we rise in the morning and come together to sing the praises of God at the dawn of a new day, when we celebrate at the coming of darkness our faith in the true light of the world at evensong, when we keep vigil with the angels and the heavenly bodies of the firmament while the world sleeps, we are doing, in obedience to the command to pray always, what men and women have done since the time of Jesus. In every time, in every land and from every race: in the privacy of the home, in desert or cave, in peasant hut and hermit cell, in Gothic choir or country chapel, in concentration camp or jungle mission-station; at every hour around the clock someone raises his or her voice

[2]Niceta of Remesiana, *Writings* (The Fathers of the Church, New York: The Fathers of the Church Inc., 1949) 62.

in the prayer of the Church, to join with the heavenly and earthly choirs down through the ages in the glorification of almighty God. In our age of narcissistic individualism one often hears people say they "don't get anything out of going to Church." What one "gets out of it" is the inestimable privilege of glorifying almighty God.

Of course to profit from the hours as a true spirituality, a school of prayer, one must be a person who prays and whose life is penetrated with the Scriptures. The Bible is a story of God's ceaseless calling, drawing, gathering, and of his people's constant waywardness. And the Fathers and monks of the early Church, in their meditation on this ever-repeated story, know that *they* were Abraham, *they* were Moses. *They* were called forth out of Egypt. *They* were given a covenant. They knew the wandering across the desert to the Promised Land was the pilgrimage of their life, too. The several levels of Israel, Christ, Church, us, are always there. And the themes of redemption, of exodus, of desert and faithful remnant and exile, of the Promised Land and the Holy City of Jerusalem, are all metaphors of the spiritual saga of our own lives.

The offices of the Church can be lived fully only by one whose life is permeated by such a *lectio divina* of the Bible. Contemporary biblical scholarship is rightly interested in the *Sitz im Leben* of what is recounted in the biblical text. But in the life of the Church there is also a *Sitz im Gottesdienst*, and in the spiritual life there is a *Sitz in meinem Leben*. As Jean Daniélou has said:

> The Christian faith has only one object, the mystery of Christ dead and risen. But this unique mystery subsists under different modes: it is prefigured in the Old Testament, it is accomplished historically in the earthly life of Christ, it is contained in mystery in the sacraments, it is lived mystically in souls, it is accomplished socially in the Church, it is consummated eschatologically in the heavenly kingdom. Thus the Christian has at his disposition several registers, a multidimensional symbolism, to express this unique reality. The whole of Christian culture consists in grasping the links that exist between Bible and liturgy, gospel and eschatology, mysticism and liturgy. The application of this method to Scripture is called exegesis; applied to liturgy it is called mystagogy. This consists in reading in the rites the mystery of Christ, and in contemplating beneath the symbols the invisible reality.[3]

St. Paul tells us, "Whatever was written in the past has been written for our instruction" (Rom 15:4). But it will not be for our instruction unless we constantly engage the biblical text in the personal dialogue of our

[3]My trans. from "Le symbolisme des rites baptismaux," *Dieu vivant* 1 (1945) 17.

private contemplation. For unless our psalmody is a response to such a *lectio divina*, a true *meditatio* in the original sense of slowly going over and over the revealed text to savor it in its depths in relation to ourselves, then of course the Divine Office will never reach its full meaning in our lives.

Just as the *lectio* penetrates our lives with a vision of human existence rooted in salvation history, the psalmody of the office is its cosmic and eschatological response. For it is in the office, above all, that we evoke that vision of a saved universe transformed into that hymn of cosmic praise before the throne of the Lamb read of in the final chapters of the New Testament (Rev 19—22):

> I heard what seemed to be the loud voice of a great multitude in heaven, crying, "Halleluiah! Salvation and glory and power belong to our God, for his judgments are true and just. . . . And from the throne came a voice crying, "Praise our God, all you his servants, you who fear him, small and great." Then I heard what seemed to be the voice of a great multitude . . . Halleluiah! For the Lord our God the Almighty reigns. Let us rejoice and exult and give him the glory, for the marriage of the Lamb has come, and his Bride has made herself ready. . . ." And the angel said to me, "Write this: Blessed are those who are invited to the marriage supper of the Lamb." . . .
>
> Then I saw a new heaven and a new earth; for the first heaven and the first earth had passed away, and the sea was no more. And I saw the holy city, new Jerusalem, coming down out of heaven from God, prepared as a bride adorned for her husband; and I heard a loud voice from the throne saying, "Behold, the dwelling of God is with men. He will dwell with them; and they shall be his people. . . . He will wipe away every tear from their eyes, and death shall be no more, neither shall there be mourning nor crying nor pain any more, for the former things have passed away." . . .
>
> And I saw no temple in the city, for its temple is the Lord God the Almighty and the Lamb. And the city has no need of sun or moon to shine upon it, for the glory of God is its light, and its lamp is the Lamb. By its light shall the nations walk; and the kings of the earth shall bring their glory into it, and its gates shall never be shut by day— and there shall be no night there; they shall bring into it the glory and the honor of nations. . . .
>
> Then he showed me the river of the water of life, bright as crystal flowing from the throne of God and of the Lamb through the middle of the street of the city; also, on either side of the river, the tree of life . . . and the leaves of the tree were for the healing of the nations. There shall no more be anything accursed, but the throne of God and of the Lamb shall be in it, and his servants shall worship him; they

shall see his face, and his name shall be on their foreheads. And night shall be no more; they need no light of lamp or sun, for the Lord God will be their light, and they shall reign for ever and ever.

This is what our end is to be, and the Liturgy of the Hours, like other symbols of Christian life, provides us with the awesome privilege of anticipating it now.

# Select Topical Bibliography

## 1. GENERAL AND EARLY:

Bacht, H. "Agrypnia. Die Motives des Schlafentzugs im frühen Monchtum." In *Bibliothek-Buch-Geschichte*. Kurt Köster zum 65. Geburtstag, ed. G Pflug and others, 353–369. Frankfurt: Vittorio Klostermann, 1977.

Baumstark, A. *Nocturna laus. Typen frühchristlicher Vigilienfeier und ihr Fortleben vor allem im römischen und monastischen Ritus*. Aus dem Nachlass hrsg. von O. Heiming. LQF 32. Münster: Aschendorff, 1956.

Beckwith, R. T. "The Daily and Weekly Worship of the Primitive Church in Relation to its Jewish Antecedents." In *Influences juives sur le culte chrétien*, R. T. Beckwith and others, 89–122. Textes et études liturgiques 4. Louvain: Mont César, 1981.

Bradshaw, P. *Daily Prayer in the Early Church*. ACC 63. London: SPCK, 1981, and New York: Oxford, 1982.

_____. *The Origins of the Daily Office*. Alcuin Club Annual Reports, 1978.

Calati, B., and others. *La preghiera nel tempo. Introduzione alla liturgia delle ore*. Quaderni di Vita monastica 7 (= *Vita monastica* 123, Oct.–Dec., 1975; 124–125, Jan.–June, 1976). Camaldoli, 1976.

Msgr. Cassien, B. Botte, *La prière des heures*. Lex orandi 35. Paris: Cerf, 1963.

Chadwick, O. "The Origins of Prime." JTS 49 (1948) 178–182.

Dekkers, E. "Were the Early Monks Liturgical?" *Collectanea Cisterciensia* 22 (1960) 120–137.

de Vogüé, A. "Le sens de l'office divin." In ch. 8 of *La Règle de s. Benoît, VII: Commentaire doctrinal et spirituel*, 184–248. SC hors série. Paris: Cerf, 1977.

(*The Rule of St. Benedict. A Doctrinal and Spiritual Commentary.* Trans. J. B. Hasbrouck. CS 54, 127–172. Kalamazoo: Cistercian Publications, 1983).

Dugmore, C. W. *The Influence of the Synagogue upon the Divine Office.* ACC 45. Westminster: The Faith Press, 1964.

Froger, J. *Les Origins de Prime.* BEL 19. Rome: Edizioni liturgiche, 1946.

———. "Note pour réctifier l'interpretation de Cassien *Inst.* 3, 4; 6 proposé dans *Les Origines de Prime.*" ALW 2 (1952) 96–102.

Goltzen, H. "Nocturna laus. Aus Arbeiten zur Geschichte der Vigil." *Jahrbuch für Liturgik und Hymnologie* 5 (1960) 79–88.

Grisbrooke, W. J. "The Divine Office in Public Worship." *Studia liturgica* 8 (1971–1972) 129–168; 9 (1973) 3–18, 81–106.

Guillaumont, A. "Le problème de la prière continuelle dans le monachisme ancien." In *L'expérience de la prière dans les grands religions,* ed. H. Limet and J. Ries, 285–293. Homo religiosus 5. Louvain-la-Neuve: Centre d'histoire des religions, 1980.

Hadidian, D. Y. "The Background and Origin of the Christians Hours of Prayer." *Theological Studies* 25 (1964) 59–69.

Hanssens, J.-M. *Aux origines de la prière liturgique. Nature et genèse de l'office des matines.* Analecta Gregoriana 57. Rome: Pontifical Gregorian University, 1952.

———. "Nature et genèse de matines." *Gregorianum* 34 (1953) 434–440.

———. "Nocturna Laus." *Gregorianum* 39 (1958) 747–756.

Hausherr, I. "Comment priaient les pères?" *Revue d'ascétique et de mystique* 32 (1956) 33–58, 284–296.

———. *The Name of Jesus.* CS 44. Kalamazoo: Cistercian Publications, 1978, ch. 3.

———. "Opus Dei." OCP 13 (1947) 195–218; English trans. in *Monastic Studies* 11 (1975) 181–204.

Heiming, O. "Die altmailändische Heiligenvigil." In *Heilige Überlieferung.* Festschrift I. Herwegen, ed. O. Casel, 174–192. Münster: Aschendorff, 1938.

———. "Zum monastischen Offizium von Kassianus bis Kolumbanus." ALW 7 (1961) 89–156.

Jeremias, J. "Daily Prayer in the Life of Jesus and the Primitive Church." In *The Prayers of Jesus,* 66–81. Studies in Biblical Theology, series 2, no. 6. London: SCM Press, 1974.

Jungmann, J. A. "The Origin of Matins." In *Pastoral Liturgy,* 105–122. New York: Herder, 1962.

Leeb, H. *Die Gesänge im Gemeindegottestdienst von Jerusalem (vom 5. bis 8. Jahrhundert).* Weiner Beiträge zur Theologie 28. Vienna: Herder 1970.

Marcora, G. *La vigilia nella liturgia. Ricerche sulle origini e primi sviluppi* (sec. I–VI). Archivo ambrosiano 6. Milan: Ambrosius, 1954.

Mateos, J. "The Morning and Evening Office." *Worship* 42 (1968) 31–47.

———. "Office de minuit et office du matin chez S. Athanase." OCP 28 (1962) 173–180.

_____."L'office dominical de la Résurrection." *Revue du clergé africain*, mai 1964, 263–288.

_____."L'office du soir. Ancienne structure et réalisations concrètes." *Revue du clergé africain*, jan. 1964, 3–25.

_____."L'office monastique à la fin du IV^e siècle: Antioche, Palestine, Cappadoce." OC 47 (1963) 53–88.

_____."The Origins of the Divine Office." *Worship* 41 (1967) 477–485.

_____. "Quelques anciens documents sur l'office du soir." OCP 35 (1969) 347–374.

_____. "Quelques aspects théologiques de l'office du matin." *Revue du clergé africain*, juillet 1965. 335–349.

_____. "La vigile cathédrale chez Egérie." OCP 27 (1961) 281–312.

Mearns, J. *The Canticles of the Christian Church Eastern and Western in Early and Medieval Times*. Cambridge: The University Press, 1914.

Raes, A. "Les complies dans les rites orientaux." OCP 17 (1951) 133–145.

Schneider, H. "Die biblischen Oden." *Biblica* 30 (1949) 28–65, 239–272, 433–452, 479–500.

Storey, W. G. "The Liturgy of the Hours: Cathedral vs. Monastery." *Worship* 50 (1976) 50–70.

Taft, R. *The Liturgy of the Hours in the Christian East: Origins, Meaning, Place in the Life of the Church*. Cochin, Kerala (India): K. C. M. Press, 1984.

_____. "Praise in the Desert: the Coptic Monastic Office Yesterday and Today." *Worship* 56 (1982) 130–158.

_____. "*Quaestiones disputatae* in the History of the Liturgy of the Hours: the Origins of Nocturns, Matins, Prime." *Worship* 58 (1984) 130–158.

_____. "*Thanksgiving for the Light*. Toward a Theology of Vespers." *Diakonia* 13 (1978) 27–50.

van der Mensbrugghe, A. "Fausses pistes de recherche sur les origines des vigiles et des matines." In *Überlieferungsgeschichtliche Untersuchungen*, ed. F. Paschke, 553–572. TU 125. Berlin: Akademie-Verlag, 1981.

_____. "Prayer Time in Egyptian Monasticism." *Studia Patristica* 2/2, 435–454. TU 64. Berlin: Akademie-Verlag, 1957.

Veilleux, A. *La liturgie dans le cénobitisme pachômien au quatrième siècle*. Studia Anselmiana 57. Rome: Herder, 1968.

Walker, J. Hazelden, "Terce, Sext and None. An Apostolic Custom?" *Studia Patristica* 5, 206–212. TU 80. Berlin: Akademie-Verlag 1962.

Winkler, G. "New Study of the Early Development of the Office." *Worship* 56 (1982) 27–35 (see also 56:264–267).

_____. "Das Offizium am Ende des 4. Jahrhunderts und das heutige chaldäische Offizium, ihre strukturellen Zusammenhänge." *Ostkirchliche Studien* 19 (1970) 289–311.

_____."Über die Kathedralvesper in den verschiedenen Riten des Ostens und Westens." ALW 16 (1974) 53–102.

_____. "Ungelöste Fragen im Zusammenhang mit den liturgischen Gebräuchen in Jerusalem," *Handes Amsorya* 101 (1987) 303–315.

Zerfass, R. *Die Schriftlesung im Kathedraloffizium Jerusalems*. LQF 48. Münster: Aschendorff, 1948.

## 2. ARMENIAN:

The Book of Hours or the Order of Common Prayers of the Armenian Apostolic Orthodox Church. Evanston: Ouzoomian House, 1964.

Breviarium Armenium sive dispositio communium Armeniacae Ecclesiae precum a sanctis Isaaco patriarcha, Mesrobio doctore, Kiudio atque a Joanne Mantagunensi habita. Venice: Mechitarist Press, 1908.

Conybeare, F. C. Rituale Armenorum, being the administration of the sacraments and the breviary rites of the Armenian Church . . . Oxford: Clarendon Press, 1905.

Raes, A. "Note sur les anciennes matines byzantines et arméniennes." OCP 19 (1953) 205–210.

Winkler, G. "The Armenian Night Office I." Journal of the Society for Armenian Studies 1 (1984) 93–113; II: Revue des études arméniennes n.s. 17 (1983) 471–551.

―――――. "Nochmals das armenische Nachtoffizium und weitere Anmerkungen zum Myrophorenoffizium," Revue des études arméniennes n.s. 21 (1988–1989) 501–519.

## 3. ASSYRO-CHALDEAN

Dalmais, I.-H. "Le thème de la lumière dans l'office du matin des Eglises syriennes-orientales." In Noël, Epiphanie, retour du Christ, ed. B. Botte and others, 257–276. Lex orandi 40. Paris: Cerf, 1967.

Gelineau, J. "Données liturgiques contenues dans les sept madrošé 'de la nuit' de saint Ephrem." OS 5 (1960) 107–121.

Husmann, H. Die Melodien des chaldäischen Breviers Commune. OCA 178. Rome: PIO 1967.

―――――. "Die Tonarten der chaldäischen Breviergesänge." OCP 35 (1969) 215–248.

Jammo, S. H. "L'office du soir chaldéen au temps de Gabriel Qatraya." OS 12 (1967) 187–210.

Maclean, A. J. East-Syrian Daily Offices. London: Revington, Percival & Co., 1894.

―――――. "The East Syrian or Nestorian Rite. The Evening, Night and Morning Services with the Propria of the Liturgy, as said on the Feast of the Epiphany, from the Gazza of the Library of the Propaganda Fide in Rome." In F. C. Conybeare, Rituale armenorum, 298–388. Oxford: Clarendon Press, 1905.

Mateos, J. Lelya-Ṣapra. Les offices chaldéens de la nuit et du matin. OCA 156. Rome: PIO, 1976².

―――――. "Les différentes espèces de vigiles dans le rite chaldéen." OCP 27 (1961) 46–67.

―――――. "Les matines chaldéennes, maronites et syriennes." OCP 26 (1960) 51–73.

―――――. "Un office de minuit chez les chaldéens." OCP 25 (1959) 101–113.

―――――. "L'office divin chez les chaldéens." In La prière des heures, ed. Msgr. Cassien and B. Botte, 253–281. Lex orandi 35. Paris: Cerf, 1963.

―――――."L'office paroissial du matin et du soir dans le rite chaldéen." LMD 64 (1960). 65–89.

Molitor, J. *Chaldäisches Brevier. Ordinarium des ostsyrischen Stundengebets.* Düsseldorf: Patmos-Verlag, 1961.

Pathikulangara, V. "Divine Office in Malabar Liturgy." EL 88 (1974) 131–141.

Pudichery, S. *Ramsa. An Analysis and Interpretation of the Chaldean Vespers.* Dhamaram College Studies 9. Bangalore: Dhamaram College, 1972.

Taft, R. "On the use of the Bema in the East-Syrian Liturgy." *Eastern Churches Review* 3 (1970) 30–39.

Vellian, J. *East Syrian Evening Services.* Kottayam: Indian Institute for Eastern Churches, 1971.

Winkler, G. "Das Offizium am Ende des 4. Jahrhunderts und das heutige chaldäische Offizium, ihre strukturellen Zusammenhänge." *Ostkirchliche Studien* 19 (1970) 289–311.

4. WEST-SYRIAN AND MARONITE:

Baumstark, A. *Festbrevier und Kirchenjahr der syrischen Jakobiten.* Studien zur Geschichte und Kultur des Altertums, Bd. 3, Heft 3–5. Paderborn: F. Schöningh, 1910.

_____. "Das syrische-antiochenische Ferialbrevier." *Der Katholik* (1902) II: 401–427, 538–550; (1903) I: 43–54.

*The Book of Common Prayer of the Antiochian Syrian Church.* Trans. Bede Griffiths. New York: John XXIII Center, Fordham University, n. d.

Breydey, M. "L'édition Assémanienne du bréviaire maronite. Histoire et valeur obligatoire." OC 42 (1958) 105–109.

_____. *L'office divin dans l'église syro-maronite.* Beyrouth: Imprimerie catholique, 1960.

_____. *Kult, Dichtung und Musik im Wochenbrevier der Syro-Maroniten.* 3 vols. Kobayath, Lebanon, 1971.

Brock, S. "The Fenqito of the Monastery of Mar Gabriel in Tur 'Abdin." *Ostkirchliche Studien* 28 (1979) 168–182.

Cody, A. "The Early History of the Octoechos in Syria." In *East of Byzantium: Syria and Armenia in the Formative Period,* ed. N. G. Garsoïan, T. F. Mathews, and R. W. Thomson, 89–113. Washington: Dumbarton Oaks, 1982.

_____. "L'eucharistie et les heures canoniales chez les Syriens jacobites. Une description des cérémonies." OS 12 (1967) 55–81, 151–186.

_____. "L'office divin chez les Syriens jacobites," POC 19 (1969) 293–319.

Dalmais, I.-H. "L'hymnographie syrienne." LMD 92 (1967) 63–72.

Francis Acharya, *Prayer with the Harp of the Spirit.* Vols. 1–3. Vagamon, Kerala (India): Kurisumala Ashram, 1980, 1982, 1985; 2d. ed. of vol. 1, 1983.

Gemayel, P. "La structure des vêpres maronites." OS 9 (1964) 105–134.

Heiming, O. *Syrische 'Eniānē und griechische Kanones.* LF 26. Münster: Aschendorff, 1922.

———. "Die 'Enajānēhirmen der Berliner Hs. Sachau 349." OC ser. 3, 5 (1930) 19–55.

Husmann, H. "Die melkitische Liturgie als Quelle der syrischen Qanune iaonaie. Melitene und Edessa." OCP 41 (1975) 5–56.

———. "Die syrischen Auferstehungskanones und ihre griechischen Vorlagen." OCP 38 (1972) 209–242.

———. "Eine alteorientalische christliche Liturgie: altsyrisch-melkitisch." OCP 42 (1976) 156–196.

———. "Syrischer und byzantinischer Oktoechos. Kanones und Qanune." OCP 44 (1978) 65–73.

Jeannin, J. "L'Octoèchos syrien." OC n.s. 3 (1913) 177–298.

——— and Leclercq, J., "Octoèchos syrien." DACL 12, 1888–1900.

Mariani, B. *Breviarium syriacum seu Martyrologium syriacum saec. IV juxta cod. SM. Musaei Brit. Add. 12150 . . .* Rerum eccl. doc. Series minor: Subsidia studiorum 3. Rome/Freiburg: Herder, 1956.

Mateos, J. "Une collection syrienne de 'prières entre les marmyata.'" OCP 31 (1965) 53–75, 305–335.

———. "Le 'Gloria in excelsis' du début des offices maronites." OS 12 (1967) 117–121.

———. "L'invitatoire du nocturne chez les syriens et les maronites." OS 11 (1964) 353–366.

———. "Les matines chaldéennes, maronites et syriennes." OCP 26 (1960) 51–73.

———. "Prières initiales fixes des offices syrien, maronite et byzantin." OS 11 (1966) 488–498.

———. "Prières syriennes d'absolution du VIIᵉ-IXᵉ siècle." OCP 24 (1968) 252–280.

———. "Le ramšo maronite." In *De officio matutino et vespertino in ritibus orientalibus*, 60–69. Pro manuscripto. Rome: S. Anselmo, 1968–1969.

———. "'Sedre' et prières connexes dans quelques anciennes collections." OCP 28 (1962) 239–287.

———. "Les strophes de la nuit dans l'invitatoire du nocturne syrien." In *Mémorial Mgr. G. Khouri-Sarkis*, 71–81. Louvain: Imprimerie orientaliste, 1969.

———. "Trois recueils anciens de prooemia syriens." OCP 33 (1967) 457–482.

*The Prayer of the Faithful according to the Maronite Liturgical Year.* Ed. B. Gemayel. Vols 1–3. Brooklyn: Diocese of St. Maron, 1982, 1984, 1985. .

Puyade, J. "Composition interne de l'office syrien." OS 2 (1957) 77–92; 3 (1985) 25–62.

———. "Les heures canoniales syriennes et leur composition." OS 3 (1958) 401–428.

Raes, A. "Les deux composantes de l'office divin syrien." OS 1 (1956) 66–75.

Tabet, J. "L'eschatologie dans l'office commun maronite." *Parole de l'Orient* 2 (1971) 5–30.

———. *L'office commun maronite. Etude du lilyō et du ṣafrō.* Bibliothèque de l'Université S.-Esprit. Kaslik, Lebanon: Université S.-Esprit, 1972.

———. "Les trois prières variables au début des complies maronites." *Parole de l'Orient* 1 (1970) 11–26.

_____. "Le témoignage de Bar Hebraeus (+1286) sur la vigile cathédrale." *Melto* 5 (1969) 113–121.

_____. "Le témoignage de Sévère d'Antioche (+538) sur la vigile cathédrale." *Melto* 4 (1968) 6–12.


## 5. Coptic:

*The Agpeya,* being the Coptic Orthodox Book of Hours according to the present-day usage in the Church of Alexandria. Los Angeles: Sts. Athanasius and Cyril of Alexandria Orthodox Publications, 1982.

'Abdallah, A. *L'Ordinamento liturgico di Gabriele V, 88° Patriarca copto (1409–1427).* Studia orientalia christiana: Aegyptiaca. Cairo: Edizioni del Centro francescano di studi orientali christiani, 1962.

'Abd-al-Masih, A. "Doxologies in the Coptic Church." *Bulletin de la Société d'archéologie copte* 4 (1938) 97–113; 5 (1939) 175–191; 6 (1941) 19–76; 7 (1942) 31–61.

Ballin, C. *L'office copte. L'office des heures, l'offrande de l'incens, la psalmodie annuelle.* Unpublished licentiate thesis. Rome: PIO, 1979.

Baumstark, A. "Palästinensisches Erbe im byzantinischen und koptischen Horologion." *Rivista di studi bizantini e neoellenici* 6 (1940) 463–469.

Borsai, I. "Y a-t-il un *Octoechos* dans le système du chante copte?" In *Studia Aegyptiaca* I. Recueil d'études dédié a V. Wessetzky, 39–53. Budapest, 1974.

Brogi, M. *La santa salmodia annuale della chiesa copta.* Traduzione, introduzione e annotazione di Marco Brogi. Studia orientalia christiana: Aegyptiaca. Cairo: Edizioni del Centro francescano di studi orientali cristiani, 1962.

Burmester, O. H. E. "The Canonical Hours of the Coptic Church." OCP 2 (1936) 78–100.

_____. *The Egyptian or Coptic Church. A Detailed Description of her Liturgical Services and the Rites and Ceremonies observed in the Administration of her Sacraments,* 31–45, 96–111. Publications de la Société d'archéologie copte: textes et documents. Cairo: Printing Office of the French Institute of Oriental Archaeology, 1967.

_____. "Four Parchment Folios of a Bohairic Horologion from Scetis." *Bulletin de la Société d'archéologie copte* 17 (1963–1964) 49–56.

_____. "Fragments of a Ṣaʿidic Horologion from Scetis." *Bulletin de la Société d'archéologie copte* 18 (1965–1966) 23–45.

_____. "The Greek Kîrugmata. Versicles and Responses, and Hymns in the Coptic Liturgy." OCP 2 (1936) 363–394 (on the office, 387ff.).

_____. *The Horologion of the Egyptian Church.* Coptic and Arabic text from a medieval manuscript, translated and annotated. Studia orientalia christiana: Aegyptiaca. Cairo: Edizioni del Centro francescano di studi orientali cristiani, 1973.

_____. "The Ṭurūḥāt of the Coptic Church." OCP 3 (1937) 78–109.

_____. "The Ṭurūḥāt of the Coptic Year." OCP 3 (1937) 505–549.

———. "The Ṭurūḥāt of the Saints." *Bulletin de la Société d'archéologie copte* 4 (1938) 141–194; 5 (1939) 85–157.

Cramer, M. *Koptische Hymnologie in deutscher Übersetzung.* Wiesbaden: Harrassowitz, 1969.

———. *Koptische Liturgien. Eine Auswahl.* Sophia 11. Trier: Paulinus-Verlag, 1973.

———. "Monastische Liturgie in den koptischen Klostern." *Jahrbuch für Liturgiewissenschaft* 14 (1934) 230–242, esp. 235–240.

———. "Zum Aufbau der koptischen Theotokie und des Difnars. Bermerkungen zur Hymnologie." In *Probleme der koptischen Literatur,* ed. P. Nagel, 1.(K2), 197–223. Wissenschaftliche Beiträge der Martin-Luther-Universität Halle-Wittenberg, 1968.

Euringer, S. "Der mutmassliche Verfasser der koptischen Theotokien und des äthiopischen Weddâsê Mârjâm." OC n. s. 1 (1911) 215–226.

———. "Die Sonntagsteotokie; ein Marienhymnos der koptischen Kirche." *Passauer theologische-praktische Monatsschrift* 19 (1909) 407–412, 480–485.

Evelyn-White, H.G. *The Monasteries of the Wâdi 'n Natrûn,* part II: *The History of the Monasteries of Nitria and Scetis.* New York: The Metropolitan Museum of Art Egyptian Expedition, 1932.

Giamberardini, G. "Il *Sub tuum praesidium* e il titolo *Theotokos* nella tradizione egiziana." *Marianum* 31 (1969) 324–369.

———. *La croce e il crocifisso presso i Copti. Studia orientalia christiana: Collectanea* 7 (Cairo, 1962) 45–100 + Pl. v-xxx (on the office, 58–67, 71–80).

John, Marquis of Bute. *The Coptic Morning Service for the Lord's Day.* Christian Liturgies. London: Cope and Fenwick, 1908.

———. *The Coptic Morning Service for the Lord's Day.* Translated into English by John, Marquess of Bute, K. T., with the original Coptic of those parts said aloud. London, 1882.

Lauzière, M. E. "Les théotokies coptes." *Echos d'Orient* 39 (1940–1942) 312–327.

Malak, H. "Les livres liturgiques de l'église copte." In *Mélanges E. Tisserant,* vol. III. 2, 1–35. ST 233. Vatican: Typis polyglottis Vaticanis, 1964.

Mallon, A. "Les théotokies ou office de la Sainte Vierge dans le rite copte." *Revue de l'Orient chrétien* 9 (1904) 17–31.

Muyser, J. "Le 'Psali' copte pour la première heure du Samedi de la joie." *Le Muséon* 65 (1952) 175–184.

O'Leary, De Lacy. "The Coptic Theotokia." In *Coptic Studies in Honor of W. E. Crum,* 417–420. Bulletin of the Byzantine Institute 2. Boston: The Byzantine Institute, 1950.

———. *The Coptic Theotokia. Text from Vatican Cod. Copt. xxxviii, Bibl. Nat. copte 22, 23, 35, 69 and other MSS. including fragments recently found at the Dêr Abû Makâr in the Wadi Natrun.* London: Luzac & Co., 1923.

———. *The Daily Office and Theotokia of the Coptic Church.* London, 1910.

———. *The Difnar (Antiphonarium) of the Coptic Church,* 3 vols. London: Luzac & Co., 1926, 1928, 1930.

_____. "On a Directory Fragment recently Discovered in the Wadi n-Natrun." JTS 24 (1923) 428–432.

*La Prière quotidienne dans l'église copte.* Collection "Liturgie et catéchèse," cahier no. 4. Cairo: Institut catéchètique, n.d.

Quecke, H. "Dokumente zum koptischen Stundengebet." In *XVII. Deutscher Orientalistentag vom 21. bis 27. Juli 1968 in Würzburg,* 392–402. *Zeitschrift der Deutschen Morgenländischen Gesellschaft,* Supplementa 1. Wiesbaden, 1969.

_____. "Erhebet euch, Kinder des Lichtes!" *Le Muséon* 76 (1963) 27–45, 266.

_____. "Fragmente einer Handschrift des koptischen Horologions in den Bibliotheken zu Leipzig und Berlin (Cod. Tisch. XXI und Ms. or. fol. 2556g)." *Orientalia* n. s. 36 (1967) 305–322.

_____. "Neue griechische Parallelen zum koptischen Horologion." *Le Muséon* 77 (1964) 285–294.

_____. "Eine griechische Strophe in koptischer Überlieferung." OCP 32 (1966) 265–270.

_____. "Ein koptisch-arabisches Horologion in der Bibliothek des Katharinenklosters auf dem Sinai (Cod. Sin. ar. 389)." *Le Muséon* 78 (1965) 99–117.

_____. "Das *Sub tuum praesidium* . . . im koptischen Horologion." *Enchoria. Zeitschrift für Demotistik und Koptologie* 1 (1970).

_____. *Untersuchungen zum koptischen Stundengebet.* Publications de l'Institut orientaliste de Louvain 3. Louvain: Université catholique de Louvain, 1970.

Taft, R. "Praise in the Desert: the Coptic Monastic Office Yesterday and Today." *Worship* 56 (1982) 513–536.

Turaev, B. A. "K voprosu o proiskhozhdenii koptskikh Theotokia." *Vizantijskij Vremennik* 14 (1907) 189–190.

_____. "Paskhalnaja sluzhba Koptskoj Tserkvi," In *Commentationes Philologicae in Honour of E. B. Pomjalovskie.* St. Petersburg, 1897.

Uspenskij, Porfirij. *Verouchenie, bogosluzhenie, chinopoluzhenie i pravila-tserkovnago blagochenija egipetskikh khristian (Koptov).* St. Petersburg: Imp. Akad. Nauk, 1856.

Viaud, G. *La liturgie des coptes d'Egypte.* Paris: Maisonneuve, 1978.

Villecourt, L. "Les observances liturgiques et la discipline du jeûne dans l'Eglise copte (ch. XVI–XIX de la *Lampe des ténèbres)." Le Muséon* 36 (1923) 249–292; 37 (1924) 201–282; 38 (1925) 261–320.

6. Ethiopian:

Bolotov, V. Review of B. Turaev, *Chasoslov efiopskoj tserkvi. Khristianskoe chtenie* 205 (1898) 189–198.

Kidane, Habtemichael. *L'ufficio divino della Chiesa Etiopica.* Unpublished licentiate thesis. Rome: PIO, 1984.

Lepsia, T. "The Three Modes and the Signs of the Songs in the Ethiopian Liturgy." In *Proceedings of the Third International Conference of Ethiopian Studies,* Addis Ababa 1966, vol. 2, 162–187. Addis Ababa: Institute of Ethiopian Studies, Haile Selassie I University, 1970.

Salaville, S. "La prière de toutes les heures dans la littérature èthiopienne." In *id.*, *Studia orientali liturgico-theologica*, 170–185. Rome: EL, 1940.

Turaev, B. *Chasoslov efiopskoj tserkvi.* Izdal i perevël na osnavanii neskol'kikh rukopisej B. Turaev. Memoires de l'Académie impériale des sciences de St.-Pétersbourg, VIII$^e$ série, Classe historico-philologique, vol. 1, no. 7. St. Petersburg, 1897.

van Lantschoot, A. S. Congregazione "Pro Ecclesia Orientali" Prot. N. 293/1937: *Horologion Aethiopicum iuxta recensionem Alexandrinam Copticam.* Vatican: Typis polyglottis Vaticanis, 1940.

Velat, B. *Etudes sur le me'erāf: Commun de l'office divin éthopien. Introduction, traduction française, commentaire liturgique et musicale,* PO 33.

―――. *Ṣoma deggua,* PO 32/3–4: Introduction pp. vii–xviii.

## 7. BYZANTINE:

(The bibliography on the Byzantine office is enormous. The following is a selection of some of the older classics and most important recent works. For a more complete list, including translations of the offices, see the bibliography appended to R. Taft, "The Byzantine Office in the *Prayerbook* of New Skete" listed below.)

Arranz, M. "La liturgie des heures selon l'ancien Euchologe byzantin." In *Eulogia: Miscellanea liturgica in onore di P. Burkhard Neunheuser,* 1–19. Studia Anselmiana 68, Analecta liturgica 1. Rome: Editrice Anselmiana, 1979.

―――. "Le sacerdoce ministeriel dans les prières secrètes des vêpres et des matines byzantines." *Euntes docete* 24 (1971) 186–219.

―――. "Les grandes étapes de la Liturgie Byzantine: Palestine-Byzance-Russie. Essai d'aperçu historique." In *Liturgie de l'église particulière et liturgie de l'église universelle,* 43–72. BELS 7. Rome: Edizioni liturgiche, 1976.

―――. "Les prières presbytérales de la 'Pannychis' de l'ancien Euchologe byzantin et la 'Panikhida' des défunts." OCP 40 (1974) 314–343; 41 (1975) 119–139.

―――. "Les prières presbytérales de la Tritoektî de l'ancien Euchologe byzantin." OCP 43 (1977) 70–93, 335–354.

―――. "Les prières presbytérales des matines byzantines." OCP 37 (1971) 406–436; 38 (1972) 64–115.

―――. "Les prières presbytérales des Petites Heures dans l'ancien Euchologe byzantin." OCP 39 (1973) 29–82.

―――. "Les prières sacerdotales des vêpres byzantines." OCP 37 (1971) 85–124.

―――. "L'office de l'Asmatikos Hesperinos ('vêpres chantées') de l'ancien Euchologe byzantin." OCP 44 (1978) 107–130, 391–412.

―――. "L'office de l'Asmatikos Orthros ('matines chantées') de l'ancien Euchologe byzantin." OCP 47 (1981) 122–157.

―――. "L'office de la veillée nocturne dans l'Eglise grecque et dans l'Eglise russe." OCP 42 (1976) 117–155, 402–425.

_____. "N. D. Uspensky: The Office of the All-Night Vigil in the Greek Church and in the Russian Church." *St. Vladimir's Theological Quarterly* 24 (1980) 83–113, 169–195 (translation of the previous title).

Balfour, D. "La réforme de l'*Horologion*." *Irénikon* 7 (1930) 167–180.

Baumstark, A. "Palästinensisches Erbe im byzantinischen und koptischen Horologion." *Rivista di studi bizantini e neoellenici* 6 (1940) 463–469.

_____. "Das Typikon der Patmos-Handschrift 266 und die altkonstantinopolitanische Gottesdienstordnung." *Jahrbuch für Liturgiewissenshaft* 6 (1926) 98–111.

Bernhard, L. "Der Ausfall der 2. Ode im byzantinischen Neunodenkanon." In *Heuresis*. Festschrift für Andreas Rohracher, 91–101. Salzburg: Vittorio Klostermann, 1969.

Borgia, N. *Horologion. Diurno delle chiese di rito bizantino.* Orientalia Christiana 56 = 16/I, 152–254. Rome: PIO, 1929.

Bonnet, G. *La mystagogie de temps liturgiques dans le Triodion.* Unpublished dissertation. Paris: Sorbonne, 1978.

Calì, L. "Le ipakoè dell'octoichos bizantino." *Bollettino della Badia Greca di Grottaferrata* 19 (1965) 161–174.

Cappuyns, N. *Le Triodion. Etude historique sur sa constitution et sa formation.* Unpublished dissertation. Rome: PIO, 1935.

Di Salvo, B. "Considerazioni sugli Sticherà del vespero e delle laudi dell' októechos bizantino della domenica." *OCP* 33 (1967) 161–175.

Dölger, F. "Lumen Christi. Der christliche Abendhymnus *Phôs hilaron.*" *AC* 5 (1936) 1–43.

Egender, N. Introduction to *La prière des heures: Hôrologion.* La prière des églises de rite byzantin 1. Chevetogne: Editions de Chevetogne, 1975.

Ehrhard, A. "Das griechische Kloster Mâr-Saba in Palästina: seine Geschichte und sein literarischen Denkmäler." *Römische Quartalschrift* 7 (1893) 32–79.

Frazee, C. "St. Theodore of Stoudios and Ninth Century Monasticism in Constantinople." *Studia monastica* 23 (1981) 27–58.

Grosdidier de Matons, J. "Kontakion et canon. Piété populaire et liturgie officielle à Byzance." *Augustinianum* 20 (1980) 191–203.

_____. *Romanos le Mélode et les origines de la poésie religieuse à Byzance.* Beauchesne religions. Paris: Beauchesne, 1977.

Hannick, C. "Etude sur l'akolouthia asmatiké (avec quatre figures)." *Jahrbuch der österreichischen Byzantinistik* 19 (1970) 243–260.

_____. *Studien zu den Anastasima in den sinaitischen Handschriften.* Unpublished dissertation. Vienna, 1969.

_____. "Le texte de l'Oktoechos." In *Dimanche. Office selon les huit tons: Oktôêchos,* 37–60. La prière des églises de rite byzantin 3. Chevetogne: Editions de Chevetogne, 1968.

Husmann, H. "Hymnus und Troparion. Studien zur Geschichte der musikalischen Gattungen von Horologion und Tropologion." *Jahrbuch des Staatlichen Instituts für Musikforschung Preussischer Kulturbesitz.* Berlin: Merseburger, 1971.

Janeras, S. "I vangeli domenicali della resurrezione nelle tradizioni liturgiche agiopolita e bizantina." In *Paschale Mysterium. Studia in memoria dell'Abate Prof. Salvatore Marsili (1910-1983)*, 55-69. Studia Anselmiana 91, Analecta liturgica 10: Editrice Anselmiana, 1986.

(Archimandrite) Kallistos, "Historikê episkopêsis tou Triôdiou, to schedion kai ho katartismos autou." *Nea Siôn* 29 (1934) 44-61, 153-161, 177-184, 330-346, 452-467, 502-516, 553-570, 609-615.

Karabinov, I. A. *Postnaja Triod. Istoricheskij obzor eja plana, sostava, redaktsii i slavjanskikh perevodov.* St. Petersburg: V. Smirnov, 1910.

Korakidês, A. S. *Archaioi hymnoi:* 1. *Hê epilychnios eucharistia "Phôs hilaron. . . ."* 2. *Ho aggelos hymnos (Gloria)* . . . . Athens, 1979, 1984.

Korolevskij, C. "La codification de l'office byzantin. Les essais dans le passé." OCP 19 (1953) 25-58.

Leeb, H. *Die Gesänge im Gemeindegottesdienst von Jerusalem (vom 5. bis 8. Jahrhundert).* Wiener Beiträge zur Theologie 28. Vienna: Herder, 1979.

Leroy, J. "La conversion de s. Athanase l'Athonite à l'idéal cénobitique et l'influence studite." In *Le millénaire du Mont Athos, 963-1963. Etudes et mélanges,* vol. 1, 101-120. Chevetogne: Editions de Chevetogne, 1963.

_____. "Le cursus canonique chez. S. Théodore Studite." EL 68 (1954) 5-19.

_____. "La réforme studite." In *Il monachesimo orientale* 181-214. OCA 153. Rome: PIO, 1958.

_____. *Studitisches Mönchtum. Spiritualität und Lebensform.* Geist und Leben der Ostkirche 4. Graz/Vienna/Cologne: Styria, 1969.

_____. "La vie quotidienne du moine studite." *Irénikon* 27 (1954) 21-50.

Longo, A. "Il testo integrale della *Narrazione degli abati Giovanni e Sofronio* attraverso le Hermêneiai di Nicone." *Rivista di studi bizantini e neoellinici* 12-13 (1965-1966) 223-267.

Mansvetov, I. *Tserkovnyj ustav (Tipik), ego obrazovanie i sud'ba v grecheskoj i russkoj tserkvi.* Moscow: Tip. Lissnera i Romana, 1885.

(Mother) Mary, K. Ware. *The Festal Menaion.* London: Faber and Faber, 1969, 1977.

_____. *The Lenten Triodion.* London and Boston: Faber and Faber, 1978.

Mateos, J. "Un horologion inédit de Saint-Sabas. Le Codex sinaïtique grec 863 (IXᵉ siècle)." In *Mélanges E. Tisserant,* vol. III. 1, 47-76. ST 233. Vatican: Typis polyglottis Vaticanis, 1964.

_____. "Prières initiales fixes des offices syrien, maronite et byzantin." OS 11 (1966) 488-498.

_____. "La psalmodie dans le rite byzantin." POC 15 (1965) 107-126 (reprinted in OCA 191, 7-26).

_____. "La psalmodie variable dans le rite byzantin." In *Acta philosophica et theologica* 2, 327-339. Societas Academica Dacoromana. Rome, 1964.

_____. "Quelques anciens documents sur l'office du soir." OCP 35 (1969) 347-374.

_____. "Quelques problèmes de l'orthros byzantin." POC 11 (1961) 17-35, 201-220.

_____. "La synaxe monastique des vêpres byzantines." OCP 36 (1970) 248-272.

_____. *Le Typicon de la Grande Eglise,* 2 vols. OCA 165-166. Rome: PIO, 1962-1963.

Minisci, T. "I typica liturgica dell'Italia bizantina." *Bollettino della Badia Greca di Grottaferrata* n. s. 7 (1953) 97–104.

Palachkovsky, V. "L'économie du salut dans l'Office divin byzantin." EL 94 (1980) 311–322.

―――. "S. Théodore le Confesseur et l'office choral." In *Studia patristica* 13/2, 387–390. TU 116. Berlin: Akademie-Verlag, 1975.

Raes, A. "Note sur les anciennes matines byzantines et arméniennes." OCP 19 (1953) 205–210.

Rougeris, P. "Ricerca bibliografica sui typica italo-greci." *Bollettino della Badia Greca di Grottaferrata* n. s. 27 (1973) 11–42.

Schmemann, A. *Introduction to Liturgical Theology.* Crestwood, N.Y.: St. Vladimir's Seminary Press, 1966.

Skaballanovich, M. *Tolkovyj Tipikon. Ob"jasnitel'noe izlozhenie Tipikona s istoricheskim vvedeniem,* 3 vols. Kiev: N. T. Korchak-Novitskij, 1910, 1913, 1915.

Smothers, E. R. "Phôs hilaron." *Recherches de sciences religieuses* 19 (1929) 266–283.

Strunk, O. "The Antiphons of the Oktoechos." *Journal of the American Musicological Society* 13 (1960) 50–67.

―――. "The Byzantine Office at Hagia Sophia." *Dumbarton Oaks Papers* 9–10 (1956) 175–202.

Taft, R. "The Byzantine Office in the *Prayerbook* of New Skete: Evaluation of a Proposed Reform." OCP 48 (1982) 336–370.

―――. "Mount Athos: A Late Chapter in the History of the 'Byzantine Rite,'" *Dumbarton Oaks Papers* 42 (1988) 179–194.

Tardo, L. "L'ottoeco nei mss. melurgici." *Bollettino della Badia Greca di Grottaferrata* n. s. 1 (1947) 26–38, 133–143; 2 (1948) 26–44.

Tillyard, H. J. W. *The Hymns of the Octoechus,* Parts I–II. Monumenta musicae byzantinae, Transcripta 3 and 5. Copenhagen: E. Munksgaard, 1940–1949.

―――. *The Hymns of the Pentecostarium.* Monumenta musicae byzantinae, Transcripta 7. Copenhagen: E. Munksgaard, 1960.

Tomadakis, E. "Un problema di innografia bizantia: il rimaneggiamento dei testi innografici." *Bollettino della Badia Greca di Grottaferrata* n. s. 26 (1972) 3–30.

Trempelas, P. *Akolouthia kai taxeis hagiasmou hydatôn, egkainiôn, orthrou kai hesperinou kata tous en Athênais idia kôdikas, 147–274. Mikron Euchologion,* vol. 2. Athens, 1955.

Tripolitis, A. "Phôs hilaron. Ancient Hymn and Modern Enigma." *Vigiliae Christianae* 24 (1970) 189–196.

Uspenskij, N. D. "Pravoslavnaja vechernja. (Istorichesko-liturgicheskij ocherk)." *Bogoslovskie trudy* 1 (1959) 5–52.

―――. "Chin vsenochnogo bdenija na pravoslavnom vostoke i v Russkoj Tserkvi." *Bogoslovskie trudy* 18 (1977) 5–117; 19 (1978) 3–69.

Vailhé, S. "Le monastère de S.-Sabas." *Echos d'Orient* 2 (1898–1899) 332–341; 3 (1899–1900) 12–28, 168–177.

―――. "Les ećrivains de Mar-Saba." *Echos d'Orient* 2 (1898) 1–11, 33–47.

8. ITALY, ROME, WESTERN OFFICES IN GENERAL (SEE ALSO SECTION 1):

Addleshaw, G. W. O. *The Early Parochial System and the Divine Office.* Alcuin Club Prayer Book Revision Pamphlets 15. London: Mowbray, n. d.

Albareda, A. M. *Bibliografia de la Regla benedictina.* Montserrat: Monestir de Montserrat, 1933.

Battifol, P. *History of the Roman Breviary.* London and N. Y.: Longmans, Green and Co., 1912.

Baudot, J. *The Roman Breviary. Its Sources and History.* St. Louis: B. Herder/ London: Catholic Truth Society, 1909.

Bäumer, S. *Geschichte des Breviers. Versuch einer quellenmässingen Darstellung des altkirchlichen und des römischen Officiums bis auf unsere Tage.* Freiburg/B.: Herder, 1895. French trans. *Histoire du Bréviaire.* Paris: Letouzey et Ané, 1905.

Brou, L. "Où en est la question des 'Psalter Collects?'" *Studia Patristica* 2/2, 17–20. TU 64. Berlin: Akademie-Verlag, 1957.

_____ and Wilmart, A. *The Psalter Collects from V–VI Century Sources.* HBS 83. London: Harrison and Sons, 1949.

Callewaert, C. *Sacris erudiri.* Steenbrugge: Abbatia S. Petri, 1940.

Cattaneo, E. *Il breviario ambrosiano. Note storiche ed illustrative.* Milan, 1943.

Chevalier, U. *Repertorium hymnologicum. Catalogue des chants, hymnes, proses, séquences, tropes en usage dans l'Eglise latine depuis les origines jusqu'à nos jours.* 2 vols. Louvain: Lefever, 1892.

de Bhaldraithe, E. "The Morning Office in the Rule of the Master." *Regulae Benedicti studia. Annuarium internationale* 5 (1976) 201–223.

de Sainte Marie, H. "The Psalter Collects." EL 65 (1951) 105–110.

de Vogüé, A. *La Règle du Maître.* 3 vols. SC 105–107. Paris: Cerf, 1964-1965.

_____. *The Rule of St. Benedict, a Doctrinal and Spiritual Commentary.* Trans. J. B. Hasbrouck. CS 54. Kalamazoo: Cistercian Publications, 1983.

Gamber, K. *Sacrificum vespertinum. Lucernarium und eucharistisches Opfer am Abend und ihre Abhängigkeit von den Riten der Juden.* Studia patristica et liturgica 12. Regensburg: F. Pustet, 1983.

Heiming, O. "Zum monastischen Offizium" (see section 1).

Hofmeister, P. "Zur Geschichte des Chordienstes." *Liturgisches Jahrbuch* 12 (1962) 16–31.

Hughes, A. *Medieval Manuscripts for Mass and Office. A Guide to their Organization and Terminology.* Toronto-Buffalo-London: University of Toronto Press, 1982.

Jasmer, P. "A Comparison of the Monastic and Cathedral Vespers up to the Time of St. Benedict." *The American Benedictine Review* 34 (1983) 337–360.

Jaspert, B. *Bibliographie der Regula Benedicti 1930–1980. Ausgaben und Übersetzungen.* Regulae Benedicti studia, Supplementa 5. Hildesheim: Gerstenberg Verlag, 1983.

Jungmann, J. A., ed. *Brevierstudien.* Trier: Paulinus-Verlag, 1958.

Korhammer, M. *Die monastischen Cantica im Mittelalter und ihre altenglischen*

*Interlinearversionen: Studien und Textausgabe.* Münchener Universitäts-schriften: Philosophische Fakultät, Bd. 6. Munich: W. Fink, 1976.

Leahy, E. G. "Archivio di San Pietro, Cod. B. 79, and Amalarius: Notes on the Development of the Medieval Office." *Manuscripta* 28 (1984) 79–91.

Leeb, H. *Die Psalmodie bei Ambrosius.* Wiener Beiträge zur Theologie 18. Vienna: Herder, 1967.

Mitchell, N. "The Liturgical Code in the Rule of Benedict." In *RB 1980. The Rule of St. Benedict in Latin and English with Notes,* ed. T. Fry, 379–414. Collegeville: The Liturgical Press, 1981.

Mohrmann, C. "Apropos des collectes du psautier." *Vigiliae Christianae* 6 (1952) 1–19.

Monachino, V. *La cura pastorale a Milano, Cartagine e Roma nel secolo IV.* Analecta Gregoriana 41. Rome: Pontifical Gregorian University, 1947.

———. *S. Ambrogio e la cura pastorale a Milano nel secolo IV.* Milan: Centro Ambrosiano di documentazione e studi religiosi, 1973.

Neufville, J. and de Vogüé, A. *La Règle de S. Benoît. 7 vols. SC 181–196; vol. 7 hors série.* Paris: Cerf, 1972–1977.

Pascher, J. *Das Stundengebet der römischen Kirche.* Munich: K. Zink, 1954.

———. "Der Psalter für Laudes und Vesper im alten römischen Stundengebet." *Münchener theologische Zeitschrift* 8 (1957) 255–267.

Pinell, J. *La Liturgia delle Ore.* Anamnesis 5. Genoa: Marietti, 1990.

Righetti, M. *Storia liturgica.* vol. 2. Milan: Ancora, 1955.

Salmon, P. *The Breviary through the Centuries.* Collegeville: The Liturgical Press, 1962.

———. *L'office divin au moyen âge. Histoire de la formation du bréviaire du IX<sup>e</sup> au XVI<sup>e</sup> siècle.* Lex orandi 43. Paris: Cerf, 1967.

Vandenbroucke, F. "Sur la lecture chrétienne du psautier au V<sup>e</sup> siècle." *Sacris erudiri* 5 (1953) 5–26.

van Dijk, S. J. P. and Walker, J. Hazelden. *The Origins of the Modern Roman Liturgy. The Liturgy of the Papal Court and the Franciscan Order in the Thirteenth Century.* Westminster Maryland: Newman/London: Darton, Longmann and Todd, 1960.

Winkler, G. Über die Kathedralvesper" (see section 1).

## 9. Latin Offices outside Italy (see also sections 1 and 8):

Beck, H. G. *The Pastoral Care of Souls in South-East France during the Sixth Century.* Analecta Gregoriana 51. Rome: Pontifical Gregorian University, 1950.

Bernal, J. "Primeros vestigios del lucernario en España." In *Liturgica* 3, 21–50. Scripta et documenta 17. Abadia de Montserrat, 1966.

Bishop, W. C. "The Breviary in Spain." In *The Mozarabic and the Ambrosian Rites,* 55–97. Alcuin Club Tracts 15. London, 1924.

Brou, L. "Le psautier liturgique wisigothique et les éditions critiques des psautiers latins." HS 8 (1954) 88–111.

Curran, M. *The Antiphonary of Bangor and the Early Irish Monastic Liturgy.* Dublin: Irish Academic Press, 1984.

Fernández Alonso, J. *La cura pastoral en la España romanovisigoda.* Madrid: Estades artes gráficas, 1955.

Heiming, O. "Zum monastischen Offizium" (see section 1).

Jungmann, J. A. "The Pre-monastic Morning Hour in the Gallo-Spanish Region in the 6th Century." In *Pastoral Liturgy,* 122–157. New York: Herder, 1962.

Martín Patino, L. "El Breviarium mozárabe de Ortiz. Su valor documental para la historia del oficio catedralico hispanico." *Miscelanea Comillas* 40 (1963) 207–297.

Meyer, W. *Die Preces der mozarabischen Liturgie.* Abhandlungen der königlichen Gesellschaft der Wissenschaften zu Göttingen. Philologisch-historische Klasse, n. F. Bd. 15. Nr. 3. Berlin: Weidmannsche Buchhandlung, 1914.

Monachino, V. *La cura pastorale a Milano, Cartagine e Roma* (see section 8).

Morin, J. "Explication d'une passage de la règle de saint Colomban relatif à l'office des moines celtiques (antiphona, chora, psalta)." RevB 12 (1895) 200–201.

Pinell i Pons, J. *De liturgiis occidentalibus, cum speciali tractatione de liturgia hispanica.* Pro manuscripto. Rome: S. Anselmo, 1967.

_____. "El 'matutinarium' en la liturgia hispana." HS 9 (1956) 61–85.

_____. "El oficio hispáno-visigótico." HS 10 (1957) 385–427.

_____. "Las horas vigiliares del oficio monacal hispánico. Estudio y edición critica," In *Liturgica* 3, 197–340. Scripta et documenta 17. Abadia de Montserrat, 1966.

_____. "Las 'missas,' grupos de cantos y oraciones en el oficio de la antigua liturgia hispana." *Archivos Leonenses* (Léon) 8 (1954) 145–185.

_____. *Liber orationum psalmographicus. Colectas de salmos del antiguo rito hispánico.* Monumenta Hispaniae sacra, serie litúrgica 9. Barcelona-Madrid: Consejo Superior de Investigaciones Científicas, 1972.

_____. "San Fructuoso de Braga y su influjo en la formación del oficio monacal hispánico." *Bracara Augusta* 22, fasc. 5–54 (63–66). Braga, 1968.

_____. "Una exhortación diaconal en el rito hispánico: La supplicatio." *Analecta sacra Terraconensia* 36 (1963) 3–23.

_____. "Vestigis del lucernari a occident." In *Liturgica* 1, 91–149. Abadia de Montserrat, 1956.

Porter, A. W. S. "Cantica mozarabici officii." EL 49 (1935) 126–145.

_____. "Early Spanish Monasticism." L 10 (1932) 1–15, 66–79, 156–167; 11 (1933) 199–207; 12 (1934) 31–52.

_____. "Monasticismo español primitivo. El oficio monastico." HS 6 (1953) 1–34 (translation of the section of the previous entry concerning the office).

_____. "Studies in the Mozarabic Office." JTS 35 (1934) 266–286.

Rocha, P. R. *L'office divin dans l'église de Braga: originalité et dépendences d'une liturgie particulière au moyan âge.* Cultura medieval e moderna 15. Paris: Fundação Calouste Gulbenkian/ Centro Cultural Português, 1980.

Szövérffy, J. *Iberian Hymnody. Survey and Problems.* Classical Folia Editions, 1971.

Winkler, G. "Über die Kathedralvesper" (see section 1).

10. SIXTEENTH-CENTURY AND MODERN REFORMS OF THE OFFICE:

Alexander, J. N. "Luther's Reform of the Daily Office." *Worship* 57 (1983) 348–360.

Bartolomiello, F. "La Liturgia delle Ore nell'esperienza delle varie comunità." In *Esperienze cristiane della preghiera, 76–91.* Milan: Edizioni O. R., 1979.

Blom, J. M. *The Post-Tridentine English Primer.* Catholic Record Society Monograph Series, vol. 3, 1982.

Bugnini, A. *La riforma liturgica (1948–1975).* BELS 30. Rome: Edizioni liturgiche, 1983.

Dehne, C. "Roman Catholic Popular Devotions." In *Christians at Prayer,* ed. J. Gallen, 83–99. Liturgical Studies. Notre Dame/London: University of Notre Dame Press, 1977.

Grisbrooke, W. J. "The 1662 Book of Common Prayer: its History and Character." *Studia liturgica* 1 (1962) 146–166.

Gy, P.-M. "Projets de réforme du Bréviaire." LMD 21 (1950) 110–128.

Jungmann, J. A. "Why was the Reform Breviary of Cardinal Quiñonez a Failure?" In *Pastoral Liturgy* 200–214. New York: Herder, 1962.

Legg, J. W., ed. *The Second Recension of the Quignon Breviary.* 2 vols. HBS 35, 42. London: Harrison and Sons, 1908, 1912.

*The Liturgy of the Hours. The General Instruction on the Liturgy of the Hours,* with a commentary by A.-M. Roguet. Collegeville: The Liturgical Press, 1971.

Old, H. O. "Daily Prayer in the Reformed Church of Strasbourg 1525–1530." *Worship* 52 (1978) 121–138.

Quentin, C. "La prière du matin à l'église." *Questions liturgiques* 61 (1980) 149–150.

_____. "Retour aux vêpres." *Questions liturgiques* 61 (1980) 37–42.

Ratcliff, E. C. "The Choir Offices." In *Liturgy and Worship. A Companion to the Prayer Books of the Anglican Communion,* ed. W. K. Lowther Clarke and C. Harris, 257–295. London: SPCK, 1932.

Reinhart, S. "Das Gebet der Kirche. Stundengebet mit der Gemeinde. Ein Erfahrungsbericht." *Gottesdienst* B-18/19 (1979) 142–143.

Salmon, P. *L'office divin au moyen âge* (see section 8).

Schnitker, Th. A. *Publica oratio. Laudes matutinae und Vesper als Gemeindegottesdienste in diesem Jahrundert. Eine liturgiehistorische und liturgietheologische Untersuchung.* Dissertation. Münster, 1977.

Storey, W. "The Liturgy of the Hours" (see section 1).

# Index of Liturgical Pieces (= ILP)

# Index of Patristic Citations (=IPC)

# General Index

(*Note:* technical terms are listed under "terminology")

Abbeloos, J. B., 226
Abbott, W. M., 347
'Abdallah, S., 381
'Abd al-Masih, 381
Addleshaw, G. W. O., 297, 387
agape, 18, 21–22, 24–29, 37, 167, 332; monastic, 332
Albareda, A. M., 388
Alexander, J. N., 319, 391
Alexandria, 14–17, 34–36, 40, 88, 167. *See also* Coptic, Egypt
alleluia, 103, 111–13, 124–30, 139, 154, 157, 227, 230, 234, 241–45, 263–64; with psalm units 59–61, 88–89, 125, 149
alleluia psalms, 18, 59–61, 102, 111, 118, 125, 128
all-night vigil. *See* vigils, agrypnia, pannychis
Alypius of Thegaste, 94
Amatowni, S., 220
Ambrosian Rite 74. *See also* Milan
Amélineau, E., 252
Anderson, W. B., 185
Andreu, F., 302
Andrieu, M., 132
angelic theme in vigils/nocturns, 16, 29, 35, 81–82, 171, 357, 370–71
Antioch, Antiochia, 13, 26, 40, 42–48, 50–51, 239; cursus, 83–84, 195; monastic office, 80–84, 91, 195, 203, 208–9; vigils, 167, 169–70, 175, 195. *See also* Syria
antiphonal psalmody, nature of, 139. *See also* psalmody
antiphons. *See* terminology, psalmody

antiphons, responds, etc., excluded in 16th c. reformed offices, 311, 320, 323; reinserted in modern reforms 321–22, 324
Arles, cathedral office, 151–56, 180–82; monasteries, 101–2; monastic office, 102–13, 128, 167, 209; rules of, 100–102, 122, 152, 154, 178, 182; see Aurelian, Caesarius, and rules of in IPC
Armenian Rite, 53, 217, 219–24; resurrection vigil of, 89
Arranz, M., xiii, 32, 274, 284, 384–85
Arras, V., 71
asmatikos office of Constantinople, 254–55, 262, 384
Assyro-Chaldean Rite, 51, 54, 88, 194, 217, 221, 225–37; breviary, 228, 237; characteristics, 235, 237; disposition of church (bema), 229–30, 235, (symbolism) 232; no readings in office, 33
Athanasius, 88, 167, 178
Aubineau, M., 88
Aucher, J. B., 220
Audet, J. P., 13
Augustine, 94, 101, 178
Aurelian of Arles, 96, 100–13, 148–49, 154–55, 182, 187, 203, 209
Ayrouth, H. H., 250

Bacht, H., 354, 375
Bäumer, S., xii, 149, 388
Baldovin, J., 183
Balfour, D., 385
Ballin, C., 255–56, 381

lucernarium, light ritual, 18, 26–28, 36–38, 55–56, 117, 189, 211–12, 351, 355–56, 385, 388; Armenian, 223, 24; Assyro-Chaldean, 232, 235–36; Byzantine, 155, 277–78, 281, 285–87; Ethiopian, 268–71; Iberian, 116–17, 156–61; *in:* Antioch, 43, 83; Cappadocia, 36–39; Cyprus, 39; Easter Vigil, 37; Gaul, 104–5, 110–11; Jerusalem, 49, 169, 277; reformed, 316, 320–22, 325; Rome, 143–44; urban monastic vespers, 90, 94, 97; Jewish, 37, 348–49; Malankarese, 245; pagan origins, 36–37. *See also* light theme, orientation
Luther and office, 269, 319–20
Lutheran Book of Worship, 316, 320–22, 324; office, 320–22

McCarthy, M. C., 100
Maclean, A. J., 33, 227, 378
Macomber, W. F., 239–40, 270
Macrina, 36–38, 146, 168
Mai, A., 206
Malabar Rite, 225, 237
Malak Hanna, 251, 382
Malankara Rite, 239, 244–46
Mallon, S., 382
Mansi, J. D., 102, 145, 148–50, 157–60, 166
Mansvetov, I., 386
Marcora, C., 165–66, 191, 376
Mariani, B., 380
Martín Patino, L., 390
Mary (Mother), 386
Maraval, P., 36, 156
Maronite tradition, 51, 54, 239–43, 246–47; matins, 89, 240–41; vespers, 241–43
Maspero, G., 72
Mateos, J., xiii, xvii, 22–23, 37–38, 40, 50, 53–54, 57, 81, 84, 88–89, 107, 139, 173, 188, 190–91, 193, 198, 205, 221, 226–28, 230–33, 236–37, 240–41, 275, 277, 283, 315, 376–78, 380, 386
Mathews, T. F., 379
matins, morning praise, morning prayer, 6, 9–11, 14–18, 22–27, 84; psalms of 11–13 (*see also* lauds *and* Pss 148–150 in ILP); purpose, 56, 65–66, 353–54, 357–58, 370; statutory, 17–18, 21, 28, 61; terminology, 77; theology/symbolism, 10, 14, 20, 23–24, 28, 56, 85–87, 142, 211–12, 233, 236–37, 352–54; time of celebration (*see* nocturns)
cathedral, 33, 55, 191–209; *in:* Antioch, 42–48; Cappadocia, 39–41, 84–87, 168; Constantinople, 48, 186; Cyprus, 41; Gaul, 104–5, 110–13, 145–56 passim, esp. 151–55, 159; Palestine/Bethlehem, 77, 79; Iberian Peninsula, 157–63; Italy, 142–44, 175, 186, 192–94, 200–209 passim; Jerusalem, 49–51, 54, 274; N. Africa, 143–45, 186; origins, 191–209; structure, 44–47, 212
today: Anglican/Episcopal, 323–25; Armenian, 222–23; Assyro-Chaldean, 232–33; Byzantine, 128, 173, 199, 206, 274–83, 288–89; Coptic, 201–2, 252, 255, 257; Ethiopian, 264–65, 271; Lutheran, 320–21; Malankarese, 245–46; new Roman, 314; W. Syrian and Maronite, 240–41, 246
urban (hybrid) monastic, 192–209; festive/Sun., 103, 111–13; *in:* Antioch, 82–84, 195–209; Gaul, 97–104, 197, 200–201, 208–9; Palestine, 77, 79, 97–100, 128, 195–209; RB/Rome, 128, 133–37, 200–201, 208–9, 312; RM, 123–30, 200–201, 208–9; time of celebration, *see* nocturns
Mattathil, M., 244
matutini hymni, 49, 99, 145, 147–48, 193–94, 201; cf. 82, 106. *See also* matins
Mearns, J., 90, 377
meditation, 66–67, 71, 73, 110, 116, 120, 131, 142, 154, 174, 179, 181, 189, 258, 368–72; original meaning, 372; *See also* lectio divina
Meinardus, O. F. A., 250
Melloh, J. A., xvii, 316, 353
mesonyktikon (monastic midnight hour), 77, 166, 189; Byzantine Sabaitic, 206; Coptic, 252; Ethiopian, 270; Iberian, 119–20; in